LIFE
APPLICATION®
BIBLE
COMMENTARY

JOHN

Bruce B. Barton, D. Min.
Philip W. Comfort, Ph.D.
David R. Veerman, M. Div.
Neil Wilson, M.R.E.

Series Editor:
Grant Osborne, Ph.D.

Tyndale House Publishers, Inc.
WHEATON, ILLINOIS

Editor: Philip Comfort, Ph.D.
Contributing Editors: James C. Galvin, Ed.D. Linda C. Taylor, and Ronald A. Beers

Life Application is a registered trademark of Tyndale House Publishers, Inc.

The "NIV" and "New International Version" trademarks are registered in the United States Patent and Trademark Office by International Bible Society. Use of either trademark requires the permission of International Bible Society.

Scripture quotations marked (NIV) are from the *Holy Bible,* New International Version®. Copyright © 1973, 1978, 1984 by International Bible Society. Used by permission of Zondervan Publishing House. All rights reserved.

Scripture quotations marked NKJV are from The New King James Version. Copyright © 1979, 1980, 1982, Thomas Nelson Inc., Publishers.

Scripture quotations marked NRSV are from the New Revised Standard Version of the Bible, copyrighted, 1989 by the Division of Christian Education of the National Council of the Churches of Christ in the United States of America, and are used by permission. All rights reserved.

(No citation is given for Scripture text that is exactly the same wording in all three versions—NIV, NKJV, and NRSV.)

Scripture quotations marked NASB are taken from the *New American Standard Bible,* © 1960, 1962, 1963, 1968, 1971, 1972, 1973, 1975, 1977 by The Lockman Foundation. Used by permission.

Scripture verses marked TLB are taken from *The Living Bible,* copyright © 1971 owned by assignment by KNT Charitable Trust. All rights reserved.

Scripture quotations marked RSV are from the *Holy Bible,* Revised Standard Version, copyright © 1946, 1952, 1971 by the Division of Christian Education of the National Council of the Churches of Christ in the United States of America, and are used by permission. All rights reserved.

Scripture verses marked TJB are from The Jerusalem Bible, Copyright © 1966, 1967 and 1968 by Darton, Longman & Todd Ltd and Doubleday & Company, Inc.

Scripture verses marked Phillips are taken from *The New Testament in Modern English* by J. B. Phillips, copyright © J. B. Phillips, 1958, 1959, 1960, 1972. All rights reserved.

Scripture verses marked NEB are taken from *The New English Bible,* copyright © 1970, Oxford University Press, Cambridge University Press.

Library of Congress Cataloging-in-Publication Data
John / Bruce B. Barton . . . [et al.]
      p.   cm.—(Life application Bible commentary)
     Includes bibliographical references and index.
     ISBN 0-8423-2892-0   ISBN 0-8423-2893-9 (pbk.)
     1. Bible.   N.T.   John—Commentaries.   I. Barton, Bruce B.
II. Series.
BS2615.3.J64   1993
226.5'07—dc20   93-22472

Printed in the United States of America
99 98 97 96 95
 8   7   6   5   4   3   2

CONTENTS

gratis

123514

FOREWORD

The Life Application Bible Commentary series provides verse-by-verse explanation, background, and application for every verse in the New Testament. In addition, it gives personal help, teaching notes, and sermon ideas that will address needs, answer questions, and provide insight for applying God's Word to life today. The content is highlighted so that particular verses and phrases are easy to find.

Each volume contains three sections: introduction, commentary, and reference. The introduction includes an overview of the book, the book's historical context, a timeline, cultural background information, major themes, an overview map, and an explanation about the author and audience.

The commentary section includes running commentary on the Bible text with reference to several modern versions, especially the New International Version and the New Revised Standard Version, accompanied by life applications interspersed throughout. Additional elements include charts, diagrams, maps, and illustrations. There are also insightful quotes from church leaders and theologians such as John Calvin, Martin Luther, John Wesley, A. W. Tozer, and C. S. Lewis. These features are designed to help you quickly grasp the biblical information and be prepared to communicate it to others.

The reference section includes a harmony of the four Gospels, bibliography of other resources, and an index.

INTRODUCTION

He spoke, and galaxies whirled into place, stars burned the heavens, and planets began orbiting their suns—words of awesome, unlimited, unleashing power.

He spoke again, and the waters and lands were filled with plants and creatures, running, swimming, growing, and multiplying—words of animating, breathing, pulsing life.

Again he spoke, and man and woman were formed, thinking, speaking, and loving—words of personal and creative glory.

Eternal, infinite, unlimited—he was, is, and always will be the Maker and Lord of all that exists.

And then he came in the flesh to a tiny spot in the universe called planet Earth—the mighty Creator becoming part of his creation, limited by time and space and susceptible to age, sickness, and death. Propelled by love, he came to rescue and save, offering forgiveness and life.

He is the Word: he is Jesus Christ.

It is this truth that the apostle John presents in this book. John's Gospel is not a life of Christ; it is a powerful argument for the incarnation, a conclusive demonstration that Jesus was, and is, the very heaven-sent Son of God and the only source of eternal life.

AUTHOR

John the Apostle, son of Zebedee and Salome, and younger brother of James.

Thunder evokes fear and images of a pending storm. We use *thunder* to describe a deafening sound, such as in "thunderous applause"; approaching danger, as in "thundering herd"; and explosive anger, as in "thundered response." So we would expect someone nicknamed Son of Thunder to be powerful, loud, and unpredictable.

That's what Jesus named two of his disciples—Zebedee's sons, James and John (Mark 3:17)—for he knew their tendency to explode. Sure enough, when Jesus and the Twelve were rebuffed by a Samaritan village, these rough fishermen suggested calling down fire from heaven to destroy the whole village. Jesus had to calm down the outspoken brothers and explain that vengeance was not his way (Luke 9:52-56). Just before that incident, John had told Jesus that he had tried to stop a man from driving out demons "because he is not one of us." Jesus had explained that he didn't have an exclusive club, "for whoever is not against you is for you" (Luke 9:49-50 NIV).

In addition to being forceful and angry, James and John also seem to have been quite self-centered. They implored Jesus "to do for us whatever we ask." Then they requested seats of honor and power in the kingdom. When the other disciples heard about what James and John had said, they became indignant (Mark 10:35-44).

Yet Jesus also saw potential in these thundering brothers—he knew what they would become. So Jesus brought both, with Peter, into his inner circle, allowing them to see him transfigured on the mountain (Mark 9:2-13). And as Jesus was dying on the cross, he entrusted Mary, his mother, to John's care (John 19:26-27).

John was following in his father Zebedee's footsteps as a fisherman when Jesus called him (Matthew 4:21; Mark 1:19-20). His mother was Salome (Matthew 27:55-56; Mark 15:40). His brother, James, was also one of the Twelve and the first apostle to be martyred (Acts 12:2). They fished on the Sea of Galilee with Peter and Andrew.

One might predict that someone with a personality like John's would self-destruct. Certainly this person would die in a fight or in a clash with the Roman government. At the very least, he would be discarded by the church as self-seeking and power-hungry.

But such was not the case. Instead, John was transformed into someone who was strong but gentle, straightforward but loving, courageous but humble. There is no dramatic event to account for John's transformation—it must have come from being with Jesus, being accepted, loved, and affirmed by the Lord, and then being filled with the Holy Spirit. So overwhelmed was John by Jesus that he did not mention himself by name in the Gospel that bears his name. Instead, he wrote of himself as "the disciple whom Jesus loved" (John 13:23; 19:26; 20:2; 21:20, 24). What a humble change for one who, at first, had wanted power and recognition.

John stands as a great example of Christ's power to transform lives. Christ can change anyone—no one is beyond hope. Jesus accepted John as he was, a Son of Thunder, and changed him into what he would become, the apostle of love.

John's ministry. John was a Palestinian and a Galilean. He was not from Jerusalem, but from the country. This is why John shows such familiarity in his writing with the geography of the area and perhaps why John singles out the system of religious leaders who were in control in Jerusalem.

Many believe that John was first a disciple of John the Baptist. His mentor pointed him to Jesus when Jesus passed by. Then Jesus and John spent the day together (1:35-39). At that time, John must have become a part-time disciple, for later we find him back fishing with his brother, James, and their father, Zebedee. But the next time Jesus called them, John and James left everything, father and boat included, and followed him. This was after Jesus had turned water into wine (2:1-11), had cleared the temple the first time (2:12-25), and had been visited by Nicodemus at night (3:1-21). It was also after Herod had imprisoned John the Baptist (Luke 3:19-20), Jesus had spoken with the woman at the well (4:1-26), and Jesus had been rejected at Nazareth (Luke 4:16-30).

In the Gospels, John is mentioned by name when he was selected as one of the Twelve and called a Son of Thunder (Mark 1:19; 3:13-19), when he saw Jesus transfigured (Luke 9:28-36), when he told Jesus about stopping a man who was driving out demons (Luke 9:49), when he asked Jesus about calling down fire on the Samaritan village (Luke 9:52-56), when he asked Jesus about sitting next to him in the kingdom (Mark 10:35-44), and when he was sent with Peter by Jesus to make preparations for the Last Supper (Luke 22:8). But as a member of the Twelve, John was an eyewitness to the miracles, an "ear-witness" to the parables and confrontations with the Pharisees and other leaders, and a student of Jesus' special words of instruction. John was at the Last Supper and in the Garden of Gethsemane. And he was the only one of the Twelve at the cross. John also saw the empty tomb and was in the upper room, on the beach, and at the Ascension.

We read more about John in the first chapters of Acts. There he is numbered among the Twelve (Acts 1:13) when they chose a replacement for Judas. Then we see him ministering with Peter at the temple (Acts 3:3-11) and in the confrontation with the Sanhedrin (Acts 4:1-31). During the growing persecution, after many believers had been scattered, Peter and John were sent by the other apostles to verify the validity of the conversions in Samaria (Acts 8:14-25). John is mentioned only one other time in Acts (in 12:2), as the brother of James, who was executed by King Herod.

Beyond being a leader in the Jerusalem church (as mentioned

in Galatians 2:9), little is known of John's ministry. When John wrote his epistles to Gentile congregations (1 John), "the chosen lady" (2 John NIV), and Gaius (3 John), he simply identified himself as "the elder." So it is thought that John must have been the only surviving apostle at that time. He wrote those letters from Ephesus about A.D. 85–90, just before writing his Gospel. In about A.D. 94, John was banished to the island of Patmos during the reign of Domitian. There, this wise and elder apostle received the dramatic vision of the future from Jesus, given to us as the book of Revelation. John probably returned to Ephesus during Nerva's reign and then died there during the reign of Trajan, around A.D. 100.

John provides a powerful example of a lifetime of service to Christ. As a young man, John left his fishing nets to follow the Savior. For three intense years he watched Jesus live and love, and listened to him teach and preach. John saw Jesus crucified and then risen! John's life was changed dramatically, from an impetuous, hot-tempered youth, to a loving and wise man of God. Through it all, John remained faithful, so that at the end of his life, he continued to bear strong witness to the truth and power of the gospel.

How strong is your commitment to Christ? Will it last through the years? The true test of an athlete is not in the start but the finish. So too with faithfulness to Christ—how will you finish that race?

The Gospel mentions no author by name, but the evidence (both from textual and historical sources) points to John as the author. Certainly the writer had to be an eyewitness of the events and one of Jesus' close associates. Irenaeus (A.D. 120–202) wrote, "Afterwards, John, the disciple of the Lord, who also had leaned upon his breast, did himself publish a gospel during his residence at Ephesus in Asia." John's authorship of this Gospel was also affirmed by other early church fathers: Clement of Alexandria, Origen, Hippolytus, Justin Martyr, and Tertullian. Those who proposed a late writing (middle of the second century) were disproved when the Ryland Papyrus (a fragment of John's Gospel) was discovered and dated from A.D. 110–125.

SETTING

Written between A.D. 85–90 from Ephesus, after the destruction of Jerusalem (A.D. 70) and before John's exile to the island of Patmos

The Gospel of John contains no references concerning where it was written. But according to the earliest traditions of the church, John wrote his Gospel from Ephesus. The church at Ephesus had been founded by Paul on his second missionary journey in A.D. 52 (Acts 18:19-21). The church grew under the ministry of Apollos, Priscilla, and Aquila (Acts 18:24-26). Paul returned to Ephesus on his third missionary journey and had an incredible ministry there (Acts 19:1–20:1). Later, during his first Roman imprisonment, Paul wrote the letter to the Ephesians (about A.D. 60). That church is described in Revelation 2:1-7.

We don't know how old John was when Jesus called him. But assuming that John was a little younger than Jesus, John would have been in his eighties when writing this Gospel, quite old for a time when the life expectancy was much shorter. And considering the fact that all the other apostles had died as martyrs, John was indeed the church's elder statesman. We can imagine him teaching and counseling the Christians in this well-established church, as well as doing some writing.

AUDIENCE

New Christians and searching non-Christians.

John does not reveal his audience directly, but several characteristics of the book provide insight into the people he was trying to reach.

1. The Gospel of John differs greatly from the other three Gospels in content and approach. Matthew, Mark, and Luke present much historical data with few explanations or interpretations. John, however, selected key events and took time to explain and apply them. (See, for example, 11:51-52 and 12:37-41.) In addition, John chose to write about a few important, miraculous signs (20:30-31) in order to give a clear picture of the person of Christ.

2. John illustrates the tension between faith and unbelief and emphasizes the importance of responding to Christ. He states this fact at the very beginning and carries it throughout the book—"Yet to all who received him, to those who believed in his name, he gave the right to become children of God" (1:12 NIV).

3. John uses simple vocabulary but chooses special words and loads them with meaning—for example, *word, truth, light, darkness, life, and love.*

4. John repeats four main points: the true identity of Jesus, the necessity of responding to Christ in faith, the gift of eternal life, and the church's mission to the world.

5. John explains his purpose clearly: "But these are written that

you may believe that Jesus is the Christ, the Son of God, and that by believing you may have life in his name" (20:31 NIV).

These unique characteristics of the book seem to indicate that John was trying to convince people of the truth about Christ. Written almost as an evangelistic tract, John presents the evidence for Jesus as the God-man and the Savior of the world, and he challenges readers to follow his Lord. So we can conclude that John wrote to unbelieving Asian Jews and Gentiles.

But John also wrote to Christians, to help strengthen their faith. John was the last surviving apostle and one of the few still living who had seen Jesus in the flesh. It would be easy for young believers—removed from Christ's life, death, and resurrection by a generation and surrounded by a hostile government and unbelieving neighbors—to have doubts and second thoughts about their faith. Remember, this is the late eighties, after the terrible persecutions by Nero (A.D. 54–68) and the total destruction of Jerusalem (A.D. 70). The church had flourished under persecution, but believers needed reassurance of the truth of Christianity. John, the venerable eyewitness to all that Jesus had done and faithful follower of his Lord, would give that assurance through his personal account of the gospel story.

PURPOSE

John gives a clear and straightforward statement of his purpose for writing this book: "But these are written that you may believe that Jesus is the Christ, the Son of God, and that by believing you may have life in his name" (20:31 NIV). To achieve this purpose, John shows, throughout the Gospel, that Jesus was, in fact, the Christ of God, the prophesied one, and the only source of salvation. This is the dominant theme of the entire book.

The Gospel of John was written to convince those who had not seen Jesus to believe in him, to help believers deepen their faith, and to convince unbelievers to trust in Jesus Christ as their Savior. In addition, John has several other emphases worth noting:

1. John shows that the Jewish leaders were completely wrong in rejecting Jesus as the Messiah. John 1:11 makes this clear: "He came to that which was his own, but his own did not receive him" (NIV). John continues this emphasis throughout the book. Consider, for example, Jesus' discussion with the Jews in 8:33-59. There Jesus calls them "illegitimate children" whose real father is the devil. Then the Jews accuse Jesus of being "demon-possessed." Finally, after Jesus says, "I tell you the truth, before Abraham was born, I am!" the Jews pick up stones to kill him—

but Jesus escapes their deadly intent. In chapter 9, we find another confrontation with the Pharisees after Jesus heals a man who has been blind since birth. These incidents and many others are found only in the Gospel of John.

2. John shows that Jesus is much greater than John the Baptist. It may be that some followers of John the Baptist were still claiming that he was more important than Jesus. Whatever the reason, John emphasizes the preeminence of Christ and John the Baptist's special role in preparing the way for him (see 1:6-8, 15-18, 19-27, 35-38; 3:25-30).

3. John emphasizes the deity and humanity of Jesus. This awesome mystery is expressed in the words of the prologue: "The Word was God, and . . . the Word became flesh" (John 1:1, 14). Elsewhere in the Gospel, Jesus himself declares that he was one with the Father—even the visible expression of the Father (10:30; 14:9-11). And at the end of the Gospel, Thomas makes the wonderful acclamation to Jesus, "My Lord and my God!" (20:28). While emphasizing Jesus' divinity and heavenly origin, John also presented Jesus as a real man. It is possible that he did this to confront a docetic heresy promoting the false notion that Jesus only seemed to be living a human life—that he was not fully human. So John states directly that "the Word became flesh and made his dwelling among us" (1:14 NIV). John also mentions Jesus' family ties (2:12; 7:3-5), explains how Jesus became tired (4:6), and shows that Jesus really died on the cross (19:33-34). John clearly presents Jesus as the God-man.

4. John shows how people misunderstood Jesus' actions and words. For example, Jesus' listeners misunderstood the identification of his body with the temple (2:18-22), the new birth (3:3-10), spiritual, living water (4:10-15), spiritual "bread," obedience to God (4:32-34), Jesus' authority (5:31-47), the true bread of life (6:30-36), and the true origin of Jesus (7:25-29). Jesus often explained deeper, spiritual truths by using physical examples. Often, however, his listeners couldn't make the connection; they couldn't get beyond the physical to the spiritual understanding.

5. John describes the work of the Holy Spirit, assuring believers of the presence of the risen Christ. Through the Holy Spirit, Christians have Christ with them; they don't have to face life alone. John records Jesus teaching that the Spirit would be sent to "convict the world of guilt in regard to sin and righteousness and judgment" (16:8 NIV), to guide believers into all truth (16:13), and to bring glory to Christ (16:14). John speaks of the work of the Holy Spirit more than any other Gospel writer.

6. John reminds believers that unbelief and opposition to God

and his plans do not surprise God or thwart his purposes. This includes the betrayal by Judas (foretold by prophets and known by Jesus—6:64; 13:18; Psalm 41:9), the death of Jesus on the cross (a necessary part of God's salvation plan—3:14-18), and the rejection of Christ by unbelievers (1:10-11). Although conflicts are inevitable, God is sovereign and in control, and his goals will be accomplished.

Because of John's special purpose for writing this book, he describes many incidents in the life of Christ that are not recorded in the other Gospels. These events include: John the Baptist declaring Jesus to be the Messiah, Jesus turning water into wine, Nicodemus visiting Jesus at night, Jesus talking to a Samaritan woman at the well, Jesus healing a government official's son, Jesus healing a lame man by the pool, Jesus' brothers ridiculing him, Jesus healing the man who was born blind, Jesus raising Lazarus from the dead, Jesus teaching about the Holy Spirit, Jesus teaching about the vine and the branches, and Jesus appearing to Thomas and reinstating Peter after his resurrection.

John, the Son of Thunder turned evangelist, knew that people needed to know about the *real* Jesus. He also knew that as a contemporary of Christ and one of the chosen Twelve, he was uniquely suited to tell the story. So, compelled by love and under the inspiration of the Holy Spirit, John wrote the Gospel.

MESSAGE

"Jesus Christ, Son of God," "eternal life," "believing," "Holy Spirit," "resurrection"—because John's purpose was to convince people to believe in Christ, it's not surprising that his message follows the themes listed here. In order to trust Christ, a person must understand Jesus' true identity, the promise of eternal life, the necessity of faith, and the resurrection of Christ. And to live for Christ, a person must understand the person and work of the Holy Spirit.

Jesus Christ, Son of God (1:1-18; 2:1-11; 4:46-54; 5:1-15; 6:5-14; 6:16-21; 9:1-12; 11:1-44; 19:1–20:30).

Because this is a "Gospel," the entire book tells about Jesus. But in relating the life of the Lord, John chose eight "signs" (miracles) that illustrate and prove Jesus' true identity as God's Son. These chosen signs (seven miracles plus the Resurrection) display Christ's glory and reveal his true nature.

1. 2:1-11—Jesus turns water into wine at the wedding at Cana. John concludes this story by explaining, "This, the first of his miraculous signs, Jesus performed at Cana in Galilee. He thus

revealed his glory, and his disciples put their faith in him" (NIV). Evidently this miracle was an important turning point for the disciples. They trusted Jesus and began to understand that he was more than just a great teacher.

2. 4:46-54—Jesus heals the royal official's son. Back in Cana, Jesus encountered a Roman official who asked Jesus to heal his son. In addition to demonstrating Christ's power over sickness, this incident also shows that Jesus was the Savior for all people, not just the Jews. John states that this was the second miraculous sign (4:54).

3. 5:1-15—Jesus heals the invalid by the pool at Bethesda. This was a significant miracle because the man had been disabled for thirty-eight years! It was also important because Jesus performed the healing on the Sabbath, incurring the wrath of many Jews. John explains: "For this reason the Jews tried all the harder to kill him; not only was he breaking the Sabbath, but he was even calling God his own Father, making himself equal with God" (5:18 NIV).

4. 6:5-14—Jesus feeds the five thousand. This miracle had a tremendous effect on the multitudes. "After the people saw the miraculous sign that Jesus did, they began to say, 'Surely this is the Prophet who is to come into the world'" (6:14 NIV). Jesus had fed thousands from only five barley loaves and two small fish!

5. 6:16-21—Jesus walks on water. In this dramatic event, Jesus displayed his power over nature. Seasoned fishermen like John knew the great difficulty of guiding a boat over wind-tossed seas. Yet Jesus encountered no resistance from the sea and defied all they knew about sinking and floating as he strolled across the waves.

6. 9:1-41—Jesus heals a man blind from birth. Although all the healings recorded by John were wonderful miracles, they increase in dramatic effect and significance throughout the book. First we read about a very sick boy being cured, then a man who had been an invalid for thirty-eight years. Here we find Jesus restoring sight to a man who had been *born* blind—incredible!

7. 11:1-44—Jesus raises Lazarus from the dead. For those impressed by Jesus healing the blind man, John tells of a miracle even more amazing—raising a dead man to life. Surely this was the Son of God!

8. 20:1-29—The greatest sign of all, of course, is the Resurrection. By conquering death, Jesus gave final, definite proof that what he said is true, that he is the Son of God, that our sins can be forgiven, and that we can have eternal life through him. John was an eyewitness—he was one of the first to the empty tomb

(20:3-9), and he saw Jesus alive again (20:19-29; 21:1-24). John's readers did not have that privilege, but they too could believe. In fact, as Jesus had told Thomas, "Because you have seen me, you have believed; blessed are those who have not seen and yet have believed" (20:29 NIV).

In addition to these signs, in every chapter Jesus' deity is revealed. John also underscores Jesus' true identity through the titles he is given—Word, the One and Only, Lamb of God, Son of God, true bread, life, resurrection, vine. And the formula is "I am." When Jesus used this phrase, he was affirming his preexistence and eternal deity. Jesus said, *"I am* the bread of life" (6:35); *"I am* the light of the world" (8:12; 9:5); *"I am* the gate" (10:7); *"I am* the good shepherd" (10:11, 14); *"I am* the resurrection and the life" (11:25); *"I am* the way and the truth and the life" (14:6); and *"I am* the true vine" (15:1).

John shows us that Jesus is unique as God's special Son, yet he is fully God. Because he is fully God, Jesus is able to reveal God to us, clearly and accurately.

Importance for Today. The person and work of Christ form the core of Christianity and give us our hope for forgiveness and eternal life. John affirms that Jesus is the God-man—that is, he is fully God and fully man. This truth, of course, is impossible for our finite minds to comprehend. John does not try to explain it; he just presents the facts—Jesus, the incarnate Word, living as one of us and dying for us.

Because Jesus is God, he has the nature, ability, and right to offer eternal life. When he died on the cross, he was the perfect sacrifice and only mediator between God and people (14:6). Because Jesus became a man, he identified fully with us, enduring temptation, persecution, hardship, and suffering. And when he died on the cross, he *really died;* he wasn't pretending. Through the Incarnation, the infinite, holy, and all-powerful God demonstrated his love for us—"For God so loved the world that he gave his one and only Son" (3:16 NIV).

As believers in Christ, we must affirm both sides of his nature and not exclude or diminish one side in favor of the other. Jesus is fully God and fully man.

Eternal life (3:15-16, 36; 4:14, 36; 5:24, 39-40; 6:27, 40, 47, 54, 58; 8:51; 10:10, 27-30; 11:25-26; 12:25, 49-50; 20:30-31).

Jesus came to bring us life, eternal life. This life begins now, on this earth, through faith in Christ. Jesus said, "I have come that they may have life, and have it to the full" (10:10 NIV). Eternal life is not just a promise for the future; believers have it now (see 3:36; 5:24; 6:47).

The life that Christ offers also continues beyond death, in heaven: "Whoever believes in him shall not perish but have eternal life" (3:16 NIV); "In my Father's house are many rooms; if it were not so, I would have told you. I am going there to prepare a place for you. And if I go and prepare a place for you, I will come back and take you to be with me that you also may be where I am. . . . I am the way and the truth and the life. No one comes to the Father except through me" (14:2-3, 6 NIV).

Eternal life is life that does not end, so it has a quantitative meaning. But eternal life also has a qualitative sense, referring to the very life of God himself. John emphasizes both meanings.

Because Jesus is God, he lives forever. Before the world began, he lived with God (1:1-2), and he will reign forever with the Father (14:1-4). In John we see Jesus revealed in power and magnificence even before his resurrection.

Obtaining eternal life is not automatic or magic. People aren't saved just because Jesus became a man and died and rose again. Individuals must believe in Jesus; they must trust in him. John presents Jesus as the Good Shepherd who lays down his life for the sheep (10:11, 15, 17). His death is said to be a saving death— he is the Lamb of God who takes away the sin of the world (1:29, 36). But his sacrifice is applied only to those who repent and believe (1:12; 2:11; 3:15-16, 18, 36; and many other passages).

Importance for Today. Life on earth is short, and filled with struggles, suffering, and hardships. Of course there are moments of ecstasy and joy, but for many those moments are very few. And because all human beings are mortal, eventually everyone dies. That description is not mere pessimism, but truth.

But God offers hope amidst the suffering—eternal life. Through faith in Christ, we have abundant life now and life unending after we die. The assurance of eternal life gives hope, meaning, and purpose as we live each day.

Jesus offers eternal life to us. We are invited to begin living in a personal, eternal relationship with him that begins now. Although we must grow old and die, we can have a new life that lasts forever by trusting Jesus.

Believing (1:12, 50; 2:11, 23; 3:15-18; 4:39-42, 48-53; 5:24, 47; 6:30, 47, 64; 8:24, 31; 9:38; 10:25-42; 11:25-27; 12:37-46; 14:11-14; 16:9; 17:8, 20; 20:25-30).

Belief in Jesus as the Messiah and Son of God is the central theme of this book and the desired response from all who read it. Knowing that Jesus is the Son of God and that eternal life is available only through him, people must believe in Jesus as their Savior and Lord. John chose eight signs (miracles) that show the nature of Jesus' power and love to convince people to believe in Christ. John explains this as he states his purpose: "But these are written that you may believe that Jesus is the Christ, the Son of God, and that by believing you may have life in his name" (20:31 NIV).

John wrote to a skeptical world. The Jews were looking for their Messiah whom they thought would be a mighty hero, one who would free them from Roman tyranny and restore Israel to her former glory. Jews found it difficult to believe in a gentle rabbi who taught love and servanthood. The religious Jews were especially skeptical of Jesus. After all, he exposed their hypocrisy and called people to a personal relationship with God through him alone (14:6). Greeks, with their history of philosophical dialogue and intellectual acumen, would be naturally skeptical of a man claiming to be God in the flesh. And what about the Romans? With their multitude of gods, they would find it difficult to embrace one who claimed to be the *only* way. So John presents the evidence, facts to support the claims of Christ, to convince readers that Jesus is the Messiah, the Son of God.

The first step toward eternal life is to believe the facts about Jesus. Through the eight signs and other incidents in the life of Christ, John presents these facts, not as statements about Jesus, but as scenes of Jesus in action. And he describes the effects on those who witnessed each event. "Many of the Samaritans from that town believed in him because of the woman's testimony, 'He told me everything I ever did.' So when the Samaritans came to him, they urged him to stay with them, and he stayed two days. And because of his words many more became believers. They said to the woman, 'We no longer believe just because of what you said; now we have heard for ourselves, and we know that this man really is the Savior of the world'" (4:39-42 NIV).

But having saving faith ("believing") involves much more than mental assent to the truth. John emphasizes Jesus' strong teaching that those who *truly* believe in Christ turn from their sin, follow him closely, and obey his teachings. Jesus told the crowds, "I am the light of the world. Whoever follows me will never walk in darkness, but will have the light of life" (8:12 NIV), and, "I tell you the truth, if anyone keeps my word, he will never see death" (8:51 NIV). When the formerly blind man believed, he worshiped Jesus (9:38). At another time Jesus taught the disciples, "The man who loves his life will lose it, while the man who hates his life in this world will keep it for eternal life. Whoever serves me must follow me; and where I am, my servant also will be. My Father will honor the one who serves me" (12:25-26 NIV).

The person who puts his or her faith in Christ (believes the facts about him, trusts him, follows close to him, and obeys his commands) is forgiven and gains eternal life. "Whoever believes in him is not condemned, but whoever does not believe stands condemned already because he has not believed in the name of God's one and only Son" (3:18 NIV).

Importance for Today. Believing is active, living, and continuous trust in Jesus as God. When we believe in his life, his words, his death, and his resurrection, we are cleansed from sin and receive power to follow him. But we must respond to Christ by believing. This believing begins with the facts about Jesus, but it must go deeper, involving total commitment to him. Do you *truly* believe in Jesus?

Remember, too, that we also live in a world of skeptics. Most people won't believe that something is true simply because we tell them, especially regarding religion. They need to see Jesus in action, to read about his claims and his miracles, and to understand his teachings. As we explain to relatives, friends, neighbors, and coworkers about how they can have eternal life, we need to present the evidence that Jesus is the Son of God and their only hope.

Holy Spirit (1:32-34; 3:5; 6:63; 7:39; 14:16-26; 15:26; 16:7, 15).

The first mention of the Holy Spirit in the Gospel of John is John the Baptist's explanation that when he baptized Jesus, he saw, "The Spirit come down from heaven as a dove and remain on him" (1:32 NIV). He adds that Jesus will "baptize with the Holy Spirit" (1:33 NIV). We know, therefore, that Jesus possessed the Spirit.

In addition, we read in John's Gospel that a person must be born "of water and the Spirit" (3:5 NIV) and that "the Spirit gives life" (6:63 NIV). In other words, when we believe in Christ, the Holy Spirit gives us new birth into the family of God. John also explains that the Holy Spirit was not fully given to believers until after Christ had been glorified (7:39).

The main teaching about the Holy Spirit in the Gospel of John, however, describes him as the Paraclete. This Greek word (*parakletos*) is also used to describe Jesus. Its literal meaning is "the one who comes alongside" and can also be translated "counselor." Therefore, the Holy Spirit is like Jesus; he comes alongside believers to guide and teach them, working for them and with them.

The main works of the Holy Spirit as the Paraclete are these:

1. He would come and abide in the disciples after the departure

of Jesus, to teach them, remind them of his words ("But the Counselor, the Holy Spirit, whom the Father will send in my name, will teach you all things and will remind you of everything I have said to you"—14:26 NIV), and show them the truth ("But when he, the Spirit of truth, comes, he will guide you into all truth"—16:13 NIV).

This work of the Holy Spirit is very important in understanding the doctrine of inspiration. In these passages, Jesus is promising his disciples that the Holy Spirit would help them recall what he had taught them and the important incidents in his life. The Holy Spirit would also open their eyes to understand Christ's true identity. This would ensure that their records of Christ's life would be accurate.

2. He would bear witness to Jesus through the disciples before the world ("When the Counselor comes, whom I will send to you from the Father, the Spirit of truth who goes out from the Father, he will testify about me. And you also must testify, for you have been with me from the beginning"—15:26-27 NIV) and will do his convicting work in the hearts of men and women in the world ("Unless I go away, the Counselor will not come to you; but if I go, I will send him to you. When he comes, he will convict the world of guilt in regard to sin and righteousness and judgment: in regard to sin, because men do not believe in me; in regard to righteousness, because I am going to the Father, where you can see me no longer; and in regard to judgment, because the prince of this world now stands condemned"—16:7-11 NIV).

All of these actions of the Holy Spirit are parallel to the work of Jesus on earth. Jesus claimed to be the way, the truth, and the life (14:6), and he preached about sin (8:24), righteousness (8:42-47), and judgment (9:39).

Jesus taught his disciples that the Holy Spirit would come after he left the earth. The Holy Spirit would then indwell, guide, counsel, and comfort those who follow Jesus. Through the Holy Spirit, Christ's presence and power are multiplied in all who believe.

Importance for Today. God has sent the Holy Spirit into the world to draw people to himself and to work in the lives of believers. As we read and study God's Word, the Holy Spirit will guide us into the truth (16:13), helping us understand about Christ and about God's principles for living. One of our responsibilities as believers is to testify about Christ in the world (15:27), passing on what the Holy Spirit tells us (15:26). As we do this, we can be confident that the Holy Spirit will be working in the lives of men

and women, convicting them of their sin and their need to trust
Christ as Savior (16:7-11).

We must know the Holy Spirit to understand all Jesus taught.
We can experience Jesus' love and guidance as we allow the
Holy Spirit to work in us.

Resurrection (20:1–21:23).
The final and greatest sign presented by John of the divinity of
Jesus is his resurrection from the dead. Just as Jesus really lived
as a man on the earth, he really died on the cross. The witnesses
to Jesus' death were many: the Roman soldiers (19:23-24, 32-34),
the chief priests and other Jewish religious leaders (19:21), the
crowd (19:20), a small collection of his loyal followers (19:25-
27), and those who buried him, Joseph of Arimathea and Nicodemus (19:38-42).

Jesus was dead, and with his death, all hope seemed to vanish
from the disciples. Most of them fled and followed from a distance (Matthew 26:56; John 18:15). Peter denied even knowing
Jesus (18:15-18, 25-27). They were a disorganized and fearful
group (20:19).

But Jesus' death was not the end of the story. He arose, triumph-
phant over death. Mary Magdalene, John, and Peter found the
tomb empty (20:1-9). Then Mary Magdalene met the risen Christ
face to face (20:10-18). Later, the disciples saw Jesus alive
(20:19-29; 21:1-23).

The fact of the Resurrection changed the disciples' lives
from fearful men who fled danger to courageous witnesses who
took the gospel to every corner of their world, from discouraged
and disillusioned followers to hopeful and joyful "Christ-ones"
(i.e., "Christians"—ones belonging to Christ).

The fact that Jesus rose from the dead is the foundation of the
Christian faith.

Importance for Today. The resurrection of Christ from the
dead is important for us for several reasons.

1. *Truth.* Because Jesus rose from the dead, we know that he is,
in fact, the Son of God and that all he taught is true. People
choose religions for a variety of reasons (for example, to please
parents, to feel good, to advance socially, or to earn their way to
heaven); but the most important and basic reason for becoming a
Christian is because the gospel is true. Jesus said that he was the
truth (14:6), and his resurrection confirmed it!

2. *Hope.* Jesus taught that whoever believes in him will have
eternal life (3:16-18). Because Jesus is God and truthful, we
know that his promise of eternal life is also true. In the face of
danger, disease, and death, we can remember the words of Jesus

to Martha at Lazarus's tomb: "I am the resurrection and the life. He who believes in me will live, even though he dies; and whoever lives and believes in me will never die" (11:25-26 NIV). We can hope.

3. *Presence.* Jesus is alive, therefore we worship and serve a living Savior. Jesus promised his followers that he would be with them always (Matthew 28:20). He said that when he left the world, he would send his Spirit to us (16:7). When Jesus rose from the dead and ascended to heaven, he sent the Holy Spirit to be with us and in us.

4. *Confidence.* After the Resurrection, the disciples were confident and bold, knowing that with God for them, no one could stand against them (Romans 8:31). They also knew that they also would rise from the dead. We can be changed as the disciples were and have the confidence that someday our bodies will be raised to live with Christ forever. The same power that raised Christ to life can give us the ability to follow him each day.

VITAL STATISTICS

Purpose: To prove conclusively that Jesus is the Son of God and that all who believe in him will have eternal life.

Author: John the apostle, son of Zebedee, brother of James, called a "Son of Thunder"

To whom written: New Christians and searching non-Christians

Date written: Probably A.D. 85–90

Setting: Written after the destruction of Jerusalem in A.D. 70 and before John's exile to the island of Patmos

Key verses: "Jesus did many other miraculous signs in the presence of his disciples, which are not recorded in this book. But these are written that you may believe that Jesus is the Christ, the Son of God, and that by believing you may have life in his name" (20:30-31, NIV).

Key people: Jesus, John the Baptist, the disciples, Mary, Martha, Lazarus, Jesus' mother, Pilate, Mary Magdalene

Key places: Judean countryside, Samaria, Galilee, Bethany, Jerusalem

Special features: Of the eight miracles recorded, six are unique (among the Gospels) to John, as is the "Upper Room Discourse" (chapters 14–17). Over 90 percent of John is unique to his Gospel—John does not contain a genealogy or any record of Jesus' birth, childhood, temptation, transfiguration, appointment of the disciples, nor any account of Jesus' parables, ascension, or great commission.

OUTLINE OF JOHN

A. BIRTH AND PREPARATION OF JESUS, THE SON OF GOD (1:1–2:11)
B. MESSAGE AND MINISTRY OF JESUS, THE SON OF GOD (2:12–12:50)
    1. Jesus encounters belief and unbelief from the people
    2. Jesus encounters conflict with the religious leaders
    3. Jesus encounters crucial events in Jerusalem
C. DEATH AND RESURRECTION OF JESUS, THE SON OF GOD (13:1–21:25)
    1. Jesus teaches his disciples
    2. Jesus completes his mission

John's story begins as John the Baptist ministers near Bethany beyond the Jordan (1:28ff). Jesus also begins his ministry, talking to some of the men who would later become his 12 disciples. Jesus' ministry in Galilee began with a visit to a wedding in Cana (2:1ff). Then he went to Capernaum, which became his new home (2:12). He journeyed to Jerusalem for the special feasts (2:13) and there met with Nicodemus, a religious leader (3:1ff). When he left Judea, he traveled through Samaria and ministered to the Samaritans (4:1ff). Jesus did miracles in Galilee (4:46ff) and in Judea and Jerusalem (5:1ff). We follow him as he fed 5,000 near Bethsaida-Julias beside the Sea of Galilee (6:1ff), walked on the water to his frightened disciples (6:16ff), preached through Galilee (7:1), returned to Jerusalem (7:2ff), preached beyond the Jordan in Perea (10:40), raised Lazarus from the dead in Bethany (11:1ff), and finally entered Jerusalem for the last time to celebrate the Passover with his disciples and give them key teachings about what was to come and how they should act. His last hours before his crucifixion were spent in the city (13:1ff), in the Garden of Gethsemane (18:1ff), and finally in various buildings in Jerusalem during his trial (18:12ff). He would be crucified, but he would rise again as he had promised.

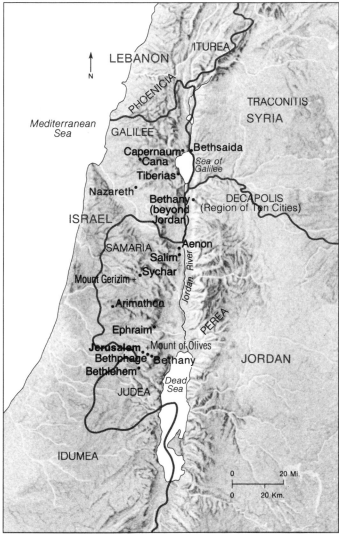

LEBANON

ITUREA

N

PHOENICIA

Mediterranean
Sea

TRACONITIS
SYRIA

GALILEE

Capernaum• •Bethsaida
•Cana   *Sea of*
Tiberias•   *Galilee*

Nazareth•

DECAPOLIS
(Region of Ten Cities)

ISRAEL

Bethany
(beyond
Jordan)

SAMARIA   •Aenon
Salim•
•Sychar

Mount Gerizim +

•Arimathea

Ephraim•

Jerusalem •Mount of Olives
Bethphage• •Bethany
Bethlehem•

JUDEA

*Dead
Sea*

Jordan River

PEREA

JORDAN

IDUMEA

0   20 Mi.

0   20 Km.

Modern names and boundaries are shown in gray.

John 1

Jesus revealed his essential nature in what he taught and did. John wrote about Jesus as fully human and fully God. Although Jesus took upon himself full humanity and entered history with the limitations of a human being, he never ceased to be the eternal God, eternally existing, the Creator and Sustainer of all things, and the source of eternal life. John's Gospel tells the truth about Jesus, the foundation of all truth. If we cannot or do not believe in Jesus' true identity, we will not be able to trust our eternal destiny to him. John wrote his Gospel to build our faith and confidence in Jesus Christ so that we might believe that Jesus truly was and is the Son of God (20:30-31).

John starts at the "beginning," with the first eighteen verses of John, called the *prologue*. Many commentators consider the prologue to be a poem or, at least, rhythmical prose. Some commentators suggest that verses 1-5, 10-12, and 14-18 may have been parts of one or several early Christian hymns. Others have thought that verses 14-18 were used as an early church confessional statement, to which John added his stamp of approval.

Furthermore, the prologue to John's Gospel provides a miniature of the entire Gospel. John's goal and guiding purpose in writing can be found in almost every phrase of his work. The prologue highlights most of the insights and truths that we find in the rest of the Gospel. John introduced key terms: *the Word, God, life, light, darkness, witness, the world, rejection/reception, belief, regeneration* (becoming a child of God), *incarnation* (the Word become flesh), *the one and only Son of the Father, glory, grace, truth, fullness.* In the rest of the Gospel, John expanded and illustrated each of these from Jesus' life and ministry.

THE REAL JESUS
Throughout John's Gospel, Christ is presented in the following ways:
- the one who expresses God (the Word)
- God himself
- the giver of eternal life to those who believe
- the bringer of light into a dark world
- the giver of grace to those who receive him
- the unique Son sharing an intimate relationship with his Father
- the bearer of heavenly truth
- the expression of God's glory and fullness.

1:1 In the beginning. When John wrote of *the beginning,* he was paralleling the words of the creation account. He stressed that "the Word" already existed at the time of creation (as is translated in the NEB). More likely, John was thinking of a beginning before "the beginning" in Genesis 1:1, a timeless beginning. Thus, we could translate the first part of the verse as "in eternity the Word existed."

BEGINNINGS
Each of the Gospel writers chose a different starting point for their accounts of the life of Jesus. Matthew began with Abraham, showing how Jesus came from Abraham's family and was the fulfillment of God's promise to Abraham. Mark skipped most of the preliminaries and moved right to the action, beginning with the ministry of John the Baptist. Luke began with a review of his research method and rooted Jesus' life in the wider historical events of his time. But John presented the largest perspective of all, describing Jesus as the very source of everything we understand as beginning. His purpose was to record, in outline form, the biography of the Son of God, who even in becoming a human being accomplished so much that "if every one of them were written down, I suppose that even the whole world would not have room for the books that would be written" (21:25 NIV).

The Word. John called the Son of God, who was with God his Father in the beginning, *the Word.* John did not identify this person immediately, but described his nature and purpose before revealing his name (see vv. 14, 17). As the Word, the Son of God fully conveys and communicates God. What does John mean by "the Word"? Theologians and philosophers, both Jews and Greeks, used the term *word* in a variety of ways. The Greek term is *logos.* In the Hebrew language of the Old Testament, "the Word" is described as an agent of creation (Psalm 33:6), the source of God's message to his people through the prophets (Hosea 1:2), and God's law, his standard of holiness (Psalm 119:11).

The Greeks used "the Word" in two ways. It could mean a person's thoughts or reason, or it might refer to a person's speech, the expression of thoughts. As a philosophical term, *logos* conveyed the rational principle that governed the universe, even the creative energy that generated the universe.

In both the Jewish and Greek conceptions, *logos* conveyed the idea of beginnings—the world began through the Word (see Genesis 1:3ff., where the expression "God said" occurs repeatedly). John may have had these ideas in mind, but his description shows clearly that he spoke of Jesus as a human being he knew and loved (see especially 1:14), who was at the same time the Creator of the universe, the ultimate revelation of God, and also the living picture of God's holiness, the one in whom "all things hold together" (Colossians 1:17 NIV). Jesus as the *logos* reveals God's mind to us.

To strict Jewish readers, "the Word was God" sounded like blasphemy. Strongly monotheistic, they found it difficult to even speak about God without running the danger of offending the One and Only. Certainly God "spoke" words, but to say "the Word was God" equated the two realities; the Hebrew mind resisted any such thinking about God. One of the most compelling reasons to believe the doctrine of the Trinity comes from the fact that it was revealed through a people most likely to reject it outright. In a world populated by many gods, it took the tough-minded Hebrews to clarify the revelation of God's oneness expressed through Three-in-oneness. We humbly bow before the one God, but we do not presume to easily comprehend his essential being.

To John, this new understanding of "the Word" was gospel, the Good News of Jesus Christ. Although it had been right in front of philosophic minds for centuries, they had been blind to it. Jesus revealed the truth in the light of his identity. He is the image of the invisible God (Colossians 1:15), the express image of God's substance (Hebrews 1:3), the revealer of God, and the reality of God. The theme of the real identity of Jesus dominates the Gospel of John. We should be grateful that the Son of God has expressed the Father to us and made him real to us. Otherwise, we could not know God intimately and personally.

The Word was with God. By using this expression, John was explaining that the Word (the Son) and God (the Father) already enjoyed an intimate, personal relationship in the beginning. The last verse of the prologue (1:18) tells us that the Son was at the Father's side; and in Jesus' special prayer for his followers (chapter 17), he expressed that the Father loved him before the foundation of the world.

The Word was God. Not only was the Son with God, he was himself God. According to the Greek, this phrase could be translated "the Word was divine." John's Gospel, more than most books in the New Testament, asserts Jesus' divinity. Jesus is called "God" in 1:1; 1:18; and 20:28.

BAD NEWS
Often little words become large issues. Cults like Jehovah's Witnesses attempt to insert an indefinite article in verse 1, making it "and the Word was a god" (New World Translation, a specific "translation" by Jehovah's Witnesses). It is a small addition with devastating results. The added *a* serves to bolster the teaching that Jesus was a created being who "earned" divine qualities that are attainable by the rest of us. If Jesus is only a god, then the so-called gospel is only bad news. However, John was writing not about gods but about God, and he clearly claimed that "the Word was God"!

1:2 He was in the beginning with God.^{NKJV} The second verse of the prologue underscores the truth that the Word coexisted with the Father from the beginning. A wrong teaching called the "Arian heresy" developed in the fourth century of Christianity. Arius, the father of this heresy, was a priest of Alexandria (in Egypt) during the reign of Emperor Constantine. He taught that Jesus, the Son of God, was not eternal but was created by the Father. Therefore, Jesus was not God by nature; Christ was not one substance with the Father. He also taught that the Holy Spirit was begotten by the *logos*. Arius's bishop, Alexander, condemned Arius and his followers. But Arius's views gained some support. At the Church Council in Nicea in 325 A.D., Athanasius defeated Arius in debate and the Nicene Creed was adopted, which established the biblical teaching that Jesus was "one essence with the Father." Yet this controversy raged until it was defeated at the Council of Constantinople in 381 A.D.

This heresy still exists, however, in several so-called Christian cults (see box above). Yet John's Gospel proclaims simply and clearly that the Son of God is coeternal with the Father.

1:3 All things came into being through him.^{NRSV} The New Testament portrays the Son of God as the agent of creation, for all things were created through him (see 1 Corinthians 8:6; Colossians 1:16; Hebrews 1:2). Everything came into being through Christ and ultimately depends upon him.

SOMETHING FROM NOTHING
When God created, he made something from nothing. Because he created us, we have no basis for pride. We must remember that we exist only because God made us, and we have special gifts only because God gave them to us. With God we have value and uniqueness; apart from God we have nothing, and if we try to live without him, we will miss the purpose he designed us to fulfill.

1:4 In him was life. Creation needs to receive life from the Word— for he is the source of *life*. Christ gives physical life to all. But he also gives eternal life to all those who believe in him. The Greek term used for "life" is *zoe;* it is always used to describe the divine, eternal life in the Gospel of John. Jesus used this specific term during the Last Supper when he told his disciples, "I am the way and the truth and the life. No one comes to the Father except through me" (14:6 NIV).

That life was the light of men.^{NIV} The divine *life* embodied in Christ brought unique *light* to people—revealing divine truth and exposing their sin. Everywhere Christ went, he brought light (see 3:21; 8:12). *Light* means understanding and moral insight, spiritual vision. But more than just shining or reflecting, the light of Jesus penetrates and enlightens hearts and minds. Everyone who comes into contact with Christ can be enlightened.

Christ is the one universal light. There is no other. As Creator, Jesus not only provides light but he also makes people light sensitive. The blindness Jesus later attributes to the Pharisees (9:35-41) includes an intentional turning away from the light, pretending to "see" something else.

What is seen by the light of Jesus? When Christ's light shines, we see our sin and his glory. We can refuse to see the light and remain in darkness. But whoever responds will be enlightened by Christ. He will fill our minds with God's thoughts. He will guide our path, give us God's perspective, and drive out the darkness of sin. John illustrates the action of Christ's light, in the chapters that follow, through the examples of the disciples, Nicodemus, the Samaritan woman, and the blind man whom Jesus healed.

1:5 The light shines in the darkness.^{NRSV} John used the past tense in the previous sentence, saying that Jesus *was* the light of all people by virtue of being their Creator; but John shifted to the present tense: *the light shines in the darkness.* The timeless light has invaded our time, and we can see it in our darkness. Christ's life and message are still effective. John could see it around him in his day as he witnessed the strength of the Christian church—planted, thriving, growing. And it is still present tense today—for Christ's light still shines in our dark world. As the light shines, it drives away the darkness for the unsaved world is blinded by the prince of this world (2 Corinthians 4:4; Ephesians 5:8).

> I believe in Christianity as I believe that the Sun has risen not only because I see it but because by it I see everything else.
> *C. S. Lewis*

The darkness did not overcome it.^{NRSV} Christ's light shined to a hardened, darkened humanity—and he continues to shine. But the *darkness did not overcome it*—the darkness could not grasp, comprehend, or extinguish the light. The NEB uses the word *mastered* to convey the dual areas of meaning carried by the Greek *katalambano.* On one hand, this word can refer to physical restraint, controlling, or conquering. On the other hand, the word can allude to a mental grasping or understanding. John may well have meant both. Unbelievers did not comprehend Christ's true identity and tried to conquer him. Thus, darkness failed on both counts to master Christ!

> There is enough light for those who only desire to see the light, and enough darkness for those who only desire the contrary.
> *Blaise Pascal*

This statement indicates the struggle between the darkness and the light. The *darkness*—unregenerate humanity under the influence of Satan, the prince of darkness—has not accepted the light and even resists the light. Thus, "darkness" indicates ignorance and sin, active rejection of God's will. Those in darkness reject Christ, his light, and his followers. But no matter how deep the darkness, even a small light can drive it back. The power of Christ's light overcomes any darkness in the world.

1:6 There was a man sent from God, whose name was John.^{NKJV} Leaping over several millennia, John abruptly introduces Jesus' forerunner and herald, John the Baptist. Actually, the startling shift in time dramatically illustrates the eternal light suddenly shining in the darkness.

God sent John the Baptist to prepare the way for the Messiah.

John the Baptist has a prominent position in the prologue because his ministry prepared the way for the Messiah—he pointed people to Jesus.

LIGHTEN UP
The darkness of evil never has and never will overcome or extinguish God's light. Jesus Christ is the Creator of life, and his life brings light to mankind. In his light we see our true identity (sinners in need of a Savior). When we follow Jesus, the true Light, we can avoid walking blindly and falling into sin. Christ lights the path ahead of us so we can see how to live. He removes the darkness of sin from our lives. Have you allowed the light of Christ to shine into your life? Let Christ guide your life, and you'll never need to stumble in darkness.

1:7-8 He came as a witness to testify to the light, so that all might believe through him.NRSV John the Baptist's function was to be a channel whereby people could come to Christ. Jesus called John the Baptist the greatest man ever born (Luke 7:28) because he fulfilled the highest privilege; he was the first to point people to Christ, so in a very real sense, all who have come to believe have done so because of his witness. He was first in a line of witnesses that stretches through the centuries to this day.

John himself was not the light, but he came to testify to the light.NRSV John stressed the difference between John the Baptist and Jesus, even though to many it might have been obvious, because even during Paul's travels, he encountered believers who only knew about John the Baptist but not about Jesus (see Acts 18:25; 19:1-7). John the Baptist influenced the people of Ephesus where John had written this Gospel. John wanted to ensure that all believers worship Christ, not his messenger.

REFLECTORS
Like John the Baptist, we are not the source of God's light; we merely reflect that light. Jesus Christ is the true Light; he helps us see our way to God and shows us how to walk along that way. But Christ has chosen to reflect his light through his followers to an unbelieving world, perhaps because unbelievers are not able to bear the full blazing glory of his light firsthand. The word *witness* indicates our role as reflectors of Christ's light. We are never to present ourselves as the light to others, but are always to point them to Christ, the Light.

1:9 The true light, which enlightens everyone, was coming into the world.NRSV How has Christ enlightened everyone? The word *everyone* here could be nationalistically inclusive, referring to both Jews and Gentiles, or it could refer to all individuals. Every person has life from God, thus they have *some* light; creation reveals God's power and divinity (1:3; Acts 14:17; Romans 1:19-20; 2:14-16); and our conscience also bears witness to God's existence. The Gospel writer's description captures the transition between the ministry of John the Baptist as herald and the ministry of Jesus, *the true light.* Jesus, as opposed to any other "luminaries," is the true and exclusive revelation of God to man. Because of this, we can count on him.

1:10 The world did not recognize him. [NIV] John notes one of the greatest tragedies: the world—humankind—did not recognize its own Creator. They were blinded and could not see his light. Although Christ created the world, the people he created didn't recognize him. He was denied the general acknowledgment that should have been his as Creator.

> Man does not recognize the place he should fill. He has obviously gone astray. He has fallen from the true status, and he cannot find it again. So he searches everywhere anxiously but in vain, in the midst of great darkness. *Blaise Pascal*

1:11 He came to His own. [NKJV] In Greek this reads, "He came to his own things"—that is, he came to that which belonged to him. The expression can even be used to describe a homecoming. This phrase intensifies the description of Christ's rejection. Jesus was not welcome in the world, or even his home. *His own* refers to God's chosen nation, Israel, which was particularly Christ's.

His own did not receive Him. [NKJV] According to the Greek, this means that his own family did not receive him. The Greek word for *receive* means "to welcome." The Jews did not welcome Jesus. Those who should have been most eager to welcome him were the first to turn away. As a nation, they rejected their Messiah. This rejection is further described at the end of Jesus' ministry (12:37-41). Isaiah had foreseen this unbelief (Isaiah 53:1-3).

In spite of the rejection described here, John steers clear of passing sentence on the world. Instead, he turns our attention on those who did welcome Christ in sincere faith.

1:12 But as many as received Him. [NKJV] Though the rejection of Christ was universal, individuals did respond personally. The Greek root word translated "received" here is also used in verse 11 in the sense of welcoming (*paralambano*); here it carries the sense of accepting *(lambano)*. To receive Jesus is to welcome and acknowledge him as our Savior and Lord.

INSIDE OUT
All who welcome Jesus Christ as Lord of their lives are reborn spiritually, receiving new life from God. Through faith in Christ, the Holy Spirit changes us from the inside out—rearranging attitudes, desires, and motives. Being born makes us physically alive and places us in our parents' family (1:13). Being born of God makes us spiritually alive and joins us with God's family (1:12). The question then becomes, Have you received Christ in order that he can make you a new person? God makes this fresh start in life available to all who believe in Christ.

To them He gave the right to become children of God, to those who believe in His name.[NKJV] In Greek *right* means "authority or permission." In this context, it speaks of God granting the right or giving the privilege for the new birth. No one can attain this new birth by his or her own power, merit, or ability. Only God can grant it.

The Greek word for *children* emphasizes the idea of birth, which Jesus expands in chapter 3. The new birth comes only *to those who believe.* To believe in Jesus' name is to believe in his person—who he is and what he represents.

RECEIVING AND BELIEVING
"To believe" parallels "receive" as another aspect of our relationship with Christ. It leaves no doubt that we need to make a conscious personal response. Receiving and believing indicate informed awareness, not blind or empty faith. Receiving and believing have a personal object—Jesus Christ. The object of our faith is not a system, tradition, or organization. When we receive and believe in Jesus Christ, he gives us the privilege of becoming children of God.

Many believed superficially in Jesus when they saw his miracles, but they did not believe in Jesus as the Son of God. They "believed" in him while he fulfilled their expectations of what the Messiah should be, but they left him when he defied their preconceived notions. We must believe in Jesus as Jesus, the Son of God; we must wholeheartedly believe in Jesus, not limiting him to our ideas and misconceptions; we must regard Jesus as the Bible truly presents him.

ALL IN THE FAMILY
John claims that those who do not believe in Jesus are not children of God. We expect to hear a chorus of protest: "Aren't we all children of God?"

What do we say to those who claim that every person is a child of God? We are all children of God in the sense that God has created each person and given each of us life and light. But God is more than Creator; he is the Guide and Controller. The question remains, What kind of children are we? A child can merely live in a home, partaking of benefits without love or gratitude for the father. Such a child neither cooperates nor truly helps the father. Those claiming that every person is God's child generally mean, "I want all the privileges but none of the responsibilities." God's true children follow him in commitment, gratitude, friendship, and fellowship. What kind of child are you?

1:13 Children born not of natural descent, nor of human decision or a husband's will, but born of God.^{NIV} One is not in God's family because he or she is a Jew by natural birth (or even born into a Christian family). The new birth cannot be attained by an act of human will, and it has absolutely nothing to do with human planning. It is a gift of God.

1:14 The Word.^{NKJV} Returning to the powerful term used at the beginning of the Gospel, John continues the theme of the prologue. The first thirteen verses summarize "the Word's" relationship to the world as its rejected Creator, Visitor, Light, and Savior. Yet throughout the opening paragraph, John does not identify *the Word* as being human, except in the personal pronouns.

Became flesh.^{NKJV} This phrase is striking and arresting despite its familiarity. Understanding its meaning simply increases our wonder. Many modern translators have unfortunately rendered this phrase "became a man." Of course, this is what the text means, but John purposely used the word *flesh* to combat a heresy called Docetism—a heresy that denied that Jesus truly had a human body. The Docetists claimed that the Son of God merely *seemed* human; he was not truly human. Later, in his first epistle, John wrote that any person who did not confess that Jesus Christ had come in the flesh did not belong to God (1 John 4:3). Jesus was already the divine Word, but he arrived on the earth as *flesh*.

When Jesus was born, he was not part man and part God; he was completely human and completely divine (Colossians 2:9). Before Christ came, people could know God partially. After Christ had come, people could know God fully because he

PARALLELS BETWEEN JOHN'S PROLOGUE AND HIS GOSPEL

Theme from Prologue	Parallel in John's Gospel	Significance
1. Preexisting Word (1:1-2)	17:5	Christ has equal status with God.
2. In him was life (1:4).	5:26	Christ is the source of life; we must come to him for eternal life.
3. His life is light (1:4).	8:12	Only Christ can light our path. We must follow him.
4. Darkness rejects the light (1:5).	3:19	Those bound in sin reject Christ's life and truth.
5. Darkness can never overcome the light (1:5).	12:35	The hostility of unbelievers can never destroy Christ's light.
6. Real light comes into the world (1:9).	3:19; 12:46	Christ shows us the way to have a personal relationship with God, but we must believe and follow.
7. Jesus' own people did not receive him (1:11).	4:44	We must not be like those who refused to believe.
8. Being born of God (1:13)	3:6; 8:41-42	To experience God's love we must be born again.
9. We have seen Christ's glory (1:14).	12:41	We know his real identity and his true nature as the Son of God.
10. Jesus is the one and only (1:14, 18).	3:16	Christ is the unique, unparalleled, and unrivaled Son of God.
11. Truth comes through Jesus (1:17).	14:6	Christ's life and teaching demonstrate God's revealed will. Those who listen to and follow his truth will be saved.
12. Only Jesus has seen God (1:18).	6:44-46	Christ is the ultimate authority on what God is like. We should not trust anyone else.

became visible and tangible (Hebrews 1:1-3). Christ is the perfect expression of God in human form. The two most common errors that people make about Jesus are minimizing his humanity or minimizing his divinity. Jesus is both divine and human (see Philippians 2:5-9).

John was also clarifying his use of the term *Word*. The Greek philosophical meaning of the term *word* as "reason" could refer to anything that wasn't flesh. To say "the Word became flesh" broke all the rules—which is exactly what God did!

WHAT CHRIST BECAME
By becoming human, Christ became:
   The perfect teacher—in Jesus' life we see how God thinks and therefore how we should think (Philippians 2:5-11).
   The perfect example—as a model of what we are to become, Jesus shows us how to live and gives us the power to live that way (1 Peter 2:21).
   The perfect sacrifice—Jesus came as a sacrifice for all sins, and his death satisfied God's requirements for the removal of sin (Colossians 1:15-23).

And dwelt among us.^{NKJV} The Greek word for *dwelt* means "tabernacled" or "pitched tent." To the Greek reader familiar with the Old Testament, this would have easily brought to mind the Old Testament tabernacle. In a sense, Jesus was God's new tabernacle. God, in Jesus, dwelt among people. The man living with the disciples was God incarnate! John was overwhelmed with that truth. He began his first letter by describing the experience of seeing, touching, and hearing this Word who became flesh and was *with* them (1 John 1:1-4). In Christ, God came to meet with people; through Christ we can come to meet with God.

We beheld His glory, the glory as of the only begotten of the Father, full of grace and truth.^{NKJV} This "glory" is often called the "shekinah glory" because *shekinah* denotes "in the tent"— "glory in the tent." *Glory* refers to Christ's divine greatness and shining moral splendor. (For a specific instance of "seeing his glory," see 2:11.) This is perhaps the clearest example of what John was thinking when he and two other disciples saw Jesus' transfiguration (see Matthew 17:1-13. Peter spoke of it specifically in 2 Peter 1:16-18).

Underneath Jesus' appearance as an ordinary Jewish carpenter, the disciples saw the indwelling glory of God. To the outsider, Jesus was nobody special; to those in the inner circle, he was the unique Son of God filled with glory. Too often we accuse the disciples of being slow to understand Jesus, but much of the time they were simply stunned. Jesus was always more than they could absorb. He will have the same effect on us.

THE GLORY OF CHRIST

"The glory of Christ" refers to the revelation of the character and presence of God in the person and work of Jesus Christ. It is God's divine honor, radiance, and perfection compressed, transformed, and made visible in Christ to our human understanding.

Christ's Glory Revealed	References
The shepherds witnessed the glory of God at Jesus' birth	Luke 2:9, 14
Jesus' miracles (signs) revealed his glory	John 2:11
God's glory is manifested in Jesus	John 7:18; 11:4; Hebrews 1:3
Jesus has his own unique glory	John 17:5
Jesus' glory was revealed at his transfiguration	Matthew 17:2-8; Mark 9:2-8; Luke 9:28-30
Jesus' disciples shared in his glory	John 17:22
Jesus' dedication to his sacrificial death is his glory	John 7:39; 12:23-28; 13:31; 17:5
Jesus' resurrection and ascension manifest his glory	Luke 24:26; Acts 3:13; 7:5; 1 Timothy 3:16
Jesus' glory will be completely revealed when he returns	Mark 8:38; 13:26

The Greek word for *only begotten* (*monogenous*) suggests a one and only son. The Son of God was the Father's one and only, his unique Son. Although all believers are called "children" and said to be "born of God" (1:12-13), Jesus is one of a kind and enjoys a special relationship with God. Eastern thought teaches a cycle of reincarnation. Many Hindus believe that Jesus was one in a series of reincarnations of Krishna. But John teaches that Jesus, as the unique Son of God, has a special glory and an unrivaled, unparalleled, and unrepeatable place of honor.

The phrase *full of grace and truth* modifies "the Word." It also softens the glare of *glory*. The Greek word for "grace" (*charis*) parallels a Hebrew word meaning "lovingkindness"; the word in Greek also means "that which is a free gift." The Greek word for "truth" (*aletheia*) means "reality" and "genuine"; John's Gospel connects it with the idea of divine revelation (8:32; 17:17; 18:37). Those enlightened realize Christ as the divine reality. In union with Christ, we experience his grace and truth. By his power we can show his life to others.

GLORY

Although we have not yet been granted the privilege of seeing Jesus as the disciples did, someday we will. "Now we see but a poor reflection as in a mirror; then we shall see face to face. Now I know in part; then I shall know fully, even as I am fully known" (1 Corinthians 13:12 NIV). In the meantime, we have the testimony of those who were with Jesus. Jesus prayed for those of us who would believe in him through their witness (17:20). In his prayer, Jesus anticipated the time when we would see his glory (17:24).

For now, even the "poor reflection" of his glory is enough to change us. As we allow his words to become part of us, as we obey his commands and seek to honor him, we will discover in ourselves a growing eagerness to stand before him and to experience his glory fully (Philippians 3:12-14) and share in it too (2 Corinthians 4:17).

1:15 (John testified to him . . . "This was he of whom I said, 'He who comes after me ranks ahead of me because he was before me.'")NRSV This verse interrupts the flow of the narrative—for verse 16 naturally follows the end of verse 14 ("full of grace and truth . . . and of His fullness have we all received, and grace for grace," NKJV). John probably decided to insert John the Baptist's testimony at this point to underscore a major theme in the prologue: Christ's eternal existence.

John the Baptist declared that Christ *ranks ahead of me because he was before me.* Although Jesus was humanly born after John the Baptist, Jesus existed from eternity past. For this reason, Jesus outranked John the Baptist.

1:16 Of His fullness.NKJV The Greek word for *fullness* is *pleroma;* it indicates superabundance and completeness. John used a root form in verse 14, "full (*pleres*) of grace and truth" (NKJV). John stretched the language to its very limit in attempting to capture the facts about Jesus and, at the same time, the lasting impact Jesus had on those who followed him. When John spoke of Jesus' "fullness," he was affirming that he had never found Jesus lacking in any way. John's description conveys a subtle invitation for us to trust Jesus' ability to meet our needs.

> It is a greater work of God to bring men to grace, than being in the state of grace, to bring them to glory; because sin is far more distant from grace than grace is from glory.
> *John Trapp*

FULLNESS
The Gnostics used the word *fullness* to describe the totality of all deities. Gnosticism was the widest known of the so-called mystery cults. Although exclusive in membership, the Gnostics were inclusive in theology. Instead of receiving the truth that "the Word became flesh," they invented a religion of "the word became secret." They made "fullness" a protected mystery; but Jesus made "fullness" a living reality!

Both John and Paul used *pleroma* to describe Christ—proclaiming that Christ embodies the fullness of God (see Ephesians 1:23; 3:19; Colossians 1:19; 2:9). Because all of God's fullness dwells in Christ, we can find every spiritual reality we need in him. He embodies all of God's power, wisdom, mercy, and love. He fills everything in every way (Ephesians 1:23). The infinite God allows us to draw on all of his attributes and resources.

We have all received.NKJV At this point, John includes all the believers, not just himself and the apostles (for whom he was spokesman—1:14). All believers receive Christ's fullness, but no single believer can receive *all* of Christ; it takes the whole body of Christ to appropriate his fullness and to express it (see Ephesians 1:23).

Nothing can deplete Christ—no matter how much the believers receive of him, he keeps on giving. His strength is not diminished by helping us. Believers do not need to seek any other source of spiritual power but Christ. Paul said: "For in Him dwells all the fullness of the Godhead bodily; and you are complete [or made full] in Him" (Colossians 2:9-10 NKJV). Christ himself fulfills our Christian life; we do not need to seek anything beyond him.

Grace upon grace.NRSV The Greek text literally says "grace in place of grace," which could mean "grace replenishing grace" (a continual supply of Christ's loving-kindness) or New Testament grace replacing Old Testament grace—in the sense that Christ's dispensation of grace supersedes Moses' or anticipated grace is replaced with fulfilled grace (see next verse). Either way, we need to realize that the grace given by Christ can never be exhausted because he is full of grace. When we are exhausted and "on empty," Christ is always present to fill us with his grace.

1:17 For the law was given through Moses, but grace and truth came through Jesus Christ.NKJV This statement presents a contrast and begs the question: Can the law given through Moses

and the grace and truth from Jesus Christ be complimentary?
John introduced one of the central questions Jesus would answer:
Because law and grace seem to contradict, what action should
people take?

Both law and grace express God's nature. Moses emphasized
God's law and justice, while Jesus Christ came to highlight God's
mercy, love, and forgiveness. Moses could only be the giver of
the law, while Christ came to fulfill perfectly the law (Matthew
5:17). The law revealed the nature and will of God; now Jesus
Christ reveals the nature and will of God. Rather than coming
through cold stone tablets, God's revelation ("truth") now comes
through a person's life. As we get to know Christ better, our understanding of God will increase.

1:18 No one has ever seen God.^{NRSV} This statement seems to contradict passages like Exodus 24:9-11, which says that the elders of
Israel "saw God." What then does John
mean? Very likely, he is affirming the
fact that no human being has seen the
essential being of God—i.e., no one
has seen God as God. Some men experienced "theophanies" (special appearances of God in various forms), but no
one saw the essential being of God. As
Calvin put it, "When he says that none
has seen God, it is not to be understood
of the outward seeing of the physical
eye. He means generally that since God dwells in inaccessible
light, he cannot be known except in Christ, his lively image."
Only the Son, who is himself God, can communicate his glory
to us.

> In the Scriptures there is
> a draught of God, but in
> Christ there is God
> Himself. A coin bears the
> image of Caesar, but
> Caesar's son is his own
> lively resemblance. Christ
> is the living Bible.
> *Thomas Manton*

God the One and Only.^{NIV} This is more precisely rendered, "an
only one, God." All the earliest manuscripts support this reading;
other manuscripts read, "the only begotten Son." The first reading is preferred. Whatever the translation, all the earliest manuscripts indicate that Jesus is called *God,* as well as *the One and
Only.* Thus, Jesus' deity is again affirmed (see 1:1).

Who is in the bosom of the Father.^{NKJV} This picturesque language portrays the Son as a child in close dependence on his
Father—enjoying a close and warm relationship with him. It also
reflects the image of two close companions enjoying a meal
together. According to an ancient custom, the one who reclined
next to the master at a meal was the one dearest to him.

Has made him known.ᴺᴵⱽ The Greek reads, "He has explained
[him]." This tells us that the Son is God's explainer; he came to
earth and lived among men to explain God to us—with his words
and by his person. No one can know God apart from Christ,
God's explainer. Again, this mirrors verse 1, where the Son is
called "the Word"—the expression of God, the communicator of
God.

JOHN THE BAPTIST DECLARES HIS MISSION / 1:19-28 / **19**

His stirring summary accomplished, John launched into telling
the gospel. He had already introduced John the Baptist in the prologue. His overall description of the wilderness preacher leaves
out the physical notes of the other Gospels (see Mark 1:1-11;
Luke 1:5-25, 57-80; 3:1-20) but focuses instead on his unique
role as herald of the Messiah. The messianic expectations of the
time, combined with his initial success in attracting large crowds,
made John the Baptist the subject of speculation: Could he be the
Messiah?

In the encounter recorded in this Gospel, John the Baptist
accomplished three objectives: (1) he firmly denied being the
Christ; (2) he identified himself as the herald predicted by Isaiah,
who would announce the Messiah; (3) he announced the presence of the Messiah, yet he did not publicly identify Jesus even
though he baptized Jesus and heard God's verbal stamp of
approval on him. As the ministry of Jesus begins, we see the final
days of the ministry of John the Baptist.

1:19-21 **This is the testimony given by John when the Jews sent
priests and Levites from Jerusalem to ask him, "Who are
you?"**ᴺᴿˢⱽ John the Baptist's calling in life was described to his
father even before John was conceived. An angel had told John's
father, Zechariah:

■ *Your wife Elizabeth will bear you a son, and you will name him
John. You will have joy and gladness, and many will rejoice at
his birth, for he will be great in the sight of the Lord. He must
never drink wine or strong drink; even before his birth he will
be filled with the Holy Spirit. He will turn many of the people of
Israel to the Lord their God. With the spirit and power of Elijah
he will go before him, to turn the hearts of parents to their children, and the disobedient to the wisdom of the righteous, to
make ready a people prepared for the Lord. (Luke 1:13-17*
NRSV*)*

John's mission was to give testimony to Jesus Christ (1:7). He was Christ's first and most important witness. John disavowed any personal status; he constantly pointed men to Christ.

The Jews, as used here and in many other places in John, designated the Jewish leaders in Jerusalem. The *priests and Levites* were respected religious leaders in Jerusalem. Priests served in the temple, assisted by the Levites. The leaders who came to see John were Pharisees (1:24), a group that both John the Baptist and Jesus often denounced. Many Pharisees outwardly obeyed God's laws in order to look pious, while inwardly their hearts were filled with pride and greed.

These leaders came to see John the Baptist for several reasons: (1) As guardians of the faith, they needed to investigate any new preaching (Deuteronomy 13:1-5; 18:20-22). (2) They wanted to find out if John had the credentials of a prophet. (3) John's growing following presented them with a possible threat if he chose to use his influence with people against the religious leaders. (4) They were also probably jealous and wanted to see why John was so popular.

"I am not the Messiah."NRSV Their question indicates that the Jews were looking for the Anointed One (Greek, *ho Christos,* "the Christ"). John wanted to make it perfectly clear that he was not the Christ; rather, he was one who prepared the way for the Christ.

"Are you Elijah?"NRSV John's role and actions reminded these religious leaders of what had been written of Elijah (see 2 Kings 2:11). The Old Testament predicted that Elijah would come to prepare the way for the Messiah (see Malachi 3:1; 4:5-6). John the Baptist, in the spirit of Elijah (Luke 1:17), had come to prepare the way for the Christ, but he did not claim to be Elijah.

"Are you the prophet?"NRSV In the Pharisees' minds, there were four options regarding John the Baptist's identity: He was (1) the prophet foretold by Moses (Deuteronomy 18:15), (2) Elijah (Malachi 4:5), (3) the Messiah, or (4) a false prophet. John denied being the first three personages. His questioners wanted him to claim a special identity; he was perfectly content in his role. He simply called himself, in the words of the Old Testament prophet Isaiah, "The voice of one crying in the wilderness: 'Prepare the way of the LORD'" (Isaiah 40:3 NKJV).

The leaders kept pressing John to say who he was because people were expecting the Messiah to come (Luke 3:15). But John emphasized only *why* he had come—to prepare the way for the Messiah.

The Pharisees missed the point. They wanted to know who John was, but John insisted on pointing them toward Jesus.

1:22 "Who are you? Give us an answer to take back to those who sent us."NIV Those sent by the religious leaders of Jerusalem confronted a man sent by God; they had run out of stereotypes and were ready to listen. Although their attentiveness was hostile, John gave them an answer.

1:23 "I am 'The voice of one crying in the wilderness: "Make straight the way of the LORD,"' as the prophet Isaiah said."NKJV John quoted Isaiah 40, a portion that introduces the Messiah's forerunner and herald. In Isaiah 40:3-11, this herald announced the coming of the divine Shepherd. In ancient times, a herald (or forerunner) would go before a dignitary to announce his coming and to clear the way before him. John was the Messiah's herald and forerunner; he came on the scene to announce Jesus' coming and to exhort people to prepare the way to receive him.

MAKE IT MATTER
Whenever you are tempted to feel indispensable, remember John the Baptist. The fact that God uses us to do his work is no excuse for pride. God does not need us or have to keep us around. So we should make the most of the time we have. John remained a loud "voice in the wilderness" right up until his death. His sacrifice presents us with a question: Was a shortened life too high a price to pay for hearing God say, "Well done, good and faithful servant"?

1:24-25 Some Pharisees who had been sent questioned him.NIV This reading (found in the earliest manuscripts) indicates that some of the emissaries were Pharisees who began to question John further. Because John had publicly made some kind of claim about his role, he was subject to being grilled.

"Why then are you baptizing if you are neither the Messiah, nor Elijah, nor the prophet?"NRSV Since John did not claim to be the Christ, the prophet, or Elijah, the Pharisees wanted to know why John was baptizing. John had not invented baptism. Gentiles converting to Judaism were baptized as an initiation rite. But John was calling upon *Jews* to be baptized. Since this was new, they demanded an explanation from John.

1:26 "I baptize with water."NIV After this, we expect a reference to Jesus' baptism "in the Spirit" because this is stated in the Synoptic Gospels after the mention of water baptism. But the announcement of Jesus' baptism in the Spirit does not come until 1:33. It was John's function to provide the means for God's cleansing through water baptism; it would be Jesus' function to provide the people with an infusion of the Spirit. John was merely helping the people perform a symbolic act of repentance. But soon one would come who would truly *forgive* sins, something only the Son of God—the Messiah—could do.

"Among you stands one whom you do not know."[NRSV] The Son of God had taken up his abode among his own people, the Jews; but they did not realize it. This recalls John's tragic words in the prologue (1:11-12): Jesus' own people did not recognize him or receive him.

1:27 "I am not worthy to untie the thong of his sandal."[NRSV] In ancient times, a slave would perform many menial tasks for his master, but unstrapping a sandal was considered an extremely menial task and was usually done by oneself, not a slave. In saying that he was not even worthy to untie Jesus' sandals, John vividly pictured his subordination to Christ.

> A man is humble when he stands in the truth with a knowledge and appreciation for himself as he really is.
> *Anonymous*

John knew who he was in comparison to Jesus—even though Jesus called him the greatest man ever born (Luke 7:28). We, by comparison, are far less qualified. We should never have a high opinion of ourselves; like Paul, we are "less than the least" (Ephesians 3:8 NKJV).

1:28 This all happened at Bethany on the other side of the Jordan.[NIV] *Bethany* is the reading in the earliest manuscripts. The reading was changed from "Bethany" to "Bethabara" in some manuscripts because scribes did not want readers thinking this was the Bethany near Jerusalem. The exact location of a "Bethany on the other side of the Jordan" has never been determined. All we know is that it was east of the Jordan River.

JOHN THE BAPTIST PROCLAIMS JESUS AS THE MESSIAH / 1:29-34 / **20**

The opening portion of John's narrative provides two witnesses to Jesus Christ's identity. The first witness is John the Baptist; this is covered in verses 19-36. John the Baptist's witness had been briefly mentioned in the prologue (1:7, 15) and is here expanded. The second witness comes from Jesus' first disciples—John (the Gospel writer), Andrew, Peter, Philip, and Nathanael.

Both John the Baptist and the disciples declare and affirm that Jesus is the Christ, the Son of God.

1:29 "Behold! The Lamb of God."^{NKJV} The title "Lamb of God" would be associated in the minds of the Jews with the Passover lamb (Exodus 12) and the lambs used in the daily sacrifices for the sin offerings (see Leviticus 14:12, 21, 24; Numbers 6:12). In calling Jesus the Lamb of God, John pointed to Jesus as the substitutionary sacrifice provided by God. Had the Jews considered the Messiah would be a lamb led to the slaughter (Isaiah 53:7ff.)?

PAID IN FULL
Every morning and evening, a lamb was sacrificed in the temple for the sins of the people (Exodus 29:38-42). Isaiah 53:7 prophesied that the Messiah, God's servant, would be led to the slaughter like a lamb. To pay the penalty for sin, a life had to be given—God chose to provide the sacrifice himself. When Jesus died as the perfect sacrifice, he removed the sin of the world and destroyed the power of sin itself. Thus God forgives our sin (1 Corinthians 5:7).
   The "sin of the world" means the sin of each individual. Jesus paid the price of *our* sin by his death. We claim the forgiveness he provided by first taking ownership of our sin. If we insist we have no sin, then we gain no forgiveness. Repentance precedes forgiveness. If you don't think you need to repent, check your life again. The Ten Commandments can help you evaluate how you're doing by God's standards.

"Who takes away the sin of the world!"^{NKJV} The Greek word for "takes away" can also mean "take up." Jesus took away our sin by taking it upon himself. This is the image depicted in Isaiah 53:4-9 and 1 Peter 2:24.

1:30 "This is he of whom I said, 'After me comes a man who ranks ahead of me because he was before me.'"^{NRSV} This verse, which reiterates 1:15, is here put in its chronological context. Although John the Baptist was a well-known preacher who attracted large crowds, he was content that Jesus take the higher place. John demonstrated true humility, the basis for greatness in preaching, teaching, or any other work we do for Christ. Accepting what God wants us to do and giving Jesus Christ the honor for it allows God to work freely through us.

1:31 "I myself did not know him."^{NRSV} Since John and Jesus were cousins, John must have known Jesus before this time. But this statement means that John had not realized that Jesus was God's

Son, the Messiah, until God provided the sign of the Spirit descending upon Jesus.

"The reason I came baptizing with water was that he might be revealed to Israel."[NIV] Though John had not yet clearly seen the Messiah, he knew that the Messiah was coming and that his mission was to prepare the nation of Israel for the Messiah's arrival. But, as John would soon explain, he had been instructed to baptize, and as he was baptizing he saw a sign that indicated the arrival of the one he had come to announce.

1:32 **"I saw the Spirit come down from heaven as a dove and remain on him."**[NIV] Evidently, the action of the Spirit descending from heaven in the form of a dove was a sign for John. Only John and Jesus saw this (see Matthew 3:16). The other Gospel writers tell us that a voice accompanied this divine sign: A voice came out of heaven saying, "This is My beloved Son, in whom I am well pleased" (Matthew 3:17 NKJV). John the Baptist did not add this detail; rather, he himself declared—"this is the Son of God" (1:34 NIV).

1:33 **"I would not have known him, except that the one who sent me to baptize with water told me"**[NIV] The phrase, *I would not have known him* repeats the statement in verse 31. *The one who sent me* is God, who had sent John to baptize and to prepare the way for the Messiah. This same God would reveal the Messiah to John by sending his Spirit upon the Messiah.

"The man on whom you see the Spirit come down and remain is he who will baptize with the Holy Spirit."[NIV] In well-known prophetic passages, the Messiah was depicted as having the Spirit resting upon him (see Isaiah 11:1-2; 61:1ff.). The statement that *he will baptize with the Holy Spirit* foretells Jesus' divine mission. It does not just point to the Day of Pentecost on which Jesus sent the Holy Spirit to baptize the disciples (see Luke 24:49; Acts 1:8; 2:4); it characterizes Jesus' entire ministry. Jesus came to give eternal life to those who believe in him. But no one could actually receive that life apart from receiving the life-giving Holy Spirit.

John the Baptist's baptism with water was preparatory because it was for repentance and symbolized the washing away of sins. Jesus, by contrast, would baptize with the Holy Spirit, imparting not only forgiveness but also eternal life. He would send the Holy Spirit upon all believers, empowering them to live and to teach the message of salvation. This outpouring of the Spirit came after

Jesus had risen from the dead and ascended into heaven (see 20:22; Acts 2).

All true believers have been baptized by Jesus in the Holy Spirit (see Romans 8:9). As such, we have been immersed in Jesus' Spirit. Now we can experience the life-giving Spirit and enjoy his presence day by day.

1:34 **"I have seen and I testify that this is the Son of God."**NIV John was declaring Jesus' special position with God. God had told John that he would reveal his sent one to John—the Spirit would descend upon the Messiah and remain upon him. John saw this and declared his belief in Jesus as God's identified Son. Those who receive the Spirit can also declare that Jesus *is the Son of God,* for the Spirit enables us to believe and confess (see 1 Corinthians 12:3).

INTRODUCTION
Today people are looking for someone to give them security in an insecure world. We must point them to Christ and show them how Christ satisfies their need. They must hear it first from us. We cannot pass on to others what we do not possess. If we know Jesus, we will want to introduce others to him.

THE FIRST DISCIPLES FOLLOW JESUS / 1:35-51 / 21

This last section of John 1 records how the earliest believers became disciples of Jesus; it is a drama of salvation revealing the formation of Jesus' first band of disciples. Andrew and John became Jesus' followers through the testimony of their teacher, John the Baptist. Peter, Andrew's brother, became a follower through the testimony of Andrew. Philip became a disciple by Jesus seeking him out and calling him to follow him. And Nathanael became a believer through the testimony of Philip and the revelation Jesus gave to him. This progression provides a model for evangelism.

1:35-36 **John again was standing with two of his disciples.**NRSV These disciples of John the Baptist were Andrew (see 1:40) and John, the writer of this Gospel. Both these men had followed John the Baptist until he pointed them to the Lamb of God, Jesus Christ. Why did these disciples leave John the Baptist? Because that's what John wanted them to do—he was pointing the way to Jesus, the one John had prepared them to follow.

"Behold the Lamb of God!"NKJV This was the second time John made this declaration (see comments on 1:29).

1:37 The two disciples . . . followed Jesus.NIV These disciples followed Jesus in two ways. They literally turned and walked after him, and they also became two of Jesus' close followers, or disciples. This was a great tribute to John the Baptist's preaching—they heard John and followed Jesus.

TIMED RELEASE
The opportunity to be an example or leader to others has its benefits. It is affirming when people depend upon us. But if we have led someone to faith in Jesus Christ, the time will come when they must follow Jesus beyond the influence of our relationship with them. Both mentor and disciple grow when the time for release arrives. John allowed his disciples to follow Jesus and in that act sealed his obedience to God. The disciples did follow Jesus, demonstrating that they had benefited from John's teaching.

In our relationship with other Christians, we must keep a healthy balance between dependence and independence. Mentors are helpful, but they cannot replace Jesus in our lives. We must also encourage those who follow us to keep their eyes on Christ.

1:38-39 Jesus . . . asked, "What do you want?"NIV Those coming to Christ, whether for the first time or each day in worship, should ask themselves this question—"What do I want? What do I expect to receive from Jesus?"

"Where are you staying?"NIV This indicates that John and Andrew were serious followers. They wanted to know where to find Jesus. This indicates a commitment, not an experiment. Curiosity about Christ or occasional spiritual interest is not enough; we must follow him for the right reasons. To follow Christ for our own purposes would be asking Christ to follow us—to align with us to support and advance our cause, not his. We must examine our motives for following him. Are we seeking his glory or ours?

They came and saw where he was staying, and they remained with him that day. It was about four o'clock in the afternoon.NRSV John recalls the

> You are standing in front of God and in the presence of the hosts of angels. The Holy Spirit is about to impress his seal on each of your souls. You are about to be pressed into the service of the great king.
> *Cyril of Jerusalem*

exact time he first stayed with Jesus. It must have been a special opportunity for John and Andrew—a time never to be forgotten. We can only imagine their wonder as they spent those hours alone with Jesus. From this time forward, these two men became his followers.

1:40-42 The first thing Andrew did was to find his brother Simon and tell him, "We have found the Messiah."[NIV] After spending a day with Jesus, Andrew immediately went to find his brother Simon (who would later be named Peter) and tell him that he had found the *Messiah* (the Hebrew term), or "the Christ" (the Greek translation of "Messiah," meaning "Anointed One"; see Isaiah 61:1).

He brought Simon to Jesus.[NRSV] Andrew appears two more times in this Gospel; each time he is bringing people to Jesus (see 6:4-9; 12:20-22). The idea that we must somehow convince people about Jesus places too much importance on what we say and do. We must trust God's Spirit to work in a person and understand that our part may be little more than bringing that person into contact with Jesus. The question "What do you think of Jesus?" ought to fit in our conversations.

> Dost thou live close by them, or meet them in the streets, or labour with them, or travel with them, or sit and talk with them, and say nothing to them of their souls, or the life to come? If their houses were on fire, thou wouldst run and help them; and wilt thou not help them when their souls are almost at the fire of hell?
> *Richard Baxter*

Jesus looked at him and said, "You are Simon son of John. You will be called Cephas" (which, when translated, is Peter).[NIV] Jesus changed Simon's name to *Cephas,* the Aramaic word for "stone," because Jesus foresaw that Peter would become a pillar and a foundation stone in the building of the first-century church (see Matthew 16:16-18; Galatians 2:9; Ephesians 2:20; 1 Peter 2:4-5).

1:43 The next day Jesus decided to leave for Galilee. Finding Philip, he said to him, "Follow me."[NIV] Jesus' first two disciples (Andrew and John) sought out Jesus. Andrew brought the third disciple, Peter, to Jesus. Jesus sought out the fourth disciple, Philip. Jesus looked for him, found him, and called him to follow.

1:44-46 Philip, like Andrew and Peter, was from the town of Bethsaida.[NIV] This tells us that Philip must have known Andrew and Peter before he began to follow Jesus.

Philip found Nathanael.^{NIV} Earlier, Andrew had found Simon (his brother) and had brought him to Jesus. Philip does the same with Nathanael.

In the list of disciples in the other Gospels, Philip and Bartholomew are listed together (Matthew 10:3; Mark 3:18); here, Philip and Nathanael are paired up. Thus, it stands to reason that, since Bartholomew is not mentioned in the fourth Gospel and Nathanael is not mentioned in the synoptic Gospels, Nathanael is none other than Bartholomew.

"We have found the one Moses wrote about in the Law, and about whom the prophets also wrote—Jesus of Nazareth, the son of Joseph."^{NIV} In saying *we,* Philip was probably referring to himself, Andrew, and Peter. If this was the case, the first five disciples (John, Andrew, Peter, Philip, and Nathanael) may have been acquainted or even friends. What a delightful experience for a Christian to witness a circle of friends or to see a family be drawn to Jesus.

The language referring to Jesus as *the one Moses wrote about* indicates that Philip was also a thoughtful seeker—one who read the Old Testament Scriptures and was looking for the Messiah. Moses had written about the Messiah in the Law (see Deuteronomy 18:15-18), and the prophets had foretold his coming.

The son of Joseph refers to Jesus' family line; in other words, this was how Jesus was known among the people (see Luke 3:23—it was supposed that Jesus was Joseph's son). In reality, Jesus was not Joseph's son; he was (and is) God's Son.

"Nazareth! Can anything good come from there?"^{NIV} Nathanael's statement does not necessarily mean that there was anything wrong with the town. Nazareth was possibly despised by the Jews because a Roman army garrison was located there. Some have speculated that an aloof attitude or a poor reputation in morals and religion on the part of the people of Nazareth led to Nathanael's harsh comment. Nathanael's hometown was Cana, about four miles from Nazareth.

Nathanael's expression seems to indicate that he did not expect that anything related to God's purpose could come from that place because Nazareth is not mentioned in the Old Testament. The prophets, moreover, never said that the Messiah would come from Nazareth. The Messiah was to be born in Bethlehem (Micah 5:2); and, in fact, Jesus *was* born in Bethlehem. But his parents' flight to Egypt and soon return to Galilee, where Jesus was raised, gave Jesus the reputation of being a Galilean, even a Nazarene. This was offensive to many Jews because they could not accept a Messiah who had not come from Bethlehem.

"Come and see."^{NIV} Philip chose the best alternative. He did not argue with Nathanael about Jesus; he brought him to Jesus. Fortunately for Nathanael, he went to meet Jesus and became a disciple. If he had stuck to his prejudice without investigating further, he would have missed the Messiah! We must not let people's stereotypes about Christ cause them to miss his power and love. We must invite them to come and meet Jesus themselves.

1:47 When Jesus saw Nathanael approaching, he said of him, "Here is a true Israelite, in whom there is nothing false."^{NIV} Jesus' statement about Nathanael reveals that Nathanael was an honest man. The Greek word for *false,* also translated "guile" (*dolos*), means "deceit, cunning, falsehood." Nathanael was void of such characteristics.

Jesus' direct, intimate knowledge of him must have taken Nathanael by surprise. He was not offended, just intensely curious. If we remember that God's grace and love come to us even though he knows all about us, we may find ourselves being even more grateful to him.

GOD KNOWS
Jesus knew about Nathanael before the two ever met. Jesus also knows what we are really like. An honest person will feel comfortable with the thought that Jesus knows him or her through and through. A dishonest person will feel uncomfortable. We can't pretend to be something we're not. God knows who we really are and wants *us* to follow him.

1:48 "I saw you while you were still under the fig tree before Philip called you."^{NIV} Here Jesus unveiled his omniscience to Nathanael. Jesus had been aware of Nathanael's exact location before Philip called him. According to Jewish tradition, the expression "to sit under the fig tree" was a euphemism for meditating on the Scriptures. Thus, Jesus had seen Nathanael studying the Scriptures before Philip had called him to come and see Jesus.

The early disciples of Jesus were well versed in the Scriptures. Life in the small towns of Israel revolved around the synagogue, where the Old Testament was constantly read, taught, and argued. Unlike many of the studied religious leaders of the day, these simple men understood the Scriptures, and knew what to look for. So when the Messiah came, they recognized him!

1:49 **"Rabbi, you are the Son of God! You are the King of Israel!"**[NRSV] Instantaneously, Nathanael realizes that Jesus is *the Son of God* (see Psalm 2:7) and *the King of Israel* (see Psalm 2:6; Zephaniah 3:15).

GET TO KNOW JESUS BETTER
These new disciples used several names for Jesus: Lamb of God (1:36), Rabbi (1:38), Messiah (1:41), Son of God (1:49), and King of Israel (1:49). As they got to know Jesus, their appreciation for him grew. The more time we spend getting to know Christ, the more we will understand and appreciate who he is. We may be drawn to him for his teaching, but we too will come to know him as the Son of God.

Although in just a few days these disciples began regularly calling Jesus the Son of God, they would not fully understand him until three years later (Acts 2). What they so easily professed had to be worked out in experience. We may also find that words of faith come easily, but deep appreciation for Christ comes from living by faith.

1:50-51 **"You shall see greater things than that. . . . You shall see heaven open, and the angels of God ascending and descending on the Son of Man."**[NIV] Jesus now speaks to all the disciples there present. He tells that they would hereafter see the angels ascending and descending upon him, the Son of Man (a messianic title, see Daniel 7:13). As students of the Old Testament, his disciples would have realized that Jesus was alluding to Jacob's vision of the ladder connecting heaven to earth (see Genesis 28:12ff.). Jacob had left home, having lied to his father and cheated his brother of the birthright. Yet in his dream Jacob saw a vision of angels ministering to him. If God could reveal himself to a sinner like Jacob, surely he could reveal himself in an even greater way to Nathanael. To Nathanael and the others, the heavens would be opened—i.e., they would be given insight into the things of heaven (Acts 10:11; Rev. 4:1; 19:11). Furthermore, they would realize that Jesus, as the Son of Man, was the vehicle of communication between heaven and earth. Just as God had appointed Jacob to be the father of the twelve tribes (under the new name Israel), God had appointed Jesus to be the founder of the new spiritual kingdom.

John 2

Beyond the startling and miraculous transformation of water into wine by Jesus, this incident includes two important statements concerning Christ: (1) "My time has not yet come"; and (2) Jesus "revealed his glory."

First, from Jesus we hear, "My time has not yet come" (2:4). In John's Gospel, Jesus' "time" refers to the time of his glorification when he would receive his true place and position as the Son of God. This glorification would include his death and resurrection. Everything Jesus said and did pointed toward that "time." Jesus' words emphasized his life purpose. Each of the Gospels expresses this unique self-awareness of Jesus in a different way. For example, in Luke's Gospel, Jesus states, "Didn't you know I had to be in my Father's house?" (Luke 2:49 NIV; see also Matthew 3:13-15; Mark 1:14-15).

Second, John portrayed through the miracle of turning water into wine how Jesus "revealed his glory" (2:11). After his death and resurrection, Jesus would be fully glorified—and all people would (or should) know that he is the Son of God. But until that time, Jesus would reveal his identity by miracles—even though he would have preferred for people to believe in him because of his words (see, for instance, 20:29). Transforming the water into wine revealed Jesus' glory by showing his tremendous power. This small display of divine nature was enough to convince the disciples of his identity and initiate their trust in him (2:11), though later events demonstrated that they only partially understood Jesus' purpose.

The miraculous supply of wine is the first of thirty-five miracles, or signs, recorded in the Gospels. This particular miracle is recorded only in John, perhaps because all the disciples had not yet been called, thus Matthew was not present. It was a private miracle done, not to alleviate suffering, but to avert social embarrassment. But in the long run, it accomplished far more, for it strengthened the faith of the first disciples and fulfilled Jesus' promise to Nathanael (1:50-51). The miracle was a display of God's power within a practical context of human need, a characteristic to be found in all of Christ's miracles.

For a list of all Jesus' miracles recorded in the Gospels, see the chart on page 411.

2:1-2 There was a wedding in Cana of Galilee.^{NKJV} Wait—

2:1-2 There was a wedding in Cana of Galilee.[NKJV] A wedding celebration could last as long as a week (see Genesis 29:27-28). Cana was a town about nine miles north of Nazareth. Curiously, John mentions that the wedding occurs on the **third day.** This probably refers to the third day after the departure from the place of Jesus' baptism (see also 1:29, 35, 43). This creates a mood of urgency and determination at the beginning of Jesus' ministry. Parallels with other biblical sequences, like the Creation account, have been noted by scholars, but do not present themselves obviously to the reader. Hidden meanings are always possible in Scripture, but they should not be sought at the expense of the plain meaning of the passage. Unless we grasp the direct meaning of the text, our insights and applications will tend to be weak or wrong. The point here is simply that Jesus included a wedding in his travel plans.

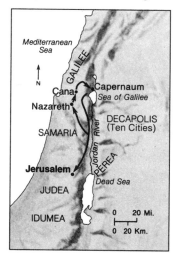

The only references to the town of Cana are found in John's Gospel. Two of Jesus' miracles are connected with that location: creating wine from water (2:1-11) and healing a nobleman's son (4:46-54). Nathanael, one of the twelve disciples, is described as a native of Cana (21:2). The town has not survived into the present but is thought to have been between Nazareth and Capernaum, in the northwest region of the Sea of Galilee.

Jesus' First Travels. After his baptism by John in the Jordan River and temptation by Satan in the wilderness (see Mark 1:9-13 and the Harmony on page 413 for other events of his life prior to this), Jesus returned to Galilee. He visited Nazareth, Cana, and Capernaum, and then returned to Jerusalem for the Passover (2:13).

Jesus' mother was there.[NIV] Perhaps Mary was the hostess at this wedding, because she was the first to know about the lack of wine, and she directed the servants to follow Jesus' orders.

Jesus and his disciples had also been invited.[NIV] When a wedding was held, the entire town was invited, and most made the effort to come (it was considered an insult to refuse an invitation to a wedding). Cana was Jesus' home region, so he may have known the bride and groom. In any case, his presence was intentional.

LET'S CELEBRATE!
Jesus was on a mission to save the world, the greatest mission in the history of mankind. Yet he took time to attend a wedding and take part in its festivities. We may be tempted to think we should not take time out from our "important" work for social occasions. But we need to see these social occasions as part of our mission. By participating in these events, Jesus was able to be involved with people, the very ones he came to save. Likewise, our efforts to represent Christ should not exclude joyous times of celebration with others. We can develop balance in our lives by bringing Jesus into times of pleasure as well as times of work.

Jesus' attendance and his actions at this wedding indicate his approval of the celebration. (See Jesus' comments about marriage in Matthew 5:31-32; 19:3-9.) Images of Jesus as a dour-faced Messiah, passing judgment on all in his path simply fail to account for the biblical evidence that he was completely at home in festive occasions. In fact, part of his rejection by religious leaders was based on their perception that he enjoyed being with sinners more than was appropriate (see Mark 2:15-16 and Luke 5:30). Jesus' life is the most profound statement ever made against joyless spirituality.

2:3-4 When they ran out of wine.^{NKJV} The week-long weddings in Jesus' time must have had about the same impact on family budgets as weddings do today. Banquets were prepared for many guests, and everyone spent several days celebrating the new life of the married couple. To accommodate the guests, careful planning was needed. Running out of wine meant more than embarrassment; it broke the strong unwritten laws of hospitality. Jesus was about to respond to a heartfelt need.

Jesus' mother said to him, "They have no more wine."^{NIV}
Mary was probably in a position of responsibility, since she was one of the first to know that the wine was gone. She told Jesus of the predicament, perhaps expecting him to do something about it.

NO MORE WINE
Mary's simple action illustrates that receiving our Lord's filling and healing begins with recognizing our need. For Mary, it was easy—the wine was gone. It may be more difficult for us to identify our problem. But left to our own resources, we will run dry. Life is too complex, its problems too challenging, and our own strength too limited to allow us to cope without help. Defining the exact need may not be as crucial as admitting our incompleteness. But recognizing our emptiness before Christ will allow him to work a miracle in us. He will apply his powerful resources to our lives. Have you expressed to God your lack that only he can fill? Are you willing to do what he asks of you?

Some believe Mary was not assuming that Jesus would perform a miracle; she was simply hoping that her son would help solve this major problem and find some wine. Tradition says that Joseph, Mary's husband, was dead, so she probably was used to depending on her son's help in certain situations. Although Mary did not know what Jesus was going to do, she trusted him to handle the problem. Those who believe in Jesus but run into situations they cannot understand must continue to trust that he will work in the best way. Real trust focuses on the source rather than on the shape of the help that will be supplied. We trust *that* God will help, not knowing how the help will come.

Others point out that Mary had known for a long time about her son's divine commission. Perhaps she wanted Jesus to do something in the presence of her relatives and/or friends (who may have heard some reports about Jesus) that would prove he was the Messiah. The tension between Jesus' verbal response and his later actions leave the question of Mary's expectations undecided. But Mary's trust is unmistakable!

CLEAR VIEW
What Mary expected her son to do with the problem must be left to speculation. Jesus' answer to her portrays the thought-provoking responses he gave to those who approached him with ambivalent comments. For instance, Jesus responded to Nicodemus's nebulous compliment about his miraculous powers (3:3) by getting to the heart of the matter, that one must be born again in order to enter God's kingdom. Jesus constantly clarified how other people viewed him, confronting them with his divine nature and their spiritual needs. John's Gospel gives us a helpful and reliable view of Jesus as Lord. We need to ask ourselves how clearly we understand the Jesus we claim to know.

"Woman, what does your concern have to do with Me? My hour has not yet come."^{NKJV} It may have been improper, in this time period, for Jesus to address his mother with a more familiar term in public. In any case, Jesus made it clear to his mother that his life was following a different timetable; he lived to carry out his Father's business, according to his Father's plans. Whatever Jesus' intended response to the problem at hand, he expressed to his mother a firm reminder that his priorities were different from hers. At another time in this Gospel, Jesus gave the same response to his brothers (see 7:3-6; also 7:8, 30; 8:20). Later, Jesus would also say that his hour *had* come (see 12:23; 13:1; 17:1).

The *hour* to which Jesus referred was the time of his glorification, when he would receive his true place and position, not as an earthly king, but as the Messiah, God's Son, Savior of mankind, seated at God's right hand (see 7:30, 39; 12:23-24; 17:1). This glorification would occur after his death and resurrection, for it would be only through death and resurrection that Jesus could accomplish what he came to earth to accomplish—to offer salvation to all people.

2:5 "Do whatever he tells you."^{NRSV} Mary was not promised any kind of action but realized that Jesus might do something about the situation, even though his remark in verse 4 must have limited her expectations. Nevertheless, Mary's words show her respect for Jesus' authority.

DO IT!
We would do well to follow Mary's command to the servants to "Do whatever he tells you" every moment of our lives. No one could have guessed what Jesus was about to do. But Mary's willingness to obey was settled beforehand. We, too, must decide that our first reaction will be to obey rather than to question what God directs us to do. Like the servants, we will rarely be told beforehand all the details of what God plans to do.

Are you ready to do what he says? Ask yourself:
- Is there a cherished sin? Confess and forsake it.
- Is there a broken relationship? Seek to heal it.
- Is there a service opportunity Christ has placed before you? Step out and do it.
- Is there a need you feel convicted to fill? Be strong and meet it.
- Is there a higher level of commitment that Christ directs you to make? Welcome his call with all your heart.

2:6-8 Six stone water jars, the kind used by the Jews for ceremonial washing.^{NIV} The six stone water jars were normally used for the ceremonial washing of hands as part of the Jewish purification rites before and after meals (see Matthew 15:1-2). According to the Jews' ceremonial law, people became symbolically unclean by touching objects of everyday life. Before eating, the Jews would pour water over their hands to cleanse themselves of any bad influences associated with what they had touched. When full, each jar would hold twenty to thirty gallons.

The number *six* and the *water jars* have been allegorized by various commentators throughout church history. The fact is, Jesus did not make random choices of objects when they were used in miraculous actions. Even the miracles operate under a system of consistency (see 2:9). It is often enlightening to inquire about the reasons behind Jesus' use of elements like mud, spittle, bread, water, fish, etc., in his miracles. In this case, the empty water jars (normally used by the Jews to purify themselves) may symbolize the emptiness of Jewish ritual when true faith is absent. Jesus had come to give content to an empty religion. The jars help visualize what Jesus meant when he talked about his relationship to the law: "I have come not to abolish but to fulfill" (Matthew 5:17 NRSV). Personally, it pictures what Christ's presence means in our life: He fills us with his Spirit and goodness when we are empty and lacking.

MORE THAN WE NEED
Jesus did not come to earth solely to satisfy our desires or to make us happy, as this first miracle might lead some to conclude. Jesus did perform a miracle, but it was in his time and in his way. Jesus provided as much as 180 gallons of choice wine. The lavish supply of wine was a picture of the salvation he came to offer, and a revelation of who he was. What God gives is given in abundance. In Christ we are promised life, the abundance of that life is indicated by the fact that it is *eternal!*

They filled them to the brim.[NIV] This filling *to the brim* showed that nothing could be added to the water. When Jesus performed the miracle, *all* the water was changed to wine; wine was not added to the water. It portrays the abundance of Christ's gracious work; it also indicates the wholeheartedness of the servants' obedience.

"Draw some out."[NRSV] The servants were now commanded to dip deep down into the jars and draw out the water that had been miraculously changed to wine.

HUMAN AGENTS
Jesus did not require the help of the servants nor the filled jars in order to perform his miracle. The filling of the jars could itself have been part of the miracle. But as Jesus demonstrated repeatedly in dealing with people, God honors us with significant roles in his work. We are not indispensable, but graciously included. For another outstanding example, note the resurrection of Lazarus (11:43-44) where Jesus gives life, but friends unwrap and clean up what must have been a completely shocked Lazarus! Does your work carry the imprint of Christ upon it? Do you fulfill your responsibility, sensing how Christ is using you?

2:9-10 The master of the banquet tasted the water that had been turned into wine.ᴺᴵⱽ The servants did as they were told. They filled the jars to the brim, then drew out some of the liquid and took it to the master of the banquet. The water had been given a new identity as wine, and the jars had been given a wider usefulness as containers of Jesus' gift.

"Everyone brings out the choice wine first and then the cheaper wine . . . but you have saved the best till now."ᴺᴵⱽ It was customary to give the best wine first and the poorer wine last because peoples' taste buds grow less sensitive with more and more drinks. The water turned into wine was of such quality that the master of the banquet made a point of mentioning this to the bridegroom, who also probably reacted in surprise. Neither of them knew where this wine came from, but Mary, the servants, and the disciples were aware of what had happened.

This miracle illustrated the emptiness of the Jewish rituals versus what Jesus came to bring (see 4:13; 7:38-39). The water of ceremonial cleansing has become the wine of the messianic age. Have we tasted the new wine?

YOU CAN HAVE THE BEST NOW
People look everywhere but to God for excitement and meaning. For some reason, they expect God to be dull and lifeless. Just as the wine Jesus made was the best, so life in him is better than life on our own. Why wait until everything else runs out before trying God? Don't save the best until last.

2:11 The first of his signs.ᴺᴿˢⱽ The Gospels record thirty-five miracles, or *signs* performed by Jesus. In the Gospel of John, each miracle was a sign intended to point people to the truth

MIRACLES RECORDED IN JOHN'S GOSPEL AND THEIR SIGNIFICANCE

Jesus' miracles were always performed to show his nature—his compassion and love for people. But more than that, they revealed his glory. They were his "credentials," but they weren't done for show. The miracles were performed to help people believe that Jesus was the promised Messiah. The miracles also reveal Jesus' great power over the temporal world. (All verses are quoted from NRSV.)

Passage and Miracle	*Significance*
Jesus turns water into wine (2:1-11). "Jesus . . . revealed his glory; and his disciples believed in him."	*Reveals Jesus' power over nature*
Jesus heals an official's son (4:46-54). "Jesus said to him, 'Go; your son will live.' The man believed the word that Jesus spoke to him and started on his way. As he was going down, his slaves met him and told him that his child was alive. So he asked them the hour when he began to recover, and they said to him, 'Yesterday at one in the afternoon the fever left him.' The father realized that this was the hour when Jesus had said to him, 'Your son will live.' So he himself believed, along with his whole household."	*Reveals that Jesus' power is not limited by time or space*
Jesus heals a lame man (5:1-16). "At once the man was made well, and he took up his mat and began to walk. . . . The man went away and told the Jews that it was Jesus who had made him well."	*Reveals Jesus' power over disease and disability*
Jesus feeds over five thousand people (6:5-14). "When he looked up and saw a large crowd coming toward him, Jesus said to Philip, 'Where are we to buy bread for these people to eat?' He said this to test him, for he himself knew what he was going to do. . . . Andrew . . . said to him, 'There is a boy here who has five barley loaves and two fish. But what are they among so many people?' . . . When they were satisfied, he told his disciples, 'Gather up the fragments left over.' . . . So they gathered them up, and . . . filled twelve baskets."	*Reveals Jesus' power to supply humanity*
Jesus walks on the water (6:17-21). "The sea became rough because a strong wind was blowing. When [the disciples] had rowed about three or four miles, they saw Jesus walking on the sea and coming near the boat, and they were terrified. But he said to them, 'It is I; do not be afraid.' Then they wanted to take him into the boat."	*Reveals Jesus' power over the forces of nature*

Jesus heals a man born blind (9:1-7).
"As he walked along, he saw a man blind from birth.
His disciples asked him, 'Rabbi, who sinned, this man
or his parents, that he was born blind?' Jesus
answered, 'Neither this man nor his parents sinned;
he was born blind so that God's works might be
revealed in him. . . . As long as I am in the world, I am
the light of the world."

*Reveals Jesus'
power over birth
defects*

Jesus raises Lazarus from the dead (11:1-45).
"Jesus said to her, 'Did I not tell you that if you
believed, you would see the glory of God?' So they
took away the stone. And Jesus looked upward and
said, 'Father, I thank you for having heard me. I knew
that you always hear me, but I said this for the sake of
the crowd standing here, so that they may believe
that you sent me.'. . . Many of the Jews . . . believed
in him."

*Reveals Jesus'
power over death*

**Jesus gives the disciples a second miraculous
catch of fish** (21:1-14).
"Just after daybreak, Jesus stood on the beach; but
the disciples did not know that it was Jesus. Jesus
said to them, 'Children, you have no fish, have you?'
They answered him, 'No.' He said to them, 'Cast the
net to the right side of the boat and you will find
some.' So they cast it, and now they were not able to
haul it in because there were so many fish. That
disciple whom Jesus loved said to Peter, 'It is the
Lord!' . . . This was now the third time that Jesus
appeared to the disciples after he was raised from the
dead."

*Reveals Jesus'
power over
creation*

---

that Jesus is the divine Son of God come down from heaven.
These signs were remarkable actions that displayed the presence and power of God. According to John's Gospel, this was
Jesus' first sign—and it was performed in Cana of Galilee (his
own region). His second was also performed in Galilee (see
4:46-54).

Many have wondered why Jesus would "waste" his powers on
performing a miracle of providing wine for a wedding feast, a
party. But all of Jesus' miracles had a purpose beyond alleviating
suffering; they revealed Jesus' glory.

Revealed his glory.[NRSV] The miracles recorded in John's Gospel
(and indeed all the miracles recorded by the other Gospel writers)
demonstrated God's great love for people and his concern for
their individual needs. But on a deeper level, they also *revealed*
Jesus' *glory*—Jesus' unique, divine nature portrayed in such a

way as to claim our loyalty and reverence. The sign of turning water into wine was a partial unveiling of Jesus' full identity. His power over nature, death, sin, and evil revealed him to be the promised Messiah. As Nicodemus said, "We know you are a teacher who has come from God. For no one could perform the miraculous signs you are doing if God were not with him" (3:2 NIV).

WHY JESUS PERFORMED MIRACLES

Miracles are not merely superhuman events, but events that demonstrate God's power. Almost every miracle Jesus did was a renewal of fallen creation—restoring sight, making the lame walk, even restoring life to the dead. We are to believe in Christ, not because he is a superman, but because he is the God who continues his creation, even in those of us who are poor, weak, crippled, orphaned, blind, deaf, or with some other desperate need for re-creation.

It was true that many people followed him for no deeper reason than to see miracles, or they "believed" but "intended to come and make him king by force" (6:14-15 NIV). Jesus responded to those misguided efforts by slipping away. But those followers who could look more deeply, who could understand more clearly, realized that Jesus was truly the Messiah, doing just what he was predicted to do: "Here is my servant, whom I uphold, my chosen one in whom I delight . . . I, the Lord . . . will keep you and will make you to be a covenant for the people and a light for the Gentiles, to open eyes that are blind, to free captives from prison and to release from the dungeon those who sit in darkness" (Isaiah 42:1, 6-7 NIV). The impact of Jesus' miracles has passed from the eyewitnesses to those who first read John's Gospel and down to us.

GLORY!

What was this glory of Jesus that people glimpsed in the miracles? It was as if, for a moment, the miracles drew back the curtain and allowed people to see a fuller view of Jesus, including his divine power and authority. Jesus' divine nature became apparent to those willing to see. The sight was dazzling, compelling, and overwhelming. The Gospel writer summarizes what those who were with Jesus came to understand: "We have seen his glory, the glory as of a father's only son, full of grace and truth" (1:14 NRSV). John's invitation to us is to look through the eyes of the disciples and allow ourselves to be convinced, as they were, by the glory of Jesus.

His disciples believed in him. NRSV To this point, the disciples
(those who had been called thus far) were following Jesus for their
own reasons. Others may have been questioning who Jesus was
and were following him to find out. John says that when the disciples saw the miracle, they believed in him. The miracle demonstrated Jesus' power over nature and revealed the way he would go
about his ministry—helping others, speaking with authority, and
being in personal touch with people. God may confront us in any
number of ways with our need to believe in his Son. We will be
held accountable for whether or not we have believed.

MIRACLES TODAY
Sincere believers wonder whether or not God works miracles
today. Certainly God knows what each person requires in order
to believe in him. The New Testament accounts record a basic
human characteristic that is still true today: people who insisted
on a miracle in order to believe remained unconvinced after witnessing the miracle, or were told by Jesus that miracles would
not help them. The person who requires God to prove himself
may be hiding his or her unwillingness to believe.
    In coming to a personal conviction about miracles today, we
can make several affirmations:
- *God can perform miracles.* We must not confuse two questions: *Does* God perform miracles today? and *Can* God perform miracles today? The first is a reasonable question; the
second implies a loss of power on God's part and questions
his ability. We cannot, by definition, impose limitations on
God. God can and will do miracles anywhere and anytime he
wishes.
- *Miracles tend to be more obvious where the gospel makes
new impact.* This is because miracles primarily confront ignorance rather than unbelief. Most reports of miracles today
come from missionaries on the "outposts" of God's work. It is
entirely possible, as Western society sinks into a morass of
religious ignorance, that God will, in fact, increase the fre-
quency of miracles in this part of the world.
- *God uses people to do his miraculous work.* In the past, there
were many basic acts of healing and helping that required
God's direct intervention, for there were no other options.
Advances in medicine, mental health, and science (which
themselves strike us as miraculous at times) now allow us to
carry out what previously required God's intervention.
- *We must expect counterfeits in a fallen world.* All the miracles
recorded in the Bible were not given a divine stamp of
approval (for instance, Pharaoh's magicians' snakes—see
Exodus 7:8-13). Trusting in God's ability and willingness to do
miracles today may make believers seem gullible. But denying God's willingness to do miracles may place believers in
the even more precarious position of doubting God's power.

JESUS CLEARS THE TEMPLE / 2:12-25 / *23*

The magnificent temple that Jesus entered with his disciples was the one rebuilt by the remnant of Israelites who had returned from Babylon under Ezra and Nehemiah; it was later enlarged by Herod. The Jews considered the temple to be God's house. The temple in Jerusalem was a familiar place to Jesus. Luke 2:41 mentions yearly visits by Mary and Joseph to the Holy City. Presumably, Jesus frequently accompanied them. On one of these occasions, Jesus called the temple his Father's house.

But the arrival of Jesus and the beginning of his ministry signaled a change. The glory of God, which had filled the holy shrine since the days of the Exodus and the tabernacle, was no longer in the building; that glory was in Jesus, though veiled within his humanity. A day would come, however, when that glory would be revealed—the day of Jesus' resurrection, the day when the Son of Man would be glorified.

2:12-13 **Capernaum** became Jesus' home base during his ministry in Galilee. Located on a major trade route, it was an important city in the region, with a Roman garrison and a customs station. At Capernaum, Matthew was called to be a disciple (Matthew 9:9). The city was also the home of several other disciples (Matthew 4:13-19) and a high-ranking government official (4:46). It had at least one major synagogue. Although Jesus made this city his base of operations in Galilee, he condemned it for the people's unbelief (Matthew 11:23; Luke 10:15).

The Passover of the Jews.[NKJV] The Passover celebration took place yearly at the temple in Jerusalem. Every Jewish male was expected to make a pilgrimage to Jerusalem during this time (Deuteronomy 16:16). This was a week-long festival—the Passover was one day, and the Feast of Unleavened Bread lasted the rest of the week. The entire week commemorated the freeing of the Jews from slavery in Egypt (Exodus 12:1-14).

Some commentators say John made a point of saying "of the Jews" because it had become a ceremonial holiday void of spiritual reality—a Passover belonging no longer to God but to custom, much like some people today might celebrate Easter or Christmas without recognizing God's place in those holidays. John may have spoken this way in anticipation of the following narrative.

Jesus went up to Jerusalem. Jerusalem was both the religious and the political seat of Palestine, and the place where the Messiah was expected to arrive. The temple was located there, and many Jewish families from all over the world traveled to Jerusalem during the key feasts. The temple was on an imposing hill overlooking the city. Solomon had built the first temple on this same site almost one thousand years earlier (949 B.C.), but his temple had been destroyed by the Babylonians (2 Kings 25). The temple was rebuilt in 515 B.C., and Herod the Great had recently remodeled it.

2:14 In the temple courts he found men selling cattle, sheep and doves, and others sitting at tables exchanging money.[NIV] God had originally instructed the people of Israel to bring from their own flocks the best animals for sacrifice (Deuteronomy 12:5-7). This would make the sacrifice more personal. But the temple priests instituted a market for buying sacrificial animals so the pilgrims would not have to bring their animals on the long journey. Given the distances traveled by pilgrims to Jerusalem, the provision of a local animal supply probably was well intended, but what had begun as an informal farmer's market along the road coming into Jerusalem had gradually become institutionalized until it took up the very place of worship.

In addition, the merchants and money changers were dishonest. The business people selling these animals expected to turn a profit. The price of sacrificial animals was much higher in the temple area than elsewhere. In order

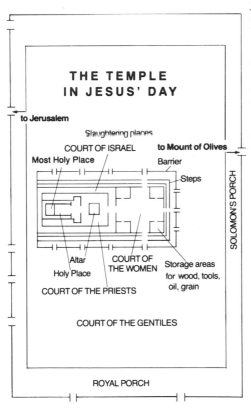

The Temple in Jesus' Day.

to purchase the animals, travelers from other lands would need local currency, and the temple tax had to be paid in local currency; so money changers exchanged foreign money, but made huge profits by charging exorbitant exchange rates. Jesus was angry at the dishonest, greedy practices of the money changers and merchants, and he particularly disliked their presence on the temple grounds. They were making a mockery of God's house of worship. The effect was somewhat like having loan officers at the back of our churches so that worshipers could obtain money to place in the offering plate.

Besides that, they had set up shop in the Court of the Gentiles, making it so full of merchants that foreigners found it difficult to worship—and worship was the main purpose for visiting the temple. With all the merchandising taking place in the area allotted for the Gentiles, how could they spend time with God in prayer? No wonder Jesus was angry!

WHY DO YOU GO TO CHURCH?
Too many churches today do everything they can to make the time of worship convenient for people. And some people attend church because they see it as a place for personal contacts or business advantage. But worshiping God is not always convenient; it demands true devotion and self-sacrifice. Nor is it for our own earthly advancement. Our focus should be on God alone. We are to worship sincerely, reverently, and humbly. That is not to say we cannot be excited, even zealous, about God. But we are always to worship with reverence—recognizing and remembering who God is.

Many radio and television ministries have become little more than marketplaces for religion. Some of these programs spend a great deal of air time discussing premiums and offers we can receive by sending in a donation that will be used to continue and increase programming so that more people can be contacted to send more money. Jesus would not condemn all fundraising; but when "worship" services are broadcast for no apparent reason other than to raise money, we should be suspect. Check with your church leaders to make sure the ministry you would like to support has validity.

2:15 He made a whip out of cords.NIV Jesus' response to the desecration of the temple was deliberate and forceful. He was intent on scouring the temple. This messianic purging of the temple was foretold in Malachi 3:1-3:

■ *"Then suddenly the Lord you are seeking will come to his temple; the messenger of the covenant, whom you desire, will come," says the* LORD *Almighty. But who can endure the day of his coming? Who can stand when he appears? For he will be like a refiner's fire or a launderer's soap. He will sit as a refiner and purifier of silver; he will purify the Levites and refine them like gold and silver. Then the* LORD *will have men who will bring offerings in righteousness. (NIV)*

This cleansing was significantly appropriate during Passover because that was the time when all the Jews were supposed to cleanse their houses of all leaven (yeast). Yeast was used in making bread, but as God was preparing his people for their hasty exodus from Egypt, he told them to make bread without leaven because they would be eating quickly and would not have time to wait for bread to rise. During the Feast of Unleavened Bread, no leaven was used in any baking and, in fact, was not even to be found in the Israelite homes (Exodus 12:17-20).

And drove all from the temple area . . . he scattered the coins of the money changers and overturned their tables.NIV Jesus did not lose his temper; his action expressed anger, but he was clearly in control of himself. Jesus was zealous for the reverence due to God the Father, and he knew that the irreverent marketplace within the very courts of God's temple would not be expelled without the use of force. Any view of God that subtly makes him incapable of anger reduces him to a status equal with pagan gods. The God who is love, who *chooses* whether or not to be angry, is quite different from a god who is incapable of being angry. One is worthy of our respectful fear; the other is an impotent idol. When sin required anger, Jesus exercised the appropriate response.

2:16 "Stop making my Father's house a marketplace!"NRSV Jesus saw the temple as belonging to his Father. His own rightful claim to ownership was unmistakable. But the religious leaders of that day were trespassers—turning it into a place of business and money-making. People had created an environment that, in essence, put a price on what God intended to be free. Access to God is not for sale. Giving the impression that God's favor can be bought shows disrespect toward both God and those he loves.

According to the other three Gospels, Jesus visited the temple again and cleansed it during his final visit to Jerusalem during the Passover, just prior to his crucifixion (see Matthew 21:12-17; Mark 11:15-19; Luke 19:45-46).

CHEAP WORSHIP
We have so many opportunities for worship that we may trivialize its importance. We frankly have a difficult time identifying with believers elsewhere in the world who worship under threat of pain, imprisonment, even death. The faith of these believers is portrayed by exuberance, seriousness, and reverence in worship, despite their environment. Too often for us, worship seems to be nothing more than Christians getting together for fellowship, to learn from each other, and to help each other. While all that is good, it may not be true worship. If God is not the focus, the church is in danger of becoming nothing more than a service club.

Then what is true worship? True worship focuses on God, the one who is to be worshiped. When Christians gather to worship—that is, to meet with God—then their deepest needs and hungers are satisfied, for they are in touch with the Creator.

We dare not cheapen this truly miraculous and intimate privilege called worship. Jesus was angered by actions and attitudes that cheapened worship, and we must take care not to let such actions and attitudes into our church. How would Jesus respond to the worship in your church if he were to visit this Sunday?

2:17 It was written, "Zeal for Your house has eaten Me up."^{NKJV} This quote from Psalm 69:9 was thought to refer not only to the psalmist but also to the coming Messiah. His incredible zeal for God and for purity of worship would endanger his life. In fact, Jesus was perceived as a threat to the religious establishment, and this was a direct cause of his death. The disciples, probably as much as any of the people then present, must have been shocked at Jesus' display of anger. But John reported that they remembered God's Word and saw the action as God-ordained. The exact time when they recalled God's Word is unclear. In any case, they didn't fully understand the implication of Jesus' words until later.

The **Jews**, as John calls them, were less than eager to agree with Jesus' implied judgment. Offended by Jesus' action, they demanded a sign to prove his right to act in such a rash way. John regularly makes use of the term *Jews* to stand for "leaders or representatives of the Jews." Its use is not so much an indictment of the nation as a whole but of those leaders who were guilty of misleading the people.

2:18 "What miraculous sign can you show us?"^{NIV} The hardhearted people of Jesus' day continually required Jesus to give them some spectacular sign to prove his authority and demonstrate that he was the Messiah. The Jews were so notorious for being sign-

WHEN IS ANGER GOOD?
Jesus was obviously angry at the merchants who exploited those who had come to God's house to worship. There is a difference between uncontrolled rage and righteous indignation—yet both are called anger. We must be very careful how we use the powerful emotion of anger. It is right to be angry about injustice and sin; it is wrong to be angry over trivial personal offenses.

Jesus made a whip and chased out the money changers. Does his example permit us to use violence against wrongdoers? Certain authority is granted to some, but not to all. For example, the authority to use weapons and restrain people is granted to police officers, but not to the general public. The authority to imprison people is granted to judges, but not to individual citizens. While we want to live like Christ, we should never try to claim his authority where it has not been given to us.

seekers that Paul could say, "Jews demand miraculous signs" (1 Corinthians 1:22 NIV). In his parable of the rich man and Lazarus (Luke 16:19-31), Jesus made the point that those unwilling to believe will not be convinced by signs. His application was both pointed and prophetic: "If they do not listen to Moses and the prophets, neither will they be convinced even if someone rises from the dead" (Luke 16:31 NRSV). Jesus would not give his generation the kind of sign they demanded; he himself was the sign, for he was the Son of God come from heaven to earth. This would be known to all after his resurrection. This would be the ultimate sign he would give Israel and all mankind.

2:19 **"Destroy this temple, and in three days I will raise it up."**^{NRSV} Jesus answers the Jewish leaders' challenge with a counter-challenge that the disciples later understood to be a prediction of his own death and resurrection (2:22). Jesus' opponents saw only the absurdity of such a claim. But as John clues us in: "He was speaking of the temple of his body" (2:21 NRSV). Jesus' ambiguous statement is a good example of how he encouraged people to think and inquire more deeply. Along with his parables, these statements accomplished the dual task of frustrating the half-hearted and self-righteous while at the same time piquing the curiosity of those who were sincere seekers.

It was quite common for people in New Testament times to speak about death in terms of the destruction of the body. Paul used this imagery in 2 Corinthians 5:1-4, and Peter in 2 Peter 1:13-14. The physical body is a temporary dwelling place for one's real person; death dissolves that dwelling place. Jesus' temporal life would be destroyed through crucifixion, but he would rise again with a new, glorified body—a body suited to his new spiritual existence (see 1 Corinthians 15:42-45). All who believe in Christ receive a new spiritual body.

This would be the sign the Jews required, even if they did not recognize it. They would destroy his body, and he would raise it up in three days. At another time when the Jews asked Jesus for a sign, he told them that the only sign he would give them was that of Jonah the prophet, who spent three days and three nights in the belly of a great fish before God delivered him (see Matthew 12:39-40). In like manner, Jesus would be killed and after three days rise from the dead.

PURITY OF WORSHIP
Jesus was zealous for the purity of worship—worship that he was going to make universally available through his death. Only by clarifying how the old system was intended could the new system have a place. Only by "destroying the temple" would Jesus be able to offer all believers personal access to God. Only by fulfilling the system of sacrifice could he become the perfect and final sacrifice for all mankind. The eventual destruction of the temple in 70 A.D. was the final evidence that the old system had been superseded by Jesus' work on the cross and in the lives of those who believe in him.

2:20-21 **"It has taken forty-six years to build this temple, and will You raise it up in three days?" But He was speaking of the temple of His body.**NKJV The Jews understood Jesus to mean the temple where he had just driven out the merchants and money changers. This was the temple Zerubbabel had built more than five hundred years earlier, but Herod the Great had begun remodeling it, making it much larger and far more beautiful. It had been forty-six years since this remodeling had started (20 B.C.), and it still wasn't completely finished. They understood Jesus' words to mean that this imposing building could be torn down and rebuilt in three days, and they were openly skeptical.

2:22 **After he was raised from the dead, his disciples remembered that he had said this; and they believed the scripture and the word that Jesus had spoken.**NRSV The *scripture* probably means the whole Old Testament as it testifies to Christ's death and resurrection (passages such as Psalm 22:7-17). After Christ's resurrection, the Spirit illuminated these Scriptures (14:26), so the disciples believed and understood. As Jesus predicted, they *did* destroy his body (the temple), and he *did* raise it up in three days.

RESURRECTION
For believers, the Resurrection places a confirming stamp on Jesus' life and words. It is not just one of many miracles of Jesus. Instead, it is the key to understanding God's plan; it is the central, foundational fact of Christianity. As Paul put it, "If Christ has not been raised, our preaching is useless and so is your faith" (1 Corinthians 15:14 NIV). Whenever we are troubled about what Jesus said or did, it usually indicates that we have drifted from our understanding of his resurrection. With the Resurrection settled, the rest of the record seems possible; but doubting the Resurrection makes the rest improbable. Do you accept his credentials as the risen Lord?

2:23-25 While he was in Jerusalem at the Passover Feast.^{NIV} This was during the same week that Jesus purged the temple in Jerusalem (see 2:13ff.). It was the week-long Feast of Unleavened Bread that followed the day of Passover.

Many people saw the miraculous signs he was doing and believed in his name.^{NIV} John did not recount any of the particular miracles Jesus performed in Jerusalem; he simply said that many people believed in Jesus when they saw the miracles he did. But, as the next verse indicates, this belief was not complete. The people believed in Jesus as a miracle worker or a political messiah, but not necessarily as the true Messiah, the Son of God.

DEFICIENT FAITH
Faith in Jesus can be deficient in at least two ways. The first occurs when we base our faith on the wrong motives. We should not believe in Jesus because of what he can do for us (or for what miracle he may have done for us); we should believe in him for who he is—the Christ, the Son of God. The second deficiency of faith pictures trust as a point of arrival rather than a point of departure. John described the disciples' attitude toward Jesus as belief, even though there was a great deal of room for growth. Either of these deficiencies leads to incomplete and immature faith. Does your faith rest on what Christ does for you or on who he is?

But Jesus on his part would not entrust himself to them.^{NRSV} John used the Greek verb *pisteuo* to make a wordplay. In 2:23, John said that many believed (*episteusan*) in him; in 2:24, John said that Jesus did not entrust (*episteusen*) himself to them. Another way to word this would be, "many trusted in his name, . . . but he did not entrust Himself to them." The reason for Jesus'

lack of trust then follows—**because he knew all people.**NRSV In
other words, many people trusted in him, but Jesus did not
entrust himself to them, for he knew that people are not trustworthy. Jesus was realistic about the depth of trust in those who were
now following him. Some would endure; others would fall away
(6:66). It is worth noting, however, that Jesus did not give up on
them; they gave up on him.

PATIENCE
How easy it is to give up on those around us or in our ministry!
Yet Jesus had the patience to wait for the disciples to develop
and mature. He had the courage to face spiritual loneliness with
no one around him who was able to understand his experience.
How patient are we with those who are struggling to keep on
track spiritually? How well do we do in those dry times when
there are no others with whom we can relate at the same spiritual level? We can see Christ's example in the Gospels, and we
can experience his patience in our own lives. Practice Christ's
patience with those to whom he has called us to minister.

**Needed no one to testify about anyone; for he himself knew
what was in everyone.**NRSV Jesus did not need to be told about
human nature; he knew the motives behind people's actions
because he thoroughly knew the human makeup. He knew how
fickle people were (and are). Jesus was well aware of the truth of
Jeremiah 17:9: "The heart is deceitful above all things and
beyond cure. Who can understand it?" (NIV—see also 1 Samuel
16:7; Psalm 139; Acts 1:24). Jesus was discerning, and he knew
that the faith of some followers was superficial. Some of the
same people who claimed to believe in Jesus at this time would
later yell, "Crucify him!"

JESUS KNOWS
It's easy to believe when there is excitement and everyone else
seems to believe the same way. But sooner or later the opportunities will come to discover whether our faith is firm when it isn't
popular to follow Christ. It is comforting to know that Jesus sees
through our efforts to be more confident or perfect than we really
are. In fact, we will not fully appreciate his grace until we recognize that he sees us and knows us exactly as we are, and he
loves us anyway. Part of trusting Jesus is acknowledging that he
understands us better than we understand ourselves.

John 3

It would be difficult to find any other portion of Scripture as well known as John 3:16 or any other statement of Scripture more applied than "You must be born again" (v. 7, NKJV). When Jesus revealed the necessity of the new birth to Nicodemus, he exposed mankind's ultimate hope.

This evening interview is the first of a series of individual encounters between Jesus and persons who fit the description given at the end of chapter 2—those who approached Jesus with an inadequate faith. Nicodemus (vv. 1-15), the Samaritan woman (4:1-42), and the nobleman from Capernaum (4:43-54) illustrate a certain view of who Jesus was and what he could do. But meeting Jesus face to face changed their views. It also changed their lives.

Wherever Jesus went, changes occurred. He challenged systems, powers, and individuals. He helped people see that they couldn't see. He invited men and women to follow him as if he expected them to drop everything and do just that. To our surprise (not his) many of them did follow. The invitation to transformation is still open. If we are listening, we can hear it in the darkness as did Nicodemus. Or it comes to us at noon, when we, like the woman at the well, are slipping through life, desperate to avoid any more troubles than we have already gotten ourselves into. Or it comes to us with shattering directness in the face of death or suffering around us, as the nobleman discovered. When the invitation comes, trust Jesus and follow him.

3:1 There was a man.^{NKJV} Each of the next segments of the Gospel revolve around Jesus and one other person. From his collection of Jesus' memorable conversations, John chose several to highlight the character of the Lord.

Though John seems to shift from the summary description of Jesus as the center of interest in Jerusalem to the interview with Nicodemus, there is a connection between 2:23-25 and 3:1. Nicodemus is spotlighted as a person who was either a typical example of someone to whom Jesus *could not* entrust himself (2:24) or he was an exception to the rule—a person to whom Jesus *could* entrust him-

PROMINENT JEWISH RELIGIOUS AND POLITICAL GROUPS

Name and Selected References	Description	Agreement with Jesus	Disagreement with Jesus
PHARISEES Matthew 5:20 Matthew 23:1-36 Luke 6:2 Luke 7:36-47	Strict group of religious Jews who advocated minute obedience to the Jewish law and traditions. Very influential in the synagogues.	Respect for the law, belief in the resurrection of the dead, committed to obeying God's will.	Rejected Jesus' claim to be Messiah because he did not follow all their traditions and associated with notoriously wicked people.
SADDUCEES Matthew 3:7 Matthew 16:11-12 Mark 12:18	Wealthy, upper class, Jewish priestly party. Rejected the authority of the Bible beyond the five books of Moses. They, along with the Pharisees, were one of the two major parties of the Jewish council.	Showed great respect for the five books of Moses, as well as the sanctity of the temple.	Denied the resurrection of the dead. Thought the temple could also be used as a place to transact business.
TEACHERS OF THE LAW Matthew 7:29 Mark 2:6 Mark 2:16	Professional interpreters of the Law—who especially emphasized the traditions. Many teachers of the Law were Pharisees.	Respect for the Law. Committed to obeying God.	Denied Jesus' authority to reinterpret the Law. Rejected Jesus as Messiah because he did not obey all of their traditions.
HERODIANS Matthew 22:16 Mark 3:6 Mark 12:13	A Jewish political party of King Herod's supporters.	Unknown. In the Gospels they tried to trap Jesus with questions and plotted to kill him.	Afraid of Jesus causing political instability.
ZEALOTS Luke 6:15 Acts 1:14	A fiercely dedicated group of Jewish patriots determined to end Roman rule in Israel.	Concerned about the future of Israel. Believed in the Messiah but did not recognize Jesus as the One sent by God.	Believed that the Messiah must be a political leader who would deliver Israel from Roman occupation.
ESSENES none	Jewish monastic group practicing ritual purity and personal holiness.	Emphasized justice, honesty, commitment.	Believed ceremonial rituals made them righteous.

self. Both these possibilities have been defended. But, in the end, neither is as important as the clearer indication of John's immediate purpose: to illustrate the truth that Jesus "knew what was in everyone" (NRSV). Jesus did not endorse every gesture of belief in himself, but he did nurture those with weak faith. Because Jesus knew what was in every person, he knew exactly when to confront Nicodemus. His knowledge of us is just as intimate.

Of the Pharisees named Nicodemus, a member of the Jewish ruling council.^{NIV} Nicodemus was one *of the Pharisees*—the most strict, conservative, and traditional Jewish sect of those times. The Jewish religious leaders were divided into several groups. Two of the most prominent groups were the Pharisees and the Sadducees. The Pharisees separated themselves from anything non-Jewish and carefully followed both the Old Testament laws and the oral traditions handed down through the centuries. The Sadducees, on the other hand, were the elite priestly class who freely mixed their political agenda with the power they wielded as religious leaders. John the Baptist criticized the Pharisees for being legalistic and hypocritical, following the letter of the law while ignoring its true intent. Jesus' cleansing of the temple was a direct affront to the power of the Sadducees, who profited from the marketing of religion.

Nicodemus was also *a member of the Jewish ruling council.* Although the Romans controlled Israel politically, the Jews were given some authority over religious and minor civil disputes. The Jewish ruling body was the council (sometimes called the Sanhedrin) made up of seventy-one of Israel's religious leaders. They functioned in a way similar to the Supreme Court in the United States, handling civil and religious issues. Thus Nicodemus was a very prominent figure in Israel, representing the "cream" of the nation; in fact, Jesus called him "a teacher of Israel" (3:10 NRSV).

3:2 He came to Jesus.^{NRSV} What motivated Nicodemus to come to Jesus? Very likely Nicodemus was both impressed and curious about Jesus and chose to form his opinions about him from firsthand conversation. Most Pharisees were intensely jealous of Jesus because he undermined their authority, challenged their views, and threatened their tenuous position under Roman rule. But Nicodemus tracked down Jesus and met him personally. It is even possible that their conversation was witnessed by both Jesus' disciples and students of the Jewish leader.

> It is by the heart that God is perceived and not by reason. So that is what faith is: God perceived by the heart, not by the reason. *Blaise Pascal*

AT LEAST HE CAME
The meeting between Nicodemus and Jesus was not by accident. Nicodemus did not stumble over Jesus, but sought him out. He made it a point to find and be with Jesus. Often we are guilty of allowing our relationship with God to degenerate into occasional chance meetings where God has had to seek us out. Do we only turn to Christ in crises, finding little place or time for him in our daily lives? How often at night, when the hustle of the day settles down, do we think of Jesus in the silence and seek him out in prayer?

At night.NIV Why did Nicodemus come to Jesus by night? It is possible that he did not want to be seen with Jesus in broad daylight because he feared reproach from his fellow Pharisees (who did not believe in Jesus as the Messiah). But it may not have been fear that brought Nicodemus at night; it is also possible that he chose a time when he could talk alone and at length with the popular teacher who was often surrounded by people.

NECESSITY OF A SEARCHING HEART
Nicodemus was searching, and he believed that Jesus had some answers. A learned teacher himself, he came to Jesus to be taught. No matter how intelligent and well-educated we are, we must come to Jesus with an open mind and heart so he can teach us the truth about God. A searching heart is marked by several characteristics:

- *Humility* in seeking and admitting personal need.
- *Perseverance* in overcoming obstacles that may keep us from finding and following Christ.
- *Insight* in recognizing that the gospel message relates to our lives.
- *Willingness* to submit to the lordship of Christ.
- *Obedience* in going beyond mental assent to active dependence on God's promises and guidance.

"Rabbi, we know you are a teacher who has come from God."NIV Nicodemus respectfully addressed Jesus as a teacher (a *rabbi*) who had *come from God.* While true, the title reveals Nicodemus's limited understanding of Jesus. He was far more than just another rabbi. Yet Nicodemus's complimentary start gives us little idea of what he intended to ask Jesus. It is to his credit that he at least understood that Jesus came *from God,* as opposed to many of his fellow Pharisees who attributed Jesus' power to Satan (Matthew 9:34). Instead, Nicodemus identified Jesus' miracles as a revelation of God's power.

> **QUESTIONS/ANSWERS**
> It is quite common to find people treating spiritual questions as if asking them was a perfectly valid pursuit, even if they had no real hope of getting an answer. That kind of treadmill leads to despair. If we are not serious about answers, questions—even hard questions—are a waste of time.
>
> We don't know exactly what questions Nicodemus planned to ask Jesus, but we do know he went to the right source. If all we want to do is ask questions, any ear will do. But if we are hungry for answers, God will be our source. He has provided his Word, his presence, and the freedom of prayer to place any question before him. Others who have brought their questions and quests to God can also provide valuable help to us. Jesus wants to be more than just an item of discussion. He has answers for the heart and soul.

Nicodemus's expression indicates that he saw himself representing a significant number of Jews (thus his use of *we*), the people over whom he was a leader and teacher. But no sooner did Nicodemus get this compliment out than Jesus responded with a statement that must have rocked the Pharisee back on his heels. With one stroke Jesus reversed the flow of discussion from his identity as a God-sent teacher to the crucial question of the destiny of each person. Jesus made it clear that his own qualifications were not up for debate, but that Nicodemus ought to be concerned about where he stood before God.

3:3 "No one can see the kingdom of God."^{NRSV} Jesus' words are unmistakable: *No one*—that is, not the Jews, not the pious Pharisees or Sadducees. No one who is relying on his or her own merits can *see the kingdom of God*.

Although the Bible does not explicitly state what the kingdom of God is, Jesus made it very clear what it isn't: "My kingdom is not from this world" (18:36 NRSV). God's kingdom is the sphere of God's rule in heaven and on earth. The Old Testament does not use the term *kingdom of God*, but it clearly refers to the kingship of God. When the last of the judges, Samuel, was an old man, the people of Israel decided they wanted a new form of government. They approached Samuel with the demand that he appoint a king. God's response to Samuel about this request is instructive: "And the Lord told him: 'Listen to all that the people are saying to you; it is not you they have rejected, but they have rejected me as their king'" (1 Samuel 8:7 NIV). This tension between the recognized or rejected kingship of God and its final resolution cannot be missed in the Old Testament (see also Exodus 15:18; Psalm 93:1; 103:19; Isaiah 9:6-7; Daniel 2:44).

THE KINGDOM OF GOD

Statement	Scripture
To enter you must confess and repent of sin.	*Matthew 4:17*
Those persecuted for the faith will receive rewards there.	*Matthew 5:10-12*
Not all who talk about it belong there.	*Matthew 7:21*
Small beginning but great results	*Matthew 13:31-32*
Worldwide impact	*Matthew 13:33*
Priceless value	*Matthew 13:44-46*
Cannot judge who will be in it	*Matthew 13:47-49*
Good news to all	*Luke 4:43*
Equally available to all	*Luke 10:21*
Must be the believer's top priority	*Luke 12:31*
The door is now open to all, but one day it will close.	*Luke 13:22-30*
To enter you must be born again.	*John 3:3*

So, what could Jesus expect Nicodemus to know about the kingdom? From the Scriptures he would know that the kingdom would be ruled by God, it would eventually be restored on earth, and it would incorporate God's people. Jesus revealed to this devout Pharisee that the kingdom would come to the whole world (3:16), not just the Jews, and that Nicodemus wouldn't be a part of it unless he was personally born again (3:5). This was a revolutionary concept: the kingdom is personal, not national or ethnic, and its entrance requirements are repentance and spiritual rebirth. Jesus later taught that God's kingdom has *already begun* in the hearts of believers (Luke 17:21). It will be fully realized when Jesus returns again to judge the world and abolish evil forever (Revelation 21–22).

During Jesus' earthly ministry, the kingdom of God was present with him (Luke 17:21). To "see" the kingdom of God means, in part, to have a special perception or insight concerning God's absolute control. But a sense of belonging, or citizenship, is also included. The "seeing" is not simply for purposes of examination; it represents participation. Part of this picture is clarified by the description of vital faith in Hebrews: "All these people were still living by faith when they died. They did not receive the things promised; they only saw them and welcomed them from a distance. And they admitted that they were aliens and strangers on earth" (Hebrews 11:13 NIV). The image here is of people, stranded in a foreign land, whose citizenship is elsewhere. Paul wrote, "Giving thanks to the Father, who has qualified you to share in the inheritance of the saints in the kingdom of light. For he has rescued us from the dominion of darkness and brought us into the kingdom of the Son he loves, in whom we have redemption, the forgiveness of sins" (Colossians 1:12-14 NIV). To "see," then, is to be a citizen without yet being able to exercise all the rights and privileges of that citizenship. Nicodemus was being taught that Israel was a chosen people to be a vehicle of God's message to the world, not to be the only beneficiaries of that relationship.

IN OR OUT
Just as earthly citizenship is a right of birth or is granted to a person, so citizenship in the kingdom of God is a right of new birth. A person can take steps toward citizenship in the kingdom, but one's actual position is either in or out. Jesus told one perceptive man, "You are not far from the kingdom of God" (Mark 12:34). Evidently, a person can approach yet still not "see" or be part of the kingdom of God. We need to prayerfully consider before God the exact location of our citizenship. If we have not been born again into God's kingdom and submitted to his rule in our lives, we cannot assume that we are citizens.

"Without being born from above."[NRSV] The Greek word translated here as "from above" can also be rendered "again." It seems that Jesus was speaking of a birth "from above" because he later used the analogy of the wind (coming from some unknown [heavenly] source) to illustrate spiritual rebirth (see 3:7-8). But Nicodemus clearly thought that Jesus was speaking of a second physical birth.

3:4 "How can anyone be born after having grown old? Can one enter a second time into the mother's womb and be born?"[NRSV] English translations of Jesus' statement tend to put the conditional clause ("without being born from above") after the primary clause ("No one can see the kingdom of God"), but they are reversed in Greek. Nicodemus either stopped listening after Jesus' opening phrase, or he chose to address the first curious statement he heard. These questions that focused solely on birth—whether spoken sincerely or sarcastically—show that Nicodemus did not perceive the spiritual intent of Jesus' words. He saw only the literal meaning and questioned its absurdity. But with all his learning he should have understood that God *can* and *will* give spiritual rebirth. The prophets had spoken about this spiritual regeneration (see Ezekiel 36:25-27; see also Jeremiah 31:31-34; Joel 2:28-32).

STARTING OVER
Most people, at one time or another, wish they could start life over again. But second thoughts usually bring us to the conclusion that another trip through life would involve just as many opportunities for mistakes as the first time. Nicodemus saw only complications and impossibilities in Jesus' challenge. But Jesus later made the point in discussing the possibility of salvation with his disciples that "with man this is impossible, but not with God; all things are possible with God" (Mark 10:27 NIV). The only way a person can really start over in life is by being born from above—"born again" by receiving God's eternal life and the regenerating Holy Spirit. Starting over may be naturally impossible; but Jesus makes it a supernatural possibility.

3:5 **"No one can enter the kingdom of God without being born of water and Spirit."**[NRSV] This statement has perplexed and divided commentators for many centuries. Some traditions have taught that the *water* denotes physical birth (referring to the "water" of amniotic fluid or even semen) and *Spirit* to spiritual birth—in which case Jesus would be saying that a person has to have two births: one physical and the second, spiritual. This view builds upon the preceding context when Nicodemus referred to physical birth. It also points to the parallel Jesus makes in verse 6: "Flesh gives birth to flesh, but the Spirit gives birth to spirit" (NIV). According to this position, Jesus would have been granting the Pharisee's point in order to highlight the nature of the second birth as spiritual. Two strengths of this interpretation are that it avoids making the physical act of water baptism a necessity and that it avoids bringing almost a "third birth" idea into the discussion. If *water* doesn't refer to natural birth, say its defenders, then Jesus seems to be saying that a person must be born of their parents, born of water, and born of the Spirit.

Several weaknesses undermine this view: (1) the Greek grammatical construction does not separate *water* and *Spirit*—together they replace the single expression *anothen* ("again" or "from above" in verse 3); (2) there is no evidence that *water* was specifically connected with physical birth in Jesus' and Nicodemus's cultural context; and (3) it would be reasonable to expect that if Jesus was explaining *water* and *Spirit* as separate terms in verse 6, he could have said, "Water gives birth to water and spirit gives birth to spirit." This interpretation turns out to be based on better motives than reasons. The concerns over making this verse say more than is true about the nature and place of water baptism are valid, but not best served by this approach.

Other traditions have taught that the *water* refers to baptism and the *Spirit* to spiritual regeneration—thus, Jesus would have been saying that a person must both be baptized and receive the Spirit in order to enter the kingdom of God. This view is at times influenced by the belief that the sacrament of baptism is itself a requirement for salvation.

A parallel view makes *water* refer to baptism but places the emphasis on teaching two steps of baptism; one by water, the other by the Spirit. For support, these views point to the larger context in John where John the Baptist and water baptism are mentioned just preceding the events in Cana and following this encounter with Nicodemus. They also rely on the tendency of previous generations of Christians to equate the mention of water with baptism. But in the first seven chapters of John, water appears in some way (naturally or symbolically) in each chapter. To associate water and baptism too closely makes baptism a higher priority than the Scriptures give it. Here, for instance, if Jesus was speaking of two completely separate acts, two baptisms, it is odd that the rest of the discussion between Jesus and Nicodemus never again refers to the subject but revolves entirely around the work of God's Spirit.

> This possibility of conversion, regeneration, opens a new and astonishing possibility to men—that men need not remain as we are; that we can have a new birth in this birth, another chance when we have muffed this business of living; . . . a new blood transfusion from the Son of God.
>
> *E. Stanley Jones*

Still other traditions have taught that Jesus' reference to *water* is not physical in either the sense of birth or baptism. The term *water* is simply another description of the Spirit—or the Spirit's activity of cleansing and life-giving action of the Spirit (see John 7:37-39).

3:6 "Flesh gives birth to flesh, but the Spirit gives birth to spirit."[NIV] This is also written: "That which is born of the flesh is flesh; and that which is born of the Spirit is spirit" (NKJV). Human beings (the *flesh*) can produce only more human beings; this answers Nicodemus's question in verse 4. Only God, the divine Spirit, can give the believer spiritual life. At the same time God puts his Spirit into us, we are given a new regenerated human spirit. It is God's Spirit, not our effort, that makes us children of God (1:12). Jesus' description corrects human hopes that we might somehow inherit goodness from parents, or earn it by good behavior, church background, or correct associations. At some point we must be able to answer the question: Have I been born of the Spirit?

WHO IS THE HOLY SPIRIT?
God has revealed himself as three persons in one—the Father, the Son, and the Holy Spirit. God became a man in Jesus so that Jesus could die for our sins. Jesus was raised from the dead to guarantee God's offer of salvation to all people through spiritual renewal and rebirth. When Jesus ascended into heaven, his physical presence left the earth, but he promised to send the Holy Spirit so that his spiritual presence would still be among his people (Luke 24:49). The Holy Spirit first became available in this special way to all believers at Pentecost (Acts 2). Whereas in Old Testament days the Holy Spirit empowered specific individuals for specific purposes, now all believers have the power of the Holy Spirit available to them. For more on the Holy Spirit, read 14:16-28; Romans 8:9; 1 Corinthians 12:13; and 2 Corinthians 1:22.

3:7 "You must be born from above."^{NRSV} Jesus' statement to Nicodemus that evening has been heralded to all the world ever since. Both Jew and Gentile have heard the divine mandate: You must be born again. Without the new birth, one cannot see or enter into the kingdom of God. In those words, millions have heard Jesus speaking directly to their hearts. Behind Jesus' challenge is his invitation to each of us—"You must be born again; allow me to do that for you."

3:8 "The wind blows wherever it pleases. You hear its sound, but you cannot tell where it comes from or where it is going."^{NIV}

Perhaps at this moment in the evening a soft wind rustled the leaves outside the house or in the garden where they were talking. Jesus used the illustration of the wind to depict the effect of the Spirit in the person born of the Spirit. In Greek the same word (*pneuma*) can have several meanings: "spirit," "wind," and "breath." God's Spirit, like the wind, has free movement and, like reviving breath, has power. Jesus used this illustration to show that the reality of the Spirit living in a person is evidenced by the

> The believer shows by deed and word that an invisible influence has moved and inspired him. He is himself a continual sign of the action of the Spirit, which is freely determined, and incomprehensible by man to source and end, though seen in its present results. *Westcott*

effect of the Spirit on that person's life. People can control neither the wind nor the movement of God's Spirit.

"So it is with everyone who is born of the Spirit."^{NRSV} The image Jesus used describes the wonderful experience we can have of realizing that God actually moves in and through us by his Spirit. Just as we do not know the origin or the destination of the wind, we do not know or control the Spirit. What we do know are the effects of the wind and of the Spirit. Life in the Spirit is as radical and unexpected as being born of the Spirit.

> The new life begotten by the Spirit of God is as mysterious as the wind. That Spirit, bearing the germ of a new life, rejoices to enter each open casement and to fill each vacuum, wherever one allows it. *F. B. Meyer*

DON'T GIVE UP ON PEOPLE
It must have seemed unlikely to the disciples that Nicodemus would believe in Jesus. Are there people you disregard, thinking they could never be brought to God—such as a world leader for whom you have never prayed or a successful person to whom you have never witnessed? Don't assume that anyone is beyond the gospel. God, through his Holy Spirit, can reach anyone, and you should pray diligently for whomever he brings to your mind. Be a witness and example to everyone with whom you have contact. God may touch those you think most unlikely—and he may use you to do it.

3:9-10 A teacher of Israel.[NRSV] In response to Nicodemus's continued question, Jesus called him *a teacher of Israel* and expressed amazement at his lack of understanding. Having such a position (perhaps as the "chakam" in the Sanhedrin), Nicodemus should have known what Jesus was talking about, for the new birth is not a topic foreign to the Hebrew Scriptures (see, for example, 1 Samuel 10:6; Isaiah 32:15; Jeremiah 31:33; Ezekiel 36:25-27; 37; Joel 2:28-29). Jesus' question must have exposed Nicodemus, who perhaps thought that he and Jesus were teachers who would discuss spiritual matters from an equal level of learning and understanding (see 3:2). This Jewish teacher of the Bible knew the Old Testament thoroughly, but he didn't understand what it said about the Messiah. Knowledge is not salvation (see 5:39 for Jesus' further indictment of those who have the Scriptures yet miss their primary purpose). People may know the Bible and even study it regularly, but unless they understand and respond to the God whom the Bible reveals and the salvation that he offers, the Scriptures will only be a priceless relic rather than a life-changing treasure.

3:11-12 "We speak of what we know and testify to what we have seen."[NRSV] Commentators do not agree as to whom the pronoun *we* refers to. Most likely, it refers to all those prophets who have spoken to Israel (including John the Baptist [see 5:33] and Jesus himself) and/or to Jesus and his Father.

"You people do not accept our testimony."ᴺᴵⱽ Israel (of which Nicodemus was a representative) did not receive the corporate testimony either from Jesus (speaking on behalf of the Father— hence, the plural *our*), or from the prophets.

"I have told you about earthly things."ᴺᴿˢⱽ *Earthly things,* such as the wind, can be "sensed"—that is, felt and heard. Jesus had spoken in an "earthly" analogy, and if Nicodemus could not understand *that,* how would he understand or believe when Jesus spoke to him of **heavenly things.** These are the truths that pertain to the heavenly realm and heavenly kingdom (for example, the more abstract theological topics such as the Trinity or Jesus' coming glory).

HEAVENLY MINDED
These "heavenly things" cannot be sensed; they must be revealed by God and believed in faith. They are not conclusions to which we are naturally drawn. Quite often Jesus did not speak of these things directly because his listeners would not be able to understand. Instead, Jesus used parables to help those whose ears and hearts were open to grasp God's revelation.

Even today the depths of Christ's teaching escapes the bored and inattentive. As Jesus pointed out, many of us have ears to hear, but do not listen. Sometimes the simple discipline of repeatedly reading a chapter of Scripture can help us see and receive what God has stored there for our benefit.

3:13-15 **"No one has ever gone into heaven except the one who came from heaven."**ᴺᴵⱽ This statement, following the last part of verse 12, tells us why Jesus was uniquely qualified to speak about heavenly matters. His authoritative message about heaven was based on personal experience. He *came from heaven!* It was the home he left on his mission to rescue us. No other man could claim the same.

The Son of Man is the term Jesus always used as his self-designation (1:51; see also Daniel 7:13; Matthew 26:64).

The words, *who came from heaven* (or, "who is in heaven," NKJV) that end verse 13 in some translations, are not found in the earliest manuscripts. However, the words were known to several early church fathers and are included in later manuscripts. Moving the phrase to the margin in modern translations does require explanation because it is known by those familiar with the Authorized Version. There is a possibility that the statement was recorded by John and then excised by several early copyists because of its enigmatic meaning: that is, how could the Son of Man who was then and there on earth also be in heaven? But it is also difficult to place it in Jesus' conversation. The phrase fits best as an early marginal reflection by a copyist, noting that the same Jesus who was claiming to have come from heaven was now back in heaven. Those who accept this phrase as original generally interpret it to be Jesus' reference to his very present connection with heaven. He was on earth, while at the same time one with the Father in heaven. While this is true, it does not help the flow of Jesus' conversation. It is difficult to understand what Jesus might have wanted Nicodemus to see.

"As Moses lifted up the snake in the desert, so the Son of Man must be lifted up."[NIV] The Son of Man came from heaven and became flesh in order to die—but his death would have special importance. That significance had been "taught" by God throughout the experiences of his chosen people. To illustrate this, Jesus compared his coming death to a story well known to Nicodemus, for it came from Jewish history.

According to Numbers 21:6-9, while the Israelites were wandering in the wilderness, God sent a plague of snakes to punish the people for their rebellious attitudes. But God also gave the remedy for the poisonous snakebites—he told Moses to erect a pole upon which he was to attach a bronze snake. Those bitten by the poisonous snakes could be healed by obeying God's command to look up at the elevated bronze snake and by believing that God would heal them. Their healing came when they looked upon this lifted-up, bronze snake.

Jesus used this incident to picture his coming salvation work on the cross. To be *lifted up* in Jesus' time—according to the usage in John (see 8:28; 12:32-34)—was a euphemism for death on the cross (the victim was literally lifted up above the earth); it also spoke of his subsequent glorification.

"Everyone who believes in him may have eternal life."[NIV] In Numbers 21:6-9, the perishing Israelites looked upon the lifted-up snake and lived. Similarly, salvation happens when we look up to Jesus, believing he will save us. God has provided this way for us to be healed of sin's deadly bite. The Israelites were spared their lives; the believer in Jesus is spared eternal destruction and given eternal life.

THE REQUIRED RESPONSE

Three times in this context the idea of "believing in him" is used to describe the required response by a person to Christ. The word translated "believe" comes from *pisteo* which means "faith" or "belief." The way this word is used means more than mental assent. Rather, it has been paraphrased: to have a firm faith; to accept trustfully; to be fully convinced; to place confidence in; to wholeheartedly accept. There is a danger, however, in emphasizing only the idea of "belief," since belief without an object is merely wishful thinking. The importance of a Christian's belief is not in the believer, but in the one believed. A person may have a strong belief in a lie, but that faith will not change the lie to truth. Believers anchor their trust in Jesus Christ, who identified himself as truth (14:6). Does our faith depend on our ability to trust or does it rest on the trustworthiness of Jesus?

3:16 "For God so loved the world that He gave His only begotten Son, that whoever believes in Him should not perish but have everlasting life."[NKJV] The entire gospel comes to a focus in this verse. God's love is not just to a certain group of individuals—it is offered to *the world.*

God's love is not static or self-centered; it reaches out and draws others in. Here God's actions defined the pattern of true

ALL THE GREATEST

God.	*the greatest Lover*
So loved	*the greatest degree*
The world	*the greatest number*
That he gave	*the greatest act*
His only begotten Son	*the greatest gift*
That whoever	*the greatest invitation*
Believes	*the greatest simplicity*
In Him.	*the greatest person*
Shall not perish	*the greatest escape*
But	*the greatest difference*
Have.	*the greatest certainty*
Eternal life	*the greatest destiny*

— *J. Edwin Hortell*

love, the basis for all love relationships—when you love someone, you are willing to sacrifice dearly for that person. Sacrificial
love expresses itself without assurance that the love will be
returned in kind. The timing of that love was highlighted by
Paul's words, "But God demonstrates his own love for us in this:
While we were still sinners, Christ died for us" (Romans 5:8 NIV).

Sacrificial love is also practical in seeking ways to meet the
needs of those who are loved. In God's case, that love was infinitely practical, since it set out to rescue those who had no hope
of rescuing themselves. God paid dearly to save us; *He gave His
only begotten Son,* the highest price he could pay. The term translated "only begotten" (*monogene*) expresses Jesus' unique value
and position as God's only Son. The salvation God offers freely
was costly to him.

This offer is made to *whoever believes.* To "believe" is more
than intellectual agreement that Jesus is God. It means putting
our trust and confidence in him that he alone can save us. It is to
put Christ in charge of our present plans and eternal destiny.
Believing is both trusting his words as reliable and relying on
him for the power to change.

Jesus accepted our punishment and paid the price for our sins
so that we would *not perish. Perish* does not mean physical
death, for we all will eventually die. Here it refers to eternity
apart from God. Those who believe will receive the alternative,
the new life that Jesus bought for us—*everlasting life* with God.

THE CHOICE
John 3:16, along with the rest of the New Testament, assumes
that apart from God's intervention, people perish (see Mark
4:38; Luke 13:3, 5; John 10:28; Romans 2:12; 1 Corinthians
1:18; 2 Peter 3:9). The word adds a sense of hopelessness to
the fact of dying—"to perish" is to come to a dead end. In this
verse, escape from the tragic fate of perishing is promised to
those who believe in God's Son. Instead of perishing, they will
have "eternal life," or "life in the ageless age." Perishing is not
an end to be desired, for it removes from the picture any ves-
tige of what we could call life. But this verse makes it clear that
those who refuse to choose Christ and the life he offers have
chosen to perish. Eternal life awaits our decision.

One of the distinctives of John's Gospel is its awareness of the
reader. John often includes reflective and explanatory statements
that help us understand events more clearly. For instance, in 2:17
John explained the insight given to the disciples about Jesus'
actions and words in the temple. Further on, in 2:23-24, John

summarized Jesus' general ongoing relationship with people. As an eyewitness, John wanted us to know not only the facts of God's human visit to earth, but also the eventual lessons and conclusions that came to light from those facts.

With this characteristic of John's Gospel in mind, some commentators have concluded that Jesus' direct speaking stopped with 3:15, and that John added the following inspired words (3:16-21) by way of further explanation. Either way, no other verse in all the Bible so encapsulates the basic message of the gospel: God so dearly loved all the people in the world that he gave his only Son so that we could have eternal life.

LIVING FOREVER DOESN'T SOUND SO GREAT . . .
Some people are repulsed by the idea of eternal life because their lives are miserable with pain, hunger, poverty, or disappointment. But eternal life is not an extension of a person's mortal life; eternal life is God's life embodied in Christ given to all believers now as a guarantee that they will live forever. Not only will we be changed, almost everything else will also be changed (Revelation 21:1-4). In eternal life there is no death, sickness, enemy, evil, or sin. When we don't know Christ, we make choices as though this life is all we have. In reality, this life is just the introduction to eternity. Receive this new life by faith and begin to evaluate all that happens from an eternal perspective.

3:17-18 "For God did not send His Son into the world to condemn the world."[NKJV] Why condemn an already condemned world? All people are already under God's judgment because of sin—specifically the sin of not believing in God's Son (16:9). The only way to escape the condemnation is to believe in Jesus, the Son of God, because he came **"that the world through Him might be saved."**[NKJV] He who believes in him is saved from God's judgment. And God *wants* people to believe: He is patient, "not willing that any should perish but that all should come to repentance" (2 Peter 3:9 NKJV).

When we consider ways to communicate the gospel, we should follow Jesus' example. We do not need to condemn unbelievers; they are condemned already. We must tell them about this condemnation, and then

> If I live my life like there is a God, and find in the end that there isn't, I have gained much and lost little. But if I live my life like there isn't a God, and find out in the end that there is, I've gained little and lost everything.
> *Blaise Pascal*

offer them the way of salvation—faith in Jesus Christ. When we
share the gospel with others, our love must be like Jesus'—willingly giving up our own comfort and security so that others
might join us in receiving God's love.

GOOD NEWS

The gospel truly is good news! It is not always seen as good
news because people are often afraid it is too good to be true.
Moments of honest reflection usually confront us with the hopelessness of our lives. We know we are far from perfect. The
bad news is so bad that we can hardly stand it. So we try to protect ourselves from our fears by putting our faith in something
we do or have: good deeds, skill, intelligence, money, possessions. Since perfection is far out of reach, we are tempted to
settle for effort. We end up living barely a step ahead of
despair. To those who can see their predicament, the gospel is
welcomed good news. Only God can save us from the one
thing that we really need to fear—eternal condemnation. We
believe in God by recognizing the insufficiency of our own
efforts to find salvation and by asking him to do his work in us.

3:19-20 **"This is the judgment."**NRSV Or "this is how the judgment
works" (TEV). What follows describes the grounds for judgment:
**"Light has come into the world, and people loved darkness
rather than light because their deeds were evil."**NRSV This is
the same conflict between light and darkness that John presented
in the prologue (1:5, 9-11). The full arrival of the light in the
world signals that God has carried out his plan for the salvation
of his creation. *Light has come* means that with the coming of
Jesus we have: (1) an absolute source of truth; (2) condemnation
of sin; (3) guidance for our daily decisions; and (4) illumination
to learn about God more clearly.

What a tragedy that people have turned away from God's
offer, embracing instead the darkness in hopes of covering up
evil actions. There is probably no more painful moment than
when we honestly confront our tendency to love darkness, to
twist or withhold the truth. The Son did not come to judge, but in
the light of his character the sharp shadows of our sinfulness
stand out.

**"All who do evil hate the light and do not come to the light, so
that their deeds may not be exposed."**NRSV The people who fear
exposure from the light are those who are doing evil. Paul wrote,
"Everything exposed by the light becomes visible, for it is light
that makes everything visible" (Ephesians 5:13-14 NIV). Evil

deeds are revealed by the light, so people who want to do evil must do it in the dark so they cannot be caught in the act.

TURN OFF THE LIGHTS!
Many people don't want their lives exposed to God's light because they are afraid of what will be revealed or because of the demands the light places on them. They don't particularly want to be changed. We should not be surprised when these same people are threatened by our desire to obey God and do what is right—they are afraid that the light in us may expose some of the darkness in their lives. Rather than giving in to discouragement, we must keep praying that they will come to see how much better it is to live in light than in darkness.

3:21 **"But those who do what is true come to the light, so that it may be clearly seen that their deeds have been done in God."**[NRSV] According to the context, to *do what is true* is to come to Christ, the light; the result of coming to the light and living in the light will be clearly seen in believers' lives. Christ's life in us will make our lives able to stand exposure to bright light, for our deeds will be honest, pure, and truthful. John wrote about this at length in 1 John 1:5-7.

LIVING IN THE LIGHT
Graciously, God does not reveal everything about us that needs changing at once. But as we move toward the light, as our lives become filled with God's presence, we become more aware of sin as well as more aware of the benefits God brings to us. Like people in a dark room when the lights suddenly come on, it takes time for our "eyes" to grow accustomed to seeing. But as Jesus points out later in 16:7-11, the presence of the Holy Spirit in us will make us specially sensitive to sin and the need for continued cleansing. Once we are in the light, we must also guard against the temptation to "close our eyes tight" when God is showing us something by the light of his Word (Psalm 119:105).

JOHN THE BAPTIST TELLS MORE ABOUT JESUS / 3:22-36 / **25**

This section begins with an abrupt change of scene to Aenon, near Salim, in the land of Judea. Two groups were baptizing: John the Baptist with his disciples, and Jesus with his disciples. Both Jesus and John—the two prominent figures in the new movement of God—were gathering disciples; but more were coming to Jesus than to John. This seems to have troubled John's disciples, who began to wonder why more disciples were going to Jesus than to their leader, John. As for John, he was perfectly aware of what his position was in God's plan. He was the herald of the Messiah-King—to put it in his own words, the friend of the bridegroom (3:29). John was content to prepare for the bridegroom and then fade quietly into the background while the bridegroom received all the attention. John knew that he would become less important and less noticed and that Jesus would receive increased recognition and importance. John rejoiced to see this happen.

3:22-23 Jesus and his disciples went out into the Judean countryside ... and baptized. Now John also was baptizing at Aenon near Salim.^{NIV} These verses tell us that two groups were baptizing at the same time: one in Judea, the other at *Aenon near Salim,* which may have been in northern Samaria. Aenon, which means "a place of many springs," helps explain the statement, **there was plenty of water.**^{NIV}

While John was baptizing in northern Samaria, the disciples of Jesus under his direction (for Jesus himself did not baptize, according to 4:2) were also baptizing. Since John's baptism prepared the way for people to come to the Messiah, we can postulate that Jesus' disciples carried out the same kind of baptism as did John—one that prepared people to receive Christ and enter into his kingdom.

3:24 (This was before John was put in prison.)^{NIV} This statement clarifies the chronology of events. At the time John wrote this Gospel (A.D. 90s), his readers may not have known when John the Baptist's ministry ended—especially in relationship to Jesus' ministry.

3:25 A discussion about purification arose between John's disciples and a Jew.^{NRSV} Given the immediate context, the argument over purification probably involved some debate about the authority of John's baptism and how it related to the baptisms connected with Jesus. This topic was still controversial years later during one of the final confrontations between Jesus and the teachers of the law (Luke 20:1-8). Jesus asked his questioners about John's authority to baptize: "Was it from heaven, or from men?" (Luke 20:4 NIV).

The Jews sought purification through various sacrifices and washings prescribed by God through Moses. But centuries of human "adjustments" had transformed the way of humility before God into a hopeless maze of human effort. The huge system was bent on self-preservation rather than in truly serving God. Thus, for many religious leaders, John's effrontery in preaching simple repentance and requiring public baptism was unacceptable as a form of purification.

THE REAL NEED
The conflict between the message of John and the system of ceremonial religion into which he stepped literally did prepare the way for the Messiah. The response of crowds repenting and seeking forgiveness was evidence of spiritual life without reality. People didn't need a religious system as much as they needed salvation. They longed for an inner purity that could not be provided by ceremonial washing. John was pleased to point them to the Savior. People today still have the same need. Our role is to point them to Jesus.

3:26 **"That man who was with you on the other side of the Jordan—the one you testified about—well, he is baptizing, and everyone is going to him."**[NIV] John's disciples exposed their competitive spirit—this is certain because of the way John responded to them in the following verses. These disciples of John must have lost sight of their mission—which was to join John in preparing people for Christ. They should not have been surprised (much less, dismayed) that people were going to Christ—they were supposed to!

Why did John the Baptist continue to baptize after Jesus came onto the scene? Why didn't he become a disciple too? John explained that because God had given him his work, he had to continue it until God called him to do something else. John's main purpose was to point people to Christ. Even with Jesus beginning his own ministry, John could still point people to Jesus.

"CHRISTIAN" COMPETITIVENESS
We Christians must always remember the primary focus of our ministry: to exalt Christ and point people to him. Healthy relationships with other Christians will include our recognition of certain leaders, pastors, and teachers. But we must always remember that they, too, have the same commission. We should not allow ourselves to become prideful of the particular church, group, or leader with which we are associated. And we must do our utmost to resist any kind of competitive spirit. All of us are under the sovereignty of God. Envious or bitter comparisons make us ineffective. Our task is to follow Christ and see that he is exalted.

3:27 "No one can receive anything except what has been given from heaven."^{NRSV} John's reply to his disciples was the response of a man who knew his place in God's plan. He knew that a person is not able to do anything unless it has been given to him or her from God. He knew how to give glory where glory was due! If all the people were going to Christ, if Christ's ministry was expanding, then it must be God's plan. John exemplifies the kind of exuberant endorsement that ought to come from us when we hear that someone is being effective as a servant of Christ.

REAL SUCCESS
To what degree is success the mark of God's blessing or approval? If God guarantees success to those who really serve him, is he limited to fulfilling their expectations of success? The answer in both cases is clearly no. Both John and Jesus were successful in their missions, but the first lost his head; the second was crucified. God's idea of blessing is quite different from ours. God calls us to be faithful where we are, with his plan for us. We are not to carry out anyone else's plan. Someday we will probably be amazed at the variety of people to whom God says, "Well done, good and faithful servant!" (Matthew 25:21 NIV). Let's make sure we share in the delight of hearing those words directed at us. That objective will require that we center our living on what God directs us to do through his Word rather than trying to live up to the expectations of neighbors or our culture.

3:28 "I am not the Messiah, but I have been sent ahead of him."^{NRSV} Here John reiterated what he had told the disciples earlier: "I am not the Messiah" (1:20 NRSV). John had always been forthright in declaring his position; he did this so that the distinction between himself and the Messiah would be unmistakably clear.

3:29 "He who has the bride is the bridegroom. The friend of the bridegroom, who stands and hears him, rejoices greatly at the bridegroom's voice."^{NRSV} John employed a beautiful metaphor to depict the way he saw his relationship with Jesus the Christ. He described himself as being the bridegroom's friend—or, as we would say today, "the best man." As the best man, John enjoyed seeing his friend, the bridegroom, honored. He insisted that all the attention should go to the bridegroom and his bride.

Who are we? We are not just those going to heaven. But we are even now the wife of God. We are at this moment the bride of Christ. And what does our divine bridegroom want from us? He wants from us not only doctrinal faithfulness, but our love day by day.
Francis Schaeffer

3:30 **"He must become greater; I must become less."**^{NIV} What a realization John had! He knew that his work was destined to decrease—even that he himself would have to decrease. John's willingness to decrease so that Jesus would increase reveals unusual humility. It also reveals how much he was like Jesus in character.

3:31 **"The one who comes from above is above all."**^{NRSV} As used in Greek, the word for *all* could be "all things" or "all men." In either case, John's statement revealed his attitude about Christ's superiority and preeminence over him. The same word (*anothen*) that appears here was used in 3:3. Jesus, then, is the one who *comes from above,* while we are people who must be "born from above" if we hope to see the kingdom of God.

BRIDES, BRIDEGROOMS, AND BELIEVERS
John's metaphor of himself as the friend of Jesus the "bridegroom" was a theological picture with a history behind it. In the Old Testament, God was likened to a bridegroom and his people to a bride (see Isaiah 62:5; Jeremiah 3; Ezekiel 16; Hosea 2). In fact, it was one of God's most revealing self-descriptions. He used it to express his anger and disappointment over the rebelliousness of his people; he employed it to express the nature of his long-suffering and faithful love.
In saying that Jesus was the bridegroom who had the bride, John was implying that Jesus was the divine husband of God's people. As such, all of God's people belonged to him—or, as John said it, all of the increase belonged to him. In the New Testament, Jesus spoke of himself as the bridegroom (Matthew 9:15; Mark 2:19-20); and then later, Paul compared Christ and the church to husband and wife, bridegroom and bride (2 Corinthians 11:2; Ephesians 5:22-32; Revelation 19:7; 21:2).

"The one who is of the earth belongs to the earth and speaks about earthly things."^{NRSV} John, whom Jesus himself called the greatest man born among men (Matthew 11:11), was still a man of the earth (see 1 Corinthians 15:47).

"The one who comes from heaven is above all."^{NIV} Christ's heavenly origin gives him superiority over every person.

Verse 31 begins and ends with a parallel doxology about Jesus. The only difference is the use of "from above" in the first part of the verse and "from heaven" at the end of the verse. The repetition is worshipful and the small change is instructive. "From above" emphasizes Jesus' divine nature, while "from heaven"

BECOMING LESS
Pastors and other Christian leaders may be tempted to focus more on the success of their ministries than on Christ. Others may project a false humility or even a destructive self-hatred. Healthy humility, as modeled by John, defines itself in truthful comparison. John did not say he was nothing. He identified himself in relation to the most important person in his life. Because of John's profound understanding of his purpose in life, he eagerly pointed to the greatness of Jesus. John welcomed the success of Jesus' revelation as the Messiah even though he realized his own moment in the spotlight was passing. The more Jesus was recognized, the more John could enjoy his own success. Humility combines the persistence to do and be what God has called us to be, the wisdom to recognize those things we cannot do and be, and the vision to always see ourselves in relation to God's greatness.

indicates his preexistence. In other words, Jesus already was in what we call the beginning; he was with God and he was God. From every perspective Jesus proved to be the one who is above all. The depth of our understanding and gratitude for the new birth that God offers us in Christ will always be shaped by our vision of what Jesus set aside when he came to earth. The one who was "above all" set aside all that was rightfully his in exchange for the single privilege of being our Savior. Paul echoed this wonder when he wrote, "Who, being in very nature God, did not consider equality with God something to be grasped, but made himself nothing, taking the very nature of a servant, being made in human likeness" (Philippians 2:6-7 NIV).

> Wouldst thou comprehend the height of God? First comprehend the lowliness of God. Condescend to be humble for thine own sake, seeing that God condescended to be humble for thy sake too, for it was not for his own. *Augustine*

While there are some ancient manuscripts that do not include the second "is above all," John's emphasis on highlighting the nature and character of Jesus argues for the authenticity of the phrase. Repetition can be redundant, but it can also be emphatic. John does not want us to miss even a little of what we are able to grasp about Christ.

3:32 "He testifies to what he has seen and heard."[NIV] Throughout his Gospel, John emphasized the fact that Jesus spoke what he had heard from the Father (8:14-30). He was the Father's representative in word and action.

"But no one accepts his testimony."[NIV] This is a great condemnation upon mankind—especially the people who lived when Jesus did, for they were the ones who heard his testimony and rejected it (see 1:10-11; 3:11; 12:37ff.).

3:33 "Whoever has accepted his testimony has certified this, that God is true."[NRSV] By way of contrast with verse 32, this verse indicates that some did receive Jesus' testimony. Those who received Jesus' testimony believed that he was the Son of God come from heaven, the Messiah. Their belief in his testimony was their "stamp of approval" on the truthfulness of God's action (sending his Son). In other words, they tested the testimony and found it to be true. "To set one's seal" to something was a way of saying, "I have identified with this." In ancient days, a person would impress his personal mark on a seal and thereby label the object so sealed as belonging to him or her.

TAKING OFFENSE
The worship of pluralism and tolerance in our own time has once again made the claims of Christ stand out in sharp relief. Jesus did not accept the mere tolerance of others in his own day, and neither will he in ours. Jesus helps us recognize that tolerance is often nothing more than thinly veiled rejection. Nicodemus's opening words can be read as complimentary tolerance. Jesus' response pushed Nicodemus to declare himself plainly, to make a choice. Jesus received the open acceptance or rejection of people, but he refused to be simply tolerated.

Repeating the absolute claims of Jesus today is liable to bring heated responses not unlike those Jesus himself experienced. Doubts about this can be easily settled by mentioning in social company that Jesus said, "I am the way, and the truth, and the life. No one comes to the Father except through me" (John 14:6 NRSV). Responses will almost always vary from "Really?" to "He must not have meant it like it sounds," to "Yes, but . . ." to "That's just narrow-minded, fundamentalist thinking—Jesus was certainly above that sort of thing!" The world persists in wanting to categorize Jesus as nice, wise, or even great—almost anything short of bowing before him in repentance and worship.

Christians who allow tolerance in exchange for the confrontation of genuine love have made many reject Christianity as irrelevant. When truth is sacrificed on the altar of tolerance, no one hears the truth of what God did for us by sending his Son to die on the cross. The fear of risking offense ought to make us examine whether or not we really believe what we think we believe.

When we read a famous document like the American Declaration of Independence, we usually are drawn to the names of those who signed. Some are well known; others are practically forgotten. But by their signature, they identified themselves with that proclamation. In the case of God's declaration, only his signature was required to make it valid. It was true whether or not anyone else ever witnessed to its truth. The gospel is the invitation from God to add ourselves to those who have staked their lives on Christ, the Truth.

> The people who hanged Christ never, to do them justice, accused him of being a bore—on the contrary, they thought him too dynamic to be safe. It has been left for later generations to muffle up that shattering personality and surround him with an atmosphere of tedium. *Dorothy Sayers*

ETERNAL LIFE INSURANCE
In the light of John 3:33, one way of understanding the gospel is by imagining that God provided for us in Christ an eternal life insurance policy. Full payment was made on the cross by Jesus' death. The Bible tells us that even though we don't deserve the privilege or opportunity, God offers to make us beneficiaries of the policy. We enter our names on the blank line through trust in Christ.

3:34 **"For the one whom God has sent speaks the words of God."**[NIV] This statement authenticates what was said in verse 32. God's Son, Jesus Christ, does not speak his own words, but the words of God (see 5:19ff.).

"For God gives the Spirit without limit."[NIV] God gave the immeasurable Spirit to his Son. As such, the Son was the recipient of the immeasurable Spirit for his prophetic ministry (see Isaiah 11:1ff.). But unlike the Old Testament prophets who were anointed with the Holy Spirit only when they were speaking for God, Jesus always had the Spirit and therefore always spoke the words of God. We can trust the words of Jesus.

3:35 **"The Father loves the Son and has placed everything in his hands."**[NIV] The Father committed all of his divine plan to the care of his beloved Son. What a glorious privilege and awesome responsibility! By the end of his ministry, Jesus told the Father that he had accomplished everything the Father had wanted him to do (17:1-4).

COMPELLED TO BELIEVE
Jesus' testimony was trustworthy because he had come from
heaven and was speaking of what he had seen there. His
words were the very words of God. Our whole spiritual life
depends on our answer to one question: Who is Jesus Christ?
If we accept Jesus as only a prophet or teacher, we will actually
have to reject his teaching, for he clearly claimed to be God's
Son—God himself. The heartbeat of John's Gospel is the
dynamic truth that Jesus Christ is God's Son, the Messiah, the
Savior, who was from the beginning and will continue to live forever. This same Jesus has invited us to accept him and live
with him eternally. When we understand who Jesus is, we are
compelled to believe what he said.

3:36 **"Whoever believes in the Son has eternal life."**^{NRSV} Believers
need not wonder whether or not they have eternal life (or wait for
the future judgment to see if eternal life will be granted or not).
He who has the Son *has* (as in present ownership) eternal life
(1 John 5:11). Thus, eternal life begins at the moment of spiritual
rebirth. The question for individual believers, then, is: How does
our way of living demonstrate the fact that we expect to live eternally?

"Whoever disobeys the Son."^{NRSV} The NIV uses "rejects" to
translate *apeithon* (disobeying) and summarizes the intent of the
verb *disobeys* in the NRSV. To disobey the Son is to reject him. To
reject the Son's testimony and the gospel is to cut ourselves off
from the benefits available only through him.

"Will not see life."^{NRSV} To *not see life* means to not experience
God's eternal life.

"But must endure God's wrath."^{NRSV} John, the author of this Gospel, has been demonstrating that Jesus is the true Son of God. Jesus
sets before us the greatest choice in life. We are responsible to
decide today whom we will obey (Joshua 24:15). God wants us to
choose him and life (Deuteronomy 30:15-20). God's wrath is his
final judgment and rejection of the sinner. To put off the choice is
to choose not to follow Christ. Indecision is a fatal decision.

John 4

Jesus had to pass through Samaria on his way to Galilee. In Jesus' encounter with the Samaritan woman and with the Samaritans in Sychar, he revealed that he is "the gift of God" (4:10), who gives "a fountain of water springing up into everlasting life" (4:14 NKJV) to each believer. He also revealed that he is the expected Messiah (4:25-26). Furthermore, Jesus pointed the Samaritans to the truth about salvation, God's nature, and the worship of God: Salvation comes from among the Jews (the Messiah is a Jew), God is spirit, and God must be worshiped in spirit and in truth.

EAR WITNESS
To our knowledge, no one was present during the conversation between Jesus and the Samaritan woman. The details of the exchange must have come to John, therefore, from one of the two. Given the woman's eagerness to proclaim to everyone that Jesus was "a man who told me everything I ever did" (4:29 NIV), we can assume that she shared with the disciples the details of that conversation.

Hearing the experiences of other believers significantly affects our spiritual growth. The Bible itself is a collection of the firsthand experiences with God that people like us had in the past. As Christians we have the privilege of passing on to others what we have learned from God. Insights, lessons, and corrections that we receive from God can help and encourage other believers. We must be eager to tell others about the most important person in our lives!

4:1-2 The Pharisees heard that Jesus was gaining and baptizing more disciples than John.[NIV] Somehow Jesus realized that his popularity had come to the attention of the Pharisees. They had scrutinized the activities of John the Baptist and sent emissaries to question him about his identity (1:19-28). John always pointed his followers

> We don't care who gets the credit as long as God gets the glory!
> *Gerry Fosdal*

to a greater one, the coming Messiah. Because the greater one had come and was in fact drawing the crowds away from John, the Pharisees began to watch Jesus closely.

Jesus had gained many more disciples than just the Twelve. We know that he had at least seventy-two committed disciples (Luke 10:1-17). We are also told that various disciples came and went, especially when times were difficult or when Jesus predicted troubles ahead (Luke 9:57-62; John 6:66).

Part of the information received by the Pharisees was incorrect because **it was not Jesus who baptized, but his disciples.**[NIV] This parenthetical remark helps to explain John the Baptist's statement in 1:33 that the Messiah would baptize in the Holy Spirit—in contrast to John who baptized in water. Thus, Jesus never personally performed water baptism; his disciples continued to perform that task during the early years of the church. These baptisms, still following the pattern set by John the Baptist, indicated repentance and confession of sin (see Matthew 3:6). The other Gospels summarize John's and Jesus' messages as being almost identical, requiring the same personal application: "Repent, for the kingdom of heaven is near" (Matthew 3:2 NIV). Later, in Acts, we find the disciples carrying out Jesus' command to make disciples of those who believed in him by baptizing them in his name (see Matthew 28:18-20; Acts 2:37-41; 8:12, 36-38).

THE MEMBER GAME
Competition can be created when none is intended. John and Jesus were not competing. But as others compared their ministries, their analysis gave the impression of competition. Similarly, two churches in a city that both have effective programs in reaching their community for Christ may begin to be compared to each other and described as if they were competing for converts. This not only distorts the purpose of the church, it also trivializes the importance of the eternal destiny of persons. The real issue is not which church wins the "member game" but whether the gospel is being communicated and people are responding. If Christ is not becoming "greater," then whoever or whatever else is growing doesn't really matter. Don't foster the false impression of competition by artificial comparisons.

4:3 He left Judea and started back to Galilee.[NRSV] Knowing that the Pharisees (in Jerusalem) had heard about his popularity and that they would begin watching him closely, and at the same time knowing that his "hour" had not yet come (see also 2:4),

Jesus wisely decided to withdraw from possible conflict by leaving Judea and returning to Galilee. Thus, Jesus' first Judean visit had come to an end—a visit begun by his coming to Jerusalem for the Passover (see 2:13). The other Gospels do not record this visit.

4:4 He needed to go through Samaria.NKJV Literally, "and it was necessary for him to pass through Samaria." Since the Samaritans were hated by the Jews, many of the strict Jews traveling

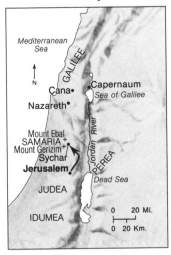

from Judea to Galilee took a route around Samaria (through Perea, east of the Jordan River, see the map on this page), even though that route took more time. But for those who were trying to make the best time, it was faster to go through Samaria to Galilee. The context does not indicate that Jesus was in a hurry to get to Galilee (see 4:40, 43). Thus, the necessity must be understood in a different way: Jesus went to Samaria to give the Samaritans what he had given to Nicodemus—the offer of eternal life by being born again. And, furthermore, by going to Samaria and bringing the gospel to the despised Samaritans, he showed that he was above the Jewish prejudices.

The Visit in Samaria. Jesus went to Jerusalem for the Passover, cleared the temple, and talked with Nicodemus, a religious leader, about eternal life. He then left Jerusalem and traveled in Judea. On his way to Galilee, he visited Sychar and other villages in Samaria. Unlike most Jews of the day, Jesus did not try to avoid the region of Samaria.

Where did these prejudices come from? Samaria was a region between Judea and Galilee where Jews of "mixed blood" lived. In Old Testament days, when the northern kingdom of Israel, with its capital at Samaria, fell to the Assyrians, many Jews were deported to Assyria. King Sargon of Assyria repopulated the northern kingdom with captives from other lands to settle the territory and keep the peace (2 Kings 17:24). These captives eventually intermarried with the few Jews who remained in the land to form a mixed race of people who became known as Samaritans. The Jews hated the Samaritans because they were no longer "pure" Jews. The Jews who lived in the southern kingdom felt these Jews had betrayed their people and nation through intermarriage with foreigners. And the hatred continued down through the years. For example, when a remnant of Jews returned from captivity in Babylon, they refused the Samaritans living in the land any participation in rebuilding the temple or the city of Jerusalem, even though the Samaritans claimed to have the same God as the Jews (see Ezra 4:1-6, where the Samaritans are called "enemies"). The Samaritans had adopted the Pentateuch as their Scriptures and set up a place for worship on Mount Gerizim using for their guidelines Deuteronomy 11:26-29; 27:1-8. Although they knew about a coming Messiah, they were far from having an accurate knowledge of the truth.

4:5-6 He came to a town in Samaria called Sychar, near the plot of ground Jacob had given to his son Joseph.[NIV] According to Genesis 33:19, Jacob purchased a piece of land in this vicinity and then later gave Joseph some land in Shechem (Genesis 48:22). Joshua 24:32 says that Joseph was buried on that land (the Jews had brought Joseph's bones with them when they made their exodus from Egypt). **Jacob's well was there**[NIV] indicates that the land must have included the parcel on which Jacob's well was dug. Thus, this well was highly valued by the Samaritans who claimed Jacob (also called Israel) as their father (4:12), just as the Jews do.

Jesus, tired as he was from the journey.[NIV] The trip was laborious and made Jesus tired. He had walked from Judea to Sychar—a trip that probably took two days. Jesus' weariness shows his true humanity. He waited while his disciples, more rested, or hungrier, than he, went to find food. He never seemed to worry that the limitations he took in becoming human might somehow undermine his claims to be the Son of God. Such expressions about Jesus' humanity help us identify with him.

It was about the sixth hour.[NIV] It was noontime, the hottest part of the day.

4:7 A Samaritan woman came to draw water.[NRSV] Two facts are unusual about the woman's actions: (1) she could have gone to a closer well (scholars have identified wells that were closer to Sychar at Ain Asker—Sychar or Ain Defne at Balata); (2) women generally drew water later in the day, when the temperature was cooler. This woman, whose reputation seems to have been well known in the small town (4:18), probably chose the well farther away from home and came to that well at an unusual hour in order to avoid contact with other women.

A VALUED GIFT
The woman came to the well with shame on her mind. She was avoiding human contact, but the stranger at the well was probably little more than an inconvenience. How often at the supermarket, gas station, or even in church do we pass by people loaded down with guilt. They find themselves having to pursue life's necessities, hoping to avoid anyone who knows their real needs. Dreading judgment and rejection, they live in fear. And yet, when shown real concern, when gently confronted, these same people find great relief in unburdening themselves. When you greet someone with "How are you?" do you stop long enough to show him or her that you really want to know? Simple caring is a gift valued infinitely more than it costs to give.

Jesus said to her, "Will you give me a drink?"ᴺᴵⱽ Again, this statement reveals Jesus' true humanity; he was really thirsty. And since Jesus did not have any container, he asked the woman for a drink. Even though such a request startled her (4:9), it drew her into a conversation with Jesus.

4:8 (His disciples had gone into the town to buy food.)ᴺᴵⱽ This parenthetical statement serves to inform the reader that Jesus was alone with this woman. Jesus could not ask his disciples to help him get water, for they had gone into Sychar to buy food. Their intention, of course, was to share this food with Jesus (4:31). Thus, we see Jesus, weary from his journey, depending on others for food and drink.

4:9 The Samaritan woman said to him, "How is it that you, a Jew, ask a drink of me, a woman of Samaria?"ᴺᴿˢⱽ The Samaritan woman was very surprised—first, that a Jew would even speak to a Samaritan; second, that a Jewish male would speak to a Samaritan woman (she also had a bad reputation and this was a public place); third, that a Jew would drink from a Samaritan's cup. The surprise is explained by the Gospel writer who clues us in on the relationship between Jews and Samaritans: **(Jews do not share things in common with Samaritans.)**ᴺᴿˢⱽ This explanatory sentence is also rendered "For Jews do not associate with Samaritans" (ᴺᴵⱽ). The Greek word translated "associate" literally means "to share the use of." Some commentators, therefore, think John was saying that Jews and Samaritans would not share the same utensils or facilities. This interpretation is reflected in the ᴛᴇⱽ: "Jews will not use the same dishes that Samaritans use." The Jewish ceremonial laws described not only certain people as ceremonially unclean, but also anything they touched. In strict religious terms, many Jews of Jesus' time considered the Samaritans to be permanently unclean.

NO PREJUDICES ALLOWED
This woman (1) was a Samaritan, a member of the hated mixed race, (2) was known to be living in sin, and (3) was in a public place. No respectable Jewish man would talk to a woman under such circumstances. But Jesus did. The attitude of the Jews toward the Samaritans in Jesus' day is not unlike that which has been frequently displayed in America by whites toward blacks. In the past, whites have not allowed blacks to share the same public facilities with them. For Jesus to ask for a drink of water from a utensil belonging to a Samaritan woman was to go against the accepted prejudices of the time.

The gospel is for every person, no matter what his or her race, social position, religious orientation, or past sins. We must be prepared to share this gospel at any time and in any place. We must also be prepared to deal with those who may be accustomed to being ill-treated and who are not sure of our motives. Jesus crossed all barriers to share the gospel, and we who follow him must do no less—even if misunderstood.

4:10 **Jesus answered her, "If you knew the gift of God and who it is that asks you for a drink, you would have asked him and he would have given you living water."**[NIV] The woman was ignorant of God's gift—the gift of life, represented by "living water"—and she did not know the giver, Jesus the Messiah. Jesus makes an extraordinary offer to this stranger—living water that would quench her thirst forever.

4:11 **"Sir, you have no bucket, and the well is deep. Where do you get that living water?"**[NRSV] Jesus' remark concerning "living water" produced several practical questions in the mind of the Samaritan woman. Like Nicodemus, she did not immediately sense the depth of Jesus' words. Obviously, she thought, if this "living water" was in some way the water at the bottom of this spring-fed well, Jesus was in no position to offer it because he had no container for drawing it. The woman assumed that Jesus would not want to use her jar because of the strong prejudice (see 4:9). She began to wonder if Jesus had access to some source of water other than Jacob's well. Yet she could clearly see that he had no container with which to get or store this "living water." So she began to probe the identity of the stranger.

4:12 **"Are you greater than our ancestor Jacob, who gave us the well, and with his sons and his flocks drank from it?"**[NRSV] What caused this response? Perhaps the woman sensed in Jesus' words a possible dishonoring of the well provided by their great ancestor, Jacob. Or perhaps the woman was beginning to have

LIVING WATER

What did Jesus mean by "living water?" In the Old Testament, many verses speak of thirsting after God. In promising to bring living water that could forever quench a person's thirst for God, Jesus was claiming to be the Messiah. Only the Messiah could give this gift that satisfies the soul's desire. (All verses are quoted from NIV.)

Psalm 36:8-9	*"They feast on the abundance of your house; you give them drink from your river of delights. For with you is the fountain of life; in your light we see light."*
Psalm 42:1-2	*"As the deer pants for streams of water, so my soul pants for you, O God. My soul thirsts for God, for the living God. When can I go and meet with God?"*
Isaiah 55:1	*"Come, all you who are thirsty, come to the water; and you who have no money, come, buy and eat! Come, buy wine and milk without money and without cost."*
Jeremiah 2:13	*"My people have committed two sins; they have forsaken me, the spring of living water, and have dug their own cisterns, broken cisterns that cannot hold water."*
Jeremiah 17:13	*"O LORD, the hope of Israel, all who forsake you will be put to shame. Those who turn away from you will be written in the dust because they have forsaken the LORD, the spring of living water."*

some inkling of who Jesus was claiming to be. He certainly accepted her in a way that must have challenged her thinking.

4:13 "Everyone who drinks of this water will be thirsty again."[NRSV] People need water daily because thirst will always return. The water from Jacob's well would indeed satisfy the woman's thirst, but only temporarily. She would always need to return for more water. So also are all the other "drinks" of life—they never satisfy. Some of them even create more thirst. The human needs for

ARE YOU SATISFIED?
Spiritual functions often parallel physical functions. Our bodies hunger and thirst; so do our souls. But our souls need *spiritual* food and water. The woman confused the two kinds of water, perhaps because no one had ever told her about her spiritual hunger and thirst before. We would not think of depriving our bodies of food and water when they hunger or thirst. Why then should we deprive our souls? The living Word, Jesus Christ, and the written Word, the Bible, can satisfy our hungry and thirsty souls.

love, food, sex, security, and approval, even when met, do not give complete satisfaction. Attempts to find full satisfaction will lead only to disappointment and despair. The Samaritan woman would have to admit that she was not satisfied, for she had had five husbands, and the man she now lived with was not her husband.

4:14 **"Those who drink of the water that I will give them will never be thirsty."**NRSV The *water* Jesus offers quenches spiritual thirst so completely that those who drink will never be thirsty again. Jesus' "water" continually satisfies the desire for God's presence because **"the water that I will give will become in them a spring of water gushing up to eternal life."**NRSV The gift that Jesus gives—a spring *gushing up* to eternal life—suggests the availability, accessibility, and abundance of the divine life for believers. The expression *to eternal life* probably means "resulting in eternal life."

> The settled happiness and security which we all desire, God withholds from us by the very nature of the world. . . . The security we crave would teach us to rest our hearts in this world and pose an obstacle to our return to God; a few moments of happy love, a landscape, a symphony, a merry meeting with our friends, a bath or a football match, have no such tendency. Our Father refreshes us on the journey with some pleasant inns, but will not encourage us to mistake them for home.
>
> *C. S. Lewis*

TROUBLED WATERS
Many people who claim to be Christians admit they feel unhappy and dissatisfied over the same problems mentioned by nonbelievers. Feelings of low self-esteem, lack of love, loneliness, and struggles over sex, money, work, and position in life are often as severe with believers as with unbelievers. Are differences between Christians and non-Christians merely on the surface or even imaginary? Did Jesus overstate his claim? Questions like these come from interpreting Jesus' words as the Samaritan woman did—expecting that physical thirst and all other life-related needs will be satisfied by Jesus' "living water." But that is not what Jesus promised. He offered freedom within life, not freedom from life! Later he told his disciples in no uncertain terms: "In this world you will have trouble. But take heart! I have overcome the world" (16:33 NIV). Believers will experience many of the same difficulties encountered by unbelievers, but the presence of Jesus in our lives should make a significant difference in the way we respond. Living water gives us spiritual power to face the challenges of living, not escape from them.

4:15 **"Sir, give me this water so that I won't get thirsty and have to keep coming here to draw water."**[NIV] The woman's response reveals that she took Jesus' words literally. The woman must have been thrilled to think that this man could give her water that really quenches thirst and would not have to be drawn from a well. Obtaining water was hard work—requiring trips to the well twice a day and carrying heavy jars full of water home.

LIFE AFTER LIVING WATERS
The woman mistakenly believed that if she received the water Jesus offered, she would not have to return to the well each day. She was interested in Jesus' message because she thought it could make her life easier. But if that were always the case, people would accept Christ's message for the wrong reasons. Jesus did not come to take away challenges, but to change us on the inside and to empower us to deal with problems from God's perspective. Indications that living water is flowing within us come from the reality of our new life in Jesus, our awareness of the Spirit within, a sense of direction to life, the specific guidance we receive from God's Word, opportunities to love and serve others, and the comforting knowledge that we are surrounded by other believers also on the way to heaven.

4:16-18 **"Go, call your husband, and come back."**[NRSV] In response to Jesus' offer of living water, the woman expressed her desire. She still did not understand the nature of the water, but she was open to something that promised to change her life. Jesus abruptly shifted the subject from his living water to her style of living. The woman perceived her need for living water at one level; Jesus knew that her need was far deeper, so he turned the conversation to reveal his knowledge of her personal life—and her sin of adultery. Jesus wanted to make this woman see her sin and her need for forgiveness and then offer her the living water—salvation. She must have realized that this was not a man who could be fooled, for she answered transparently, **"I have no husband."** The woman spoke the truth without any explanation.

Jesus said to her, "You are right in saying, 'I have no husband'; for you have had five husbands, and the one you have now is not your husband."[NRSV] Although he confronted the woman's sinful life, Jesus managed to affirm her truthfulness. He did not accuse or excuse; he simply described her life so that she could draw some clear conclusions about the mess in which she was living. The conclusions we reach without knowing the facts will usually err in one of two directions: We will accuse others and raise their defenses, or we will excuse others and enable their denial. We see in Jesus' communication with this woman that faced with an accepting confrontation, people will often respond positively. When we speak to others about themselves, we must limit our words to what we know.

4:19 "I can see that you are a prophet."^NIV In saying this, the woman acknowledged the truthfulness of Jesus' remarks about her life. At the same time, she recognized that he must be a prophet who had the power to "see" the hidden past as well as the future. The theme of people "seeing" Jesus appears several times in John (especially in chapter 9). The persons Jesus encountered saw him many different ways, but he consistently directed their attention to recognize him for who he really was—their Savior.

Many commentators have pointed out that the woman may have been purposely attempting to avert any further disclosure of her personal, sinful life by shifting the conversation to religion. Notice how Jesus responded to her change of direction. He was not presenting a system or a gospel outline; he was having a conversation with someone who needed the living water. Jesus made no attempt to turn the discussion back to her life-style; rather, he entered into a dialogue about the true place of worship. Jesus kept the woman's interest by demonstrating his willingness to let her direct the discussion.

4:20 "Our ancestors worshiped on this mountain, but you say that the place where people must worship is in Jerusalem."^NRSV The unspoken question is, If you are a prophet, who's right? The Samaritans had set up a place for worship on Mount Gerizim, basing their authority to do so on Deuteronomy 11:26-29; 27:1-8; the Jews had followed David in making Jerusalem the center of Jewish worship. The split had come in the days of Ezra and Nehemiah (Ezra 4:1-2; Nehemiah 4:1-2) when the Samaritans had offered to help rebuild the temple in Jerusalem but had been rebuffed. So there was an ongoing debate between the two groups as to who was correct. The Scriptures authenticated Jerusalem as the place of worship (Deuteronomy 12:5; 2 Chronicles 6:6; 7:12; Psalm 78:67-68); thus, the Jews were correct and the Samaritans in error. The Samaritan woman wanted to hear what a Jewish prophet had to say about this.

4:21 "A time is coming when you will worship the Father neither on this mountain nor in Jerusalem."^NIV Both the Jews and the Samaritans were convinced the correct way to worship God depended on a particular geographical location. But Jesus pointed

to a new realm—not at Mount Gerizim or in Jerusalem, but in the
Spirit of God. He also knew that the temple in Jerusalem soon
would be destroyed. The first readers of John would have known
this as a historical fact because it would have already happened!

WORSHIP-FULL
Do you depend on a physical building or a specific setting for
the proper worship environment? God is Spirit and cannot be
confined to a building. The *location* of worship is not nearly as
important as the *attitude* of the worshipers. The specific conditions that enhance worship tend to be quite individual and
should not be legislated. By emphasizing where we worship,
we may neglect the substance of our worship where we are.

4:22 **"You Samaritans worship what you do not know; we worship
what we do know, for salvation is from the Jews."**[NIV] The
Samaritans worshiped, but their system of worship was
incomplete and flawed because it had no clear object. Because
the Samaritans only used the Pentateuch (Genesis through
Deuteronomy) as their Scriptures, they did not know what the
rest of the Old Testament taught about worship. The Jews, with
whom Jesus explicitly identified himself here, *did* know whom
they worshiped, for they had the full revelation in the Old Testament Scriptures. These Scriptures revealed that *salvation is from
the Jews,* for the Messiah would come from the Jewish race (Genesis 12:3).

Jesus' answer to the woman's religious problem is strikingly
similar to Paul's approach with the Athenians (Acts 17:16-34). In
both cases, the gospel was explained, not as a criticism of the
desire and need to worship, but as the revelation of the nature of
true worship. It's as if, in both cases, the message is: "You are
demonstrating a good quality in desiring to worship, but your
worship is misdirected; the perfect object to be worshiped, the
Messiah, has come." The living water that comes from Christ and
is ever present in the believer makes the idea of continual worship a possibility. Worship becomes, at least in part, the enjoy-
ment of our relationship with Christ wherever we are at any
moment.

4:23 **"But the hour is coming, and is now here."**[NRSV] The new worship *is now here* among Jesus' followers (including both Jews
and Samaritans who are united in Christ), although the end of
worship in the temple or on Mount Gerizim is still future—*is
coming.* Jesus announced that a new time had come, a time in

which **"the true worshipers will worship the Father in spirit and truth."**^{NRSV} *True worshipers* are to be recognized by the way they worship. After making the place of worship and order of worship secondary to our spiritual relationship with God, Jesus defined real worship. According to him, worship would take on two new aspects: It would be *in spirit* and *in truth* (see also 4:24).

The expression *in spirit* refers to the human spirit—the immaterial, inner being in each person, the God-breathed entity that corresponds to the nature of God himself, who is Spirit. Using the terms of Jesus' conversation, worship involves the person's awareness of that personal "spring of living water" that God has planted in him or her. God indwells believers—that is where true worship takes place. Our body can be anywhere, yet worship occurs as our attention and praise are turned toward God. We need to consciously focus on God when we are in a house of worship because we easily assume that our presence in church is all that we need in order to worship. We can usually remember how long the worship service lasted, but can we remember exactly when we actually worshiped the Lord?

The phrase *in truth* means "in a true way" or "with genuineness." This would speak to all people—Jews, Samaritans, and even Gentiles; all need to worship God by recognizing God's character and nature as well as our common need for him. We worship in truth because we worship what is true.

WORSHIPING IN TRUTH
If we are not worshiping "in spirit," our worship will be dry and lifeless. Worship not done "in truth" becomes deceitful or irrelevant. "In spirit" reminds us who we are worshiping. "In truth" exposes the required genuineness of those doing the worshiping. To paraphrase Jesus, "True worshipers worship truthfully." By contrast, fleshly or false worship would be: pretending to be someone or something we are not; displaying prejudice toward others who are also made in God's image; practicing self-righteousness by denying our constant need for God's mercy and grace; worshiping in ignorance or superstition without knowing the reality for ourselves; blindly worshiping out of habit with no heartfelt devotion.

4:24 **"God is spirit."**^{NRSV} In the Greek text, the word *spirit* comes first for emphasis: "Spirit is what God is." Here is a simple yet sublime definition of the nature of God. He is spirit. God is not a physical being limited to place and time as we are. He is present everywhere, and he can be worshiped anywhere, anytime.

WHAT GOD ISN'T
As spirit, God relates to us without the limitations that we possess:
■ He is never tired.
■ He is never distant.
■ He is never distracted.
■ He is not limited by time and space.
■ He can be present in all people.
■ He cannot be destroyed or overpowered.

In Christ, God experienced all our weaknesses firsthand. He knows them, but they do not control him. Someday we will leave our present limitations behind and be fully in God's spiritual presence. Worship includes saying to God, "Thank you for understanding where I am; I can hardly wait to be where you are!"

Anyone who wants to worship God must **worship in spirit.**[NRSV] There is no other way to truly worship God. Of course, a person cannot do this if his or her spirit has not been reborn by God's Spirit (3:6, 8). Worship is to spiritual rebirth what growing up is to physical birth. Our life of worship begins when we are born by God's Spirit.

ON HIS TERMS
When Jesus taught that worship must be "in spirit," he was emphasizing the proper relationship with God. We approach him on his terms, not ours. But his terms are for our benefit. If God were to invade our world openly with his glory and holiness, we would be overwhelmed. Instead, God has chosen to reveal himself generally through his creation, specifically through the prophets and writers of the Bible, and fully (though humanly) in his Son, Jesus. We worship in submission to what God has revealed of himself. Worship includes our praise to God for the ways that he has revealed himself, our confession for the sins he has allowed us to see, our thanksgiving for all he has done for us, and our requests to learn more. True spiritual worship must have God at its center.

4:25 **"I know that Messiah is coming" (who is called Christ). "When he comes, he will proclaim all things to us."**[NRSV] Talk of a new kind of worship must have reminded the Samaritan woman about the coming of the Messiah. Her comment was only loosely related to what Jesus had just said. She probably uttered it with a sigh, revealing her uncertainty about an unknown future. The Samaritans believed in the coming of "the Prophet" predicted by Moses (Deuteronomy 18:15-18), whom they called "the Restorer." The Samaritans may have also heard of the coming Messiah from John the Baptist who had been baptizing in northern Samaria (3:23). They, as with the Jews, probably did not consider "the Prophet" and "the Messiah" to be the same person. Either way, both groups were expecting someone who would be a political liberator. They could not accept the idea that the long-awaited one would be a suffering servant before he would become the conquering king.

The woman had already perceived that Jesus was a prophet (4:19); his comments made her wish for the coming Prophet who would explain everything.

ANSWER MAN
The discussion had reached a point at which the Samaritan voiced her hope that someone would eventually be able to settle all her questions and problems. Sooner or later, in a conversation on life, people will reveal their hope. They will tell us what they rely on when worldly answers fail. At those times, we certainly should reveal our hope. Peter reminds us to "quietly trust yourself to Christ your Lord, and if anybody asks why you believe as you do, be ready to tell him, and do it in a gentle and respectful way" (1 Peter 3:15 TLB). Unlike Jesus, we cannot claim to *be* the Answer, but if we believe in Jesus, we can claim to *know* the Answer. When someone says, "Someday I'll figure it all out," we ought to respond, "I know someone who has the answers today!"

4:26 **"I who speak to you am He."**NKJV Literally, "I am [he], the one speaking to you." Although Jesus avoided telling the Jews directly that he was the Christ (see 10:24ff.), he told this Samaritan woman that he, the one who sat there with her on the well, was the promised Messiah.

JESUS TELLS ABOUT THE SPIRITUAL HARVEST / 4:27-38 / *28*

The sudden arrival of the disciples interrupted the conversation. Jesus seems to have made no effort to continue the exchange. He had placed himself before the woman as the one she was expecting. What the woman would have said in response to Jesus' revelation is unknown. But what she did is clear. She immediately went and told her neighbors that she had just encountered a unique and wonderful person whom they should also meet. She knew little about

Jesus, but she knew *him*. The news she shared about the stranger at the well raised great curiosity among the townspeople.

Meanwhile, Jesus spoke to his disciples about the importance of being able to look at the world from God's perspective, seeing people as a spiritual harvest to be reaped for God. Jesus reminded his disciples of his mission to do the will of God and accomplish his work; in so doing he encouraged their participation.

4:27 Just then his disciples returned and were surprised to find him talking with a woman.[NIV] Jesus had broken two cultural taboos: (1) Jews did not speak with Samaritans, and (2) a male did not normally speak with a female stranger. Jesus' behavior amazed his disciples; yet they did not query him concerning his motives, for they must have come to realize that all of his motives were good. Anyone else would have been called to account.

4:28 Leaving her water jar, the woman went back to the town.[NIV] Beyond displaying the woman's excited state of mind, this action has several significant explanations: On the one hand, it speaks of the woman leaving behind her water jar representing her thirst for true life and satisfaction; on the other hand, it also reveals her intention to return. The water jar was a valuable and practical household object. But as useful as it was to get water from the well, it was useless for obtaining the water of life. However, she had just met someone who promised living water and who had displayed intimate knowledge of her life and profound understanding of spiritual truths. We can't be sure how much she understood of what Jesus had told her, but she was convinced that everyone in town ought to hear what he had to say.

> Let us throw off everything that hinders and the sin that so easily entangles.
> *Author of Hebrews*

4:29-30 "Come and see a man who told me everything I have ever done!"[NRSV] In essence, the Samaritan woman was saying that Jesus *could have* told her everything about her life, for in telling her about her relationships with various men, he revealed his knowledge about her history. She made no promises about what Jesus might know about everyone else, but she appealed to their curiosity. What was it about this stranger that could make a woman who had every reason to be ashamed of her life now speak publicly about her experience of transparency before him? Her invitation proved irresistible.

> The fact that I am a woman does not make me a different kind of Christian, but the fact that I am a Christian does make me a different kind of woman. *Elisabeth Elliot*

WHAT TO LEAVE BEHIND
When we return to the world of family and friends after encountering Jesus, there are two kinds of "water jars" we must leave behind:

1. We must leave behind our shame about the past. Because Jesus knows all about us, we can repent and receive his forgiveness. God may use the emptiness of our past life to help us convey to others the wonder of forgiveness. But we must not dwell on or carry guilt about the past.

2. We must leave behind former friends and activities. Certain pleasures and relationships (not bad in themselves) may hinder our telling others about Christ. The water jar would have slowed the woman down. She probably retrieved it later, but was not concerned about it in the light of her discovery.

Are there possessions that threaten to own us rather than the other way around? These we must leave with Christ. We must lay down our useless former pursuits of pleasure and personal fulfillment. Even though we know that our old way of living never truly satisfies, the tempter deceives us into believing that there still may be an instant, easy source of happiness in the old empty ways. Have you turned your back on old habits, old treasures, old pleasures in order to seek what only God can give? Leave them behind and satisfy your thirst in Christ.

"He cannot be the Messiah, can he?"NRSV In Greek speech, this is a tentative question: "Perhaps this may be the Christ?" She probably knew that her reputation preceded her, and any assertion on her part regarding her belief in this man would go unheeded. At this stage, she may also not have been fully convinced that Jesus *was* the Messiah. But her question did serve to stir up curiosity and had the desired effect—the people **came out of the town and made their way toward him.**NIV

4:31-33 **Meanwhile his disciples urged him, "Rabbi, eat something."**NIV After the woman left for the town, the disciples urged their master to eat. His response was baffling: **"I have food to eat that you do not know about."**NRSV The disciples thought he was talking about physical food; instead, Jesus was saying that he was spiritually satisfied by having shared the Good News with the Samaritan woman.

4:34 **"My food," said Jesus, "is to do the will of him who sent me and to finish his work."**NIV This statement shows that Jesus lived to please his Father and in so doing found spiritual satisfaction (17:4). *To do* God's *will* meant that Jesus submitted himself to the Father's plan and enjoyed carrying out his Father's desires. Satisfying the Father gave Jesus true satisfaction. *To finish* God's *work*

speaks of completing the task—all the way from sowing the seed
to reaping the harvest (see following verses). According to 17:4,
Jesus accomplished all that the Father wanted him to do before
leaving this earth. Preeminently, Jesus had revealed the Father to
the world.

All Christian service and acts of compassion must be done by
those who submit to God's will. It must be God's work, not ours,
and the motivation to do it will come as we are rightly related to
the Father.

HUNGRY?
Jesus spoke about the "food" that provided his spiritual nourishment. We are nourished by Bible study, prayer, and attending
church. Spiritual nourishment also comes from doing God's will
in order to be his kind of people in the world. We are nourished
not only by what we take in but also by what we give out for
God.

Recognize the spiritual hunger to which Jesus referred in
statements like, "Blessed are those who hunger and thirst for
righteousness, for they will be filled" (Matthew 5:6 NIV); and "Do
not worry, saying, 'What shall we eat?' or 'What shall we drink?'
. . . But seek first his kingdom and his righteousness, and all
these things will be given to you as well" (Matthew 6:31, 33
NIV). Don't you hunger to do God's will?

4:35 **"Four months more, then comes the harvest."**[NRSV] For farmers,
approximately four months elapsed between the end of sowing
and the beginning of reaping.

**"Lift up your eyes and look at the fields, for they are already
white for harvest!"**[NKJV] From Jesus' spiritual perspective, the
time for harvesting had already arrived. The Samaritans, who
were coming from town, were ready to be harvested. In telling
the disciples to *lift up* their eyes and *look at the fields,* Jesus may
well have been directing them to look at the approaching Samaritans. This may help explain Jesus' use of the word *white* to
describe a harvest. Harvests in Palestine do not look white, but
Samaritans often dressed in white. They were ready to be harvested.

4:36-37 **"The reaper draws his wages . . . he harvests the crop for eternal life."**[NIV] The reaper of this spiritual harvest derives satisfaction from bringing others to experience eternal life. This parallels
Jesus' experience with the Samaritan woman; he was satisfied by
offering her the gift of life.

HARVESTTIME

Sometimes Christians excuse themselves from witnessing by saying that their family or friends aren't ready to believe. But our excuses don't stand up very well before the example of the Samaritan woman, who spoke to the very people most likely to reject anything she had to say. Her message was attractive because she described how Jesus had met her needs; she did not attempt to expose *their* needs.

Jesus made it clear that a continual harvest awaits reaping. Don't make excuses. If you are watchful and available, you will find people ready to hear God's Word.

"The sower and the reaper may be glad together."^{NIV} Jesus here mentions the sower in addition to the reaper. Jesus, as both sower and reaper, sowed the seed through a single Samaritan woman and reaped a harvest from many in a Samaritan city. This sowing and reaping transpired so quickly that the sower and reaper could rejoice together. Normally, the sower's joy is hopeful, for it is based on a future harvest. The reaper's later joy is complete, for it is based on the stored harvest. But in the context of eternity, the sower and reaper will be together and can rejoice over the harvest they both accomplished.

The sower and the reaper do not have the same role—the point of the next verse: **"Thus the saying 'One sows and another reaps' is true."**^{NIV} This saying may have come from verses like Deuteronomy 20:6; 28:30; Micah 6:15; Job 31:8, but it is not a direct quotation of any known biblical passage.

SEEDS AND SHEAVES

God oversees the continual work of planting the seeds of the gospel (Luke 8:4-15) and then reaping the crop. That the fields are ripe for harvest reminds us that many are ready to receive salvation because others have sown the seed. Can you identify the process of sowing and reaping that occurred in your life? Perhaps your mother or father, a Sunday school teacher, a pastor, a camp director, or a youth group leader sowed or nourished the gospel seed in you. Then a "reaper" came along whose gospel message found you ripe to respond, and you accepted eternal life. At the moment of being "harvested," we became sowers and reapers ourselves. Our lives ought to be an effort to sow wherever and reap whenever. As was done for us, we ought to seek to do for others. In the end, the sowers, reapers, and the harvest will all rejoice!

4:38 **"I sent you to reap what you have not worked for. Others have done the hard work, and you have reaped the benefits of**

their labor."[NIV] This probably refers to the coming harvest of Samaritan believers reaped by Jesus and his disciples, as well as to the harvest that would come after Pentecost (see Acts 1:8; 2:41; 9:31; 15:3). The *others* who labored may have been some of the Old Testament prophets or, more likely, John the Baptist and his followers (see 3:23).

TAKING CREDIT
Think of all that farmers do—plowing, fertilizing, sowing, weeding, watering, harvesting. For the most part, however, farmers are a humble group when it comes to taking credit for the results. So much is out of their hands, yet what they do is vital. In spreading the gospel, God gives us a significant role, yet he deserves the credit. In fact, we can only claim to have done a small part of the job. Often we have only a slight idea of how others have contributed to what God accomplished in a person. But our testimony, kindness, encouragement, patience, or teaching of the gospel may be the turning point in someone's life. Let us make the most of all our opportunities.

MANY SAMARITANS BELIEVE IN JESUS / 4:39-42 / 29

As he has done before (1:12; 2:23; 3:18), John points out that to "believe in him" is the required response when a person encounters Jesus. As a result of Jesus' conversation with the Samaritan woman, her bold witness in town, and the people's curiosity, many became believers. The choice is a significant challenge to the whole person—mind, will, emotions, experience. The response is profound, but not complicated. At some point a person's mind must stop asking how, his will must stop asking why, his emotions must set fear aside, and his experience must not be allowed to say "Jesus can't be trusted either." Jesus' proof was compelling. John was convinced and believed; the Samaritans were convinced and believed; so have millions of others. The unavoidable question each person must ask is, "Have I believed in Jesus?"

4:39-42 Many of the Samaritans from that town believed in him because of the woman's testimony.[NIV] Many of the Samaritans who believed in Jesus were first drawn by the testimony of the woman about the mysterious man who told her everything she had ever done. They invited Jesus to stay longer, and because of that, others believed when they heard Jesus for themselves (4:41).

They said to the woman, "We no longer believe just because of what you said; now we have heard for ourselves, and we

know that this man really is the Savior of the world."NIV Many Samaritans had come to know absolutely and positively that Jesus was *the Savior of the world*. This last statement is the climax of this passage (4:1-42), for it speaks of how Jesus had come to be, not just the Jews' Messiah, but the world's Savior as well.

 ON OUR OWN
When people become new Christians, they often depend on the individual who invited them to believe in Christ. That dependence helps in the beginning, but it can cause harm if it becomes central to their understanding of Christ. Spiritual maturity grows from one's own direct relationship with God. At the human level, the giving should go both ways, not just one way. We will always be grateful to those who shared the gospel with us. But as we grow in Christ, God will help us minister to those who first ministered to us.

JESUS PREACHES IN GALILEE / 4:43-45 / 30

After his wonderful experience in Samaria, Jesus went to Cana in Galilee, where he healed a royal official's son. But along with the healing came Jesus' rebuke that the people's belief was based on seeing signs and wonders, not on trusting in Jesus himself. These events stand in contrast to Jesus' experience in Sychar (4:1-42), where without miracles and through an unexpected witness, many placed their trust in him.

4:43-44 **When the two days were over, he went from that place to Galilee.**NRSV According to verse 3, Jesus left Judea and headed for Galilee. He passed through Samaria on the way and stayed there for two days (4:40).

(Now Jesus himself had pointed out that a prophet has no honor in his own country.)NIV Some commentators argue that Jesus' native country was Judea; others have argued for Nazareth. Those who argue for Judea do so because the Galileans welcomed him. Those who argue for Nazareth do so on the strength of the synoptic Gospels (see Matthew 13:57; Mark 6:4; Luke 4:24, where the word *patridi*—"own country"—is used to describe Nazareth) and on the basis that Jesus did not leave Judea because he was unpopular. To the contrary, his popularity was increasing (see 4:2). Thus, Jesus went to the Galileans, knowing that they would welcome him as miracle-worker but not as a prophet, much less as the Messiah. In any case, the identity of the place Jesus might have thought of as *his own country* is secondary to the fact that he was rejected everywhere he went, eventually being given the highest dishonor of death on a cross. In Jesus' case, the world was his own creation; and though "he came to that which was his own" (1:11 NIV), he was not received.

4:45 When he arrived in Galilee, the Galileans welcomed him. They had seen all that he had done in Jerusalem at the Passover Feast, for they also had been there.^{NIV} This statement refers to 2:23, which says that the people assembling in Jerusalem (among whom were these Galileans) during the Passover believed in Jesus because of the signs they saw him perform.

JESUS HEALS A GOVERNMENT OFFICIAL'S SON / 4:46-54 / 31

The story of Jesus turning water into wine was still news in Cana when he returned. The local welcome was tinged with interest over what new wonders he might perform. The opportunity would soon come. A child in nearby Capernaum lay sick, and an anxious father came to Jesus, begging for help.

4:46-50 Then he came again to Cana in Galilee where he had changed the water into wine.^{NRSV} See 2:1-11.

There was a royal official whose son lay ill in Capernaum.^{NRSV} This man was very likely an official in Herod's court, serving in some capacity in Capernaum, about twenty miles from Cana. Although this miracle bears similarities with the one recorded in Matthew 8:5-13 and Luke 7:2-10 (both deal with the healing of a centurion's servant), they seem to be different incidents. All the Gospel writers imply that the miracles they recorded were nothing more than samples of Jesus' work.

When the royal official requested that Jesus **come and heal**^{NIV} his son, who was **at the point of death,**^{NKJV} Jesus responded, **"Unless you people see miraculous signs and wonders . . . you will never believe."**^{NIV} Jesus took the opportunity to address all the Galileans (2:23; 4:45) and reprimand them for being sign-seekers. But *this* Galilean was *not* merely a sign-seeker. He had a need, and he truly believed Jesus could meet that need. As a result, his need was met.

"Go; your son will live." The man believed the word that Jesus spoke to him and started on his way.^{NRSV} The official believed Jesus' word, and the healing was performed. He was the type of man whom Jesus would later call "blessed," for he had not seen and yet he believed (see 20:29). Jesus' word is a life-giving word (see 5:24-25; 6:68).

4:51-53 While he was still on the way, his servants met him with the news that his boy was living.[NIV] The details given in these verses

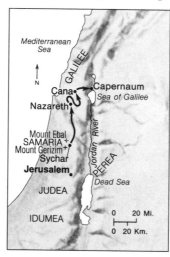

Jesus Returns to Galilee.
Jesus stayed in Sychar for two days, then went on to Galilee. He visited Nazareth and various towns in Galilee before arriving in Cana. From there he spoke the word of healing, and a government official's son in Capernaum was healed. The Gospel of Matthew tells us Jesus then settled in Capernaum (Matthew 4:12-13).

tell the reader that the healing occurred at exactly the time Jesus spoke the words, **"Your son lives!"**[NKJV] Jesus' miracles were not mere illusions, the products of wishful thinking. Although the official's son was twenty miles away, he was healed when Jesus spoke the word. Distance was no problem because Christ has mastery over space. This miracle produced faith throughout the household (including family members or servants): **So he himself believed, along with his whole household.**[NRSV] There are cultures where the word or belief of the head of the household represents what each member of the house believes. New Testament evidence points to these kinds of responses in more than one case (Acts 10:2; 16:15, 33). This strikes our individualistic culture as somewhat unusual. But, in fact, even in modern families, when one member of the family is profoundly and clearly changed by the gospel, the effects tend to spread throughout the rest of the family. How different would the state of the Christian church be today if heads of households provided real spiritual leadership in their homes?

CAN HE BE TRUSTED?
This government official not only believed that Jesus could heal, he also obeyed Jesus by returning home, thus truly demonstrating his faith. It isn't enough for us to say we believe that Jesus can take care of our problems. We need to act as if he can. We also need to leave the means, ways, and timing up to him. When we pray about a need or problem, we should live as though we believe Jesus can do what he says.

4:54 Now this was the second sign that Jesus did after coming from Judea to Galilee.^{NRSV} The first sign was changing the water into wine at the wedding in Cana (2:1-11). The second was healing a dying child. According to the Gospel of John, Jesus' miracles were "signs"—pointing the people who witnessed them to the one who performed the signs, Jesus, the Messiah, the Son of God. If the miracle produced faith in Jesus only as a miracle worker and not as the Son of God, then the people missed the miracle as the sign it was intended to be.

EXERCISE YOUR FAITH
Notice how the official's faith grew:
- He believed enough to ask Jesus to help his son.
- He believed to the point of insisting that Jesus come with him to heal his son.
- He trusted Jesus' assurance that his son would live, and he acted on it.
- He and his whole household believed in Jesus.

Faith grows as we use it.

John 5

God gives salvation freely through Jesus Christ. But to receive salvation, a person must *believe*. The lame man by the pool at Bethesda had to *want* to be healed. Then Jesus approached him later to explain to him that he needed to believe and receive spiritual healing as well. God makes the offer and God performs the miracle, but we must respond to his offer and accept it.

5:1 After this there was a feast of the Jews, and Jesus went up to Jerusalem.[NKJV] Capernaum, at the northern end of Israel, was lower in altitude than Jerusalem. Because of Jerusalem's location in the mountains, and because of its priority as the city of David, people spoke of going *up to Jerusalem*. All Jewish males were required to come to Jerusalem to attend three feasts: (1) the Feast of Passover and Unleavened Bread, (2) the Feast of Weeks (also called Pentecost), and (3) the Feast of Tabernacles. Though this particular feast is not specified, the phrase explains why Jesus was in Jerusalem. John added the expression *of the Jews* to help Gentile readers.

5:2 Now in Jerusalem by the Sheep Gate there is a pool.[NRSV] This is how most translators render the Greek. A few other translations render it this way: "Now at the Sheep-Pool in Jerusalem there is a place . . ." (NEB; see also NJB). Readers familiar with Jerusalem would have known that John was referring to the Sheep Gate (it is mentioned in Nehemiah 3:1, 32; 12:39). Recent excavations show that this site had two pools with **five covered colonnades**[NIV]. These were open structures with roofs that allowed some protection from the weather.

5:3-4 Here a great number of disabled people used to lie—the blind, the lame, the paralyzed.[NIV] The multitude of sick people lay underneath the five colonnades. In modern times similar gatherings have happened in Fatima and Lourdes. Many people make pilgrimages to these sites to receive the healing benefit of the waters. The colonnade in Jerusalem was a place of collected human suffering—people attracted by a faint hope of being

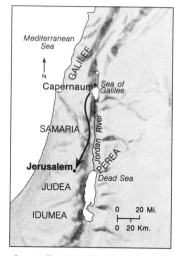

Jesus Teaches in Jerusalem.
Between chapters 4 and 5 of
John, Jesus ministered throughout Galilee, especially in Capernaum. He had been calling
certain men to follow him, but it
wasn't until after this trip to Jerusalem (5:1) that he chose his
twelve disciples from among
them.

healed. To this place Jesus was
also attracted, offering with his
presence the kind of healing that
went beyond the physical needs
of the disabled.

**Waiting for the moving of the
water. For an angel went down
at a certain time into the pool
and stirred up the water; then
whoever stepped in first, after
the stirring of the water, was
made well of whatever disease
he had.**NKJV It is very doubtful
this portion was written by John,
since it is not found in the earliest
manuscripts, and where it does
occur in later manuscripts, it is
often marked in such a way as to
show that it is an addition. The
passage was probably inserted
later by scribes who felt it necessary to provide an explanation for
the gathering of disabled people
and the stirring of the water mentioned in verse 7. It is unclear
whether an angel actually disturbed the water, or if this was just a
local superstition used to explain the natural movement in a pool
of water fed by a spring. But somehow the waters were stirred
and seemed to have had curative powers.

HURT, HOPE, AND HELP
After thirty-eight years, this man's problem had become a way
of life. No one had ever helped him. He had no hope of ever
being healed and no desire to help himself. The man was paralyzed in sight of healing. His situation looked hopeless; that is,
until the day that Jesus made his way through the crowd.
Among all those trying to be healed, Jesus found the one who
couldn't help himself.
    No matter how trapped you feel in your infirmities, God can
minister to your deepest needs. Don't let a problem or hardship
cause you to lose hope. God may have special work for you to
do in spite of your condition, or even because of it. Many have
ministered more effectively to hurting people because they
have triumphed over their own hurts.

5:5-8 When Jesus saw him lying there, and knew that he already had been in that condition a long time.NKJV This gives us a glimpse into the extent of Jesus' knowledge. Jesus knew this man's condition and how long he had suffered (he was **an invalid for thirty-eight years**).NIV

Jesus asked, **"Do you want to be made well?"**NRSV Jesus' question shows us that he will not force himself upon anyone. He seeks permission before intervening in that person's life.

Standing before a man whose desperate need was so apparent, Jesus asked an embarrassingly obvious question, *"Do you want to be made well?"* Usually these questions didn't lead to immediate explanations. In this case, Jesus waited until later to explain to the man the spiritual aspects of his sickness (5:14).

We must acknowledge our dependency and decide if we want Christ to heal us. Jesus wants more than to make some "minor" corrections in our lives—he offers radical transformation (2 Corinthians 5:17). Only when we admit our need will we receive the amazing power of his grace and the miracle of salvation and eternal life.

"I have no one to help me into the pool when the water is stirred."NIV The man indirectly answered Jesus by telling how he had not been able to be healed because others would get into the water before he did. But in making this statement, the man admitted that he needed help. His hope for healing was stuck behind his hopelessness of ever having help to get to the water in time.

BOTTOMED OUT
The paralyzed man had one important trait that many people lack: He knew he needed help. Not only was he unable to help himself, he also hadn't been able to persuade anyone else to help him. Apparently the religious leaders who were so quick to judge his failure to keep their Sabbath laws had not been nearly as quick to obey God's clear Old Testament commands about helping those in need.

In contrast, we are surrounded with so many supports and buffers that we may live without ever facing our inability to save ourselves. Jesus didn't choose the ones who were pushing forward; rather, he went directly to the person who had almost given up hope. He went to a desperate person who didn't have to be convinced he needed help. The paralyzed man had reached the end of his rope and was ready to respond. Does God have to wait until we are desperate before he hears from us?

Jesus offered help, but not the kind of help the man expected.
Jesus simply said, **"Rise, take up your bed and walk."**^{NKJV} And
the man responded immediately.

5:9 **At once the man was cured; he picked up his mat and
walked.**^{NIV} The action of carrying his mat represented this man's
freedom and became the occasion for others to impose limitations. This miracle should have revealed to the Jews in Jerusalem
that the Messiah was finally present, for Isaiah had prophesied,
"Then will the eyes of the blind be opened and the ears of the
deaf unstopped. Then will the lame leap like a deer, and the mute
tongue shout for joy" (Isaiah 35:5-6 NIV). Instead, they chose to
focus on another issue: **The day on which this took place was a**

BUILDING BRIDGES
Most people would rather avoid seeing and speaking to people
with disabilities. It's easier to politely ignore someone in a
wheelchair at a mall, or a child who struggles just to walk. But
notice what Jesus did in this story:
   He went to the place. Jesus could have entered Jerusalem
by another gate. He could have avoided walking by the pool
called Bethesda. Just as Jesus went to the pool, so the church
should go to where people with disabilities are. It's not enough
to open the church doors and wait to see who enters. Ministry
in the disabled community must be outreach-oriented to be
effective.
   He talked with the person. Jesus spoke to the man directly.
He demonstrated respect and concern, not pity. We can sometimes feel uncomfortable around people with disabilities. We
may be afraid of saying the wrong thing, so we choose to say
nothing at all. But guided by love, we can build bridges with disabled people by simply demonstrating common courtesy and
respecting human dignity. God can help us overcome our fears
so that we can ask questions and have a conversation.
   He offered specific help at a point of need. Jesus healed the
man—something we are unable to do. But we can pray for
people, refer them to competent, professional care, and offer to
help at a point of need. Specific offers are usually more well
received than general ones. If we say, "Be sure to give me a
call if there is anything I can do," we usually won't get a call.
People who are struggling with a handicap don't want to bother
anyone. Besides, how do they know we really mean what we
say? Specific offers of help are better, such as: "Would you like
me to drive you to the store on Tuesday?" or "Could I help you
with some housecleaning on Saturday?"
   Like Jesus, the church should demonstrate compassion to
people with disabilities of all kinds. Of all the help we offer, the
most important is to point people to Christ, who will one day
heal all disabilities and remove all handicaps from his people.

Sabbath.[NIV] Presumably, if the waters had been stirred on the Sabbath and he had been healed by getting in, the Jews would not have argued against his healing. But these religious leaders would not allow God in the flesh to break their rules by healing this man directly. We wonder how anyone could be so closed to God's working. But how often do our preconceived notions of how God's work should be done get in the way of it getting done!

5:10 So the Jews said to the man who had been cured, "It is the sabbath; it is not lawful for you to carry your mat."[NRSV] There is nothing in God's law to prohibit a person from carrying a mat on the Sabbath. God's law says: "Remember the Sabbath day, to keep it holy. Six days you shall labor and do all your work, but the seventh day is the Sabbath of the LORD your God. In it you shall do no work" (Exodus 20:8-10 NKJV). Car-

> Poor human reason when it trusts in itself substitutes the strangest absurdities for the highest divine concepts.
> *John Chrysostom*

rying a mat on the Sabbath did not break any Old Testament law; instead, it broke the Pharisees' legalistic application of God's command. The regulation against carrying something on the Sabbath was the last of thirty-nine rules in the "tradition of the elders" that stipulated the kinds of work prohibited on the Sabbath. This was just one of hundreds of rules the Jewish leaders had added to the Old Testament law.

We must not take the mind-set of the Pharisees in our church practice. But some still rely on "oral traditions" or "principles

SEVEN SABBATH MIRACLES
The religious leaders had created a law that people could not heal on the Sabbath because "healing" was "work." Seven times Jesus healed people on the Sabbath. In doing this, he was challenging the religious leaders to look beyond God's command regarding the Sabbath to its true purpose—to honor God by helping people in need. Would God have been pleased if Jesus had ignored these needy people?

Jesus sends a demon out of a man.	*Mark 1:21-28*
Jesus heals Peter's mother-in-law.	*Mark 1:29-31*
Jesus heals a lame man	*John 5:1-18*
Jesus heals a man with a shriveled hand	*Mark 3:1-6*
Jesus restores a crippled woman	*Luke 13:10-17*
Jesus heals a man with dropsy	*Luke 14:1-6*
Jesus heals a man born blind	*John 9:1-16*

handed down" that don't come from Scripture. Such legislature can hinder true service to God. The Bible does not stipulate what we can't do on Sunday; it does not dictate the denomination we worship in; it does not specify the kind of Christian music we use to worship God. Where the Bible does not specify rules, we should not either.

IN A BIND
Although God's truth is timeless, our application of that truth may be limited by time and circumstance. The authority of an application depends on how nearly it conveys the intended truth of Scripture. Application based on personal convictions may help a person, but it becomes tyrannical if made binding on everyone. In this case, God's command to keep the Sabbath holy was still in force, but the application of avoiding certain work activities was clearly secondary to healing a person. As Jesus said at another Sabbath healing, "You hypocrites! Doesn't each of you on the Sabbath untie his ox or donkey from the stall and lead it out to give it water? Then should not this woman, a daughter of Abraham, whom Satan has kept bound for eighteen long years, be set free on the Sabbath day from what bound her?" (Luke 13:15-16 NIV).

5:11-13 "The man who made me well said . . ." The man who was healed had no idea who it was.[NIV] In this exchange between the man who was healed and the Jewish leaders in Jerusalem, the man said he didn't know who had healed him. The man's ignorance is quite possible, for Jesus had not identified himself and had immediately **slipped away into the crowd.**[NIV] At the same time, however, the healed man seemed to be more eager to blame the healer for having him walk around with his mat than to shout about his healing. The man should have found out who healed him.

When God touches our body to heal us, we must not be so preoccupied with the miracle or even the relief from pain that we neglect to seek him out, thank him, and believe in him.

DON'T TRIP!
A man who hadn't walked for thirty-eight years was healed, but the Pharisees were more concerned about their petty rules than the life and health of a human being. It is easy to get so caught up in our man-made structures and rules that we forget the people involved. Are our guidelines for living God-made or man-made? Are they helping people, or have they become needless stumbling blocks?

5:14-15 Later Jesus found him in the temple.^{NRSV} Perhaps the man had gone there to give thanks to God for his healing. When Jesus found him, he told him, **"Do not sin any more, so that nothing worse happens to you."**^{NRSV} This statement leads to the conclusion that the man's sickness was in some way caused by sin. This does not contradict what Jesus said in 9:3 about the man born blind because Jesus did not say the blind man never sinned; rather, he was pointing out that sin had not caused

> I believe that no man is ever condemned for any sin except one—that he will not leave his sins and come out of them, and be the child of Him who is his Father. *George Macdonald*

his blindness. One of the results of sin is suffering, but not all suffering is the result of personal sin.

In this case, Jesus sought out the healed man to warn him that though he was healed physically, his thirty-eight years as an invalid would be nothing compared to something *worse*—that is, eternity in hell. The man needed to stop sinning and come to salvation in Christ. He had been lame, but now he could walk. This was a great miracle. But he needed an even greater miracle—to have his sins forgiven. The man was delighted to be physically healed, but he had to turn from his sins and seek God's forgiveness to be spiritually healed.

WHAT SIN?
What was this paralyzed man's sin that Jesus now told him to stop? Was it some kind of unhealthy behavior that had directly caused his paralysis? Was it the sin of unbelief? Was it the sin of ingratitude? Or was Jesus using the man's past illness to warn him about the dangers of falling into sin? None of these possibilities provide an absolute answer. Beyond all these questions is Jesus' warning that continuing in sin eventually leads to something worse. The various benefits of God's grace, including physical healing, must be followed by repentance and growing commitment to him. Many people focus on their physical well-being while completely neglecting the health of their souls.

After this encounter, the man told the Jewish leaders what he could not tell them before: **It was Jesus who had made him well.**^{NRSV} This report triggered the Jews' persecution of Jesus—a persecution that continued from that day onward. And why did they persecute Jesus so vehemently? John proceeds to give us the answer in verse 18.

5:16 Because Jesus was doing these things on the Sabbath, the Jews persecuted him.[NIV] The Jewish leaders were faced with a mighty miracle of healing and a broken rule. They threw the miracle aside as they focused their attention on the broken rule. As is common with those who assume authority that is not rightfully theirs, these leaders instinctively felt their power threatened by Jesus' actions, thus they resented him. John traced their subsequent efforts to humiliate, harass, and kill Jesus back to this conflict over who was in charge of the Sabbath.

5:17 "My Father is always at his work to this very day, and I, too, am working."[NIV] With this statement Jesus challenged the notion that God himself was somehow literally subject to the Sabbath rules. If God stopped every kind of work on the Sabbath, nature would fall into chaos and sin would overrun the world. Genesis 2:2 says that God rested on the seventh day; he rested from the work of creation but began the work of sustaining the creation. God has been at work and continues to work; so does his Son, Jesus. With this claim, Jesus affirmed his equality with God (see comments on 5:18). Furthermore, Jesus was teaching that when the opportunity to do good presents itself, it should not be ignored, even on the Sabbath.

Sabbath—Uncluttered time and space to distance ourselves from the frenzy of our own activities so we can see what God has been and is doing. If we do not quit work for one day a week we take ourselves far too seriously. *Sabbath-keeping*—Quieting the internal noise so we hear the still small voice of our Lord. Removing the distractions of pride so we discern the presence of Christ. *Eugene H. Peterson*

SABBATH KEEPING
Two significant principles come to us from the Bible regarding the Sabbath. By Jesus' declaration (Matthew 5:17-20), the fourth commandment (along with God's other commands) is still in force: "Remember the Sabbath day by keeping it holy" (Exodus 20:8 NIV). But Jesus gave helpful guidelines in applying the commandments (see Matthew 5:1–7:29—much of the Sermon on the Mount is Jesus' application of God's commands). In the case of Sabbath keeping he said, "The sabbath was made for humankind, and not humankind for the sabbath" (Mark 2:27 NRSV). Jesus did not release us from keeping the Sabbath; he challenged us to keep it in the right way by setting down our work, consciously taking time for rest, and under-

standing that God has a place in our work and our rest, which makes them both holy.

When you keep the Sabbath, consider the answers to the following questions:

- When I work, am I working for God?
- When I rest, am I resting for God?
- Does my "resting" refresh me for work?
- How does my time of rest include devotion to God?
- How well do I understand the fact that one person's "work" is another person's "rest"? (For example, some might find tending a rose garden tedious work, while others find it a joyful, restful act of worship.)

5:18 Therefore the Jews sought all the more to kill Him, because He not only broke the Sabbath, but also said that God was His Father, making Himself equal with God.^{NKJV} The Jews realized that Jesus' words revealed his very personal relationship with God. In saying, "My Father," he was clearly claiming to be God's Son, thus *equal with God.* For a human to claim equality with God was blasphemy; and blasphemy was a sin carrying the death penalty (Leviticus 24:15-16). People regularly misunderstood Jesus, and he was constantly correcting them. Jesus never attempted to correct the understanding that he was claiming to be God, for that was exactly what he meant. Thus the Jewish leaders sought to accuse Jesus and have him killed.

UNDERSTANDING THE HATE

To understand the hate that Jesus received from some of his own people, we must examine the larger political picture. The Roman rule over the Jews placed severe limits on most power and control exercised by native peoples. But the Romans made an important exception in matters of religion. The Romans, with their pluralistic views of religion, interpreted the religious sphere as little more than local, meaningless activity to help keep the masses under control. However, their relaxed philosophy of religion ran into serious difficulties when applied to the monotheistic Jews.

Among the Jews of Jesus' time, the highest power someone could wield was in the religious structure. The authorities Jesus confronted had worked hard to obtain and maintain their positions of prestige and power. To the Romans, their squabbles seemed trivial, but among the Jews, religious issues, whether politicized or not, were matters of life and death.

Into this arena stepped Jesus, challenging the legitimacy of the religious leadership, exposing their false pretenses, and claiming a higher authority. To those in power, his credentials were unacceptable:

- Jesus was an outsider and not from their ranks.

- Jesus was reputedly a Galilean, considered worthy of little respect.
- Jesus was young and his training was suspect.
- Jesus spoke with uncompromising clarity and authority.
- Jesus had a startling way of cutting through the technicalities of the law that preserved the position of the hierarchy.

Threatened by the loss of power if Jesus' claims were true, the religious leaders chose to reject him. When unable to discredit him, they attempted to dispose of him. But God used their attempted solution to the "Jesus problem" to solve once and for all the entire world's "sin problem."

JESUS CLAIMS TO BE GOD'S SON / 5:19-30 / **43**

The Old Testament included signs for recognizing the coming Messiah. Not surprisingly, these signs point to God himself. In this chapter, John shows how Jesus fulfilled three of these signs.

5:19-20 **"The Son can do nothing by himself; he can do only what he sees his Father doing, because whatever the Father does the Son also does."**[NIV] Jesus did not say that he *will not* do anything independent from the Father, but that he *cannot*. The Son performs the tasks the Father wants done because they are of one spirit.

> Christ encourages us to pattern our lives after his so we can become spiritually enlightened. Our most important task, then is to meditate on the life of Jesus Christ.
> *Thomas à Kempis*

"For the Father loves the Son and shows him all he does."[NIV] The Father and the Son know and love each other completely. Because of their transparent relationship, the Son always knows what the Father is doing and works in harmony with him to see it accomplished.

 IN JESUS' STEPS
Because of his unity with God, Jesus lived as God wanted him to live. Because of our identification with Jesus, we must honor him and live as he wants us to live. When we need guidance, the questions What would Jesus do? and What would Jesus have me do? may help us make the right choices.

"He will show him greater works than these."[NRSV] According to the following verses, the *greater works* are the Son's ability to give life to the dead and to execute judgment.

JESUS, THE MESSIAH

What God does	What Messiah does	What Jesus did
1. God alone judges (Psalm 7:6-17; 9:7-8; Joel 3:12)	Messiah has authority to judge (Daniel 7:13-14; Jeremiah 23:5-6)	Jesus claimed and demonstrated his authority to judge (John 5:27)

Because Jesus demonstrated his authority, we have no reason to fear judgment, or what people may do to us.

2. God alone heals (Isaiah 35:3-7)	Messiah has the power to heal (Isaiah 53:4-5; 61:1-3)	Jesus demonstrated the power to heal (John 5:8, 20, 26)

Because Jesus demonstrated his power to heal, we can claim that power in our own lives for now and eternity.

3. God alone gives life (Genesis 1:20-27; Deuteronomy 32:39; 1 Samuel 2:6; 2 Kings 5:7)	Messiah has the power to give life (Daniel 7:13-14)	Jesus claimed and demonstrated the power to give life (John 5:21, 28, 39)

Because Jesus demonstrated his power over death, we do not have to fear dying.

5:21 "Just as the Father raises the dead and gives them life, so also the Son gives life to whomever he wishes."[NRSV] This statement would have shocked Jesus' audience because it ascribes to the Son—Jesus himself—what was seen as exclusively the activity of God the Father. God alone can reverse the power of death by resurrection. That God gave that power to the Son is demonstrated in Jesus' raising of Lazarus from the dead (see 11:41-44).

5:22-23 "Moreover, the Father judges no one, but has entrusted all judgment to the Son."[NIV] The certainty of our salvation is in the hands of the Son because God entrusted him with judicial and executive authority to judge. Thus, he has equal dignity and honor with the Father—**"all should honor the Son just as they honor the Father."**[NKJV]

"Anyone who does not honor the Son does not honor the Father who sent him."[NRSV] Here Jesus was referring to that time when everyone will recognize his lordship. Paul described that event in this way: "Therefore God exalted him to the highest place and gave him the name that is above every name, that at the name of Jesus every knee should bow, in heaven and on earth and under the earth, and every tongue confess that Jesus Christ is Lord, to the glory of God the Father" (Philippians 2:9-11 NIV). The tragedy will be that many will then recognize Jesus' true nature but will have lost the opportunity to receive his saving help. Those unwilling to honor Christ now will discover that they have not been honoring the Father either. People should not say they believe in God while ignoring the power and authority of his Son.

5:24 "Whoever hears my word and believes him who sent me."NIV True hearing results in believing, for, as Paul says, "Faith comes by hearing, and hearing by the word of God" (Romans 10:17 NKJV). The gospel usually stresses believing in Jesus himself; but Jesus points to believing in the one who sent him. The statement affirms the unity of the Father and the Son. To believe in the Father is to believe in the Son he sent to earth.

> If Christ is our life, our future is not our own. Our ruling passion is not greed of life. We do not do just what we must do to keep death at bay. We begin living the eternal life here, with its endless selfless energy, vaster than we feel, and surer than we know.
>
> *P. T. Forsyth*

"Has eternal life."NRSV The believer *has* eternal life as a present possession, guaranteeing an eternal life with God. We can be certain about whether we have eternal life. John wrote in another letter, "He who has the Son has life" (1 John 5:12 NKJV). The believer **"does not come under judgment"**NRSV because the judgment has passed. Alternately, those who hear and do not believe in the one who sent Jesus do *come under judgment*. The decision we make about Jesus places eternal consequences before us. Belief in Christ means we have **"passed from death into life"**NKJV (see also 1 John 3:14). According to 3:18, God has judged this present world. We will realize the full devastation of that judgment at the final Judgment Day. Belief in Jesus provides the only escape from this judgment. For those who believe, God "has rescued us from the dominion of darkness and brought us into the kingdom of the Son he loves" (Colossians 1:13 NIV).

5:25 "I say to you, the hour is coming, and now is, when the dead will hear the voice of the Son of God; and those who hear will live."NKJV When Jesus spoke of a time that *is coming, and now is,* he saw God's wonderful future plan as happening in the present. Christ makes the same power that will resurrect the dead at his return available to all who are spiritually dead—the woman at the well, the paralyzed man, and each one of us.

In the future, the physically dead will hear the voice of the Son of God and will be raised from the grave. From verse 25, which clearly refers to those who are spiritually dead, we realize that Jesus was speaking about two kinds of life-giving power. On one level, he was speaking of the power to give life as we know it; on the other, he was speaking of the power to give life as he knows it. In saying that the dead could hear his voice, he was referring to the power to return physical life to those who had died. In fact, Jesus raised several persons who had died while he was on earth (11:38-44), though at some point they would die again. But in saying that the dead could hear his voice, Jesus was also referring to the spiritually dead who hear, understand, and accept him. Those who accept God's Word have eternal life, even though they may still experience physical death (11:25-26). After explaining briefly why he can make these promises, Jesus returns to the theme of the "coming time" when all will be gathered from death, some to eternal life and some to eternal condemnation (5:28-29).

ETERNITY NOW
Everlasting life—living forever with God—begins immediately when a person accepts Jesus Christ as Savior. At that moment, new life begins (2 Corinthians 5:17). It is a completed transaction. We will face physical death; but when Christ returns again, our body will be resurrected to live forever.

5:26 "For as the Father has life in Himself, so He has granted the Son to have life in himself."NKJV Human beings do not have life in themselves; they receive it from God. God does not receive his life from any exterior source; he is the source and Creator of life. No life exists apart from him, here or hereafter. In eternity past, the Father gave his Son the same capacity—*to have life in himself* (see 1:4, which says "in Him was life" NKJV). God does not share this uniquely divine characteristic with any created being. Because Jesus exists eternally with God the Father, he too is "the life" (14:6) through whom we may live eternally (1 John 5:11). God's gift of life comes through Christ alone (Deuteronomy 30:20; Psalm 36:9).

Jesus gives us a glimpse of the Trinity. His explanations present us with facts we must accept without being able to fully understand the nature of God. God's uniqueness renders incomplete any other object or idea we might use to fully understand his nature. God reveals enough about himself to prompt us to believe, but he withholds full understanding because we are unable to absorb the infinite. Even the claim to understand God fully would put us in danger of arrogance about our Creator. What an awesome privilege we have to know God!

5:27 **"He has given him authority to judge because he is the Son of Man."**ᴺᴵⱽ This statement seems to contradict 3:17, where Jesus is said not to have come into the world to judge it, but 8:15-16 offers an explanation. Jesus did not come to judge, but his coming led to judgment because his coming forced decision—and decision results in judgment for those who reject Jesus. The last phrase literally reads, "He is Son of Man"; as such, it emphasizes Jesus' humanity. Jesus, as man, will judge men (see Daniel 7:13-14). In this way, the Father has given all the honor to the Son, for everyone must answer to him (see Philippians 2:5-11). Jesus always kept before his audience, in word and deed, his unique dual nature as God-man.

5:28-29 **"The hour is coming."** ᴺᴿˢⱽ Compare this with verse 25, which adds the expression "and now is." Verse 28 speaks only about a future event—the coming resurrection. At that time, **"all who are in their graves will hear his voice and will come out—those who have done good, to the resurrection of life, and those who have done evil, to the resurrection of condemnation."**ᴺᴿˢⱽ Every person will be resurrected when the Lord returns, with one of two results: one will be life, the other will be condemnation. God grants eternal life to those who have come to the Light and have believed in Jesus Christ. But God will judge and condemn those who rebelled against Christ by refusing to come to the Light. God's judgment has already come upon them and will be completely executed by the Son of Man after the resurrection (see 3:18-21).

5:30 **"By myself I can do nothing; I judge only as I hear, and my judgment is just, for I seek not to please myself but him who sent me."**ᴺᴵⱽ Even though the Father committed to the Son the task of executing judgment, the Son cannot and will not perform on his own authority and by his own initiative. The distinctions within the persons of the Trinity allow each to perform certain specific functions, but the divine unity of God means that Father, Son, and Holy Spirit each do what the others would do if the roles were changed.

▨▨▨▨ *JESUS SUPPORTS HIS CLAIM / 5:31-47 / 44*

Jesus claimed to be equal with God (5:18), to give eternal life (5:24), to be the source of life (5:26), and to judge sin (5:27). These statements make it clear that Jesus claimed to be divine an almost unbelievable claim. So he called upon several witnesses to his divine being: (1) John the Baptist (5:33-35), (2) Jesus' works (5:36), (3) the Father himself (5:37), (4) the Scriptures (5:39-40), and (5) Moses (5:45-47). Any of these witnesses should have been enough, but together they supplied a compelling testimony to Jesus' claims. But many of the ones listening to Jesus were examples of how a hard heart can nullify even the most powerful argument.

5:31-32 **"If I testify about myself, my testimony is not true. There is another who testifies on my behalf, and I know that his testimony to me is true."**[NRSV] According to the Jewish law, truth or validity had to be established by two or three witnesses (Deuteronomy 17:6; 19:15). Therefore, Jesus' self-witness could not alone validate his claims, even though they were true. For these Jewish leaders, he needed the witness of another. John the Baptist was one witness, but the one to whom Jesus was referring here is his Father (see 5:36).

> The question is often asked, "If Christianity is rational and true, why is it that most educated people don't believe it?" The answer is simple. They don't believe it for the same reason that most uneducated people don't believe it. They don't want to believe it.
> *Paul Little*

5:33-34 **"You sent messengers to John, and he testified to the truth. Not that I accept such human testimony, but I say these things so that you may be saved."**[NRSV] John the Baptist was Jesus' first human witness (see 1:6-8). His testimony that Jesus was the Christ was necessary for the Jews, not Jesus.

5:35 **"He was the burning and shining lamp."**[NKJV] John the Baptist was not the Light (see 1:8); he was a reflector for the Light, not the Light itself.

"You chose for a time to enjoy his light."[NIV] Some of the Jews accepted John the Baptist and were content for a while to enjoy the light he brought to them. But they did not really understand his message or receive the illuminating revelation concerning the one to whom John gave witness—Jesus, the Son of God.

LIGHT WORK
Jesus' description of John as a "lamp" and container for the light reminds us of Jesus' description of the believers as being "the light of the world." He said, "Let your light shine before men, that they may see your good deeds and praise your Father in heaven" (Matthew 5:16 NIV). We have both the privilege and command to be carriers of the light in our corner of the world. We can hardly predict how God might use the witness we have to offer others, but we have been warned not to keep our light hidden. We simply must keep asking ourselves if those who are regularly part of our lives know of our relationship with Jesus Christ.

5:36 **"I have testimony weightier than that of John. For the very work that the Father has given me to finish, and which I am doing, testifies that the Father has sent me."**[NIV] These works signified Jesus as being the one sent from the Father. The most compelling witness about Jesus does not begin with, "Here's what Jesus can do for you," but rather, "Can I tell you what Jesus has done for me?" The work Jesus does in us still bears testimony to his special role.

5:37 **"And the Father who sent me has himself testified on my behalf."**[NRSV] The Father gave direct witness to his Son at Jesus' baptism (Matthew 3:16-17), on the Mount of Transfiguration (Matthew 17:5), before his crucifixion (12:28), and in his resurrection (Romans 1:3-4); indirect witness came through Jesus' works (see 3:2).

To recognize Jesus is to realize his divine origin and commission. Thus, to believe in Jesus is to believe in the one who sent him; to reject the sent one is to reject the sender, God.

"You have never heard his voice nor seen his form."[NIV] The Greek word for "form" is *eidos*; it is used in the Septuagint to describe the "face" of God that Jacob saw (Genesis 32:30). Moses had heard God's voice (Exodus 33:11), and so had the children of Israel (Deuteronomy 4:12).

Moses had asked to see God's glory but was not allowed to see God's face—only God's back as his glory passed by (Exodus 33:18-23). But the Jews to whom Jesus was speaking had not received any of these special revelations. In the Old Testament, God had revealed himself in many ways; now

> What have I learned? Why, I have learned what I least of all suspected, that I, who went to America to convert the Indians, was never myself converted to God!
> *John Wesley*

he reveals himself completely in his Son and in his Word (see Hebrews 1:1-3). Yet, here they had the greatest of all God's manifestations standing right before their eyes—Jesus, the Word, the visible expression of God to people.

5:38 **"You do not have his word abiding in you, because you do not believe him whom he has sent."**[NRSV] Even though the Jews to whom Jesus was speaking had not received the kinds of revelations some of their ancestors had, they still possessed the Word of God. If that Word had been abiding in their hearts (see 8:31; 15:7), they would have recognized the one to whom the Scriptures give testimony.

5:39 **"You diligently study the Scriptures."**[NIV] This could be translated, "You research the Scriptures." The Jewish scribes devoted their lives to studying the Scriptures—not so much to search for the truth but to analyze the minutia of the law. And the "scholars" studied, Jesus said, because they thought that by doing so they would **possess eternal life.**[NIV] Paul countered this notion in Galatians 3:21: "For if a law had been given that could impart life, then righteousness would certainly have come by the law" (NIV). We do not earn life by studying the Scriptures, nor do we gain great spiritual merit by possessing a certain Bible. But by studying the Scriptures we can meet the source of life: Jesus Christ, the Son of God. Jesus said, **"These are the Scriptures that testify about me."**[NIV] If we fail to see this testimony, we miss the very purpose for which the Scriptures exist. If there were no such person as Jesus Christ, the Scriptures would have little value. The Bible's chief value lies in its testimony to him.

"BIBLIOLATRY"
The proliferation of Bibles translated and paraphrased into English has brought us mixed blessings. On the one hand, people can connect with a Bible they can read and understand in the language that they speak and think. On the other hand, fierce allegiance to one or another version can border on idolatry. The doctrine of inerrancy, limited to original manuscripts, has sometimes been applied to a translation made by men. Good as it might be, it's not the inerrant Word. It is not having the right Bible that saves you; it's knowing and believing what the Bible says about Jesus that saves you.

5:40 **"You refuse to come to me to have life."**[NIV] To *refuse to come* to Jesus is to reject *life* because Christ is the giver of eternal life (1:4; 5:25; 14:6). Religious zeal—even involvement with the

Scriptures—does not bring a person eternal life. The religious leaders knew what the Bible said but failed to apply its words to their lives. They knew the teachings of the Scriptures but failed to see the Messiah to whom the Scriptures pointed. They knew

---

APPLIED TRUTH
Every other lesson and application drawn from the Bible takes second place to our personal response to Jesus Christ. Bible study and the accumulation of Bible knowledge profits us little if we are not brought face to face with our own need for salvation. All the applied principles will do us little good if we have never allowed God to give us spiritual birth!

---

the rules but missed the Savior. Entrenched in their own religious system, they refused to let the Son of God change their lives.

How foolish it would be if a doctor had the only cure for our fatal disease and was offering it free, and we decided to try every home remedy and self-help program we could find instead of making an appointment to be healed.

WHY PEOPLE REFUSE TO COME TO CHRIST
People do have reasons for rejecting Jesus. Their wrong attempts to justify themselves are often plain when they are willing to share their reasons.

- Life in Christ is *too demanding.* People think they have found an easier path. But have they?
- Life in Christ is *too humiliating.* People resist surrender to Jesus because they think it is the same as surrender to anyone else. But is it?
- Life in Christ is *too costly.* People value their power, position, or possessions too much to set them aside for Christ. But are these things really theirs?
- Life in Christ is *too disappointing.* Christ seems no different from the Christians who have been bad examples. But is the example of inadequate, failure-prone Christians an acceptable excuse before God?
- Life in Christ is *irrelevant.* It is about as significant as some people's dim memory of a visit to Sunday school or the latest talk-show discussion on religion. Is ignorance an adequate defense before God?
- Life in Christ is *for later.* Someday some people might get around to giving him serious consideration. But while they are pursuing "better things," their hearts and minds become insensitive. Will God wait forever until we are ready to listen?

5:41-43 **"I do not accept glory from human beings."**[NRSV] Just as Jesus did not receive (or need) the testimony from people (5:34), he does not need to receive praise from them.

"But I know you, that you do not have the love of God in you."[NKJV] Jesus knew the condition of the people; they did not really love God—they loved their religion. Therefore, they could not receive the Son of God.

"I have come in my Father's name, and you do not accept me."[NRSV] Jesus came as the Father's personal representative (see 14:7-11), but many of the Jews could not accept his claims of being the one sent by the Father.

THE CLAIMS OF CHRIST

Those who read the life of Christ are faced with one unavoidable question—was Jesus God? Part of any reasonable conclusion has to include the fact that he did claim to be God. We have no other choice but to agree or disagree with his claim. Eternal life is at stake in the choice.

Jesus claimed to be:	Matthew	Mark	Luke	John
the fulfillment of Old Testament prophecies	5:17; 14:33; 16:16-17; 26:31, 53-56; 27:43	14:21, 61-62	4:16-21; 7:18-23; 18:31; 22:37; 24:44	2:22; 5:45-47; 6:45; 7:40; 10:34-36; 13:18; 15:25; 20:9
the Son of Man	8:20; 12:8; 16:27; 19:28; 20:18-19; 24:27, 44; 25:31; 26:2, 45, 64	8:31, 38; 9:9; 10:45; 14:41	6:22; 7:33-34; 12:8; 17:22; 18:8, 31; 19:10; 21:36	1:51; 3:13-14; 6:27, 53; 12:23, 34
the Son of God	11:27; 14:33; 16:16-17; 27:43	3:11-12; 14:61-62	8:28; 10:22	1:18; 3:35-36; 5:18-26; 6:40; 10:36; 11:4; 17:1; 19:7
the Messiah/the Christ	23:9-10; 26:63-64	8:29-30	4:41; 23:1-2; 24:25-27	4:25-26; 10:24-25; 11:27
Teacher/Master	26:18			13:13-14
One with authority to forgive		2:1-12	7:48-49	
Lord		5:19		13:13-14; 20:28
Savior			19:10	3:17; 10:9

"If another comes in his own name, you will accept him."NRSV
Very likely Jesus was referring to other persons who claimed to
be the Messiah. Because they fit the mistaken image of what the
Messiah was supposed to accomplish (political liberation),
people eagerly received them. Many men made such a claim. For
example, in A.D. 132 Simeon ben Kosebah claimed to be the Messiah, and his claim was upheld by Akibah, the most eminent rabbi
of the day.

5:44 **"How can you believe if you accept praise from one another,
yet make no effort to obtain the praise that comes from the
only God?"**NIV This condemning word exposes why the Jewish
religious leaders could not believe: They were so dependent on
group acceptance that an individual could hardly make a stand
that differed from the rest. Instead of seeking what would honor
God and bring glory to him—which, in this case, would be to
believe in his Son—they continued to seek acceptance from their
peers.

STAMP OF APPROVAL
Whose approval do we seek? The religious leaders enjoyed
great prestige in Israel, but their stamp of approval meant nothing to Jesus. He was concerned about God's approval. This is
a good principle for us. Even if the highest officials in the world
approve of our actions but God does not, we should be concerned. But if God approves, even though others don't, we
should be content.

5:45 **"But do not think I will accuse you before the Father. Your
accuser is Moses, on whom your hopes are set."**NIV The verb
tenses here reveal that Jesus wouldn't have to go to the Father
and accuse these religious leaders because they were already
being accused by Moses. This could mean that Moses was in the
presence of God in heaven accusing them (Matthew 17:3), or it
could mean that *Moses* here stands for what Moses wrote, as is
indicated in the next two verses. To be told that Moses was accusing them was a great blow. The Pharisees prided themselves on
being the true followers of their ancestor Moses. They followed
every one of his laws to the letter and even added some of their
own. Jesus' warning that Moses was accusing them stung them to
fury.

5:46-47 **"If you believed Moses, you would believe me, for he wrote
about me. But since you do not believe what he wrote, how**

are you going to believe what I say?"[NIV] Moses had written about Christ (see Genesis 3:15; Numbers 21:9; 24:17; Deuteronomy 18:15-18; see also Luke 24:44), but since they did not believe in Christ when he came, they did not really believe in the writings of Moses. This was Jesus' final condemnation.

John 6

Once again in this Gospel, John selects a particular place for presenting a spiritual truth about Christ. Earlier, the well in Samaria was an excellent setting for Christ to teach about the fountain of living water. Here, in chapter 6, the multiplication of the loaves provides a way for Christ to present himself as the Bread of Life. This pattern parallels Jesus' point made in the last chapter when he emphasized that the Old Testament writers had foretold his coming. By readily using common places and events as examples of deeper truth, Jesus taught that the created order itself contains insights and lessons that point to him. The God who revealed himself in the Old Testament also left his fingerprints all over his creation (see Psalm 19:1-4; John 1:3-4, 9-10; Colossians 1:15-20; Hebrews 1:1-3).

This miracle was a significant turning point in the ministry of Jesus and is the only miracle recorded in all four Gospels. After this miracle and the teaching that flowed from it, many of those who had been following Jesus defected. It should also be said that some commentators see a connection between the Passover (mentioned in 6:4) and Jesus offering himself as the Bread of Life because the Passover symbolizes God's provision for life and salvation (see 1 Corinthians 5:7).

6:1 Some time after this.NIV John left unspecified how long this *some time* was (see also 5:1 and 7:1). According to the chronology that emerges when the Gospels are harmonized, the events during that time include:

- Jesus gives the Sermon on the Mount (Matthew 5–7)
- Jesus heals the Roman centurion's servant (Matthew 8:5-13; Luke 7:1-10)
- Jesus raises a widow's son to life (Luke 7:11-17)
- Jesus calms the storm (Matthew 8:23-27; Mark 4:35-41; Luke 8:22-25)
- Jesus sends demons into a herd of pigs (Matthew 8:28-34; Mark 5:1-20; Luke 8:26-39)

- Jesus heals a bleeding woman and restores a girl to life (Matthew 9:18-26; Mark 5:21-43; Luke 8:40-56)

- Jesus sends out the twelve disciples (Matthew 10:1-16; Mark 6:7-13; Luke 9:1-6)

- King Herod kills John the Baptist (Matthew 14:1-12; Mark 6:14-29; Luke 9:7-9)

Jesus crossed to the far shore of the Sea of Galilee.NIV This great body of water (which is actually a lake, thirteen miles by seven miles) was also given the name "the Sea of Tiberias" by Herod Antipas in honor of the Roman emperor Tiberias in A.D. 20.

6:2-3 A large crowd kept following him, because they saw the signs that he was doing for the sick.NRSV Even though John does not specify every act of healing, he tells us later in his Gospel that Jesus did "many other signs in the presence of his disciples, which are not written in this book" (20:30 NRSV). John chose to call the healings "signs" rather than "miracles" because, like signposts, they pointed people to the divine power behind the act— the power of God. John described certain of Jesus' many signs in his Gospel so that we, his readers, "may come to believe that Jesus is the Messiah, the Son of God, and that through believing . . . may have life in his name" (20:31 NRSV).

Jesus went up on a mountain (the Sea of Galilee is surrounded by hills) and sat down with his disciples—presumably for a time of teaching. Then **he looked up and saw a large crowd coming toward him.**NRSV The crowd had followed him even there. Though he was not always able to take time away from the crush of the crowd, Jesus regularly made the effort to do so. A popular following can tempt us to overextend ourselves; it should also warn us to set aside some time to be alone and reflect.

6:4 The Jewish Passover Feast was near.NIV John mentions three Passovers in this Gospel: the first in 2:13 (when Jesus was in Jerusalem), the second here (when Jesus remained in Galilee), and the third in 12:12 (when Jesus went to Jerusalem and was crucified shortly thereafter).

6:5-6 When Jesus looked up and saw a great crowd coming toward him, he said to Philip, "Where shall we buy bread for these people to eat?"NIV If anyone knew where to get food, Philip would because he was from Bethsaida, a town about nine miles away (1:44). Jesus was testing Philip to strengthen his faith. By asking for a human solution (knowing that there was none), Jesus highlighted the powerful and miraculous act that he was about to perform.

John clues us in: Jesus **asked this only to test him, for he
already had in mind what he was going to do.**[NIV] In usual use,
the word *test* (*peirazo*) has a neutral meaning. It refers to a proving experience like Jesus' testing in the wilderness or Abraham's
test over the sacrifice of Isaac. In all these cases, God allowed the
test to occur, not expecting failure, but placing the person in a situation where his or her faith might grow stronger. Jesus did not
want Philip to miss what he was about to do.

THE TEST
As he did with Philip, Jesus sometimes tests us by putting us in
difficult situations with no easy answers. At these times we feel
frustrated, as Philip did. However, frustration cannot be God's
intended result. The wise disciple always keeps the door open
for God to work. When the first or second look at a problem
yields no solution, do you trust God to work or assume it's
hopeless? Philip fell short because he allowed his thinking to
be limited by his own limited resources instead of seeking
God's limitless resources.

6:7-10 **"Eight months' wages would not buy enough bread for each
one to have a bite."**[NIV] This equivalent translation of Philip's literal "two hundred denarii" allows us to appreciate the expense
which would have been required to feed the crowd. A less-than-
literal translation in a place like this is sometimes chosen because
it does convey more clearly the intent of Philip's statement. *Eight
months' wages* communicates the need better than two hundred
of any currency that has been depreciated by inflation.

But, in fact, Philip did not really answer Jesus' question. The Lord
had asked him to consider the ways of supply ("Where shall we buy
bread?"), while Philip responded with what he perceived as the
larger problem—the *means* of supply. Perhaps knowing the area
gave him some idea where sufficient quantities of food might be purchased, but why send out buyers if they had no money?

IMPOSSIBLE IS NOT IN GOD'S VOCABULARY
When Jesus asked Philip where they could buy a great quantity
of bread, Philip started assessing the probable cost. Jesus
wanted to teach him that financial resources are not the most
important ones. We can limit what God does in us by assuming
what is and is not possible. Is there a seemingly impossible task
that you believe God wants you to do? Don't let your estimate of
what can and can't be done keep you from taking on the task.
God can do the miraculous; trust him to provide the resources.

At this point, Andrew (who is usually presented in the Gospels as Simon Peter's brother and takes a subordinate position to him) took advantage of an opportunity to join the discussion. Apparently a young boy who had overheard the conversation pulled out his lunch and made it available. Someone has said that the first miracle was that he hadn't eaten it yet! It was Andrew who inadvertently answered Jesus' original question. He pointed out that the only available food was the boy's lunch: **five small barley loaves and two small fish.**[NIV] (Barley loaves and fish were food for the poor.) Then Andrew adds the disclaimer: **"But how far will they go among so many?"**[NIV] Whether Andrew was speaking in humor or hyperbole we can't be sure, but we can be fairly certain that he did not expect what followed

---

LITTLE WAS ENOUGH
The disciples' skeptical reluctance contrasts with the youngster's willingness to share what he had. Others may have been withholding what they had. They certainly had more resources than the boy. But they knew they didn't have enough, so they didn't give anything at all. The boy gave what little he had, and it made all the difference. If we offer nothing to God, he will have nothing to use. But he can take what little we have and turn it into something great.

6:11-12 What was offered was enough for Jesus; he took the bread and fish, **and when he had given thanks, he distributed them . . . so also the fish, as much as they wanted.**[NRSV] The multitude numbered five thousand men, plus women and children (see Matthew 14:21).

MEALS AND MIRACLES
Thankfulness helps us appreciate both meals and miracles more fully. Jesus regularly gave thanks for food. The way in which he always paused to thank the Father made an indelible mark on the disciples. It was so characteristic of Jesus that even the two disciples with whom Jesus walked to Emmaus after the Resurrection recognized him when he gave thanks (Luke 24:30). How well are we recognized by our spiritual habits? When we give thanks for our meals we follow the example of Jesus Christ himself.

6:13 After all had eaten and were satisfied, they still had leftovers; the disciples **filled twelve baskets with the pieces of the five barley**

LEFTOVER LESSONS
We can learn from the leftovers. God gives in abundance. He takes whatever we offer him in time, ability, or resources and multiplies its effectiveness beyond our wildest expectations. If we take the first step in making ourselves available to God, he will show us how greatly we can be used to advance the work of his kingdom. Most of us want to see a great work of God, but can we take the first step of sacrifice?

loaves left over by those who had eaten.[NIV] This miracle and these leftovers reveal Jesus once again as the all-sufficient Lord. Our needs and problems are not obstacles to him, for his abundant power transcends any need or problem we place before him.

TAKING THE MIRACLE OUT OF A MIRACLE
Our "scientific age" tries to explain everything in materialistic terms. In one way the very possibility of miracles threatens a simplistic view of science. After all, if the laws of nature are not absolute, we might have to admit that something or someone out there controls the universe. Those who believe that miracles can't happen won't be objective in studying Scripture.
  Scientific materialism removes the miraculous from the miracles. It would explain this miracle meal by suggesting that the boy's generosity set in motion a wave of giving so that all the people brought out the food they had and shared it with each other. Such a view makes the "miracle" easier to swallow, but it downplays Jesus' miraculous power. The miracles, however, demonstrated the same power that raised Jesus from the dead. Those who find it difficult to accept these miracles usually find it difficult to believe in the Resurrection. When we accept the Resurrection, miracles like the multiplying of fish and loaves become part of a day's activity in the life of Jesus, the Son of God.

6:14 Then those men, when they had seen the sign that Jesus did, said, "This is truly the Prophet who is to come into the world."[NKJV] The people saw and filled their stomachs as a result of this sign—who could have missed it?—and this led them to believe that Jesus was *the Prophet* whom Moses had predicted (Deuteronomy 18:15-18). John does not say the people were wrong to think of Jesus as "the Prophet," but the next verse shows that they thought this Prophet should be a political leader. In this they were wrong.
  Elisha foreshadowed this Prophet (who was one and the same as the Messiah) to come. According to 2 Kings 4:42-44, Elisha

fed one hundred men with twenty loaves (a 5:1 ratio). But Jesus fed five thousand with five loaves (a 1000:1 ratio)! In Isaiah 25:6-9, the prophet said that the Messiah would prepare a great feast for all people, Jews and Gentiles. This miracle shows Jesus to be the Messiah.

6:15 Jesus, knowing that they intended to come and make him king by force, withdrew again to a mountain by himself.NIV During Jesus' ministry, nationalistic fervor was high; the people wanted a king, a leader who would free Israel from Rome. The people expected this of the coming Messiah-King. When Jesus realized their intentions, he left. Jesus' kingdom would not be an earthly one; his kingdom would not be established by a ground swell of popularity. This same opportunity for political power had already been offered to Jesus by Satan in the wilderness (Matthew 4:1-11). Jesus knew that the immediate opportunity was nothing compared to what God had planned. As the prophet Daniel foretold:

> ▪ *In my vision at night I looked, and there before me was one like a son of man, coming with the clouds of heaven. He approached the Ancient of Days and was led into his presence. He was given authority, glory and sovereign power; all peoples, nations and men of every language worshiped him. His dominion is an everlasting dominion that will not pass away, and his kingdom is one that will never be destroyed. (Daniel 7:13-14 NIV)*

JESUS WALKS ON WATER/6:16-21 / 97

Of the three Gospel accounts of this miracle, John's includes the fewest details. He understates the action, and apart from a brief mention of the disciples' fright, he makes little emphasis on this event. Matthew described Peter's walk on (then in) the water. Mark mentioned the difficulties being created by the wind and waves as well as the fact that when the disciples saw Jesus, he was passing by them. The focus of Matthew and Mark highlighted the miracle and its effects on those who participated in it; John included the miracle as yet another indication of the true identity of Jesus.

6:16-18 Jesus had gone up to a mountainside to be alone (6:15). The disciples went down from the hillside near Bethsaida **to the lake, where they got into a boat and set off across the lake for Capernaum,**NIV (see the map). Though it was late in the day, many of the disciples were experienced boatmen who would have felt comfortable sailing at night as well as in daylight. Jesus had called Peter to follow him after Peter and his partners had been out all night fishing (Luke 5:1-11).

This *lake*, the Sea of Galilee (or Sea of Tiberias, see 6:1), is very large. It is 650 feet below sea level, 150 feet deep, and surrounded by hills. These physical features make it subject to sudden wind-storms that cause extremely high waves. Sailors expected such storms on this lake, but the storms could still be very frightening. Such a sudden storm arose as the disciples were on their way to Capernaum: **the sea became rough because a strong wind was blowing.**NRSV

> That man is perfect in faith who can come to God in the utter dearth of his feelings and desires, without a glow or an aspiration, with the weight of low thoughts, failures, neglects, and wandering forgetfulness, and say to Him, "Thou art my refuge."
> *George Macdonald*

For those reading the Gospels with a Harmony of the Gospels, there may be some confusion about *where* the disciples were going. According to Matthew 14:22, Jesus told the disciples to get into a boat and go on ahead to "the other side." According to Mark 6:45, Jesus made the disci-ples board a boat while he dis-missed the crowds and told them to "go on ahead to the other side, to Bethsaida" (NRSV). According to Luke 9:10, Jesus and the disci-ples were in Bethsaida for the feeding of the five thousand. According to John 6:17, the disci-ples "set off across the lake for Capernaum" (NIV). One solution is that two communities were named Bethsaida. Luke 9:10 iden-tifies Bethsaida near Julias on the northeast side of the Sea of Gali-lee. In Mark 6:45-46, the name identifies a village near Caper-naum on the western shore.

Jesus Walks on the Water.
Jesus fed the five thousand on a hillside near the Sea of Galilee at Bethsaida. The disciples set out westward across the sea toward Capernaum. But they encoun-tered a storm—and Jesus came walking to them on the water! The boat landed at Gennesaret (Mark 6:53). From there they went back to Capernaum.

It was now dark, and Jesus had not yet come to them.NRSV John added the words *not yet come* for the sake of his readers, who already knew the story, and for the sake of specifying the time during the evening when the disciples encountered the storm. It was before Jesus had come to them, and it was "about the fourth watch of the night" (Mark 6:48 NIV) or between three and six in the morning.

LIGHT THINKING
Sadly, most of us quickly forget in the darkness what seemed so clear in the light. As the disciples continually learned, we depend on tangible evidence more than we ought. Our senses, though valuable gifts, have limitations. As soon as Jesus left his disciples, they forgot the amazing powers he had shown them so recently. But before we chide their lack of faith, we need to examine our own. How much of our spiritual life is a series of peak experiences of God's nearness followed by declines? When we can't *feel* God's presence, do we assume that he is not there and that he cannot help us? God's presence and help should come as a welcomed expectation, not a frightening surprise!

The Sea of Galilee is about seven miles across at its widest point, and the disciples were rowing the boat through rough waters that the wind had stirred up at the north end. They had recently encountered a bad storm in similar circumstances, except that at that time Jesus was in the boat with them (Mark 4:35-41). This time they noticed his absence.

6:19-21 They had gone **three or four miles.**NKJV According to Mark 6:45, it had taken the disciples all evening to row this short distance—evidently because the head wind was so strong. Suddenly, **they saw Jesus approaching the boat, walking on the water.**NIV Not only was Jesus walking on the water, he had walked a great distance over raging seas! Understandably, the disciples were terri-

EXPECTATIONS
Faith is a mind-set that *expects* God to act. When we act on this expectation, we can overcome our fears. Even after watching Jesus miraculously feed over five thousand people, the disciples still could not take the final step of faith and believe he was God's Son. If they had, they would not have been amazed that he could walk on water. They did not transfer the truth they already knew about him to their own lives. We read that Jesus walked on the water, and yet we often marvel that he is able to work in our lives. We must not only believe these miracles really occurred; we must also transfer the faith to our own life situations.

fied, but Jesus called over the wailing wind, **"It is I; do not be afraid."**NKJV The disciples, terrified, thought they were seeing a ghost (Mark 6:49). They were frightened—they didn't expect Jesus to come, and they weren't prepared for his help. The literal reading for "It is I" is "I am" (Greek, *ego eimi*); it is the same as saying "the I AM is here" or "I, Yahweh, am here."

John records a second miracle involved in this incident: **immediately the boat reached the shore where they were heading.**NIV Remember, the disciples were still far from the shore when Jesus met them. This miracle greatly strengthened the disciples' faith (see 6:66ff.).

STORMY WEATHER
When Jesus came to the disciples during a storm, walking on the water (three-and-a-half miles from shore), he told them not to be afraid. We often face spiritual and emotional storms and feel tossed about like a small boat on a big lake. In spite of terrifying circumstances, if we trust our lives to Christ for his safekeeping, he will give us peace in any storm.

JESUS IS THE TRUE BREAD FROM HEAVEN / 6:22-40 / **99**

The interaction occurring between Jesus and the crowd in Capernaum was strikingly similar to his conversation with the Samaritan woman at the well outside Sychar. To the Samaritan, Jesus introduced himself as the source of living water; to the crowd he identified himself as the living bread. As he had done before, Jesus used the immediate context of the miracle of the loaves and fish to point to his concern over the eternal welfare of his hearers.

As long as Jesus used his power to meet the felt needs of the crowd, they were happy to follow. They even made plans to crown him king. What better social program could be possible than miraculously feeding people every day! But that was not Jesus' purpose. The crowd quickly displayed their real allegiance by rejecting Jesus as soon as he would not do what they wanted.

6:22-25 To understand the action in these verses, we must back up and trace the movements of all the characters. Jesus performed the miracle of feeding the five thousand somewhere on the eastern shore of the Sea of Galilee (6:1). That evening, his disciples boarded a boat headed west toward Capernaum (6:17) without Jesus, who had gone up into a mountain to be alone (6:15). Then Jesus came to the disciples during the storm (6:21). So Jesus and the disciples arrived together at Capernaum (presumably before dawn).

Once the crowd realized that neither Jesus nor his disciples were there, they got into the boats and went to Capernaum in search of Jesus.NIV On the opposite shore, the crowd that had seen the disciples leave knew that Jesus hadn't gone with them and that the disciples had taken the only boat. The next morning they discovered that Jesus was gone, but they knew that he had not gone with the disciples. They assumed that he must have left to join his disciples. At some point during the day several boats arrived from Tiberias. Though it is not stated, the implication is that the crowd may have heard of Jesus' whereabouts from someone on the boats. So people from the crowd used those boats, which were probably going to head back across the sea toward Tiberias anyway, to cross to Capernaum to search for Jesus.

6:26-29 **"Very truly, I tell you, you are looking for me, not because you saw signs, but because you ate your fill of the loaves."**NRSV
The crowd, being satisfied once by what Jesus had done for them, wanted to see what else Jesus could do for them (maybe he'd provide more free meals?). But they did not realize what the miracle actually revealed to them. Even though they realized that perhaps Jesus was the Prophet (see 6:14), they were going to try to make him

> It is good to be weary and frustrated with the fruitless search for the good, so that one can reach out one's arms instead to the Redeemer.
> *Blaise Pascal*

king. Jesus refused to encourage them in their desire for the material satisfaction he could provide. His beginning response in effect was, "You were so intent on the loaves themselves that you haven't yet seen who made them." The people may not have known it, but their needs went much deeper. Jesus' signs were given to reveal that he could meet those deeper needs.

Thus, Jesus told them: **"Do not work for the food that perishes."**NRSV The bread that fills the stomach, whether produced by a miraculous sign or made at the bakery, is not spiritual or eternal. But there is another kind of food, **"food that endures for eternal life, which the Son of Man will give you."**NRSV Jesus was saying that the people should not be following him because he provided free bread, but because he provides spiritual "bread"—bread that can give them eternal life.

Jesus wanted the people to look to him as the one who could provide the food that endures to eternal life. He himself is that food. By coming to him and receiving him by faith they would

partake of the Bread of Life. This offer is the same as the offer of
living water to the Samaritan woman in chapter 4. Eternal life is
a gift; it cannot be earned, so Jesus said, "Do not work for it."
The only work to be done is to believe in Jesus.

"On him God the Father has placed his seal of approval."NIV
In those days a *seal* was a mark of ownership and authenticity.
The Son belonged to his Father; furthermore, Jesus was the
authentic Son of God—the giver of eternal life. The Father's seal
of approval was on him alone.

**Then they asked him, "What must we do to do the works God
requires?"**NIV The crowd missed Jesus' words about how he
would *give* the food that lasts for eternal life. Instead they
focused on his words about working, wanting to know what they
could do to carry out the works of God.

Jesus gave a straightforward answer: **"This is the work of
God, that you believe in Him whom He sent."**NKJV The only
"work" God requires from us is to believe in his Son. But for
some reason, we feel better somehow "earning" God's favor
rather than accepting it as a gift. But the *work* of trusting Christ is
not by works, but by faith!

THE WORK OF GOD
Many who sincerely seek God wonder what he wants them to
do. The religions of the world have many answers to this question, but Jesus' reply was brief and simple: Believe in him
whom God has sent. Satisfying God does not come from the
work we *do,* but from whom we *believe.* What does it mean to
believe? The first step is accepting Jesus' claim to be the Son
of God. We declare in prayer to Jesus, "You are the Christ, the
Son of the living God" (Matthew 16:16 NKJV). Accepting Jesus
means giving him control of every area of life. To believe
means to yield our wills, our desires, our plans, our strengths
and weaknesses to Christ's direction and safekeeping. It
means moment-by-moment obedience. Believing is a relationship with the one who promises to live within, trusting him to
guide and direct us to do his will.

6:30-31 Amazingly, the crowd then asked Jesus, **"What miraculous sign
then will you give that we may see it and believe you? What
will you do?"**NIV The crowd had just seen the miracle of the multiplication of the loaves, but they wanted more—not just one
day's supply of bread, but a guarantee of continuous supply.
Their argument was that their **ancestors ate the manna in the
wilderness**NRSV—which, of course, was available every day for

nearly forty years. And they cited their Scriptures, quoting from such verses as Exodus 16:4 and Psalm 78:24-25—**"He gave them bread from heaven to eat."**^{NKJV} A midrash (Jewish commentary) on Exodus 16:4 says that just as the former redeemer (Moses) caused manna to descend from heaven, so also the latter Redeemer will cause manna to descend. They expected this from Jesus if he was the Messiah.

6:32 **"It was not Moses who gave you the bread from heaven, but it is my Father who gives you the true bread from heaven."**^{NRSV} Moses hadn't performed the miracle, God had. And the God who gave the manna to the Israelites for forty years now gives the true bread out of heaven—Jesus. Just as the Israelites ate manna every day, so God provides the true bread for daily sustenance.

WHO IS THE SOURCE?
The Jews wanted to give Moses the credit for what God had done. Can the same kind of misunderstanding creep into our own thinking? For instance, when we speak about prayer, do we tend to take part of the credit for the work that God actually accomplishes? We hear statements such as, "She was sick, and we prayed and she was healed," or "The storm was approaching, but I prayed and it went around us." Our phrases may imply that the power was in the prayers rather than in God who hears and answers prayer. Prayer allows us to participate in God's work. We dare not get so involved in our experience of prayer that we neglect the source of our power. When prayers are answered, our attention must be on who answered rather than on who prayed.

6:33-35 **"For the bread of God is He who comes down from heaven and gives life to the world."**^{NKJV} The Jews wanted a daily supply of physical bread. God had given them his Son as the true heavenly bread to meet their daily spiritual needs. The present tense indicates the continual supply.

Unable to grasp that Jesus spoke about himself as the Bread of Life, the crowd said, **"From now on give us this bread."**^{NIV} Like the woman at the well who asked Jesus to give her the living water so she wouldn't be thirsty again and would never have to make any more long trips to the well, this crowd wanted what Jesus could give so their lives could be made easier. They missed the point. So Jesus told them directly,

"I am the bread of life."^{NKJV} If people wanted this bread, they must come to Jesus and believe in him. When Jesus used the words "I am," he was pointing to his unique, divine identity. In essence this statement says, "I the Lord God am here to provide you with everything you need for your spiritual life." Each of the "I am" statements (see chart on page 136) represent a particular aspect

> "I am the bread of life"—here is at the same time one of the greatest claims and one of the greatest offers of Jesus Christ. *William Barclay*

of this provision. For Jesus to say he is the Bread of Life is for him to say, "I am the sustenance of your life."

"He who comes to Me shall never hunger, and he who believes in Me shall never thirst."^{NKJV} Just as bread supplies our bodies with strength and nourishment, Jesus, the true bread from heaven, had come to strengthen and nourish his people—to change their lives, to bring spiritual and eternal life to all who would believe in him!

REAL SATISFACTION
Jesus offers the ultimate spiritual satisfaction: If we believe in him, we will never hunger or thirst. But we have heard the gospel wrong if we think Jesus offers an escape from life and its problems. Thousands of Christians still face physical hunger, and millions face crushing difficulties. The gospel frees us to face life. In the middle of the world's pessimism and despair, the gospel unflinchingly claims that Jesus offers infinitely more than this life can give. We will be disappointed if we expect the presence of Jesus in us to mean that we are immune to sin, struggles, and failures. There are many ways to know hunger and thirst, and we will undoubtedly experience many of them. One of Jesus' last statements was, "In the world you face persecution. But take courage; I have conquered the world!" (16:33 NRSV).

6:36 **"You have seen me and still you do not believe."**^{NIV} According to this reading (which is found in some manuscripts), this emphasizes that the crowds had seen *Jesus*, the very Bread of Life, standing before them, and yet they did not believe in him. Other manuscripts read, "You have seen and still you do not believe." This emphasizes that the crowds had seen the miracles Jesus did and still they did not believe. They had not only seen but eaten the multiplied bread and fish, but they resisted the necessary conclusion that he was divine.

Luke records Jesus telling the story of a poor man named Lazarus and how he begged for food outside the gate of a wealthy man's house (Luke 16:19-31). Lazarus's eternal reward was the company of Abraham, while the rich man found himself in hell. Eventually the rich man begged Abraham to send Lazarus back to warn his loved ones of their imminent fate. Abraham replied, "If they do not listen to Moses and the Prophets, they will not be convinced even if someone rises from the dead" (Luke 16:31 NIV). Jesus told the story to teach that miracles cannot overcome hardness of heart. Jesus offered plenty of evidence for those willing to believe.

6:37 **"All that the Father gives Me will come to Me."**^{NKJV} In the Greek, the words *all that* are neuter singular, indicating the total body of believers for all time. The Father gives this collective group to the Son (see also 17:2, 24). Only those selected by God can come to the Son and believe in him. God's Spirit enables them to come. All those who have been invited to come to Jesus and have done so can rest assured that God was at work in their lives.

"The one who comes to Me I will by no means cast out."^{NKJV} While the first part of this verse speaks of the collective group of believers, this second part speaks about the individual. God's Word assures us that Jesus will always welcome the sincere seeker, and the seeker who comes to believe will never be rejected (10:28-29).

OUR PLACE IN THE PLAN
The Father gives, the Son preserves, and we come. God's fore-knowledge is a part of his character that we must accept though we do not fully understand. We must ask ourselves: Am I one of those who has come to Christ? Whether or not we are among those whom the Father has given to the Son, or whether we are secure in Christ's protection, depends on how we answered the first question—have we come? When we come to Jesus, we find great assurance in his promise that we will never be rejected.

6:38 **"For I have come down from heaven, not to do My own will, but the will of Him who sent Me."**^{NKJV} Jesus did not work independently of God the Father, but in union with him. This should give us even more assurance of being welcomed into God's presence and being protected by him. All who respond positively to God's call can be assured of his protection (see 17:11). The protection covers them in this life and for eternity. Our spiritual hunger and thirst are satisfied in this life, and we know in the future that we will be raised from the dead to live with Jesus forever.

Yet the guarantee does not apply to superficial attachment. We must follow him wholeheartedly and commit our lives to him.

6:39 "And this is the will of him who sent me, that I should lose nothing of all that he has given me."[NRSV] As in verse 37, the Greek words for *all that* are neuter singular; they indicate the total collective entity of all believers. All those who are among this group of believers can be assured of God's promise of eternal life. Christ will not let his people be overcome by Satan. However, this commitment must not be superficial, as was the "commitment" of those disciples who turned away (see 6:66).

6:40 "All who see the Son and believe in him may have eternal life; and I will raise them up on the last day."[NRSV] While the NRSV translators chose *them* for the final phrase to indicate all believers (though the Greek word is *auton,* meaning "him"), the NIV preserves *him* because Jesus was emphasizing personal response and individual belief. The same pattern appears as in verse 37, which goes from the collective entity of believers to the individual believer. God values each person. Jesus demonstrated how valuable we are by his teaching: God sent the Son to earth; the Son came to earth; the Son promised to both preserve and to resurrect the ones he received from the Father.

THE JEWS DISAGREE THAT JESUS IS FROM HEAVEN/6:41-59 / **100**

Many of the crowd in Capernaum that day could not believe their ears. They knew this man's family, yet he claimed to be the Son of God. To them, Jesus' delusion seemed obvious. In their minds, Jesus was a local product with interesting powers and unusual authority, but was audacious when it came to speaking about himself. Jesus responded with uncompromising directness. He required then, as he requires now, an unconditional acceptance of his lordship. Any attempt to soften his claim amounts to rejection of his central message.

6:41-43 Then the Jews began to complain about him.[NRSV] When John says *Jews,* he is referring to the Jewish leaders who were hostile to Jesus, not to Jews in general. John himself was a Jew, and so was Jesus. The Jews in Jesus' audience hardly heard a word he said about selection, protection, and resurrection, for they were offended by his claim to be the bread that came down from heaven.

"I am the bread that came down from heaven."[NRSV] They said to one another, **"Is not this Jesus, the son of Joseph, whose**

JESUS SAID, "I AM"

In different settings, Jesus gave himself names that pointed to special roles he was ready to fulfill. Some of these refer back to the Old Testament promises of the Messiah. Others were ways to help people understand him.

Reference	Name	Significance
6:27	Son of Man	Jesus' favorite reference to himself. It emphasized his humanity, and it was another title for "the Messiah."
6:35	Bread of Life	Refers to his life-giving role—that he is the only source of eternal life.
8:12	Light of the World	Light is a symbol of spiritual truth. Jesus is the universal answer for people's need of spiritual truth.
10:7	Gate for the sheep	Jesus is the only way into God's kingdom.
10:11	Good Shepherd	Jesus appropriated the prophetic images of the Messiah pictured in the Old Testament. This is a claim to divinity, focusing on Jesus' love and guidance.
11:25	The Resurrection and the Life	Not only is Jesus the source of life, he is the power over death.
14:6	The Way, the Truth, and the Life	Jesus is the method, the message, and the meaning for all people. With this title he summarized his purpose in coming to earth.
15:1	The Vine	This title has an important second part, "you are the branches." As in so many of his other names, Jesus reminds us that just as branches gain life from the vine and cannot live apart from it, so we are completely dependent on Christ for spiritual life.

father and mother we know? How can he now say, 'I have come down from heaven'?"NRSV What they concluded was logical: "If we know this man's parents, how can he be from heaven?" But they *didn't* know Jesus' parentage. They missed what their own Scriptures had prophesied in Isaiah 7:14, "Therefore the Lord Himself will give you a sign: Behold, the virgin shall conceive and bear a Son, and shall call His name Immanuel" (NKJV).

Jesus had moved from Nazareth to Capernaum at the beginning of his ministry (see Matthew 4:13; Mark 1:21; John 2:12).

Most likely, his parents and siblings had gone with him. The Jews in Capernaum knew Jesus' parents, and therefore they thought they knew who Jesus was—the son of Joseph.

"Do not complain among yourselves."NIV

Jesus told the people to stop grumbling and complaining among themselves. Not one of them could know his true identity if the Father had not revealed it to him. Jesus relied on this revelation.

EXCUSE OR REASON
If we listen carefully, we will hear people admiring Jesus in some way while refusing to submit to him. They might say, "He's a great teacher, but I don't believe he's God." Some so-called Christians or a respected leader or minister may have let them down or even abused them in some way. Perhaps a parent modeled a contradictory message of religious superficiality alongside violent behavior. Pain creates very real obstacles. We must not deny the pain in ourselves or in others, but pain and disappointment must not keep people from Jesus. Beyond whatever obstacles come between us and Jesus, we must honestly ask, Is what happened an excuse to reject Jesus or a reason to run to him?

6:44-45 **"No one can come to me unless drawn by the Father who sent me; and I will raise that person up on the last day. It is written in the prophets, 'And they shall all be taught by God.' Everyone who has heard and learned from the Father comes to me."**NRSV A person cannot come to Jesus if he has not been drawn by the Father, taught by the Father, heard from the Father, and learned from the Father. God, not the person, plays the most active role in salvation. When someone chooses to believe in Jesus Christ as Savior, he or she does so only in response to the urging of God's Holy Spirit. Thus no one can believe in Jesus without God's help. If a person comes, the Father has drawn him or her.

When Jesus quoted from the prophets saying, *"They shall all be taught by God,"* he was alluding to an Old Testament view of the messianic kingdom where all people would be taught directly by God (Isaiah 54:13; Jeremiah 31:31-34). He was stressing the importance of not merely hearing, but learning. We are taught by God through the Bible, our experiences, the thoughts the Holy Spirit brings, and relationships with other Christians. Are you open to God's teaching?

6:46 **"No one has seen the Father except the one who is from God; only he has seen the Father."**ᴺᴵⱽ Jesus' previous statement about people being taught by God (and listening to and learning from the Father) does not mean that any mortal could actually see God the Father. *Only* Jesus has come from God's presence, and *only he* has seen the Father. This last statement in itself implies divine privileges—for no man has ever seen God (see 1:18; 1 Timothy 6:15-16).

6:47 **"Most assuredly, I say to you, he who believes in Me has everlasting life."**ᴺᴷᴶⱽ Jesus makes it plain that the believer has eternal life, starting now. *Believes* in these verses means "continues to believe." We do not believe merely once; we keep on believing in and trusting Jesus.

6:48 **"I am the bread of life."**ᴺᴷᴶⱽ This is one of Jesus' remarkable "I am" declarations (see the summary chart on page 136). No one else but Jesus is the Bread that gives eternal life.

6:49-50 **"Your ancestors ate the manna in the wilderness, and they died. This is the bread that comes down from heaven, so that one may eat of it and not die."**ᴺᴿˢⱽ The religious leaders frequently asked Jesus to prove to them why he was better than the prophets they already had. Earlier in this chapter (6:30-31), they had used Moses and the supply of manna in the wilderness as a standard for measuring Jesus. Jesus refused their challenge. *Manna* was a physical and temporal bread. The people ate it and were sustained for a day. But they had to get more bread every day, and this bread could not keep them from dying.

Without demeaning Moses' role, Jesus was presenting himself as the spiritual bread from heaven that satisfies completely and leads to eternal life. Again, the personal effectiveness of this Bread comes not from seeing it or from recognizing its heavenly origin, but from taking it in—eating it.

6:51 **"The bread that I will give for the life of the world is my flesh."**ᴺᴿˢⱽ To *give* of his *flesh* meant Jesus gave over his body to death on the cross, so that by his death the world could have life. To eat the living bread means to accept Christ into our lives and become united with him. We are united with Christ in two ways: (1) by believing in his death (the sacrifice of his flesh) and resurrection and (2) by devoting ourselves each day to living as he requires, depending on his teaching for guidance, and trusting in the Holy Spirit for power. Just as the Jews depended on bread for daily strength and relished it as a main part of their diet, so we should depend on and desire the living Christ in our daily lives.

6:52-53 **"Unless you eat the flesh of the Son of Man and drink his blood, you have no life in you."**ᴺᴵⱽ Instead of directly telling them how he could give them his flesh to eat (6:52), Jesus reemphasized the necessity of eating his flesh and—he here added—also drinking his blood. No one could receive his life until the giver died by shedding his own life's *blood.* Thus, Jesus wants us to accept, receive, even assimilate the significance of his death in order to receive eternal life. Christians do this frequently when they commemorate the Lord's Supper and take to heart Jesus' words, "Take, eat, this is my body . . . drink from it, all of you; for this is my blood of the covenant" (Matthew 26:26-28 ɴʀsⱽ). But Christians should not limit this to only the celebration of the Lord's Supper (or Eucharist); Christians can partake of Jesus anytime.

6:54-55 **"Those who eat my flesh and drink my blood have eternal life, and I will raise them up on the last day."**ᴺᴿsⱽ The person who feeds on Jesus' flesh (said to be the **true food,**ᴺᴿsⱽ and drinks his blood (said to be **true drink,**ᴺᴿsⱽ is one who accepts by faith Jesus' sacrificial death and thereby receives eternal life.

6:56 **"Those who eat my flesh and drink my blood abide in me, and I in them."**ᴺᴿsⱽ This is the first mention in this Gospel of "mutual indwelling" (that is, a simultaneous indwelling of two persons in each other, also known as "coinherence"). When we receive Jesus, he lives in us and we live in him.

6:57 **"Just as the living Father sent me and I live because of the Father, so the one who feeds on me will live because of me."**ᴺᴵⱽ Here Jesus pointed to his relationship with the Father as a model of the vital union he would share with each believer. As the Son depends upon the living Father for his life and lives *because of* the Father, so the believer who feeds on Jesus will live *because of* Jesus.

6:58 **"This is the bread that came down from heaven, not like that which your ancestors ate, and they died. But the one who eats this bread will live forever."**ᴺᴿsⱽ This verse summarizes the discourse and repeats the major points of Jesus' message. He again contrasted himself as the Bread that gives life with the manna that could not give eternal life to those Israelites who ate it.

6:59 **He said this while teaching in the synagogue in Capernaum.**ᴺᴵⱽ The Greek expression underlying *in the synagogue* is literally "in synagogue." The absence of the article in the Greek may indicate a gathering, not necessarily in the synagogue.

MANY DISCIPLES DESERT JESUS/6:60-71 / **101**

Those listening to Jesus were experiencing a crisis in their determination to follow him. Many of his actions thus far had been attractive, though sometimes curious. But all this talk of consuming his body and blood was difficult to stomach. Jesus' claims forced his followers to examine their real motives and the depth of their commitment.

A SAMPLING OF HARD SAYINGS

At least seventy hard sayings of Jesus have been identified in the Gospels. The following allow us to sense their impact on Jesus' followers, for they still challenge us. (All are quoted from NRSV.)

Reference	Saying
Matthew 5:22	"But I say to you that if you are angry with a brother or sister, you will be liable to judgment; and if you insult a brother or sister, you will be liable to the council; and if you say, 'You fool,' you will be liable to the hell of fire."
Matthew 5:29	"If your right eye causes you to sin, tear it out and throw it away; it is better for you to lose one of your members than for your whole body to be thrown into hell."
Mark 8:12	"He sighed deeply in his spirit and said, 'Why does this generation ask for a sign? Truly I tell you, no sign will be given to this generation.'"
Mark 9:1	"And he said to them, 'Truly I tell you, there are some standing here who will not taste death until they see that the kingdom of God has come with power.'"
Luke 12:10	"And everyone who speaks a word against the Son of Man will be forgiven; but whoever blasphemes against the Holy Spirit will not be forgiven."
Luke 14:26	"Whoever comes to me and does not hate father and mother, wife and children, brothers and sisters, yes, and even life itself, cannot be my disciple."
John 6:53	"Very truly, I tell you, unless you eat the flesh of the Son of Man and drink his blood, you have no life in you."

John made it clear that the problem of acceptance was among the disciples, not the Jewish leaders. He was warning later disciples against being superficial or shallow followers. At times the way may become difficult and confusing. When that happens, will we persevere or fall by the way?

6:60 When many of his disciples heard it, they said, "This teaching is difficult; who can accept it?"NRSV
At this time in Jesus' ministry, he had several followers who could loosely be called *his disciples* (see 4:1). These "disciples" were not the Twelve, and many of them would not receive his message.

> The Christian ideal has not been tried and found wanting. It has been found difficult, and left untried. *G. K. Chesterton*

HARSH WORDS
The motive behind Jesus' harsh words is not difficult to see—he wanted people to count the cost of following him (Luke 14:25-33). His words shocked and challenged. They were not comfortable half-truths, but hard-edged truth. Those who follow Jesus in hopes of feeling good always will be disappointed sooner or later. Only those who find in Jesus the rock-solid truth will be able to weather the difficulties of living in this fallen world. If our central motive for following Jesus isn't because he is *the Truth,* we too will be disappointed.

6:61 Jesus, knowing that his listeners were struggling, asked, **"Does this offend you?"**NKJV, or more literally, "Does this cause you to stumble?" (The Greek word *skandalizo* means "to ensnare, to trap, to cause to stumble"; it is often used in the New Testament to indicate a falling away into unbelief. See, for example, Matthew 13:21; 24:10; Mark 6:3; Romans 14:20-21.)

Earlier, in answering questions that John the Baptist had asked through messengers, Jesus made this pointed remark, "And blessed is he who keeps from stumbling over me" (Matthew 11:6 NASB). Jesus was keenly aware that those not ready to respond fully to him would stumble over him or be

> You may start out with Christ in the school of discipleship, but as the courses get harder, will you drop out? *Bruce B. Barton*

offended by him. Remember that it is possible to be offensive in the way we communicate the gospel, for which we would be at fault. But if we present Jesus lovingly and honestly, we must neither be shocked nor feel guilty if the Good News offends someone.

6:62 "Then what if you were to see the Son of Man ascending to where he was before?"NRSV They didn't believe that Jesus came down from heaven. If they saw him return and go back up to heaven, would they then believe? According to verse 65, they would not, for they were not true believers. Jesus had been purposely harsh so as to separate the true believers from those who were accompanying him for the wrong reasons. Some sought a new political party; others thought Jesus might lead a revolt against Rome; still others were simply fascinated with theological discussions. All of these thoughts were potential starting points of interest in Jesus, but they were not enough to make people real disciples.

6:63 **"The Spirit gives life; the flesh counts for nothing. The words I have spoken to you are spirit and they are life."**[NIV] This statement gives us the key to interpreting Jesus' discourse. His hearers had not understood the spiritual intent of his message. Some of them may have taken Jesus' words about eating his flesh literally; thus, Jesus' clarification, *the flesh counts for nothing*. This statement also applies to the correct mode of interpretation: A fleshly interpretation of his words would yield nothing; one must apply a spiritual interpretation to Spirit-inspired words.

> A woodenly literal, flesh-dominated manner of looking at Jesus' words will not yield the correct interpretation. That is granted only to the spiritual man, the Spirit-dominated man.
> *Leon Morris*

Jesus had used similar terms in defining the new birth to Nicodemus, "Flesh gives birth to flesh, but the Spirit gives birth to spirit" (3:6), making the point in both places that effort that begins with the desires and objectives of human wisdom cannot arrive at the kind of life that the "Spirit gives." Jesus' very words are spirit (*pneuma*) and life (*zoe*); therefore, we must depend on the life-giving Spirit to appropriate Jesus' words. Peter was one such believer who came to realize that Jesus had the words of eternal life (see 6:68).

6:64 **"But among you there are some who do not believe." For Jesus knew from the first who were the ones that did not believe.**[NRSV] From the beginning of his ministry Jesus knew that some of the ones following him were not believers in his true identity as the Son of God come from heaven.

Jesus also knew from the first **the one that would betray him.**[NRSV] This was Judas, the son of Simon Iscariot (6:70). For a moment, John interrupts with a brief word of explanation for his original readers and us. Jesus included Judas in every facet of his ministry, knowing all the time that he would not respond to the living truth. Jesus' treatment of Judas was consistent with his

own character, rather than according to what Judas deserved for
his unwillingness to believe.

**6:65 "For this reason I have told you that no one can come to me
unless it is granted by the Father."**NRSV This repeats (hence the
imperfect tense, "was saying") what Jesus had declared before
(see 6:44-45). The signs in themselves, no matter how remarkable, are not completely convincing. Some believe through seeing and others believe though not seeing, but all require God's
assistance (20:29).

**6:66 From this time many of his disciples turned back and no
longer followed him.**NIV Several followers decided to not follow
anymore. Within sight of the kingdom of heaven, privileged with
a taste of the Bread of Life, and watching the living water flow,
they nevertheless walked away. In a short sentence, John captured one of the saddest moments in the ministry of Jesus.

TEMPTED TO TURN
Why did Jesus' words cause many of his followers to desert
him?
■ They may have realized that he wasn't going to be the conquering Messiah-King they expected.
■ He refused to give in to their self-centered requests.
■ He emphasized faith, not deeds.
■ His teachings were difficult to accept, and some of his words
were offensive.
   As we grow in our faith, we may be tempted to turn away
because Jesus' lessons are difficult. When discouragement,
doubt, or confusion set in, will our response be to give up,
ignore certain teachings, or reject Christ? Instead, we must consistently ask God to show us what the teachings mean and
how they apply to our lives. We must then have the courage to
act on God's truth.

6:67 Jesus said to the twelve, "Do you also want to go away?"NKJV
According to the Greek, this question expects a negative answer.
Jesus knew their weaknesses and how little they really understood. He knew that one of them would not only go away, but
betray him also. Yet he also knew that God had chosen eleven to
believe in him.
   We can't stay on middle ground about Jesus. When he asked
the disciples if they would also leave, he was showing them that
he was not taking their faith for granted. Jesus never tried to repel
people with his teachings. He simply told the truth. The more the
people heard Jesus' real message, the more they divided into two

camps—the honest seekers wanting to understand more, and those rejecting Jesus because they didn't like what they heard.

6:68 Simon Peter answered Him, "Lord, to whom shall we go? You have the words of eternal life."[NKJV] After many of Jesus' followers had deserted him, he asked the twelve disciples if they also would leave. Peter replied, *"To whom shall we go?"* In his straightforward way, Peter answered for all of us—there is no other way. Though there are many philosophies and self-styled authorities, Jesus alone has the words of eternal life. People look everywhere for eternal life and miss Christ, the only source. There is nowhere else to go. The true disciples had found the only one who spoke the words that give eternal life.

THE SOURCE
Peter's declaration was a statement of faith, not a claim of complete understanding. He was convinced that when Jesus spoke, the truth about eternal life flowed in his words. Peter wanted what Jesus had to give. His simple affirmation presents us with two challenges:

1. Do we (or those people we would like to reach) really desire eternal life? For many, eternity is an unattractive subject. Life is going so well. Death and disease are usually distant and unreal. Relationships, pleasures, and possessions are too cherished to even think about forsaking. The fact that we will be dead infinitely longer than we have lived is denied for as long as possible.

2. Are we holding out for eternal life through another way? Some people avoid thinking about eternal life by denying its existence outright. In fact, many religious systems do not have a concept of eternal life. Those that do, make the requirements unclear or beyond attainment.

Jesus' words are the only source of eternal life: "I am the bread of life. . . . If anyone eats of this bread, he will live forever" (6:48, 51, NIV).

6:69 "We believe and know that you are the Holy One of God."[NIV] Peter's declaration parallels the one he made at Caesarea Philippi, but each of the synoptic Gospels gives a slightly different version of Peter's words (see Matthew 16:16; Mark 8:29; Luke 9:20). Peter was actually saying more than he knew. The descriptive words he blurted out to tell Jesus how he and the other disciples felt about him conveys both Peter's impulsive nature and his genuine impression of Christ. First, he called Jesus "Lord" (6:68). To this he added: (1) there's no one else like you; (2) you have the truth about eternal life; (3) we have believed; (4) we know that you are *the Holy One of God.* Peter was doing the best he could to describe Jesus in a category separate from anyone else who ever lived.

Like Peter's, our own understanding of Jesus must expand as we live for him. When we first believe in Jesus as Savior and Lord, our understanding will be real but limited. But as time passes, our awareness of the breadth and depth of Jesus' saving work and his lordship ought to grow.

6:70-71 **Jesus answered them, "Did I not choose you, the twelve, and one of you is a devil?" He spoke of Judas Iscariot, the son of Simon, for it was he who would betray Him.**[NKJV] Peter may have thought he was speaking for the Twelve, but not so. One among them—Judas Iscariot—was a *devil,* the traitor who would betray Jesus. According to 13:2 and 27, Satan put the idea into Judas's heart to betray Jesus and then entered Judas to instigate the actual betrayal. *Diabolos* (6:70) means "slanderous, devilish," and having Satan's nature and qualities. Judas gave in to evil thinking and came under the control of the devil.

John reminded his first readers about what was at stake. Almost every word of teaching uttered by Jesus was given in the context of intense spiritual drama. Heaven must have held its breath as humans tried to figure out Jesus' true identity.

HOW WILL YOU RESPOND?
In response to Jesus' message, some people left; others stayed and truly believed; and some, like Judas, stayed but tried to use Jesus for personal gain. Many people today turn away from Christ when they discern his real message. Others pretend to follow, going to church for status, approval of family and friends, or business contacts. We have only two choices for responding to Jesus—we either accept him or reject him. Have you accepted or rejected Christ?

John 7–8:11

From this chapter forward, John shows Jesus as the suffering Messiah—suffering the unbelief of his own family, the divided opinions of the crowd, and the persecution of the Jewish religious leaders in Jerusalem. Because John clearly stated his purpose for writing this Gospel (20:30-31), even the rejection of Jesus proves that "Jesus is the Christ, the Son of God, and that by believing you may have life in his name" (20:31 NIV). By portraying Jesus' rejection, John provided his first readers and us with a realistic picture of the costs of being a disciple. Those who followed did so knowingly and willingly. John encourages us to believe, to stand firm, and to resist being like those who opposed and doubted Jesus while he lived on earth.

In this chapter and that which follows, John turns our attention to the Feast of Tabernacles. During this festival the people commemorated God's provision (of water) for his people in the wilderness and presence among them (in the pillar of fire) by pouring out water on a rock and by lighting lamps. Jesus presents himself as the spiritual reality of both God's provision (the water out of the rock) and God's presence (in the light).

7:1 After this, Jesus went around in Galilee, purposely staying away from Judea because the Jews there were waiting to take his life.NIV Because the Jewish religious leaders in Jerusalem were seeking to kill him (see 5:18), Jesus stayed in Galilee for the next twelve months. He was not afraid of the Jewish leaders; rather, he knew that his time to die had not yet come (see 7:8). When God's intended time came, he would willingly give his life.

According to the synoptic Gospels, during this time Jesus ministered actively throughout Galilee (with Capernaum as his home base).

STAYING AWAY
Jesus was ready to die, but not to die prematurely before he carried out God's purposes on earth. Timing was important. Although Jesus knew his purpose was to give his life as a ransom for sinners, he did not wish to be careless or play into the hands of the religious authorities.

We may be tempted to think that our allegiance to God somehow makes us immune to danger, burnout, mistakes, and even gross sins. Many who have regarded themselves beyond temptation have failed miserably. We can keep from living recklessly by honoring God's timing in our lives. Sometimes obedience involves risk; sometimes it involves caution. We must determine to wholeheartedly cooperate with God's plans.

Therefore, we should not be driven by fear, impulsiveness, ignorance, or anxiety. Sometimes the wisest, most difficult action is the decision to wait for God's timing.

7:2 The Jewish Feast of Tabernacles was near.NIV The Feast of Tabernacles occurred about six months after the Passover celebration mentioned in 6:4. This feast commemorated the days when the Israelites wandered in the wilderness and lived in tents (Leviticus 23:43). Celebrated in the month of Tishri (September/October in our calendar), it marked the gathering of the autumn harvest including the grapes (see Exodus 23:16). During this time many Jews went to Jerusalem and built booths (or "tabernacles") in which they would live for a full week while enjoying the festivi-

EVENTS FROM JESUS' GALILEAN MINISTRY

Event	References
Jesus sent a demon out of a girl	*Matthew 15:21-28; Mark 7:24-30*
Jesus fed four thousand	*Matthew 15:32-39; Mark 8:1-9*
Religious leaders asked for a sign in the sky	*Matthew 16:1-4; Mark 8:10-12*
Jesus restored sight to a blind man	*Mark 8:22-26*
Jesus took Peter, James, and John to see his transfiguration	*Matthew 17:1-13; Mark 9:2-13; Luke 9:28-36*
Jesus healed a demon-possessed boy	*Matthew 17:14-21; Mark 9:14-29; Luke 9:37-43*
Jesus twice predicted his death	*Matthew 16:21-28; 17:22-23; Mark 8:31–9:1, 30-32; Luke 9:21-27, 44-45*
The disciples argued about who would be the greatest	*Matthew 18:1-6; Mark 9:33-37; Luke 9:46-48*

ties in the city (see Leviticus 23:33ff.). These simple dwellings helped the people remember their days of misery in the wilderness.

7:3-5 **His brothers said to him, "Leave here and go to Judea so that your disciples also may see the works you are doing; for no one who wants to be widely known acts in secret. If you do these things, show yourself to the world." (For not even his brothers believed in him.)**NRSV Jesus' brothers, the sons of Joseph and Mary, did not believe that their brother was the Messiah (see Mark 3:21, 31-35). Apparently, they did not become believers until after Jesus' resurrection. After his resurrection, Jesus appeared to his brother James (1 Corinthians 15:7), who believed and eventually became the leader of the church in Jerusalem (Acts 15:13) and the author of the book of James. The prayer meeting that followed Jesus' ascension included "Mary the mother of Jesus, as well as his brothers" (Acts 1:14 NRSV). Those brothers were James, Joseph, Simon, and Judas (Matthew 13:55). Judas (Jude) later wrote the book of Jude. Matthew writes that Jesus also had half sisters (Matthew 13:56).

FAMILY TIES
Jesus demonstrated courage with such consistency that at times we overlook it. He ignored the urging of his brothers to do something that would have been foolish. Among Jesus' teachings was the fact that real faith would divide families, and he experienced that truth firsthand. When those we love, whose approval we long to have, minimize or belittle our faith, we can recall Jesus' example. He relied on God's approval and timing, not on the expectations and demands of people around him.

Jesus' brothers' words mocked him. The *disciples* refers to the crowds who followed him, not the Twelve. Jesus' brothers scoffingly asked why he would remain in relative obscurity (in Galilee, at home with them) when he was trying to show *the world* he was the Messiah. They urged him to prove his identity by showing his wonderful works in Jerusalem, so that the world could see that Jesus was who he claimed to be. But because of their unbelief, they missed the point. The miracles had pictured Jesus' power and glory. He would reveal his true glory and power through his death and resurrection, and the time for that revelation was coming.

YOU HAVE NO EXCUSE
Jesus' brothers had a difficult time believing in him. Two would eventually become leaders in the church and New Testament letter writers (James and Jude). But for several years they were embarrassed by Jesus. After Jesus died and rose again, his brothers finally believed. Today we have every reason to believe, for we have the full record of Jesus' miracles, death, and resurrection. We also have the evidence of what the gospel has done in people's lives through the centuries. We simply can't afford to miss our opportunity to believe in God's Son.

7:6 "My time has not yet come."NKJV Usually Jesus speaks about "his hour" (*hora*) having not yet come (2:4; 7:30; 8:20 NKJV; here he speaks about his *time* or "opportune time" (*kairos*) having not yet come. The "hour" refers to the time of his crucifixion; the "opportune time" might also have referred to Jesus' ultimate goal, but only in a secondary way. Here, Jesus was simply indicating that the freedom to go up to Jerusalem had not yet come for him. As events unfolded, he did eventually go to the feast, but according to God's timetable.

> We must use the time which we have because even at best there is never enough. *Elton Trueblood*

"Your time is always here."NRSV Jesus told his brothers that they could use time as if it was theirs to squander, basing their decisions about time only on immediate opportunities, and showing no apparent desire to fit into God's plan. But Jesus' time belonged to the Father; he lived according to a different and predetermined schedule. The brothers could go to the feast whenever they chose or not go at all. But Jesus, whose every step on this earth had a purpose, would only act according to God's timetable. Whether he would go to this feast, and when he would go, would be determined by God alone, not by harassing relatives.

> If my private world is in order, it will be because I am convinced that the inner world of the spiritual must govern the outer world of activity. *Gordon MacDonald*

USING TIME
Many of us excuse our poor use of time by thinking that if we knew exactly what God wanted us to do, we would use our days more wisely. We need to ask ourselves, however, how well we have followed the many specific guidelines given in God's Word about the use of time (for example, Exodus 20:8-11; Ephesians 5:15-21; Philippians 4:4-9; Colossians 4:2, 5-6).

Perhaps God has withheld his guidance from us because we are unwilling to put into practice the directions he has already given.

7:7 "The world cannot hate you, but it hates me because I testify that what it does is evil."NIV The world at large hates Jesus because his testimony (as the Light of the World) exposes the world's evil (see 3:19-21). By *the world* John means this nonbelieving world's system of values and all those in it who have no love for or devotion to God. At this time Jesus' brothers were one with *the world* in not believing in Jesus; therefore, the world could not hate them. Rebellion loves company. People do not realize that indifference to Christ makes them partners with those who hate Christianity.

REJECTED
Whoever believes in Jesus must expect to be rejected and hated by the world (see 15:18-25). Because the world hated Jesus, we who follow him can expect that many people will hate us as well. They will consider our beliefs and life-style narrow-minded, intolerant, and prudish. We should not be surprised or embittered by the rejection of those still uncommitted to Christ. In fact, the way we accept rejection may be used by God to make a powerful impression on someone. If circumstances are going too well, we ought to ask whether or not we are following Christ as we should. We can be grateful when life goes well, but we must make sure we are not following Jesus halfheartedly or simply conforming to those around us. We must not compromise our faith in order to be accepted by our neighbors.

7:8 "I am not yet going up to this feast."NIV This reading is from the earliest manuscripts; however, other manuscripts read, "I am not going to this festival" (NRSV). Despite the early testimony for the inclusion of the word *yet,* most scholars consider the inclusion to be an addition made by scribes trying to clear the text of any contradiction (i.e., Jesus says he will not go to the feast, but then he goes—7:10). If the shorter wording "I am not going to this festival" is original, it very likely means: "I am not going up to the feast until the Father tells me to do so." (This interpretation is affirmed by the very next statement: **"for My time has not yet fully come."**NKJV) Or it could mean that Jesus was saying he did not want to go for public manifestation but that he would go as a private pilgrim.

Jesus would do nothing by coercion or persuasion of others. Whatever he did would be done for his Father's glory and on his Father's timetable. In this incident, Jesus' brothers seem to be trying to taunt him into proving he is the Messiah. But Jesus knew his mission. No one, not even his taunting brothers, would turn him away from what he had come to do and from the way he had chosen to do it.

7:9 He remained in Galilee.^{NRSV} True to his word, Jesus did not go up to Jerusalem when his brothers wanted him to. He stayed in Galilee until after they left.

JESUS TEACHES AT THE TEMPLE / 7:10-31 / *123*

Throughout this chapter John highlights the various opinions the Jews had about Jesus. Before Jesus appeared at the feast, opinions about him were swirling through the visiting crowd. Some of these Jews may have seen Jesus' miracles or heard him teach; others may have only heard of what he had done both in Jerusalem and in Galilee. That particular year, Jesus was the hot topic of conversation during the Feast of Tabernacles.

Meanwhile, Jesus was leaving Galilee for the last time. Events were moving rapidly toward "his hour," and he would have no further opportunities to travel back to the area where he had spent his childhood. This visit marked the third appearance of Jesus in Jerusalem during his ministry (2:13; 5:1).

VIEWS OF JESUS
John 7 could be titled "A Catalogue of Opinions about Jesus." Among the clearest opinions are that Jesus was:

View	Reference in John 7
A good man	*verse 12*
Deceiving the crowd into thinking he was the Messiah	*verse 12*
A great teacher	*verse 15*
Demon-possessed	*verse 20*
A doer of miraculous signs	*verse 31*
The Prophet	*verse 40*
The Messiah	*verse 41*

But the key question is, what do *you* believe about Jesus? It makes a difference, both now and for eternity.

KEEPING IT QUIET
Jesus came with the greatest gift ever offered, so why did he
act secretly? The religious leaders hated him, and many would
refuse his gift of salvation no matter what he said or did. The
more Jesus taught and worked publicly, the more those leaders
caused trouble for him and his followers. So it was necessary
for Jesus to teach and work as quietly as possible. He still had
many lessons to teach his inner circle of twelve disciples, and
much of this teaching needed to be done without the impact of
the crowds or the harassment of the authorities. Jesus' primary
objective was not to exclude the crowds, but to seclude himself
with those who were ready to move on in belief. The proclamation of the gospel is often a public effort; but training and discipleship progress more effectively in private.

7:10-12 After Jesus' mocking brothers left for the festival in Jerusalem,
Jesus **went also, not publicly, but in secret.**^{NIV} Jesus would not
go up to Jerusalem for the purpose of showing himself to be the
Christ (which was what his brothers had told him to do, see 7:3-
4). In fact, Jesus could not be found during the first few days of
the feast (see 7:11, 14).

In the events that follow, a lot happened behind the scenes. Not
only did Jesus travel to Jerusalem *in secret,* but intrigue and sub-
terfuge were at work everywhere. The crowds were buzzing with
opinions about Jesus, yet there was no clear consensus. The Jewish leaders were busily conferring and watching for the right time
to legitimately arrest him. The tension-laden atmosphere fostered
both excitement and treachery.

FREEDOM!
Today most of us can teach, preach, and worship publicly with
little persecution. But at times, these very freedoms can lull us
into complacency. Because we can practice religious freedom
whenever we desire, some of us never get around to doing it.
So our freedom means very little. In addition, our spiritual freedoms erode because our unfaithfulness and lack of diligence
have allowed generations to grow up without learning the rele-
vance of biblical truth, prayer, and personal integrity. We should
be grateful and make the most of our opportunities to proclaim
and practice the gospel while we have the freedom.

**7:13 But no one would say anything publicly about him for fear of
the Jews.**^{NIV} *The Jews* refers to the Jewish leaders in particular.
They had a great deal of power over the common people. Appar-

ently these leaders couldn't do much to Jesus at this time, but they threatened anyone who might publicly support him. They could use excommunication from the synagogue as a reprisal for believing in Jesus (9:22). Jews considered this a severe punishment. Jesus' listeners had their opinions but were afraid to express them: "The people were divided because of Jesus" (7:43 NIV). This created a power stalemate between the religious leaders and the crowds. Public opinion had not reacted strongly enough against Jesus to give the leaders a free hand in dealing with him; yet public opinion did not support Jesus enough to diminish the hopes the leaders had to eliminate him at the first opportunity.

SPEAK UP!
Everyone was talking about Jesus! But when it came time to speak up for him in public, no one said a word. All were afraid. Fear can stifle our witness. Although many people talk about Christ in church, when it comes to making a public statement about their faith, they are often embarrassed. Jesus said that he will acknowledge us before God if we acknowledge him before others (Matthew 10:32). Be courageous! Speak up for Christ!

7:14-15 Not until halfway through the Feast did Jesus go up to the temple courts and begin to teach. The Jews were amazed and asked, "How did this man get such learning without having studied?"NIV Halfway through the feast, Jesus came out from secrecy and began to teach in public, in the extremely visible outer court of the temple (indicated by the Greek word, *heiron;* see also 10:23). Jesus' delay in arriving and the crowd's divided opinion created an anticipation for his appearance and teaching. The atmosphere was tense and excitable.

When the Jews heard Jesus, they marveled at his ability to know "letters" (*grammata*), having never studied. They were not wondering about Jesus' ability to read or write; they were amazed that he could interpret the Scriptures without being trained as a rabbi. In other words, Jesus had no official human certification. He spoke with authority without relying on license or degree to legitimize his teaching. Jesus did not dress like a rabbi, but he applied the Scriptures as no rabbi they had ever heard. Matthew 7:29 reports the same amazement about Jesus. The religious leaders expressed similar surprise at the words of Peter and John in Acts 4:13, where Luke says they were called unschooled (*agrammatoi*) men.

We do not know the exact content of Jesus' public teaching during this period. Because the crowd did not react as they had in 6:60 and 66, we surmise that his teaching was probably more similar to the Sermon on the Mount (Matthew 5–7) than to his comments about himself recorded in chapter 6. Jesus may have told parables similar to those recorded in the other Gospels (Mark 4:1-34). Or he may have captivated the crowd with his prophetic statements about future events (Luke 21:5-38). From what follows this statement by John about the amazement of the crowd, we understand that the unrest among the people about Jesus' identity continued to develop. After the crowd's initial amazement, they grew restless over the issues of Jesus' identity and began to take sides.

7:16-18 **"My teaching is not mine but his who sent me."**[NRSV] Jesus' teaching was authoritative because it originated from God, not from himself. Those who knew God and sought to do his will would **know whether the teaching is from God**[NRSV] or was his own. Unlike those who **speak on their own [to] seek their own glory,**[NRSV] Jesus sought **the honor of the one who sent him.**[NIV] Jesus determined to bring God's message of salvation to humanity and thereby to bring him glory. Therefore, Jesus could rightfully claim about himself that **he . . . is a man of truth; there is nothing false about him.**[NIV] And only those who want to do God's will can recognize Jesus for who he is—God's Son.

> You can never please God without faith, without depending on him. Anyone who wants to come to God must believe that there is a God and that he rewards those who sincerely look for him. *Author of Hebrews*

TELLTALE SIGNS OF GLORY-SEEKING TEACHERS
- They insist on using their titles and credentials.
- They are preoccupied with their relative position in the program or breaches in protocol.
- They take the credit for success rather than giving it to God.
- They habitually take more than the allotted time to speak.
See 2 Corinthians 10:13-18

Jesus did not sweep away (nor did John) the need for objective evidence. Faith cannot be reduced to a mindless commitment with no basis in reality. Jesus was saying that those who examine his teaching or the signs that accompanied his ministry must be open-minded and desire to respond to God's will once it is known. Some people who demand more evidence may be covering up their refusal to submit to God. Every believer who desires to know God's will must seek it with the intention of obeying it once it has been found. Jesus firmly challenged all those who considered themselves superior to God's revealed truth or who declared themselves free to pick and choose what they wished to accept.

SPOT THE FAKE
Those who seek to know God's will and do it will be guided by the Holy Spirit to realize that Jesus told the truth about himself (14:15-21). We can test religious speakers:

- Their words should agree with, not contradict, the Bible in its entirety.
- Their words should glorify God and his will, not themselves.
- If their words are true, we will realize more deeply all that Jesus has done for us.
- Their message should not only challenge our present way of living but also show us in the light of the Bible what corrections need to be made.

7:19 **"Did not Moses give you the law? Yet none of you keeps the law. Why are you looking for an opportunity to kill me?"**[NRSV] Beginning with verse 19, Jesus alluded to the debate he had with the Jews during his last visit to Jerusalem (see 5:18ff.). Because Jesus had healed a man on the Sabbath and then directly implied his equality with God, his Father, the Jewish religious leaders wanted to kill him for Sabbath-breaking and blasphemy. The Pharisees tried to achieve holiness by meticulously keeping the rules that they had added to God's laws. Jesus' accusation that they didn't keep Moses' laws stung them deeply. In spite of their pompous pride in their accomplishments and their rules, they did not measure up, for they were living far below what the law of Moses required. By enforcing their own laws regarding Sabbath-breaking and blasphemy, they were about to break one of the Ten Commandments: "You shall not murder" (Exodus 20:13). But they didn't see this error; they so hated Jesus that they were blind to their own sin.

7:20 **"You are demon-possessed.... Who is trying to kill you?"**[NIV] In response to Jesus' charge that they were trying to kill him, the people responded with an accusation of their own and a question. We cannot know how widely spread the plot against Jesus was. But verse 25 records the fact that a certain "they" were trying to kill him, and their intentions were widely known. At this point, the crowd wanted to know whether Jesus could identify the

people behind the plot. But this crowd also blasphemed against
Jesus by charging him with being demon-possessed. Mark
records an earlier incident (Mark 3:22-30) when a similar charge
was leveled against Jesus. It was a particularly effective tactic on
the part of the religious leaders to admit the spirituality of Jesus,
but then define it as evil. This time Jesus did not even bother
refuting the obvious dishonesty of the allegations.

7:21-24 **"I did one miracle."**NIV Because Jesus was in Jerusalem, he most
likely was referring back to the miracle in 5:1-15—the healing of
the paralyzed man. Jesus mentioned that he had healed on the
Sabbath, the point of contention surrounding the miracle. Jesus
reminded the people again that their spiritual priorities were
wrong.

"You circumcise a child on the Sabbath."NIV Jesus noted that,
according to Moses' law, circumcision was to be performed eight
days after a baby's birth (Genesis 17:9-14; Leviticus 12:3). This
rite demonstrated the Jews' identity as part of God's covenant
people. If the eighth day after birth fell on a Sabbath, they still
performed the circumcision (even though it was considered
work). By referring to the patriarchs performing circumcision,
Jesus was pointing to an authority and principle prior to Moses.
By healing the whole person, Jesus demonstrated that his creative
power was equal to God's and superior to Moses'. John
explained Moses' proper relationship to Jesus. While the religious leaders allowed certain exceptions to Sabbath laws, they
allowed none to Jesus, who simply showed mercy to those who
needed healing. He demonstrated from their own practices that
they would overrule a law when two ceremonial laws came into
conflict. But the Jewish leaders were so engrossed with their regulations about Sabbath-keeping that they failed to see the true
intent of Jesus' actions. They judged his actions **by mere
appearances**NIV and failed to **make a right judgment.**NIV Their
superficial but tenacious adherence to their own traditions would
cause them to miss the Messiah, to whom their Scriptures pointed.

At first sight, it may appear that Jesus' words in verse 24 contradict his teaching in Matthew 7:1. Upon careful reflection, however, we find consistency. In the sermon beginning in Matthew
7:1 ("Do not judge, or you too will be judged," NIV), Jesus
preached against judgmentalism, the act of condemning others by
comparing them to our own "superior" behavior. Such self-righteousness would not fit with kingdom values. This teaching con-
demns false judgment based on outward appearances (superficial,

physical interpretations). Right judgment demands moral and biblical discernment in order to make a wise choice.

7:25-27 **Some of the people of Jerusalem**[NIV] had heard that the religious rulers were **trying to kill**[NIV] Jesus. But since he was speaking openly and none of the rulers attempted to stop him, they wondered if the rulers had reconsidered and had recognized that Jesus was the Christ: **"Can it be that the authorities really know that this is the Messiah?"**[NRSV] Perhaps the authorities had changed their minds about Jesus. But this seemed improbable to the crowds because even they could think of some objections.

Their reasoning? **"We know where this man is from; but when the Messiah comes, no one will know where he is from."**[NRSV] The people thought they knew where Jesus came from—Nazareth of Galilee. They saw him as a man, a neighbor, a carpenter, but they did not have a close relationship with him. They did not know that he had come from God and had been born of a virgin, heralded by angels, recognized as divine by shepherds and then by wise men from the East, and greeted joyfully as the Messiah by two aged prophets (Luke 2). Anyone who tries to dismiss Jesus as just a human being misses the point of his coming to earth and loses the forgiveness, peace, and eternal life Jesus offers.

Instead, the people were convinced that no one was supposed to know where the Messiah came from. There was a popular tradition that the Messiah would simply appear. It was just as mistaken as the belief that the Christ would be a military/political leader who would restore Israel's greatness. Those who believed this tradition were ignoring the Scriptures that clearly predicted the Messiah's birthplace (Micah 5:2). The popular tradition about the origin and appearance of the Messiah probably came from what is recorded in 1 Enoch 48:6; 4 Ezra 13:1ff., books that were not included in our Bibles because they were not considered authoritative (however, they were valued for personal study).

7:28-31 Knowing that the people did not believe in him, Jesus said: **"Yes, you know me, and you know where I am from."**[NIV] Some versions render this sentence as a question rather than a statement. The people did indeed know where he was from geographically (he grew up in Galilee), but they really did not know because, as Jesus went on to say: **"I have not come on my own. But the one who sent me is true, and you do not know him. I know him, because I am from him, and he sent me."**[NRSV] Jesus was declaring his divine origin and divine commission. From Jesus' proclamation we can gather that it is important to know, not from *where*

Jesus came, but *from whom* he came. To recognize this origin
requires revelation. But the people did not know Jesus because
they did not know the one who sent him.

**At this they tried to seize him, but no one laid a hand on
him.**NIV This was the first spontaneous attempt to restrain Jesus. A
little later there was an official attempt described in verse 32. But
Jesus could not be detained, for **His hour had not yet come.**NKJV
The verse between the two attempted arrests says, **Yet many in
the crowd believed in him.**NRSV There was turmoil in the crowd
about Jesus' true identity. People were taking sides. Some people
believed and others did not. For a while there had been general
confusion. But the confusion was resolving into belief and unbelief. Those who believed Jesus concluded that he had presented
the true credentials of the Messiah.

IN THE MIDDLE
Many consider neutrality to be a sign of maturity and objectivity.
Maintaining a neutral position toward Christ may be popular,
but it is dangerous. People stay undecided about Jesus under
the pretense of not wanting to make a hasty or wrong judgment. But Jesus never allowed indecision. He confronted men
and women with the unavoidable choice of belief or unbelief.
Today those who remain undecided must understand that they
remain, by that choice, in opposition to Christ.

RELIGIOUS LEADERS ATTEMPT TO ARREST JESUS/7:32-52 / **124**

With emotions at a fever pitch, the Pharisees thought they finally
had enough popular support for an open move against Jesus. But
they had miscalculated the division of the crowd and the impression Jesus would make on the guards sent to arrest him. One
clear example of the depth of the division about Jesus is shown
by the mention of Nicodemus, who offered at least a voice of reason to the Pharisees. His words were drowned in a chorus of prejudice.

Meanwhile, Jesus again referred to himself as the source of living water. John explained the promise as a prediction of the giving of the Spirit. It is apparent from the guards' response that
Jesus' words revealed a deep spiritual thirst in many people.
Those who were sent to imprison Jesus were themselves captivated by what he said.

7:32-34 Aware that the Jewish religious leaders were seeking to kill him, Jesus alluded to his coming death: **"I will be with you a little while longer, and then I am going to him who sent me."**ᴺᴿˢⱽ No one would be taking Jesus' life from him; rather, he would depart this life according to the preordained time and then return to his Father. Jesus' statement also served as a calm warning to those who were plotting against him that their efforts would only succeed subject to God's plan. At that time, says Jesus, **"You will look for me, but you will not find me; and where I am, you cannot come."**ᴺᴵⱽ Another way to say this is, "You will seek me and not find me because your unbelief has rendered you unable to understand where I am." Even after Jesus (the true Messiah) left, the Jews would continue to seek for the coming of the Messiah but would never find him—because he had already come!

> Life without Jesus is like a dry garden baking in the sun. It is foolish to want anything that conflicts with Jesus. What can the world give you without Jesus? His absence is hell; his presence, paradise.
> *Augustine*

In Luke 17:22, Jesus said, "The days are coming when you will long to see one of the days of the Son of Man, and you will not see it" (NRSV). The Jews who rejected Jesus would want those days back again, but the opportunity for repentance would be past.

7:35-36 The Jews, not understanding that Jesus' statement referred to his death, wondered if he was speaking about going to **our people . . . scattered among the Greeks**ᴺᴵⱽ (also called "the Dispersion," NRSV, NKJV), where he would also **teach the Greeks.**ᴺᴵⱽ The Dispersion or *Diaspora* is a technical term referring to the large number of Jews who were "dispersed" (or scattered) throughout the Roman Empire and beyond. Some of the Jews were dispersed among the Greeks. The Jews listening to Jesus

---

EVEN TO US
The mention of Greeks in this passage ought to catch the attention of those who are not Jewish. John's readers appreciated the startling and hopeful nature of Jesus' words. To appreciate the impact, we must remember that the Jewish people perceived anyone who was non-Jewish as totally isolated from God. They regarded the Greeks or Gentiles as pagans and infidels, cut off from God, without hope. But Jesus' message promises rivers of living water to "anyone" who is thirsty. If we have believed in Jesus, we have discovered that God's grace extended even to us!

---

wondered if he was about to depart Judea and go to these Jews. Their comment seems to imply that some of the Greeks themselves might be taught if Jesus were to try to work among the scattered Jews.

7:37-39 On the last and greatest day of the Feast.^{NIV} This occurred on the eighth day, the climax of the festive occasion. During the Feast of Tabernacles, the Jews celebrated the memory of how God protected their ancestors in their travels across the wilderness to the Promised Land, guiding them on their way and providing them with manna and, on one occasion, water from a rock (see Exodus 17:1-7).

On the first day of this feast, a priest read Zechariah 14:8: "On that day living water will flow out from Jerusalem" (NIV). Every day during this feast, except for the last day, a priest stood in front of the temple with a golden pitcher of water and poured the water on a rock. This commemorated the water flowing out of the rock that gave the Israelites water to drink. While the water flowed out, the people standing by chanted, "With joy you will draw water from the wells of salvation" (Isaiah 12:3 NIV). They performed this ceremony each day of the feast except the eighth, when they offered public prayers for continued rain.

The Jews felt it was necessary to pray for rain on the last day of the feast. Doing so diverted attention from their yet unfulfilled need for living water. It was as if, on the eighth day, everyone shrugged their shoulders and settled for the immediate need for rain rather than stating their need for living water. The promise still remained: No one could really take a drink; consequently, the people were still thirsty. Thus, on *the last and greatest day of the Feast*, the day when the water was *not* poured out, Jesus stood and said in a loud voice, **"If anyone thirsts, let him come to Me and drink. He who believes in Me, as the Scripture has said, out of his heart will flow rivers of living water."**^{NKJV} Jesus' words, *"Come to Me and drink,"* allude to the theme of many Bible passages that talk about the Messiah's life-giving blessings (Isaiah 12:2-3; 44:3-4; 58:11). By promising to give the Holy Spirit to all who believed, Jesus was claiming to be the Messiah, for that was something only the Messiah could do.

There is no particular verse in the Old Testament that exactly says "out of his innermost being [literally, the belly] will flow rivers of living water." Jesus was either paraphrasing a verse like Psalm 78:16 ("He brought streams out of a rocky crag and made water flow down like rivers," NIV) or a verse like Isaiah 58:11 ("You will be like a well-watered garden, like a spring whose waters never fail," NIV). The Psalm 78 passage bears the closest meaning to what Jesus said and affirms that he referred to himself as "the smitten Rock."

Jesus became the true smitten Rock by being crucified on the cross and giving forth the life-giving water. Even prior to his crucifixion, Jesus suffered the blows of persecution, insult, and unbelief. He did not retreat or withdraw in the face of suffering; rather, he took the smiting as a chance to let the living waters flow and give life to others. Our response should be to believe in Jesus so that he might give us the living water of the Holy Spirit, flowing in us and over us.

WELL-WATERED
Those listening to Jesus' words knew the importance of water. They knew, as we do, that water is essential for life and crops. Yet they did not take water for granted. Such a rare, precious commodity made an effective symbol.

All the water anyone used in their homes had to be carried from nearby springs or wells. People handled water carefully and conserved it. Because much of the country was arid, the survival of the crops was determined by rain. Late rains could cause the planted seeds not to germinate. In the cultivation of grapes, for instance, the vines require at least one hundred gallons of water in order to produce one gallon of wine.

Symbolically, water came to represent the people's deliverance in the wilderness when they were actually dying of thirst. Jesus' claims reflect both the availability and the abundance of God's provision. He promised rivers of living water and bread from heaven so that thirst and hunger would be no more.

It is pitiful not to recognize the abundance we have in Christ. We do this when

- we discount his blessings instead of depending on Christ's constant provision,
- we foolishly crave what we do not need instead of trusting Christ to determine what we really need,
- we lean on the comforts of this life and our personal gratification instead of looking to the eternal destiny that Christ has promised.

After recording Jesus' declaration in verses 37-38, John provided an explanatory note: **By this he meant the Spirit, whom those who believed in him were later to receive. Up to that time the Spirit had not been given, since Jesus had not yet been glorified.**[NIV] John explained to his readers that by "living water" Jesus meant the Holy Spirit. Everyone who believes in Jesus receives the Holy Spirit—although at that time, the Holy Spirit had not yet been given to all believers. That happened after

Jesus' resurrection and ascension (see 16:7-16). The availability of the Spirit is linked with the glorification of Jesus, for it was after Jesus' glorification through death and resurrection that the Spirit became available to believers (see 20:22).

7:40-44 Jesus' exclamatory invitation generated faith in some of the hearers. Some said, **"Surely this man is the Prophet"**NIV (meaning the Prophet predicted by Moses in Deuteronomy 18:15-18); others said, **"He is the Christ."**NIV But others could not believe. They were convinced that the Messiah would not come from Galilee. They argued, **"Does not the Scripture say that the Christ will come from David's family and from Bethlehem, the town where David lived?"**NIV These unbelievers correctly asserted that the Messiah, as David's offspring, should come from Bethlehem (see Psalm 89:3-4; 132:11; Isaiah 9:6-7; 11:1; Micah 5:2). And, in fact, Jesus was David's son (see Matthew 1:1-18; Romans 1:3-4) born in Bethlehem (see Matthew 2:1-6; Luke 2:1-11). But soon after his birth, Jesus' parents took him to Egypt to protect his life. Later they brought him to Nazareth of Galilee (the hometown of Joseph and Mary), where he grew up (see Matthew 2:13-23). Thereafter he was identified as a Galilean and a Nazarene, not a Judean or a Bethlehemite. However, Jesus never once tried to explain that his birthplace was Bethlehem. Instead, he always pointed to his divine, heavenly origin. If a person knew God, he would know that Jesus was the Christ.

> Their testimony [that of the officers who went to arrest Jesus] was expressed in few and simple words, but it has stood the test of nineteen centuries. *F. F. Bruce*

As the crowd argued about Jesus' identity, **some wanted to seize him, but no one laid a hand on him**NIV because, as it is says in verse 30, "His hour had not yet come" (NKJV).

GET OFF THE FENCE
There can be no fence sitting when it comes to deciding about Jesus Christ. By this point in the Gospel of John, it is already clear that picking and choosing what we like from the teachings and life of Jesus is unacceptable. If belief in Christ does not include his divine identity and his "hard teachings," it isn't really belief in him as he defined it. We must remember that claiming to accept the *teachings* of Christ includes accepting what he taught about himself. Jesus did not welcome fence sitting. Have you decided to follow or reject Christ as Lord?

7:45-49 The **temple guards**^{NIV} were very likely temple police under the jurisdiction of the Jewish religious rulers, not the Romans. Some of the Levites were probably assigned this duty. Although the Romans ruled Palestine, they gave the Jewish religious leaders authority over minor civil and religious affairs. The religious leaders supervised their own temple guards and gave the officers power to arrest anyone causing a disturbance or breaking any of their ceremonial laws. Because these leaders had developed hundreds of trivial rules, it was almost impossible for anyone, even the leaders themselves, not to break, neglect, or ignore at least a few of them some of the time. But these temple guards couldn't find one reason to arrest Jesus. And as they listened to Jesus to try to find evidence, they couldn't help but hear his wonderful words.

Although sent by **the chief priests and Pharisees**^{NIV} with specific orders to arrest Jesus, the guards returned empty-handed. When asked why they did not bring Jesus, they said, **"No man ever spoke like this Man!"**^{NKJV} When the officers heard Jesus, they recognized that they were listening to a man like no other, for, in fact, they were listening to the Son of God (see Matthew 7:29; Luke 4:22).

CAPTIVATED CAPTORS
Perhaps, until now, these temple guards had been protected by their duties from coming face to face with Jesus and hearing his teachings. But here they found themselves exposed. Being confronted directly with the character and words of Jesus always makes a greater impact than we may imagine. God doesn't limit his life-giving insights to the academically trained or the socially elite. Meeting and observing Jesus led these simple men to give a ringing testimony to Jesus among those who hated him. Our task is to present Christ so that others may see him in action and hear his remarkable testimony.

But the Pharisees rejected this simple testimony. They asked these officers, whose job was simply to carry out orders, if they, like the crowd, were **also deceived**^{NKJV} into believing that Jesus was the Messiah. If Jesus really were, they argued, at least some of the religious rulers would believe in him: **"Has any of the rulers or of the Pharisees believed in him? No!"**^{NIV} And since none of them did (supposedly—even if one of them did, like Nicodemus, he would be afraid to say so), then this man could not be the Messiah. Maybe the crowd believed in him, but the crowd **does not know the law**^{NKJV} (the Scriptures); therefore, they are

accursed[NKJV] for their ignorance (see Deuteronomy 28:15). But in judging the people for their supposed ignorance, they were judging themselves, for they were ignorant of God and did not know the one he sent.

7:50-52 Nicodemus, who had gone to Jesus earlier and who was one of their own number (see 3:1-21), asked, **"Our law does not judge people without first giving them a hearing to find out what they are doing, does it?"**[NRSV] Nicodemus attempted to make his fellow Pharisees adhere to the law they claimed to know (7:49) and to act fairly and justly. An accused person, according to Deuteronomy 1:16, must first be heard before being judged.

This passage offers additional insight into Nicodemus, the Pharisee who visited Jesus at night (chapter 3). Apparently Nicodemus had become a secret believer (see 12:42). Since most of the Pharisees hated Jesus and wanted to kill him, Nicodemus risked his reputation and high position when he spoke up for Jesus. His statement was bold, and the Pharisees immediately became suspicious. After Jesus' death, Nicodemus brought spices for his body (19:39). That is the last time Nicodemus is mentioned in Scripture.

But these Pharisees would not listen even to one of their own. The depth of their real allegiance to the law became clear when their position was threatened by the truth. They retorted sarcastically, **"Are you from Galilee, too? Look into it, and you will find that a prophet does not come out of Galilee."**[NIV] The Pharisees and religious rulers were confident that they could reject Jesus as having any claim as the Messiah because of his Galilean origin. To their way of thinking, the Scriptures never spoke of a prophet—much less the Christ—coming from Galilee. But they were wrong on three counts:

(1) Jesus *was* born in Bethlehem, the city of David (Luke 2:4-11; also Micah 5:2).

(2) The Scriptures *do* speak of the Messiah (called "Wonderful, Counselor, Mighty God, Everlasting Father, Prince of Peace"—Isaiah 9:6 NKJV) as a "great light" for Galilee. Isaiah said, "The land of Zebulun and the land of Naphtali . . . in Galilee of the Gentiles. The people who walked in darkness have seen a great light" (Isaiah 9:1-2 NKJV see also Matthew 4:13-16).

(3) Jonah (2 Kings 14:25) and Elijah (1 Kings 17:1) came from this region.

But they referred to the prophet of Deuteronomy 18:15. They were proud and certain that he would come from their territory, Judea.

Nicodemus tactfully confronted the Pharisees with their failure to keep their own laws. The Pharisees were losing ground—the temple guards came back impressed by Jesus (7:46), and one of the Pharisees' own, Nicodemus, was defending him. With their hypocritical motives being exposed and their prestige slowly eroding, the Pharisees renewed their efforts to protect themselves. Pride would interfere with their ability to reason, and soon they would become obsessed with getting rid of Jesus just to save face. What was good and right no longer mattered.

JESUS FORGIVES AN ADULTEROUS WOMAN / 7:53–8:11 / **125**

The earliest manuscripts of John's gospel do not include the story of the adulterous woman. It does not appear in any Greek manuscript until the fifth century, and no Greek church father comments on the passage prior to the twelfth century. Even then, the comments state that the accurate manuscripts do not contain this story. When it was inserted in later manuscripts, the story of the adulterous woman appeared in different places: after John 7:52, after Luke 21:38, at the end of John; and when it does appear it is often marked off by asterisks to signal doubt about where it belongs. The story is part of an oral tradition that was circulated in the Western church, eventually finding its way into the Latin Vulgate, and from there into later Greek manuscripts.

The evidence against John having included this particular story in his gospel is conclusive. First, many scholars point out that the vocabulary used in this passage does not match the rest of John. Second, although the setting is plausible (other similar confrontations between Jewish leaders and Jesus occurred in Jerusalem), the insertion of the story at this point in John (after 7:52 and before 8:12) disrupts the narrative flow. Third, since the account does not appear in writing until later manuscripts, its "orphan" status is evidenced by it being in several locations.

Thus, this story was not originally part of this section of John. Consequently, it is not even included in the text of some Bible versions (for example, see the first edition of the RSV). However, even though the passage was not written by John, it still may be regarded as a true story. It is unlikely that a later scribe would have made up such a story, given the strict views of the church regarding sexual immorality. The actions and words of Jesus are consistent with what we know of him from the rest of the Gospels. There is no new or unusual information in the passage that adds evidence against its inclusion. The encounter appears as an added snapshot of Jesus in John's collection, though we can tell that someone else probably took the picture. The event deserves at least consideration in teaching and preaching as an act that Jesus did at some point in his ministry, for it illustrates Jesus' compassion for sinful people (which includes us all) and his willingness to forgive any sinner; but the story should not be given the same authority as Scripture.

7:53–8:3 **The teachers of the law and the Pharisees brought in a woman caught in adultery.**^{NIV} Scribes (*the teachers of the law*) often gathered in the outer court of the temple to teach the crowds of worshipers, so it was natural for Jesus to be there. The religious leaders did not bring this woman to Jesus to promote justice; they used her to try to trap Jesus. (The others involved in this attempt simply mingled with the crowd; see a similar trap in Mark 12:13-17.) Though indignant toward this woman's sin, the religious leaders brought her to Jesus with political, not spiritual, motives in mind. They forgot the obvious fact that catching someone in the very act of adultery involves catching *two* people. Their devaluation of the woman (while ignoring the man's sin) made her no more than a pawn in their efforts to trap Jesus.

> Of course I had a deep respect, indeed a great reverence for the conventional Jesus Christ whom the Church worshipped. But I was not at all prepared for the *unconventional* man revealed in these terse Gospels. *J. B. Phillips*

How unfortunate that they were so quick to point out the sins of another and so blind to their own sins—especially the sin of not recognizing and accepting their own Messiah. But Jesus was about to teach them a lesson they wouldn't forget.

DOUBLE STANDARD
The details of this event are painfully common. Traditionally, women have borne an undue burden of blame for sins in which men participated equally. Today, radical feminism shifts the balance of blame to men. However, placing more blame on one person than the other covers a hidden motive: blaming others shifts the load of our own guilt. God stands against double or separate standards for women and men. He rejects the hypocrisy that holds others to a different standard than we hold for ourselves. When we accept our own blame, we take the first step toward experiencing forgiveness.

8:4-6 **They said to him, " . . . the law . . . commanded us to stone such women. Now what do you say?" They said this to test him, so that they might have some charge to bring against**

him.^{NRSV} The Jewish leaders had already disregarded the law by
arresting the woman without the man. The law required that both
parties to adultery be put to death (Leviticus 20:10; Deuteronomy
22:22) and specified stoning in the case of a betrothed virgin
(Deuteronomy 22:23, but see 22:24 for
an important condition). But the pro-
ceedings before Jesus had little to do
with justice. The leaders were using the
woman's sin as an opportunity to trick
Jesus and destroy his credibility with
the people. If Jesus were to say that the
woman should not be stoned, they
could accuse him of violating Moses'
law. If he were to urge them to execute her, they would report
him to the Romans, who did not permit the Jews to carry out their
own executions (18:31). But Jesus was aware of their intentions
and did not give either of the expected responses to the dilemma
they placed before him.

> Aversion for the truth
> exists in different
> degrees, but it may be
> said to exist in every one
> of us to some degree, for
> it is inseparable from
> self-love. *Blaise Pascal*

Jesus bent down and wrote with his finger on the ground.^{NRSV}
What was Jesus writing in the dirt on the ground? Many have
speculated: maybe he was listing the names of those present who
had committed adultery (and scaring them to death that he knew
it); he might have been listing names and various sins that each
person had committed; maybe he was writing out the Ten Commandments to point out that no one could claim to be without sin.
In any case, Jesus made the accusers uncomfortable.

8:7-8 **"Let anyone among you who is without sin be the first to throw
a stone at her."**^{NRSV} The religious leaders could have handled this
case without Jesus' opinion. Jesus was fully aware that the woman
was only brought to him so the Pharisees could test him. They
thought they had him in a no-win situation: no matter what he said,
he would offend someone and thus give them a crime of which to
accuse him. But Jesus' calm words caught them completely off
guard. They never anticipated his turning the tables on them.

Jesus' statement of permission balanced several crucial points
of truth. He upheld the legal penalty for adultery (stoning), so he
could not be accused of being against the law. But by requiring
that only a sinless person could throw the first stone, Jesus
exposed what was in the accusers' hearts. Without condoning the
woman's actions, he highlighted the importance of compassion
and forgiveness and broadened the spotlight of judgment until
every accuser felt himself included. Jesus knew the execution
could not be carried out.

How are we to apply Jesus' statement about only sinless persons rendering judgment? Jesus was not saying that only perfect, sinless people can make accurate accusations, pass judgment, or exact a death penalty. Nor was he excusing adultery or any other sin by saying that everyone sins. This event illustrates that wise judgment flows out of honest motives. Jesus resolved an injustice about to be committed by exposing the hypocrisy of the witnesses against the woman. By making the accusers examine themselves, he exposed their real motives.

Jesus did confront the woman's sin, but he exercised compassion alongside confrontation. As with the woman at the well (chapter 4), Jesus demonstrated to this woman that she was of greater importance than what she had done wrong.

CONFLICT OF INTEREST
The religious leaders who tried to trap Jesus were treating neither the sin nor the sinner with the necessary respect. The same blindness that caused them to not see their own sins made them unable to recognize who Jesus was. Behind their diligence to "keep the law" lay hidden the drive to protect their power. Their conflict of interest made them inept judges.
Sin calls for compassion as well as judgment. But final judgment is God's prerogative alone. Sins may be abhorrent, but sinners have been offered forgiveness in Christ. When we must confront sin, we ought not condemn, but rather present the need and opportunity for forgiveness.

After Jesus made his statement, **once again he bent down and wrote on the ground.**^{NRSV} Jesus allowed the blunt truth to sink in and have an effect. There was no further need for argument; the sides had been clearly drawn. The trap snapped shut, and those who set it found themselves caught!

8:9-11 **When they heard it, they went away, one by one, beginning with the elders.**^{NRSV} When Jesus invited someone who had not sinned to throw the first stone, the leaders slipped quietly away, from oldest to youngest. Evidently the older men were more aware of their sins than the younger. Age and experience often temper youthful self-righteousness. Each person, no matter what age, should take an honest look at his or her life. We all have a sinful nature and are desperately in need of forgiveness and transformation. None of us would have been able to throw the first stone; none of us can claim sinlessness. We, too, would have had to walk away.

The accusers slinked away **until only Jesus was left, with the woman still standing there.**^{NIV} After everyone had left, Jesus stood and spoke to the accused woman, **"Has no one condemned you?"**^{NIV} Apparently no one could claim sinlessness so as to stone this woman. Imagine the scene: anyone who tried would immediately be condemned by someone who knew of a sin that person had committed. Even those pious religious leaders—"the teachers of the law and the Pharisees" (8:3 NIV) who brought this woman to Jesus—could not save face. Jesus had exposed their hypocrisy and embarrassed them, and there was nothing for them to do but go back and try to think of some other way to trap Jesus.

HYPOCRISY
How quickly and self-righteously we bring before Jesus the sins of others while overlooking and denying our own sins. These hypocrites were guilty of sin in their own lives and were unwilling to face it. They claimed concern for truth and justice, but were arrogantly using the woman who had fallen into their hands. In their anger at Jesus they made her life cheap.

When you find yourself enraged at others, you may be on the verge of a healthy discovery. You should examine what is behind the rage. Are you covering sins or excusing faults that have made you unusually sensitive to the faults in others? What wrong motives are you masking by your anger?

No one had accused the woman, and Jesus kindly said, **"Neither do I condemn you."**^{NRSV} But there was more—she was not simply free to go her way. Jesus didn't just free her from the Pharisees, he wanted to free her from her sin, so he added, **"Go your way, and from now on do not sin again."**^{NRSV} Jesus didn't condemn the woman accused of adultery, but neither did he ignore or condone her behavior. Jesus told the woman to leave her life of sin.

TRUE LOVE AND GOOD INTENTIONS
God hates sin; we must make no mistake about that. But he loves sinners—and that includes each of us. In fact, he loves us so much he sent his Son to die—to take the penalty our sins deserved. Jesus stands ready to forgive any person, but confession, repentance, and a change of heart are the properly prepared ground for forgiveness.

Our intention must be to *not sin again.* This does not mean that God expects us to never sin again, but he does expect that our life-styles are no longer sinful. Our desire should be no longer to live for ourselves and our pleasures, but to live for God. With God's help we can accept Christ's forgiveness and stop making a practice of wrongdoing. Only then will we be really free to *not sin again.*

John 8:12-59

This section ties in closely with the previous section (7:45-52)—minus the story of the woman caught in adultery, which John didn't write. In 7:45-52, Nicodemus had recommended that the religious leaders first hear Jesus before passing judgment on him. In this section Jesus is heard, and he affirms the validity of his testimony based on his divine identity.

In no other chapter of the Bible does Jesus make so many declarations about himself. Here he asserts his divine identity through a series of "I am" statements (all are from NKJV):

- "I am the light of the world" (8:12)

- "I am not alone" (8:16)

- "I am One who bears witness of Myself, and the Father who sent Me bears witness of Me" (8:18)

- "I am from above" (8:23)

- "I am not of this world" (8:23)

- "I am He [the Christ]" (8:24, 28)

- "I AM" (8:58).

8:12-14 **"I am the light of the world. Whoever follows me will never walk in darkness but will have the light of life."**NRSV In John's original writing, this verse immediately follows 7:52. The intervening passage, 7:53–8:11, about Jesus forgiving the woman taken in adultery interrupts the narrative's continuity and is not included in the earliest manuscripts (see 7:53–8:11 for a further discussion).

Chapters 7 and 8 record the dialogues that Jesus had with the Jewish leaders in Jerusalem during the Feast of Tabernacles. As part of the ritual during this feast, water was poured over a rock in commemoration of the water supply that had gushed from the rock in the wilderness (Numbers 20:8-11), and huge lamps in the Court of Women in the temple were lit in commemoration of the pillar of fire that led the Israelites in their wilderness journey

(Numbers 9:15-23). The light from those lamps lit up much of
Jerusalem. In the context of these two rituals, Jesus presented
himself as the true source of living water (7:37-39) and as the
true light to be followed (8:12).

In declaring himself to be *the light,* Jesus was claiming divinity.
In the Bible, "light" symbolizes the holiness of God (see also Psalm
27:1; 36:9; Acts 9:3; 1 John 1:5). Jesus is not merely *a* light or
another light, he is *the one and only* true Light. As the Light, Jesus
illumines the truth, gives people spiritual understanding, and reveals
to us God himself and what he has done for us.

FIRE AND LIGHT
Jesus was speaking in that part of the temple known as the
treasury, where the offerings were collected (8:20) and huge
torches or lamps burned to symbolize the pillar of fire that led
the people of Israel through the wilderness (Exodus 13:21-22).
In this context, Jesus called himself the Light of the World. The
pillar of fire in the wilderness had represented God's presence,
protection, and guidance, though the holy flames were almost
as dangerous to the Israelites as they were to their enemies.
They were reminded that: "The LORD your God is a consuming
fire, a jealous God" (Deuteronomy 4:24 NIV).

Because we no longer depend on fire as a source of light, we
might miss the connection Jesus makes between fire and light.
In Christ, God became light personified. Jesus brought God's
presence, protection, and guidance into the world in an
approachable way. Now God could be known with an intimacy
not possible with consuming fire. How well do we know God as
a holy fire? Have we allowed Christ as God's holy light to
enlighten us?

In claiming to be the light *of the world,* Jesus defined his
unique position as the one true light for all people, not just the
Jews. Isaiah wrote, "I will also give You as a light to the Gentiles,
that You should be My salvation to the ends of the earth" (Isaiah
49:6 NKJV).

Death brings eternal darkness; but to follow Jesus means to
never walk in darkness, but . . . have the light of life. When we
follow Jesus—accepting him as Savior and Lord and following
him—we are walking in his light. We no longer walk blindly in
our sin, rather his light shows us our sin and our need of forgiveness, guides us along life's pathway, and leads us into eternal life
with him. The psalmist said, "In Your light we see light" (Psalm
36:9 NKJV). The theme of Jesus as *the light* indirectly takes up all
of chapter 9, in which Jesus heals a blind man.

After Jesus said this, **the Pharisees challenged him, "Here**

you are, appearing as your own witness; your testimony is not valid."ᴺᴵⱽ Jesus did not disagree with the Jewish law that says that two witnesses are needed for a valid testimony in a capital offense, as their charge of blasphemy was (5:31; also Deuteronomy 19:15). Instead, he claimed that his testimony was true even if no one else bore witness: **"for I know where I came from and where I am going."**"ᴺᴵⱽ Jesus knew his origin and his destiny. In other words, Jesus knows God the Father, and the words that Jesus spoke were from the Father himself. Therefore when Jesus spoke, not only was he testifying for himself, but because he spoke the words of God, God was testifying for him as well. Countless believers have discovered that their consistent exposure and memorization of the words of Jesus have deepened their awareness of his divinity. His words ring true. Not knowing or obeying Christ's words is our fault, not a reflection on their truthfulness.

8:15-16 **"You judge by human standards."**"ᴺᴿˢⱽ The religious leaders did not know Jesus' divine origin and considered him to be no more than a fake Messiah; that is, they were judging him *by human standards.* Jesus had already told them, "Do not judge by appearances" (7:24 NRSV). Yet they continued to do so. He was reminding them of the same lesson he had taught Samuel in the Old Testament: "For the LORD does not see as mortals see; they look on the outward appearance, but the LORD looks on the heart" (1 Samuel 16:7 NRSV).

APPEARANCES
People today are very willing to acknowledge the greatness of Jesus as a man but not to acknowledge him as God. By human standards, Jesus was the greatest man who ever lived. Yet human standards are not enough to portray all of Jesus' true identity. Calling Jesus "great" is faint praise in light of his identity as God. Mere admiration of Jesus as a great leader or teacher falls short. Our response should be to adore him as our Lord.

"I judge no one.""ᴺᴿˢⱽ Given the context, Jesus meant that while his accusers judged by human standards, he did not.

"Yet even if I do judge, my judgment is valid.""ᴺᴿˢⱽ Jesus reserved for himself the right to judge, though that was not the primary reason for his presence. Jesus did not come to judge, but to save. He had already told a noted Pharisee (Nicodemus), "For God did not send His Son into the world to condemn the world, but that the world through Him might be saved" (3:17 NKJV). But as the Son of Man, he has been given the authority to judge; and when the future day of judgment comes, Jesus will judge according to the Father's will (see 5:27, 45). Therefore, it could be said that while

IF YOU KNEW ME

For John, "knowing God" was a key theme of Jesus' ministry. Understanding the nature of God is not something we can do on our own. Each individual must be given the ability to recognize Jesus and God. Once given, we must grow in our knowledge of God by knowing Christ better and better. (Verses are quoted from NKJV.)

Knowledge of Christ is not innate

1:5	*"And the light shines in the darkness, and the darkness did not comprehend it."*
1:10	*"He was in the world, and the world was made through Him, and the world did not know Him."*

Knowledge of God comes to us through Christ

7:28-29.	*"Then Jesus cried out, as He taught in the temple, saying, 'You both know Me, and you know where I am from; and I have not come of Myself, but He who sent Me is true, whom you do not know. But I know Him, for I am from Him, and He sent Me.'"*
8:19	*"Then they said to Him, 'Where is Your Father?' Jesus answered, 'You know neither Me nor My Father. If you had known Me, you would have known My father also.'"*
8:55	*"Yet you have not known Him, but I know Him. And if I say, 'I do not know Him,' I shall be a liar like you; but I do know Him and keep His word."*

Knowing God is every believer's opportunity

14:7	*"If you had known Me, you would have known My Father also; and from now on you know Him and have seen Him."*
14:9	*Jesus said to him, "Have I been with you so long, and yet you have not known Me, Philip? He who has seen Me has seen the Father; so how can you say, 'Show us the Father'"?*
14:17	*"The Spirit of truth, whom the world cannot receive, because it neither sees Him nor knows Him; but you know Him, for He dwells with you and will be in you."*

Knowing the Father through the Son was the end result of Jesus' mission on earth

17:3	*"And this is eternal life, that they may know You, the only true God, and Jesus Christ whom You have sent."*
17:6	*"I have manifested Your name to the men whom You have given Me out of the world."*

Jesus did not come to judge, his coming led to judgment because it forced a decision—and a rejection of Jesus led to judgment.

8:17-18 **"The testimony of two men is valid. I am one who testifies for myself; my other witness is the Father, who sent me."**NIV The religious leaders did not understand that the Father and Son lived in each other and were with each other (see 10:38; 14:9-11; 17:21). Therefore, even though the Son came from the Father (8:14) and was sent by the Father (8:16, 18), he was not separate from the Father—for the Father who sent the Son came with him and provided testimony for him. His confirming witness was God himself. Jesus and the Father made two witnesses, the number required by the law.

8:19-20 The Pharisees, mystified about Jesus' reference to his Father, asked him, **"Where is your father?"**NRSV (see also 14:8ff.). They might as well have been saying, "Bring on the other witness; we wish to question him." If his father was the other witness, then where was he? In their very presence, Jesus affirmed that they knew neither him nor his Father. Their unwillingness to "know" him when he was among them also kept them from knowing the Father, who was just as truly among them.

Jesus had already told them that his Father was with him, but their question showed that they did not know the Son or the Father for **"if you knew me, you would know my Father also."**NRSV When Jesus speaks, the Father speaks. But this was completely lost on these religious leaders.

He spoke these words while teaching in the temple area near the place where the offerings were put.NIV This area was part of the Court of Women (a court in the temple where women were permitted to go). This court held thirteen trumpet-shaped containers for collecting various dues and offerings—seven of the boxes were for the temple tax; the other six were for freewill offerings. According to Mark 12:41-44 and Luke 21:1-4, on at least one occasion Jesus sat opposite this treasury and watched various people (including the widow who gave "two small copper coins" NRSV) deposit their offerings into these containers. This treasury was very close to the hall where the Sanhedrin met, and yet **no one laid hands on Him, for His hour had not yet come.**NKJV. The statement anticipates the fact that Jesus' "hour" would eventually come—and that those who had been pursuing him would finally get their hands on him. But the timing was under God's control, not man's.

JESUS WARNS OF COMING JUDGMENT / 8:21-30 / **127**

With chilling brevity, Jesus predicted the fate of those who fail to find him. The Pharisees continued to respond to Jesus out of rigid human standards. Because of this, they continued to be denounced by Jesus. But in this case, Jesus' hardness proved to be compassion. Only the bluntness of Jesus' vision of their condition finally broke through to some. By the end of this section, while he was speaking, "many put their faith in him" (8:30 NIV).

8:21-22 Speaking again to the Jewish religious leaders, Jesus declared, **"You will die in your sin."**NRSV If the Jewish religious leaders would not believe in Jesus while he was with them, they would run the risk of not having any further opportunity to receive eternal life. Jesus predicted that they would continue to look for a messiah, though the real one had already been among them. The leaders' fatal sin would be in rejecting the only one who could save them.

> Let them fear death who do not fear sin.
> *Thomas Watson*

WHAT DO YOU WANT?
Those questioning Jesus were convinced they understood God's plan. They thought they had a clear idea of exactly what kind of savior they needed, and Jesus did not fit that pattern.
Are you trusting Jesus to be your Savior because he knows best, or are you reserving final judgment just in case a "better" option comes along? Are you trusting God to graciously meet your needs even when you do not fully understand them, or are you clinging to the belief that you know best what God can do for you? Are you still shopping for a better offer? Only Jesus can give forgiveness and eternal life.

"Where I am going, you cannot come."NRSV Jesus was speaking of his death and his return to his Father—the religious leaders could not follow him there. The opportunity to speak with Jesus was limited; soon he would leave them having been rejected by them. Those who rejected Jesus would die without having their sins forgiven and would therefore literally not be able to go where Jesus would be.

As in 7:34-36, the Jews could not comprehend Jesus' words. They surmised that he must be speaking about death when he said, **"I am going away,"**NRSV but they could hardly believe that he might be planning to give them a simple solution to their problem. **"Will he kill himself?"**[NIV] they wondered. In Greek, the question expects a negative answer. Instead of responding to their tentative interpretation, Jesus explained why they were unable to comprehend his statements.

8:23-24 **"You are from below, I am from above; you are of this world, I am not of this world."**[NRSV] Those of this world are earthly, born of the flesh, incapable of understanding heavenly and spiritual realities (see 3:6; 1 Corinthians 2:14-15). The Pharisees were set in their faulty perspective and were unwilling to consider that they might be wrong. They were people look-

> Alas! that the farthest end of all our thoughts should be the thought of our ends. *Thomas Adams*

ing very hard—in the wrong place. Therefore, Jesus told them, **"For you will die in your sins unless you believe that I am he."**[NRSV] In the Greek the last words are *ego eimi* (I am). Translators fill out the expression by adding "he" or even "the one I claim to be " (NIV). This claim, made also in 8:28 and 8:58, was a claim to deity (see Exodus 3:14; Deuteronomy 32:39; Isaiah 43:10). By refusing to acknowledge Jesus as the divine Son of God, these people were committing spiritual suicide. To die in our sins is the worst that can happen, for it is to die without ever repenting of our sinful life-style or having our guilt and sin covered by the blood of Christ. Only by believing in Jesus and his teaching could these inquirers transcend their worldly way of thinking.

Jesus said his opponents would die in their sins, while subtly referring to his own sinless death. Still his opponents refused to acknowledge what Jesus had said about them. In verse 21 Jesus used *sin* (*hamartia*) in referring to their rejection of him; in verse 24 he used *sins* (*hamartiais*) to show that their sinful acts would confirm that they were sinners by nature. Because Jesus simply said, "I am," instead of "I am ——— [Lord, Christ, etc.]," some have wondered if he used the phrase, "I am from above," to indicate his divine nature. The broader context shows how the hearers finally understood the way Jesus was using "I am"—they attempted to stone him (8:58-59). This confirms the meaning for us also. Jesus confronted the leaders with their crucial need to recognize or reject his divinity. People today face that same need.

8:25 The Pharisees decided to try the direct approach; they asked Jesus, **"Who are you?"**[NRSV] When the Pharisees pressed Jesus to declare his identity, he answered, **"Why do I speak to you at all?"**[NRSV] Jesus' answer has also been translated as a statement: "Just what I have been saying to you from the beginning" (NKJV) or "I am the one I have always claimed to be" (TLB). Jesus simply refused to answer their question, for to do so would have created an endless argument. Jesus had already revealed his identity to them through his speeches, his miracles, and the Father's testimony about him. But the Pharisees were unable to understand because they were deaf to his word (8:43).

"I AM HE"
Jesus' claim "I am he" (*ego eimi,* see also 8:24, 58) is thought by many to refer to the name God commanded Moses to use in Exodus 3:13-14. Moses asked God what name he should use when he went before Pharaoh. God's answer was, "I AM WHO I AM" (NIV). It is just as likely, however, given the way in which Jesus used passages and concepts from Isaiah 40–55 to identify himself, that he was using the "I am" phrase from that part of the Old Testament. In any case, Jesus was pushing his hearers to recognize his full identity. The following verses highlight the primary uses of "I am he" in Isaiah (all verses are quoted from NKJV):

- Isaiah 41:4
  "I, the LORD, am the first; and with the last I am He."
- Isaiah 43:10
  "You are My witnesses," says the LORD, "and My servant whom I have chosen, that you may know and believe Me, and understand that I am He."

Isaiah 43:13
  "Indeed before the day was, I am He."

- Isaiah 43:25
  "I, even I, am He who blots out your transgressions for My own sake."
- Isaiah 46:4
  "Even to your old age, I am He."
- Isaiah 48:12
  "Listen to Me, O Jacob, and Israel, My called: I am He, I am the First, I am also the Last."

8:26 **"I have much to say about you and much to condemn; but the one who sent me is true, and I declare to the world what I have heard from him."**NRSV Jesus could have said more to them in way of judgment, but he would speak only what his Father commanded. The Pharisees claimed they wanted him to explain his identity, but Jesus knew they were simply heaping judgment on themselves. Instead of continuing an argument with these religious leaders who had already made up their minds not to believe, Jesus would say no more in condemnation. Rather, he would speak only what the Father told him to say—and he would speak, not just to the Jews, but to the world. And whatever he says is the Father's word; thus it is true, reliable, and valid (see also 8:16).

8:27 The Pharisees still **did not understand that he was speaking to them about the Father.**[NRSV] They mentally blocked out the possibility that Jesus had come from God the Father and was still accompanied by God the Father, even though Jesus mentioned this twice. Jesus was not alone; the Father who had sent him had come with him (see 8:16, 29). Jesus had not come on his own, and he did not do anything of his own initiative (see 8:28, 42). He lived to please his Father.

8:28-30 **"When you have lifted up the Son of Man, then you will realize that I am he, and that I do nothing on my own."**[NRSV] The Jews in Jesus' day understood the expression *lifted up* to signify crucifixion. That the religious leaders would realize who Jesus was does not mean that they would believe in him. Rather, it means that Jesus' claims would be proven through the Crucifixion and Resurrection. *"I am he"* refers immediately to the title *"Son of Man."*

Jesus was not on his own mission to gain glory for himself; he had come to fulfill the Father's will by dying on the cross. Jesus' death on the cross exhibited his absolute submission to the Father's will. He summed it up thus: **"I always do what is pleasing to him."**[NRSV]

The passage concludes with a crack in the wall of resistance to Jesus. **Even as he spoke, many put their faith in him.**[NIV] Even among those most unyielding to Jesus were some who surrendered to his character and words. Groups may be labeled as being solidly against Christ, but God specializes in plucking out believers from the most unexpected sources.

THE RISK WORTH TAKING
To people who fear being offensive when they express their faith, the bluntness of Jesus' statements stands as a rebuke. Sometimes we do not love people enough to risk losing their approval. Jesus took the risk because he loved the people, even those who rejected him. Among those who did respond to Jesus were some who had once been firmly set against him.

At all times Jesus was truthful, never deliberately harsh or offensive. Jesus said what people needed to hear, fully knowing that they did not want to hear it. If we wait to speak about Christ until we are sure the other person is ready to respond, we may never speak at all. Our caution will prevent us from sharing our faith with some who might astound us with their unexpected openness.

JESUS SPEAKS ABOUT GOD'S TRUE CHILDREN / 8:31-47 / **128**

Next Jesus singled out the group of people who recently had believed in him. They formed part of the scattered response from among the crowd listening to Jesus in 8:30. Difficulties with this passage arise from the fact that John called them believers in verses 30 and 31, but they proved to be faithless. Their belief in Jesus turned out to be merely superficial. Jesus tested their commitment with his first instructions; their response demonstrates their unwillingness to actually follow the one in whom they had recently declared their faith. Their arguments with Jesus proved that they had failed the condition Jesus gave in verse 31—"If . . . you are really my disciples . . ."

We must ask ourselves whether our excitement over the apparent conversion of a person stems from our genuine delight over salvation or from a selfish claim to have "led someone to Christ." Are we glad because a new life has begun, or because we have done our job? Do we close the file, or roll up our sleeves? Jesus continually asked people who followed him to count the cost. He did not hesitate to challenge immature or incomplete expressions of faith. Believing in Jesus has ongoing implications. If initial belief does not lead to obedience, it may not have been genuine.

8:31 To those who believed in him Jesus said, **"If you hold to my teaching, you are really my disciples."**NIV As the following verses demonstrate, some of these new believers did not remain his followers for long. But Jesus urged those who really wanted to remain his disciples to hold to, or continue in, his teachings. John's report of the failure of one group of followers is a strong lesson. We need to count the cost of following Jesus (see Luke 14:25-35).

The Greek expression for *hold to* (*meinete en*, also translated "abide in" or "remain in") has great spiritual significance in the Gospel of John (see especially 15:1-17). We abide in Christ when we place ourselves in him and continue there, drawing life from his words. This produces ongoing discipleship. A true and obedient disciple will find the truth by knowing the one who is the truth, Jesus himself (1:17; 14:6). This knowledge frees people from their bondage to sin (see 8:34).

8:32 **"And you shall know the truth, and the truth shall make you free."**NKJV When Jesus spoke of "know[ing] the truth," he was speaking of knowing God's revelation to man. This revelation is embodied in Jesus himself, the Word; therefore, to know the truth is to know Jesus. The truth is not political freedom or intellectual knowledge. Knowing the truth means accepting it, obeying it, and regarding it above all earthly opinion. Doing so offers true spiritual freedom from sin and death.

Believers become truly free because they are free to do God's will, and thus fulfill God's ultimate purpose in their lives. As believers, we have the Holy Spirit living within us and guiding us on our journey through life. In fact, later in 16:13, Jesus specifically identified the Holy Spirit as "the Spirit of truth" who will "guide you into all truth" (NIV).

THE TRUTH SHALL MAKE YOU FREE
Just as the Jews misunderstood what Jesus meant by "the truth shall make you free," people today still take it the wrong way. In fact, this familiar phrase has been used out of context to promote a wide range of freedoms. Universities use it on their seals to promote the value of academic knowledge. Yet around the world people who know academic truths are still in bondage. So Jesus must have had some other kind of truth and freedom in mind. For many, "knowing the truth" means personal autonomy, creativity, and freedom from oppression and ignorance, which they define as mental slavery. But Jesus didn't die to guarantee personal freedom of expression.

The error comes when we think of truth as a concept rather than God himself, which was the way Jesus used the term. Jesus clarified his meaning when he said, "So if the Son sets you free, you will be free indeed" (8:36 NIV). By interchanging *truth* and *Son*, Jesus implied that granting freedom is God's work. So Jesus promised freedom from slavery to sin. That freedom begins when we acknowledge our bondage to sin. Only God can free us through his forgiveness, which he made possible by Christ's death in our place on the cross. Jesus' sacrifice did not free us "to do our own thing;" rather he freed us *from* doing our own thing so that we could serve him!

8:33 The Jews thought that Jesus' words about their needing freedom devalued their ancestry and unique position with God, so they gave Jesus a little history lesson: **"We are Abraham's descendants and have never been slaves of anyone. How can you say that we shall be set free?"**NIV Yet the crowd's denial of the obvious seems apparent even to us. The Jewish ancestors of these people had been enslaved by the Egyptians, the Assyrians, and the Babylonians. And they were ruled by the Romans at the moment Jesus spoke. Though not actually in slavery, they were under foreign domination, and were looking for the Messiah to free them from Roman rule. But they insisted that as Abraham's descendants they were free people.

They also claimed that Abraham's righteousness guaranteed their righteousness. Their spiritual superiority made them blind to their real slavery to sin. Jesus bluntly challenged their claims.

8:34-36 Not only was the crowd wrong about their national history, they were also wrong about the meaning of Jesus' earlier statement. Jesus spoke of a different liberation—that of the soul set free from sin. He pointed out that they did indeed need to be set free, because, **"Everyone who commits sin is a slave to sin."**^{NRSV} Jesus went on to explain . . .

"A slave has no permanent place in the family"^{NIV} or "does not remain in the house forever." But **"a son belongs to it forever."**^{NIV} This statement amplifies the difference between a slave and a son. A slave has no permanent standing in the master's household because he or she can be sold to a different master (in the Roman Empire slaves had no legal status). But a son always has a place in the family. The Jews had a false sense of security because they claimed to be Abraham's children—and thus thought this guaranteed them a permanent place in God's family and household (heaven). But Jesus explained that they, along with all people, were slaves to sin. As such, they had no permanent standing in the Father's house.

"If the Son makes you free, you shall be free indeed." NKJV The Son of God alone has the power and authority to free people from their bondage to sin. Paul developed the same idea in Romans 6:12-23. Paul also wrote in Galatians, "In Christ Jesus you are all children of God through faith. . . . And if you belong to Christ, then you are Abraham's offspring, heirs according to the promise" (Galatians 3:26, 29 NRSV).

SET FREE!
Sin has a way of enslaving us, controlling us, dominating us, and dictating our actions. It manifests itself in self-centeredness, rebelliousness, possessiveness, dysfunctional love, and addictive behaviors. Jesus can free us from this slavery that keeps us from becoming the person God created us to be. Even if sin is restraining, mastering, or enslaving us, Jesus can break its power over our life. Jesus himself is the truth that sets us free (8:36). He is the source of truth, the perfect standard of what is right. He frees us from the consequences of sin, from self-deception, and from deception by Satan. He shows us clearly the way to eternal life with God. Thus Jesus does not give us freedom to do what we want, but freedom to follow God. As we seek to serve God, Jesus' perfect truth frees us to be all that God meant us to be.

8:37-38 "**I know you are Abraham's descendants.**"^{NIV} Jesus recognized that the Jews could rightfully claim to be Abraham's descendants, but they were his children only in the physical sense, not spiritually or morally, because they were **ready to kill**^{NIV} him. In seeking to kill Jesus, the true Son of Abraham (see Galatians 3:16), these leaders revealed that they were not Abraham's spiritual children. If they had been, they would have recognized their Messiah.

> There is little hope of children who are educated wickedly. If the dye have been in the wool, it is hard to get it out of the cloth.
> *Jeremiah Burroughs*

Jesus knew of their plans, and knew where those plans originated. He pointed to their evil nature and said, "**You do what you have heard from your father.**"^{NIV} In being ready to kill Jesus, the leaders betrayed their link with another *father,* namely the devil (8:44). Jesus made a distinction between hereditary children and *true* children. The religious leaders were hereditary children of Abraham (founder of the Jewish nation) and therefore claimed to be children of God. But their actions showed them to be true children of Satan, for they lived under Satan's guidance. True children of Abraham (faithful followers of God) would not act as they did. Church membership and/or family connections will not make people true children of God. Only rebirth can do that. Then they will imitate and obey their true Father.

8:39 "**If you were Abraham's children, you would be doing what Abraham did.**"^{NRSV} Sons copy their fathers, but the Jewish leaders did not behave like the one whom they claimed as their father. Jesus specifically pointed to their sin of wanting to kill him because this proved that they were not Abraham's true children. Abraham believed in and obeyed God (see Genesis 12:1-4; 15:6; 22:1-14) and welcomed God's messengers (Genesis 18:1-8).

8:40-41 "**You are determined to kill me, a man who has told you the truth that I heard from God.**"^{NIV} They could not claim to have Abraham as their father when they were seeking to kill the one who brought them truth from God, for "**Abraham did not do such things.**"^{NIV}

Instead, Jesus said, "**You are doing the things your own father does.**"^{NIV} Jesus was speaking of Satan as being their father, but they did not understand this. So Jesus made this explicit in verse 44.

The Jews protested, "**We are not illegitimate children.**"^{NRSV} Some commentators have said that this retort was a slur on Jesus' own birth, but they would not have known about his unusual origins. They all assumed Jesus was Joseph's son. Rather, they could have been claiming to be unlike the Samaritans, who were not purebred Jews or claiming to be devout monotheists untainted by spiritual fornication with other gods.

"The only Father we have is God himself."^{NIV} Since their appeal to Abrahamic privilege was either deflected or challenged by Jesus (see explanation of translation above), they appealed to their position with God. Their retort

> When God said, "Let there be light," he did not speak in order that some subordinate might hear, understand what the speaker wanted, and go and perform the task. This is what happens in human affairs. But the Word of God is creator and maker, and he *is* the Father's will. *Athanasius*

shows that they took offense at being told that their ancestry did not automatically place them in a privileged moral standing before God. But they did not truly know the one God they claimed as their Father because they did not recognize his Son who had come to give them the truth and to set them free from sin.

8:42 Jesus forcefully challenged the leaders' claim that they were God's children. **"If God were your Father, you would love me."**^{NRSV} If those people truly loved God as their Father, then they would recognize and love the Son. And he repeated for them his origin and mission: **"I came from God and now I am here. I did not come on my own, but he sent me."**^{NRSV} Jesus came as the one sent by the Father to bring God's word to his people.

8:43 **"Why do you not understand what I say?"**^{NRSV} Jesus already knew the answer to this question—but he asked the leaders so he could answer for them. They did not understand because they had already made up their minds about him, and thus could not hear and accept what Jesus had to say. Understanding was not the problem; being willing to hear and

> The devil utters falsehood as naturally and spontaneously as God utters truth. *F. F. Bruce*

accept it as the truth was their barrier. As Paul later wrote to the Corinthian church, "We have not received the spirit of the world but the Spirit who is from God, that we may understand what God has freely given us. . . . The man without the Spirit does not accept the things that come from the Spirit of God, for they are foolishness to him, and he cannot understand them, because they are spiritually discerned" (1 Corinthians 2:12, 14 NIV).

8:44 Jesus told them, **"You belong to your father, the devil, and you want to carry out your father's desire."**^{NIV} A person's actions reveal what is in his or her heart. In a later letter John wrote, "Everyone who commits sin is a child of the devil; for the devil has been sinning from the beginning" (1 John 3:8 NRSV).

The devil **"was a murderer from the beginning, not holding to the truth, for there is no truth in him. When he lies, he speaks his native language, for he is a liar and the father of lies."**[NIV] The intent to murder comes from the devil. The devil was the instigator of Jesus' murder (6:70-71; 13:27) and the perpetrator of the lies that the Jews believed about Jesus.

DANGEROUS DEAFNESS

Jesus' audience was hardened and deaf; the life-giving, enlightening word could not penetrate their closed hearts, ears, and minds. And this was very dangerous because not being open to the words of God made them receptive targets for the devil's lies. The religious leaders were unable to understand because they refused to listen. Satan used their stubbornness, pride, and prejudices to keep them from believing in Jesus.

If we fill our life with distracting and conflicting messages from the heroes we follow, the books we read, the songs we listen to, and the movies we watch, we will discover that it is harder and harder to "hear" God speaking at all. He has not stopped communicating; we are just listening to other voices.

The attitudes and actions of the Jewish leaders clearly identified them as followers of Satan, though they may not have been conscious of this. But their hatred of truth, their lies, and their murderous intentions indicate how much control the devil had over them. They were Satan's tools in carrying out his plans; they spoke the very same language of lies. Satan still uses people to obstruct God's work (Genesis 4:8; Romans 5:12; 1 John 3:12).

8:45-46 In contrast to the devil, who habitually lies, Jesus speaks only **the truth**[NIV]—and for that reason was not believed. In the end, Jesus was rejected not only because the Jews judged him to be a Sabbath breaker and blasphemer (5:18), but also because his words to them were very harsh and exposing. In light of his character and words they could not stand to see and hear the truth about themselves.

If there was a chink in Jesus' armor, his next question would have been their golden opportunity to destroy him. Jesus left himself completely open for a direct attack.

"Can any of you prove me guilty of sin?"[NIV] Of course no one could. People who hated him and wanted him dead scrutinized his behavior but could find nothing wrong. And they were grasping at straws trying to make him anything but what he claimed to be. Jesus proved he was God in the flesh by his sinless life. He was speaking the truth, but they refused to believe. And Jesus knew why.

8:47 "Whoever is from God hears the words of God. The reason you do not hear them is that you are not from God."[NRSV] Although some in his audience had heard and become believers (8:30), most remained deaf because their hearts were hardened (see 12:39-40). They refused to *hear* (or obey) the words of God because they were not God's children.

HEARING AID
Jesus' use of the word *whoever* makes his statement easily applicable to our own time. The claim to hear God speak is much easier to make than to prove. Jesus consistently taught that obedience was the indicator of hearing. Take the steps to active listening:
- Get away from distracting noise.
- Approach God in a prayerful attitude.
- Devote your full attention to his Word.
- Open your heart and mind, and be willing to obey what he said.
- Don't argue; listen.

JESUS STATES HE IS ETERNAL / 8:48-59 / *129*

At this point, the dialogue between Jesus and his Jewish audience took a decidedly angry turn. Since they had no answer for his clear diagnosis of their spiritual sickness, Jesus' audience reacted with a verbal attack against him. They charged him with two of the most offensive terms at their disposal: "Samaritan" and "demon-possessed." Name-calling usually indicates that a person or group has run out of intelligent comments. Up until this point, Jesus' opponents reserved one final accusation against him: blasphemy. But as Jesus responded to their angry tirade he finally led them to realize the full extent of his claims. He used the "I am" phrase in 8:58 to state his unequivocal claim to divinity. He left no more room for debate. The crowd took up the stones to carry out judgment for blasphemy, but Jesus removed himself from that place. He would choose the time and place for final confrontation.

8:48-50 The Jews answered him, "Aren't we right in saying that you are a Samaritan and demon-possessed?"[NIV] This is the only

instance in the Gospels where Jesus is charged with being a
Samaritan. These expressions were filled with great anger. The
Samaritans were considered beneath the Jews because of their
intermarriage with heathens and their religious impurity. The
Jews leveled this charge at Jesus because he, a fellow Jew, had
accused them of not being true descendants of Abraham (see
8:37-44). Elsewhere in John, Jesus was accused of being demon-
possessed (see 7:20; 8:52; 10:20).

Jesus did not respond to the charge of being "a Samaritan"; he
did refute the charge of being demon-possessed. **"I am not possessed by a demon . . . you dishonor me."**[NIV] Jesus told the leaders that they were dishonoring him by such a charge because
Jesus always sought to honor and glorify his Father. Jesus was
not seeking any glory for himself, but he explained, **"There is
one who seeks it, and he is the judge."**[NIV] The Father would
seek glory for his Son and judge those who dishonor him.

8:51 **"Whoever keeps my word will never see death."** NRSV To keep
Jesus' word means to hear his words and obey them. Keeping
Jesus' word includes relying on the character, ability, strength,
and truth of what he promised. When Jesus said that those who
obeyed wouldn't die, he was talking about spiritual death, not
physical death. Even physical death, however, will eventually be
overcome. Those who follow Christ will be raised to live eternally with him.

8:52-53 **"Now we know that you are demon-possessed! Abraham died
and so did the prophets, yet you say that if anyone keeps your
word, he will never taste death. Are you greater than our
father Abraham? He died, and so did the prophets."**[NIV] For
Jesus to claim that he could prevent death was for him a claim to
be greater than any person who ever lived—indeed, it meant he
was claiming to be divine. These Jews were convinced that only
a madman (someone who was *demon-possessed*) would make
such a claim.

8:54-55 **"If I glorify myself, my glory means nothing."**[NIV] Again, Jesus
deferred the matter of his divine identity to his relationship with
his Father. He could never make the kind of claims he made apart
from his union with the Father. If he had come of his own accord,
his glory would be worthless. But the Father had sent him, and
the Father would glorify him—even if the Jews didn't.

**"My Father, whom you claim as your God, is the one who glo-
rifies me. Though you do not know him, I know him. If I said
I did not, I would be a liar like you, but I do know him and**

keep his word."^{NIV} The crux of the matter was that the Jews did not know the Father from whom Jesus came, even though they claimed to know him. The one who really knew the Father and kept his word knew that these Jews were lying.

8:56 **"Your ancestor Abraham rejoiced that he would see my day; he saw it and was glad."**^{NRSV} Jesus referred to Abraham as their ancestor, but he meant it only in the physical sense. Abraham, by some revelation not directly recorded in Genesis, saw the coming day of the Messiah (cf. Hebrews 11:8-13). Several possibilities have been proposed: (1) According to rabbinic tradition, Abraham was given foresight about the future of his descendants. Jesus, perhaps knowing this tradition, pinpointed the one event that would have made Abraham rejoice—the day when the Messiah, his descendant, would come to deliver the world; (2) Genesis 17:7 mentions God's establishment of an everlasting covenant with Abraham's offspring, which some take to be a messianic promise; (3) Genesis 22:8 records Abraham's prophetic words that "God himself will provide the lamb for the burnt offering,"^{NIV} which received their complete fulfillment in Jesus. Of the three interpretations, the first makes the most sense because the text speaks of "my day"—i.e., the time of Christ's presence on earth.

8:57 **"You are not yet fifty years old, and have you seen Abraham?"**^{NRSV} Jesus had not claimed to be a contemporary with Abraham or that he had seen Abraham; instead, he said that Abraham had seen his day. The comment about Jesus being not yet fifty years old is a roundabout way of saying that he was not yet an old man.

DECISION TIME
When Jesus said that he existed before Abraham was born, he undeniably proclaimed his divinity. Not only did Jesus say that he existed before Abraham; he also applied God's holy name (*I AM*—Exodus 3:14) to himself. No other religious figure in all of history has made such claims. Either Jesus was God or he was a madman. His claim to deity demands a response. It cannot be ignored. The Jewish leaders tried to stone Jesus for blasphemy because he claimed equality with God. But Jesus *is* God. How have you responded to Jesus, the Son of God?

8:58-59 Jesus astounded them with his answer: **"Most assuredly, I say to you, before Abraham was, I AM."**^{NKJV} Abraham, as with all human beings, had come into existence at one point in time. But

Jesus never had a beginning—he was eternal and therefore God. This is evident in the words "I AM" (*ego eimi*) which he used before (see 8:28). This statement may refer to Exodus 3:14, in which God unveiled his identity to Moses with the name "I AM WHO I AM" (NKJV), and to Isaiah 45:18, "I am the LORD, and there is no other" (NKJV). Thus, Jesus was claiming to be God.

This was too much for the Jews; these words so incensed them that they **picked up stones to stone him**[NIV] for blasphemy. In accordance with the law (Leviticus 24:16), the religious leaders were ready to exercise the punishment for claiming to be God (see 5:18; 10:31). They well understood what Jesus was claiming; and because they didn't believe him, they charged him with blasphemy. In reality, *they* were really the blasphemers, cursing and attacking the God whom they claimed to serve!

But Jesus hid himself[NRSV] or "was hidden" (perhaps meaning he was hidden by God), **and went out of the temple.**[NRSV] John doesn't say it, but by now we know it—Jesus escaped their attempted stoning because his "hour had not yet come."

John 9

Thus far, Jesus has explained his identity in many ways to his listeners. Often he would use a physical object, person, or setting to depict a certain spiritual aspect of his life and purpose. For example:

- While sitting by Jacob's well and talking to the Samaritan woman, Jesus explained that he could give her "living water" (4:10 NKJV).

- After feeding over 5,000 people with two small loaves of bread, Jesus explained that he was "the bread of life" (6:35 NKJV).

- At the Feast of Tabernacles, where a symbolic act took place commemorating the time when Moses struck the rock in the wilderness and it brought forth water for the parched Israelites, Jesus told all the people, "If anyone thirsts, let him come to Me and drink" (7:37 NKJV).

- Again at the Feast of Tabernacles, another symbolic act took place commemorating the pillar of fire that guided the Israelites on their wilderness journey. Jesus told all the people, "I am the light of the world. He who follows Me shall not walk in darkness, but have the light of life" (8:12 NKJV).

All of Jesus' miracles also pointed to who he was. John follows Jesus' discourse about being "the light of the world" (8:12; 9:5) with the account of Jesus restoring sight to a man born blind. This story illustrates the spiritual truth of Christ being the Light of the World. As the blind beggar comes to "see" that Jesus is the Messiah, so Jesus offers us spiritual sight to enable us to see him as our Savior and Lord. We too are born spiritually blind and need the gift of sight that only the Light of the World can provide. The Light of the World becomes our light when we put our faith in Jesus Christ.

9:1 Now as Jesus passed by, He saw a man who was blind from birth. NKJV In ancient cultures, as in many modern cultures, blind people had no choice but to be beggars. This man probably was very poor and was begging along the roadside, thus Jesus saw him as he passed by. Because Jesus did the "seeing" and the disciples did the "asking" the implication is that perhaps Jesus pointed out the man to the disciples. Jesus may have spoken to the blind man. The wording of the following question seems to imply that the group was standing directly in front of the blind man.

A CURIOSITY
We have a tendency not to "see" those who are disabled or to treat them in ways that emphasize or trivialize their disadvantage. For instance, blind people are often treated as if they can't hear either, which is exactly what the disciples did on this occasion.
  People appreciate being genuinely cared for, but resent being treated as a "case," "problem," or "curiosity." When dealing with people who are suffering or disabled, we must try to empathize with them. We should always strive to treat others in the way we would want to be treated, were our situations reversed (see Matthew 7:12).

9:2-3 **"Who sinned, this man or his parents, that he was born blind?"**[NRSV] The disciples believed, based at least partly on Old Testament texts like Exodus 34:7, that a disability such as blindness was a punishment for sin. Many people around the world believe that suffering results from sin. People tend to believe that displeasing God leads to punishment; therefore, they assume that whenever a person seems to be undergoing punishment, there is reason to suspect wrongdoing. This assumption, for example, drove Job's friends to treat him with heavy-handed judgment.

But if suffering always indicates sin, what do we say about babies born with deformities or handicaps? If this man was *born blind,* who sinned, the man (who must have somehow sinned in the womb) or his parents?

WHY THE HURT?
In Jewish culture, many believed that all calamities and suffering resulted from sin. But this man suffered so that God could be glorified. We live in a fallen world where good behavior is not always rewarded and bad behavior not always punished; therefore, innocent people sometimes suffer. If God removed suffering whenever we asked, we would follow him for comfort and convenience, not out of love and devotion. Regardless of the reasons for our suffering, Jesus has the power to help us deal with it. When we suffer from a disease, tragedy, or disability, we should not ask, Why did this happen to me? or What did I do wrong? Instead, we should ask God to give us strength for the trial and a clearer perspective on what is happening.

The disciples were thinking about what caused the blindness. Jesus shifted their attention away from the cause to the purpose. Jesus demonstrated God's power by healing the man. Instead of worrying about the cause of our problems, we should instead find out how God could use our problem to demonstrate his power. Jesus explained that the man's blindness had nothing to do with his sin or his parents' sin: **"But this happened so that the work of God might be displayed in his life."**[NIV] These words do not mean that God heartlessly inflicted blindness on this man at birth, but simply that he allowed nature to run its course so that the victim would ultimately bring glory to God through the reception of both physical and spiritual sight (see 9:30-38).

GOD MAY USE OUR SUFFERING
How can God be at work in a desperate situation? There may be times when we have done everything possible to solve a problem. After we have explored the options, exhausted our resources, probed our motives, asked for advice, and done what was suggested, we may have found that nothing seems to have changed. We may have persisted in prayer and asked others to pray for us, and yet perceive no answer. The truth is, the solution, resolution, or answer may not ever come in this life. But it is also true that regardless of our difficulty and whether or not our burden is removed, God is still at work.

- God may use our experience to help advise and encourage others who pass through the same trials.
- God may use our suffering to break through the hardness of another person and bring about change in them.
- God may use our unresolved need to motivate others to keep searching for a solution from which others will benefit.
- God may use our endurance in suffering rather than the suffering itself to be an encouraging example to other believers.

9:4-5 **"We must do the work of him who sent me."**[NIV] This verse is also translated, "We must work the works of him who sent me" (NRSV), and some early manuscripts end the sentence in the plural, "us." Evidently, Jesus was speaking of himself and his disciples as coworkers. He wanted them to learn from him because they would continue his work as his sent ones (see 20:21). Jesus included the disciples in this work (although they actually did nothing for this blind man) because they would be the ones doing the work of God on earth after his resurrection and ascension. What a privilege to be called Christ's coworkers (see 1 Corinthians 3:9; 2 Corinthians 5:21; 6:1). We must never doubt our role or significance.

"As long as it is day."[NIV] While Christ was in the world, light was in the world; it was "day." The "day" was the time allotted for Jesus to do his work on earth. However, **"night is coming, when no one can work."**^{NIV} The night would come, that is, Jesus would soon die, and would no longer be in the world in physical form. The coming of the night speaks of the shortness of time Jesus had left to fulfill his purpose on earth.

TODAY
Jesus' words held a note of urgency. It may be "day" now, but it won't always be so. We must not put off until tomorrow what God wants us to do now. Today is the day. If God presents an opportunity and also provides the strength, skill, or other resources to do it, we ought to respond immediately. The night is coming soon enough; then our day of opportunity will end. What have you done today with eternity in mind?

"I am the light of the world."^{NIV} The healing of the blind man affirmed Jesus' identity as the Messiah, for the Old Testament predicted that the Messiah would come to heal the blind (Isaiah 29:18; 35:5; 42:7).

9:6-7 **He spat on the ground and made mud with the saliva and spread the mud on the man's eyes.**^{NRSV} Why would Jesus perform this miracle in such a strange way? This is not typical of the way Jesus performed miracles, according to John. But Mark records two incidents of miraculous healing where Jesus used his saliva—to cure a deaf and dumb man in Decapolis and to heal a blind man in Bethsaida (Mark 7:33; 8:23). John's account, however, provides the only record of Jesus spitting on the ground and forming clay from it.

From antiquity, spit or saliva was thought to have medicinal power. But the Jews were suspicious of anyone who used saliva in healing because it was associated with magical arts. It is worth noting, however, that the role of Jesus' saliva in the healing was primarily in making the mud. As has been pointed out before (see section on 2:6-8), Jesus did not use random objects without a specific purpose.

First, Jesus used the clay to help develop the man's faith (he had to do as Jesus said, which was to go and wash in a certain pool). Second, Jesus kneaded the mud with his hands in order to make the clay to put on the man's eyes. This constituted "work" on a Sabbath day and would upset the Pharisees. Jesus had much to teach them about God and his Sabbath.

"Go, wash in the pool of Siloam" (which means Sent).^{NRSV} *Siloam* is a Greek translation of the Hebrew name *Shiloah,* mean-

ing "sent." The pool of Siloam had been built by King Hezekiah.
His workers had built an underground tunnel from the Spring of
Gihon in the Kidron Valley outside of Jerusalem. This tunnel
channeled the water into the pool of Siloam inside the city walls.
Located in the southeast corner of the city, the tunnel and pool
were originally built to help Jerusalem's inhabitants survive in
times of seige. If the city were ever surrounded by enemy armies,
the people inside could always get fresh water without having to
leave the city (2 Kings 20:20; 2 Chronicles 32:30). These waters
may symbolize the work that Jesus, the sent one, had come to do.
They provided the deliverance and healing sent by God, illustrat-
ing the full deliverance from sin that Jesus provided for us.

9:8-12 These verses record the various reactions of the blind man's
neighbors to his healing. Some thought he looked like the one
who used to sit and beg. Others positively identified him as the
same man. Still others objected that this only looked like that
blind man. In response, the healed man insisted, **"I am the
man."**[NIV] Finally realizing that the person who once was blind
had received his sight, they asked, **"How then were your eyes
opened?"**[NIV] The formerly blind man testified to the healing
power of Jesus by recounting the story of how he had been
healed.

Of course, the crowd wanted to track down this healer (perhaps they assumed it was Jesus), so they asked, **"Where is this
man?"**[NIV] But the man had been blind when Jesus sent him to the
pool of Siloam; therefore, he didn't know where Jesus had gone
afterward. From this point on, the formerly blind man began to
see more clearly who Jesus was, while the Pharisees became
more spiritually blind. While sin did not cause the man to be born
blind, sin *did* cause the Pharisees' blindness.

RELIGIOUS LEADERS QUESTION THE BLIND MAN / 9:13-34 / *149*

Because the people discovered both a miracle and a mystery surrounding the healing of the blind man, they took him to what
they considered the most dependable place for exploring such
matters. The Pharisees quickly concluded that whatever else the
healer might be, he certainly wasn't from God, for otherwise he
would not work on the Sabbath. In their quest for "truth," these
Pharisees tried a number of explanations to invalidate the
miracle: (1) perhaps the blind man had not been blind from birth
or had not been totally blind; (2) perhaps God did this miracle
directly (but they would recognize no human agent).

When the formerly blind man pointed out the obvious answers that they had been so studiously avoiding, they responded by viciously berating him and expelling him from their presence.

The astonishing fact of the man's newly given vision eluded this group as if they were blind. Later Jesus pointed this out as their problem, over their strenuous objections.

9:13-15 **They brought to the Pharisees the man who had been blind.**NIV Why did they bring him to the Pharisees? The local synagogue was the equivalent of small-claims court. If formal charges had been made, the case would have gone to the Sanhedrin, the high court. But verse 14 also provides a possible answer: **the day on which Jesus had made the mud and opened the man's eyes was a Sabbath.**NIV The people had realized that Jesus had performed another miracle on the Sabbath and that the Pharisees would want to know about this event. This miracle was news because it was very unusual (9:32). Healing, along with many other actions defined as work, was strictly controlled on the Sabbath. Healing was only to occur in cases of life and death, for which the blind man did not qualify because he had been living with his blindness since birth.

The Pharisees wanted to know how this man had received his sight, and the man explained it in the simplest of terms. Because the man was still blind during the interview with Jesus, he really didn't know who Jesus was. He could only exclaim, **I washed, and now I see.**NIV But no one cheers and congratulates the man on his healing, instead they condemn the healer.

9:16-17 **"This man is not from God, for he does not observe the sabbath."**NRSV The Jewish Sabbath, Saturday, was the weekly holy day of rest. The Pharisees had made a long list of specific do's and don'ts regarding the Sabbath in an attempt to explain and put into practice what the Scriptures meant when they prohibited work on the Sabbath. Kneading the clay, anointing his eyes, and healing the man (whose life was not in danger) were all considered work and therefore were forbidden. Jesus may have purposely made the clay in order to emphasize his teaching about the Sabbath—that it is right to care for others' needs even if it involves working on a day of rest. But because Jesus broke their petty rules, they immediately decided he was *not from God.*

But some other Pharisees questioned this condemnation: **"How can a man who is a sinner perform such signs?"**NRSV There is no indication that these men were inclined to believe in Jesus; more likely, they were protecting themselves from the charge of obvious bias. Thus, **there was a division among**

them.^{NKJV} While the Pharisees conducted investigations and
debated about Jesus, people were being healed and lives were
being changed. The Pharisees' skepticism was not based on insuf-
ficient evidence, but on jealousy of Jesus' popularity and his
influence on the people.

CLEARER VISION
Our personal description of Jesus to others makes an impact.
John encourages all of us whose eyes, hearts, and minds have
been opened by Christ to speak out for the Lord. This lesson is
for us because the formerly blind man's vision of Jesus got
clearer and clearer as he reflected on what had happened and
listened to the accusers frantically trying to discredit what he
knew to be undeniably true. At first his description of Jesus
wasn't accurate, but it was heartfelt. He said what he understood. New believers often bring that quality of freshness and
earnestness to their statements about Jesus. How quickly we
forget the wonder of being able to see spiritually for the first
time!
    We can testify to the fact that we were once blind to our own
separation from God, blind to our need, blind to God's influence
in our lives, and blinded by the world around us. We may not
be able to explain in detail how Jesus has done what he has
done in our lives, but we can say with conviction: Once I was
blind; now I can see!

**What do you say about Him because He opened your
eyes?**^{NKJV} The staunchest Pharisees attacked the healed man with
a renewed attempt to break down his testimony. But this newly
sighted beggar responded with even more praise for his healer
than he had offered previously—he called Jesus **a prophet.** The
man was searching for a category in which to place the one who
healed him. At first (9:11) the healer was just a man. But under
questioning a new title came to mind: "prophet."

9:18-21 The Pharisees **still did not believe that he had been blind and
had received his sight,**^{NIV} so they called in the man's parents in
the hope that they would refute their own son's testimony. Failure
to reach quick agreement on the case meant they needed to
review the "facts." They asked the parents if this man was really
their son, and if he was really born blind. The Pharisees were
exasperated: **"How is it that now he can see?"**^{NIV} they asked,
although we may wonder what they expected the parents to
answer.
    They knew their son, and they knew his previous condition,
but how he could see, they didn't know. Instead of giving praise

for their son's healer, they responded, **"Ask him; he is of age. He will speak for himself."**^{NRSV} The parents did not deny their son's story, but neither did they support his claim as their son had done.

9:22-23 **His parents said this because they were afraid of the Jews, for already the Jews had decided that anyone who acknowledged that Jesus was the Christ would be put out of the synagogue.**^{NIV} The Greek expression for *be put out of the synagogue (aposynagogos genetai)* literally means "become de-synagogued"—similar to the idea of excommunication. The expression is unique to John's Gospel (used here and in 12:42; 16:2).

Jewish regulations stipulated two kinds of excommunication: one that would last for thirty days until the offender could be reconciled, and one that was a permanent "ban" accompanied by a curse. Because the synagogue controlled every aspect of life (civic, recreational, legal, and religious), an individual cut off from the synagogue would suffer severe isolation. Many Jews in John's day had been "de-synagogued" because they had confessed Jesus to be the Christ. (Jesus predicted this—see 16:2.) In Jesus' day, there was also a kind of informal prohibition against any Jew who would confess Jesus to be the Christ.

But why would such a harsh punishment be given people who followed this Jesus, whom the Pharisees had proclaimed as a fake Messiah? Up to this point, Jesus had been accepted by many as "the Prophet . . . [and] they intended to come and make him king by force" (6:14-15 NIV). He had done miracles that could not be ignored or explained away. Many thought he was "the Christ" (7:26 NIV). The Pharisees were facing a politically dangerous situation. If the crowds were to take Jesus by force and make him king, Rome would respond quickly and forcefully to suppress such a revolt. Roman intervention would cause incredible troubles for the Jews. So the religious leaders decided on the harsh punishment of being put out of the synagogue for anyone who dared believe in Jesus.

9:24-25 **A second time they summoned the man who had been blind.**^{NIV} Not content with their cross-examination of the healed man, the Pharisees called him in a second time with a command, **"Give glory to God!"**^{NRSV} This means "admit the truth" (see Joshua 7:19; Jeremiah 13:16). The Pharisees tried to make the man confess his wrong in proclaiming Jesus as a prophet and to make him agree with them that Jesus was a sinner.

LOOKING FOR A LOOPHOLE
In reviewing the facts of the case, the Pharisees had no intention of believing or following the one who had performed the healing. They wanted to disqualify Jesus. They avoided the truth in their quest for a loophole.

Occasionally we will meet people who only want to argue and debate the merits and claims of Jesus without ever deciding to follow him. They mask their rejection under a thin cover of inquiry. Perhaps, like the Pharisees, they have too much to lose. Prestige, power, and personal independence are hard to give up. It is easier to keep the argument on intellectual grounds than to face our spiritual and moral shortcomings. Sometimes, people have worked hard to get to their comfortable place in life and are unwilling to consider change. We must help them see that Christ gives both the power and the desire to change.

But the healed man would not give in; he would not say whether or not Jesus was a sinner. What he would say was what he had experienced: **"One thing I know: that though I was blind, now I see"**[NKJV] So many Christians, having been blind and then received spiritual sight, have testified the same! Believers don't need to know all the answers before they can share Christ with others. All they must know is how Jesus changed their lives. Each of us is our own expert on that topic! We should tell people what Jesus did for us, and trust God to help our words draw others to him.

9:26-27 **"What did he do to you? How did he open your eyes?"**[NIV] The Pharisees relentlessly asked who did the healing and how it happened. Perhaps they hoped the man would contradict his earlier story so they could accuse him.

"I have told you already and you did not listen. . . . Do you want to become his disciples, too?"[NIV] This brings out the irony of the situation. The religious leaders were making such extensive inquiry about Jesus' identity that it would appear they wanted to follow him—when actually they had no intention of becoming his disciples.

The religious leaders were unable to throttle the healed beggar's willingness to testify for Jesus. In fact, the more the Pharisees questioned this man who had received his sight, the stronger and clearer he became about Jesus. Their blind obstinacy helped his clarity. See how his vision cleared:

■ At first, the man recognized his healer as "the man called Jesus" (9:11 NRSV).

- Then he knew Jesus was "a prophet" (9:17).

- Then he saw Jesus as one who was "from God" and had performed a miracle never done before (9:32-33).

- Then finally, when confronted by Jesus, he believed that Jesus is the "Son of Man" (the Messiah), worthy of worship (9:35-38).

9:28-29 **"We are disciples of Moses!"**NIV While the Pharisees questioned the man, they persistently defended their adherence to Moses (they were confident that God had spoken to Moses). But Jesus had already told them that if they really knew Moses and understood his writings, they would know the Messiah, for Moses wrote of him (5:45-47).

"But as for this fellow, we don't even know where he comes from."NIV The word *fellow* here is derogatory—as if Jesus were just another person with no credentials. It is ironic that the Pharisees claimed not to know where Jesus was from, for that was one item they believed would be true about the Messiah: "No one will know where he is from" (7:27 NIV). They refused to accept Jesus' words or believe that the signs he did validated his claims. They chose to reject him.

9:30-31 This reasoning (and probably their insults too) astonished the healed man, so he tried to explain to them that the act of giving him sight proved that Jesus was a man whom God listened to: **"We know that God does not listen to sinners, but he does listen to one who worships him and obeys his will."**NRSV There are many Scriptures that support this man's statement:

- "For what is the hope of the godless . . . ? Will God hear their cry . . ?" (Job 27:8-9 NRSV)

- "There they cry out, but he does not answer, because of the pride of evildoers. Surely God does not hear an empty cry, nor does the Almighty regard it." (Job 35:12-13 NRSV)

- "The LORD is far from the wicked, but he hears the prayer of the righteous." (Proverbs 15:29 NRSV)

- "When you stretch out your hands, I will hide my eyes from you; even though you make many prayers, I will not listen; your hands are full of blood." (Isaiah 1:15 NRSV)

As a boy, this healed man certainly had been taught the Scriptures, and he pointed out this fact to these supposedly "learned" Pharisees. God does not listen to the requests of sin-

A COLLECTION OF ATTITUDES
Contrast the attitude of the Pharisees with the newfound attitude of the blind man.

Spiritual Blindness	*Spiritual Insight*
Pride	*Humility*
No concern for others	*Compassion for others*
Condemnation	*Forgiveness*
Hopelessness	*Hope*
Insensitivity to sin	*Desire to repent and change*
Anger	*Love*

ners, only to the requests of those devoted to him. This verse is also translated, "He listens to the godly man who does his will" (NIV).

9:32-34 **"Never since the world began has it been heard that anyone opened the eyes of a person born blind. If this man were not from God, he could do nothing."**[NRSV] Jesus had done the unprecedented, but not the unpredicted. In their fury, the Pharisees were blind to the Old Testment descriptions that specifically speak of the Messiah bringing sight to the blind (see Isaiah 29:18; 35:5; 42:7). Indeed, many thought the healing of the blind would be the messianic miracle *par excellence* because there was never any record of such a healing in the Old Testament.

The healed man's condemnation of the Pharisees' irrational rejection of Jesus proved too much for them to take, so **they threw him out**[NIV] (i.e., "they expelled him from the synagogue") with a curse about his presumed guilt from birth: **"You were born entirely in sins, and are you trying to teach us?"**[NRSV]

JESUS TEACHES ABOUT SPIRITUAL BLINDNESS / 9:35-41 / 150

Unless we have suffered rejection for our faith, we may not be able to identify with the state of this blind man whom Jesus healed. In a single day he went from being a disabled outcast to a celebrity who had miraculously received his sight, then to being a witness in court where he was treated like a criminal, and finally to being outcast again (literally) for simply telling the truth as he clearly saw it.

At this point, Jesus intervened again. He found the man, faced him, and asked a question that would uncover whether or not this man was ready to receive complete vision. The man's under-standing of the one who had healed him had already expanded considerably. Here was his chance to really see Jesus.

In the background of the man's willing trust and worship we hear the Pharisees mumbling, incensed that Jesus was unwilling to recognize their spiritual stature. Instead, Jesus diagnosed their problem as ongoing profound blindness coupled with guilt.

9:35-38 After the man was thrown out of the synagogue, Jesus found him and asked him, **"Do you believe in the Son of Man?"**[NIV] This is the reading in all the earliest manuscripts; later manuscripts read, "the Son of God." Since *Son of Man* is a title of the Christ, Jesus was asking the man if he believed him to be the Messiah. Perhaps the man instantly recognized Jesus by his voice. He expressed immediate desire to believe, which here means not intellectual recognition, but wholehearted trust.

20/20 VISION
The longer this man experienced his new life through Christ, the more confident he became in the one who had healed him. He gained not only physical sight but also spiritual sight as he recognized Jesus first as a prophet (9:17), then as his Lord. When you turn to Christ, you begin to see him differently. The longer you walk with him, the better you will understand who he is. Peter tells us to "grow in the grace and knowledge of our Lord and Savior Jesus Christ" (2 Peter 3:18 NIV). If you want to know more about Jesus, keep walking with him.

When the man asked who the Son of Man was, Jesus responded, **"You have now seen him; in fact, he is the one speaking with you."**[NIV] The words *you have now seen him* have double impact—the man could physically see Jesus with his healed eyes, and he could spiritually see because he understood that Jesus was the Messiah.

"Lord, I believe," and he worshiped him.[NIV] The man acted on his newfound belief—he worshiped. He may have just been excommunicated from the synagogue, but he had found true wor-ship. His personal belief is the culmination of the narrative. His belief sharply contrasts with the blindness of the religious leaders (9:40-41).

9:39-41 Jesus said, "I came into this world for judgment."[NRSV] Do Jesus' words here contradict his statement in 3:17: "God did not send His Son into the world to condemn the world" (NKJV)? Jesus did not execute judgment during his years on earth, although he would do that in the future. However, his words here reveal that, as the Light of the World, he sees and reveals people's innermost thoughts and deepest motives. In so doing, he "judges" or separates those who claim to have great spiritual knowledge when in fact they are blind, from those who humbly seek to follow God and who thus find the Savior.

ULTIMATE ADVENTURE!
John 9 would make a wonderful script for a play or movie. The innocent hero, a disabled victim, is expelled from his home and lives on the periphery of society. Religious people suspect his parents committed some heinous sin, possibly before he was even born!

Into our victim/hero's life steps a remarkable stranger who heals his blindness. The blind man is asked to wash off some miracle mud and loses track of the one who gave him his sight. Strangely, no one recognizes the miracle that has happened to him or shares in his joy. Instead, they treat him as if he has contracted a new disease! Even his parents maintain their distance. Finally, as he explains over and over what happened and what he thinks about the man who healed him, he finds himself thrown into the street. It is only then that he finally meets Jesus face-to-face and believes.

By relating this incident John prepares those who follow Jesus to expect opposition from unbelievers—even religious unbelievers. The trials of those who trust Jesus are real. The backlash and rejection can take financial, familial, social and religious forms. It takes courage and conviction to keep on following Christ. "Though my father and mother forsake me, the LORD will receive me" (Psalm 27:10 NIV).

"So that those who do not see may see, and those who do see may become blind."NRSV Christ spoke these words to the healed man in the presence of the Pharisees. *Those who do not see* are those who realize their need for the Savior and humbly come to him for salvation. They will *see*. But *those who do see* are the self-righteous who think they have all the answers and have no need of the Savior. They *become blind* because they have rejected the "light of the world" (8:12).

The Pharisees quickly understood that Jesus had directed this statement toward them, but they were not fully sure of the meaning of his words, so they asked, **"Surely we are not blind,**

Most high, glorious God, enlighten the darkness of my heart and give me, Lord, a correct faith, a certain hope, a perfect charity, sense, and knowledge, so that I may carry out your holy and true command. *Francis of Assisi* are we?"^{NRSV} They assumed that with their learning, reputation, and high standing, they certainly would not be counted among the "blind."

Jesus expanded his statement with the rather cryptic condemnation: **"If you were blind, you would not be guilty of sin; but now that you claim you can see, your guilt remains."**^{NIV} In contrast to the man who had received his sight, the Pharisees had sight but no light. They were spiritually blind, though they claimed to see. Those who admitted blindness could receive the light and see, but those who thought they saw would remain in their darkness. And their guilt remained, whether they felt guilty or not.

CHOOSING BLINDNESS

The Pharisees were shocked that Jesus thought they were spiritually blind. Jesus countered by saying that it was only blindness (stubbornness and stupidity) that could excuse their behavior. To those who remained open and recognized how sin had truly blinded them from knowing the truth, Jesus gave spiritual understanding and insight. But he rejected those who had become complacent, self-satisfied, and "blind."

Spiritual darkness describes the worst form of judgment. The Light of the World, Jesus, gives us a glimmer of hope. All of us need to follow the Light given to us. Otherwise we are left with nothing but our blind judgment and self-darkening opinions.

John 10

This chapter begins with an extended figure of speech or illustration (10:6), similar to a parable, about shepherds and sheep. John provides two aspects of the illustration: the "gate" (10:1-3) and the "shepherd" (10:3-5), each with its own interpretations—the "gate" is interpreted in 10:7-10, and the "shepherd" in 10:11-18. Parallelling leaders with shepherds and their people with sheep was a common analogy both in the Middle East and in the Bible (see for example 2 Samuel 5:2; 1 Kings 22:17; Zechariah 10:2). Shepherding was a common occupation; many of the Old Testament leaders were shepherds, as were most of the ancestors of the entire nation of Israel (Genesis 46:32; 47:3). God is often called a shepherd or his people the sheep (Genesis 48:15; 49:24; Psalm 23:1; 80:1; Ecclesiastes 12:11; Isaiah 40:11; 53:6; Jeremiah 31:10; 1 Peter 2:25). Several of the elements in the illustration in verses 1-18 can be readily assigned a symbolic meaning:

- the "good shepherd" is Christ
- the "sheep" are the Jewish believers
- the "sheepfold" is Judaism
- the "gate" is Jesus as the way to life
- the "other sheep" are Gentile believers
- the "gatekeeper" is probably God.

The entire passage calls to mind the imagery of Ezekiel 34, where the prophet castigated the false shepherds (Israel's evil leaders) and predicted that the true Shepherd (the Messiah) would come and provide God's people (the sheep) with genuine care and leadership. In comparison to the Pharisees, who were bad leaders of God's people, Jesus was the true Shepherd of all God's people. The healed man who believed in Jesus (in the previous chapter) represented all believers who would come out of Judaism to follow Jesus, as sheep follow their shepherd.

10:1-2 **"Anyone who does not enter the sheepfold by the gate but
climbs in by another way is a thief and a bandit."**^{NRSV} At
night, the shepherd often would gather the sheep into a fold to
protect them from thieves, bad weather, or wild animals. The
sheepfolds were caves, sheds, or open areas surrounded by
walls made of stones or branches, eight to ten feet high. Sometimes the top of the wall was lined with thorns to further dis-
courage predators and thieves. The fold's single entrance made
it easier for a shepherd to guard his flock. Often several shepherds used a single fold and took turns guarding the entrance.
In towns where many people each owned a few sheep, the combined herd was watched over by a shepherd. Mingling the animals was no problem since each flock responded readily to its
own shepherd's voice.

The *gate* (also translated "door," see NKJV) is the main
entrance. Jesus explained that anyone who tried to get in any
other way besides going through the gate would be *a thief and a
bandit*—that person would be up to no good. Most likely this
gate represents the position of Messiah because Jesus went on to
say, **"the one who enters by the gate is the shepherd of the
sheep."**^{NRSV} Only the shepherd has the right to enter the sheepfold and call his own sheep out to follow him.

Jesus rebuked those who would claim to lead God's people
without regarding the Messiah (who is in their midst, but unrecog-

WE ARE HIS SHEEP
Jesus' love for his people is contrasted with the treatment given
the people by the Jewish religious leaders of that day. That contrast would hold for any leader who attempts to use the flock of
God for his or her own selfish purposes.

Religious leaders	Jesus
Self-centered (thieves and/or hired hands)	From God, true
Strangers	Knows his sheep and they recognize him
Lead sheep away from God	Leads sheep to God
Flee when danger threatens	Provides real safety and assurance (Psalm 23)
Have no heart of compassion for the sheep	Lays down his life for the sheep (Psalm 22)
Will abandon the sheep in time of trouble	Will return for his sheep (Psalm 24)

nized by them). Such leaders have false ambitions, selfish desires, and evil intentions.

10:3-6 **"The gatekeeper opens the gate for him, and the sheep hear his voice."**[NRSV] When the shepherd arrived, he would call his sheep. Because sheep recognize the voice of their shepherd, they come and follow him out to pasture. The shepherd was also the gate or the door for the sheep—which in the illustration meant Jesus is the way to eternal life, the way into the kingdom of God.

The "sheepfold" of Judaism held some of God's people who had awaited the coming of their Shepherd-Messiah (see Isaiah 40:1-11). He **"calls his own sheep by name and leads them out"**[NRSV] of the fold. When the Shepherd came, believing Jews recognized his voice and followed him. Not all Jews were God's people; as Paul wrote: "Not all who are descended from Israel are Israel. Nor because they are his descendants are they all Abraham's children. . . . It is not the natural children who are God's children, but it is the children of the promise who are regarded as Abraham's offspring" (Romans 9:6-8 NIV).

"But they will never follow a stranger; in fact, they will run away from him because they do not recognize a stranger's voice."[NIV] It is said that shepherds in the East could name each sheep and that each sheep would respond to the shepherd calling its name. True believers, as sheep belonging to the true Shepherd, would never follow someone pretending to be their shepherd (5:43).

This illustration[NKJV] or "figure of speech" NIV. The Greek word *paroimia* can mean "proverb" or "enigmatic saying." John did not use the word *parabole* (parable), which is common in the synoptic Gospels; and the synoptic Gospels do not have the word *paroimia*. Nonetheless, both had nearly the same function: to communicate spiritual truths by a story or illustration.

IN REVERSE
From the vantage point of the Resurrection and two thousand years of church history, our position is almost exactly the reverse of what Jesus' listeners experienced. We understand better what Jesus meant, but are largely unfamiliar with the shepherding scene he described.

The challenge for us is to take Jesus' self-description seriously. He called himself the gate and the Good Shepherd. He is the entry point and the caring master. Have you responded to his voice and followed him?

10:7-9 After presenting the illustration, Jesus thought it first necessary to explain the symbolic meaning of "the gate" (10:7-10) before identifying the "shepherd" (10:11-18).

The shepherd has called together his flock and taken them to the pasture. Near the pasture is another enclosed place for the sheep. Here the shepherd sits in the doorway, acting as the "gate." The sheep can go out to the pasture or stay inside the walls of the enclosure. To go out or in is to pass by the shepherd's watchful eye.

Having realized they had not grasped what he was teaching them, Jesus said to his listeners, **"I am the gate for the sheep."**[NIV] As the gate for the sheep, he is the only way to salvation and eternal life (10:9; 14:6), and his sheep are under his watchful care.

JESUS THE PROVIDER
In this illustration Jesus used two powerful "I am" statements to show his full provision for us: "I am the gate" and "I am the good shepherd." In ancient days, the shepherd often slept before the gate so as to provide protection for the sheep. Jesus provides us with the greatest protection against eternal destruction. And it was the shepherd's responsibility to make sure his sheep were led to a plentiful pasture. Jesus, as the Good Shepherd, has provided us with abundant life.

"All who ever came before me."[NIV] This statement was not directed at Old Testament saints and prophets, but at those who had come on the scene pretending to be the Christ (see 5:43), or who had led the people away from God. By immediate context, we see that Jesus was also referring to those evil Jewish religious leaders who cared nothing about the spiritual welfare of the people, but only about their petty rules and their reputation (see Matthew 23:13; 24:5). Their treatment of Jesus had made it clear that they were far more committed to their system than to God's Word. They had invented their own gateway and had appointed themselves gatekeepers. Jesus reminded them that any other supposed "gate" to salvation is false.

"But the sheep did not listen to them."[NRSV] Though false teachers, leaders, and messiahs do have their followings, the true sheep of God do not listen to any of them because none of them possess the authentic voice of the Shepherd.

SAFELY GRAZING
Jesus described a scene of sheep safely grazing in lush pastures. The great Shepherd clearly conveyed the idea of real contentment. When we place ourselves under Jesus' care, we discover true freedom in and through him. On our own we frantically seek security, even though the threat of death overshadows us; in Christ we find the eternal life that he freely gives to us. Freedom in Christ does not mean being left to our own devices, but instead means living within the boundaries of his plans and directions.

"I am the gate; whoever enters through me will be saved."[NIV] Because Jesus was the genuine Messiah, the sheep could enter through him to find salvation, freedom (implicit in the statement **will come in and go out**[NIV]), and eternal life (14:6). The expression *will be saved* points to spiritual salvation and spiritual security. It could also be translated, "will be kept safe." The sheep **"find pasture"**[NIV] not as a result of their diligent searching, but through the gracious provision of the Shepherd.

10:10 "The thief does not come except to steal, and to kill, and to destroy."[NKJV] The *thief* (which symbolizes false messiahs) and the *hired hand* (which symbolizes corrupt religious leaders) have evil intentions. They seek to *steal, and to kill, and to destroy* the sheep. They care only about feeding themselves or making money off of the flock. Jesus pictured a heartless individual who began by taking all he could and then killing what he couldn't have. Anything else he destroyed. God's people, Israel, had suffered through more than their share of evil leaders, false prophets, and false messiahs (see, for example, Jeremiah 10:21-22; 12:10; Zechariah 11:4-17).

> All joy (as distinct from mere pleasure, still more amusement) emphasizes our pilgrim status; always reminds, beckons, awakens desire. Our best havings and wantings.
> *C. S. Lewis*

LIFE-GIVER
In contrast to the thief who takes life, Jesus gives life. The life he gives right now is abundantly richer and fuller. It lasts forever, yet it begins today. Life in Christ is on a higher plane because of his forgiveness, love, and guidance. Which would you rather face—the evil thief or the loving Shepherd?

"I have come that they may have life, and that they may have it more abundantly."^{NKJV} Jesus gives abundant life to his sheep. This speaks of the gift of divine, eternal life, a life which becomes the possession of every believer for now and for eternity. Jesus would provide his sheep with this eternal life, and it would cost him his own life.

ABUNDANT LIFE
Jesus promised to provide abundant, or full life to the sheep. One of the first images that comes to mind is the cup described in Psalm 23:5, which is described as filled to overflowing by the shepherd who is the Lord. Abundance of life points to depth of living now and length of living in eternity. It is not only life as good as it can be, but also life beyond what we can imagine!

Jesus gave this full life to the blind man who had been abandoned by his parents and rejected by the religious system (see chapter 9). It is clearly not, however, a life that denies problems and pain. Rather, it is a life that faces them and makes use of them. Instead of letting us focus on the ups and downs of life, Jesus takes us deep into life itself, where there is a calm center even in the storm.

Later Jesus told his disciples, "In this world you will have trouble" (16:33 NIV), thereby removing any last hopes that he was leading his followers into a life of guaranteed earthly happiness and prosperity. Even the beautiful pastoral scene Jesus described in this chapter does not allow us to forget the danger of thieves, the presence of death, and the daily hardships of coming in and going out.

10:11 In contrast to both the thief and the hired hand, Christ is the devoted and dedicated Shepherd—**the good shepherd.**^{NKJV} As described in the verses that follow, there are four characteristics that set this Good Shepherd apart from the false or evil shepherds:

- He approaches directly—he enters at the gate.

- He has God's authority—the gatekeeper allows him to enter.

- He meets real needs—the sheep recognize his voice and follow him.

- He has sacrificial love—he is willing to lay down his life for the sheep.

One of the historical developments within the church has come in our use of the word *shepherd*. The early Latin translation (Vulgate) used the word *pastor*, which English eventually transliterated. Based on passages such as 1 Peter 5:4, which speak of Jesus as the "Chief Shepherd" and elders as "shepherds," ministers within the church came to be known as pastors. Because Jesus is the Good Shepherd, pastors should be like him, demonstrating qualities like honesty, holiness, and sacrificial service.

By repeating it four times, Jesus pointed out that the most important trait of the Good Shepherd is that he **"gives his life for the sheep"**^{NKJV} (10:11; see also 15, 17, 18). According to the imagery in this chapter, a shepherd's life could at times be dangerous. Wild animals were common in the countryside of Judea. A good shepherd may indeed risk his life to save his sheep.

10:12-13 **"The hired hand . . . cares nothing for the sheep."**^{NIV} This person does not have a particular parallel, but is in the story as a contrast with the Good Shepherd. Because he is doing the job only to be paid, he does not have an investment in the sheep as does the shepherd. And when **the wolf** attacks, he's not about to risk his life— he'll run! Very likely, "the wolf" refers to false prophets or others who take advantage of God's people, the sheep (see Acts 20:29).

What a difference between the Good Shepherd and the thief and the hired hand! The thief steals, kills, and destroys; the hired hand does the job only for money, but readily flees when danger comes. The Good Shepherd is committed to the sheep. Jesus is not merely doing a job; he is committed to loving us and even laying down his life for us. Religious leaders who are concerned only about their reputation and their petty rules do not have this commitment. How would you characterize your ministry?

LIFE!
John emphasized the theme of "life" in his Gospel. The word was constantly on Jesus' lips. It was John who recorded Jesus saying: "I am the resurrection and the life. He who believes in me will live, even though he dies" (11:25 NIV). The following are several other aspects of life found in the Gospel of John:

Aspects of Life	Reference in John's Gospel
Life is God's gift	1:4; 10:28
Jesus is the Life	11:25; 14:6
Eternal life is living fellowship with God now and forever	3:15-16
Life is found only in trusting Christ, not just knowing about him	5:40
Life begins by believing in Jesus	20:31

10:14-16 "**I know my sheep and my sheep know me.**"NIV Just as the shepherd calls his sheep and they follow only him, so Jesus knows his people. And his followers, in return, know him to be their Messiah, and they love and trust him. Such knowing and trusting between Jesus and his followers is compared to the relationship between Jesus and the Father: "**as the Father knows me and I know the Father.**"NIV And Jesus repeated his point—that he is the Good Shepherd and that he will lay down his life for the sheep.

"**I have other sheep that do not belong to this fold.**"NRSV Jesus had already spoken of leading out his sheep from the fold of Judaism. All of his disciples came out of this fold, as did all those Jews who came to believe in him as their Messiah. Jesus knew, however, that he had *other sheep* that were not from Judaism. These *other sheep* are Gentile believers. Jesus came to save Gentiles as well as Jews. This is an insight into his worldwide mission—to die for sinful people all over the world.

"**There shall be one flock and one shepherd.**"NIV The Good Shepherd came to gather together God's people into one flock (Ezekiel 34:11-14, 23). The new Gentile believers and the Jewish believers who left Judaism would form one flock that would be altogether outside of Judaism. The flock would have one Shepherd. Furthermore, Jesus' words here foreshadow those he uttered

LIVING TO DIE

Everything about Jesus' life pointed toward a purpose. His passing through the world illustrated many spiritual truths about God and his plan, but Jesus' main reason for coming was to die in our behalf. Without Christ's death for us there would be no hope for us! (All verses are quoted from NRSV.)

Reference	Passage
Romans 5:8	"But God proves his love for us in that while we still were sinners Christ died for us."
Ephesians 5:2	"Christ loved us and gave himself up for us."
Hebrews 9:14	"Christ, who through the eternal Spirit offered himself without blemish to God."
1 Peter 2:24	"He himself bore our sins in his body on the cross, so that, free from sins, we might live for righteousness; by his wounds you have been healed."
1 Peter 3:18	"For Christ also suffered for sins once for all, the righteous for the unrighteous, in order to bring you to God."

in his prayer for the oneness of all those who would believe in
him through the disciples' message (17:20ff.)

UNITY
Jesus definitely taught unity: "There shall be one flock . . ."
(10:16). The Idea of a single flock helps determine our relationship with other Christians. We certainly desire a structural unity
among Christians to display our oneness to the world. Many
Christians work hard to accomplish that very objective. However, did Jesus have something greater in mind than organiza-
tional unity when he spoke of "one flock"?

A flock derives its unity partly by being a group of animals in
one place; but Jesus desires more than that. Each of the sheep
remains in the flock, not by being physically present, but
because the shepherd owns and cares for it. The basis for the
unity of the flock is that they all have one shepherd.

Too many efforts in structural unity among Christians focus
on building bigger, more inclusive fences rather than clarifying
to which shepherd the sheep belong. True followers of Jesus
have always managed to find and fellowship with each other
even though they live out their faith in different church structures. Genuine oneness in Jesus Christ allows for wonderful fellowship among sheep from very diverse backgrounds.

10:17-18 "**The reason my Father loves me is that I lay down my life—
only to take it up again. No one takes it from me, but I lay it
down of my own accord. I have authority to lay it down and
authority to take it up again.**"NIV The Father loved the Son for
his willingness to die in order to secure the salvation of the
believers. Jesus laid down his life of his own accord; and yet of
his own accord he would also take up his life again in resurrection. When Jesus said "I lay it down . . . and take it up again" he
was claiming authority to control his death and beyond. John's
original readers needed to remember that Jesus specifically foretold his death and resurrection. We need the same reminder. Jesus
gave up his life; it was not taken from him.

"**I have received this command from my Father.**"NRSV The
Son's authority to lay down his life and take it up again did not
originate with himself; it came from the Father.

10:19-21 **The Jews were again divided.**NIV Some of the unbelieving Jews
who heard Jesus pronounced a twofold judgment against him:
"**He is demon-possessed and raving mad.**"NIV Jesus had already
been accused of being demon-possessed (7:20; 8:48), but this is
the first and only time in John's Gospel that Jesus is accused of

being raving mad or insane. It was commonly believed that insanity went hand-in-hand with demon-possession.

Others were saying, "These are not the words of one who has a demon. Can a demon open the eyes of the blind?"NRSV Some other Jews in Jesus' audience were impressed with both Jesus' words and miraculous deeds. They had not yet forgotten the healing of the blind man (chapter 9). Thus, they disagreed with those who charged him with demon-possession.

THE RING OF TRUTH
One of the arguments for the credibility of the Gospels is that they show little defensiveness in handling contradictory reports about Jesus. John included the reactions and reasons of those who disbelieved in Christ. Other explanations for Jesus' power are faithfully recorded. The Gospels are not propaganda; they present the facts in such a way that the reader is still forced to make his or her own decision about Jesus.

The questions of doubt and unbelief are useful for clarifying our own faith. Is the Christ we trust more like someone raving mad or like the Lord of the universe? Each time we reaffirm our faith in Jesus, we become stronger and better prepared for new challenges and opposition.

RELIGIOUS LEADERS SURROUND JESUS AT THE TEMPLE / 10:22-42 / *152*

As this section begins, there has been a temporary stalemate between Jesus and his opponents. They have become divided, so they are unable for a time to mount an effective attack against him. It must have been a period of intense frustration for the Jewish religious leaders. Finally, an opportunity for confrontation developed one day while Jesus was visiting the temple.

To a direct question about his identity, Jesus briefly returned to the shepherd/sheep theme, but he concluded with a clear description of oneness between himself and God. Once again the stones used to execute blasphemers were about to be hurled, but Jesus faced down his accusers. When they tried to restrain Jesus, he left the temple and the area and traveled outside Jerusalem until the final week of his life. This strategic retreat cleared the way for the Triumphal Entry.

10:22-23 The Feast of Dedication.NIV A couple of months had passed since Jesus' last teaching to the people in 7:1–10:21. That teaching had occurred during the Feast of Tabernacles in September/October; the coming words occurred at the Feast of Dedication in December. This feast was not one of the official festivals in the Old Testament. It was instituted by Judas Maccabeus in 165 B.C. to commemorate the cleansing of the temple after Antiochus Epiphanes had defiled it by sacrificing a pig on the altar of burnt offering (see 1 Maccabees 4:36-59; 2 Maccabees 1:9; 10:1-8). This is also the present-day Feast of Lights called Hanukkah.

It was winter.NIV This added detail gives us a time frame. John may have included it to help his readers who would probably not be familiar with the Jewish calendar. Jesus was **walking in Solomon's Colonnade.**NIV Colonnades were roofed porches with tall stone columns that surrounded the temple on all sides and faced inward, forming long walkways. Solomon's Colonnade was located on the east side of the temple. It was named for Solomon because it was believed to rest on portions of the original temple built by Solomon. These were common places for teaching, so it would have been an appropriate place for Jesus to be walking and probably teaching as he walked. The earliest Christians also met and taught in the same location (Acts 3:11; 5:12). It would have been a site of deep significance to believers.

10:24 **The Jews gathered around him, saying, "How long will you keep us in suspense? If you are the Christ, tell us plainly."**NIV Many people who ask for proof do so for wrong reasons. Jesus had never plainly told the Jews in Jerusalem that he was the Christ because the term *Messiah* or *Christ* connoted a military leader or political liberator for them. Therefore, Jesus wisely avoided using that term. Most of these questioners didn't want to follow Jesus in the way that he wanted to lead them. They hoped that Jesus would declare himself the Messiah, but only if he intended to get on with their political agenda and drive out the Romans. So they wanted to hear an open declaration from Jesus' lips. Was he the Christ or not?

It is doubtful, however, that a plain declaration would have convinced them, for they had already made up their minds on the issue. Some of them hoped he would identify himself so they could accuse him of telling lies or catch him in the act of blasphemy (see 10:31, 33, 39).

10:25-26 **"I have told you, and you do not believe. The works that I do in my Father's name testify to me."**NRSV Although Jesus had never told them "I am the Christ," he had clearly indicated his unity with God the Father (5:17ff.) and his heavenly origin (6:32ff.). Besides, the *works* Jesus performed should have convinced them he was the Messiah (see Isaiah 35:3-6).

John refers to the illustration Jesus used months earlier regarding Jesus as the "good shepherd" (10:3-9, 16). Here, Jesus told the Jewish leaders surrounding him, **"You do not believe, because you do not belong to my sheep."**NRSV Only those who were given to Jesus by the Father (10:29) were his sheep.

SECURITY

Jesus' hand provides such powerful security that he pledges the full power of God to fulfill it. "No one can snatch them out of my hand" shows the impossibility of true believers being lost. This security is also promised by Jesus when he says, "I shall lose none of all that he has given me" (6:39 NIV). When facing any temptation, they are secure with God, not because of their own strength or wisdom, but because of God's power. Just as a shepherd protects his sheep, Jesus protects his people from eternal harm. While believers can expect to suffer on earth, Satan cannot harm their souls or take away their eternal life with God. There are many reasons to be afraid here on earth, because this is the devil's domain (1 Peter 5:8). But if you choose to follow Jesus, he will give you everlasting safety.

10:27-28 Of those who do believe Jesus and are his sheep, Jesus says, **"My sheep listen to my voice; I know them, and they follow me. I give them eternal life, and they shall never perish; no one can snatch them out of my hand."**NIV In this grand statement, Jesus summarized the blessings of those who truly listen to and believe the gospel. The believer in Jesus knows him personally, has eternal life, will not perish, and is secure in his care. But many of those who heard had no intention of truly listening. It is also true that those refusing to listen to Jesus' voice are not his sheep. We recognize Christ's voice when he speaks to us through the Bible. Are we truly listening for it?

10:29 **"My Father, who has given them to Me, is greater than all."**NKJV The ancient manuscripts record this statement in three ways. The first, as just cited; the second, "My Father, as to that which he has given me, is greater than all"; the third, "That which the Father has given me is greater than all." The first reading has early manuscript support and makes good sense. The second reading strains the Greek language. The last reading is the most difficult (and is therefore considered by some scholars to be the original); it speaks of the Father's gift to the Son (i.e., the believers) as being able to overcome all outside forces. In any case, the point is that God's power guards and preserves the flock for salvation.

10:30 "I and the Father are one."[NIV] Jesus did not mean that he and the Father are the same person, because the word for "one" in Greek is neuter. The Father and the Son are two persons in the Trinity, but they are one in essence. Given this essential oneness, the Father and Son act as one—what the Father does, the Son does, and vice versa. This is one of the clearest affirmations of Jesus' divinity in the whole Bible. Thus Jesus is not merely a good teacher—he is God. His claim to be God was unmistakable. The religious leaders wanted to kill him because their laws said that anyone claiming to be God should die for blasphemy. Nothing could persuade them that Jesus' claim was true.

10:31-33 Again, the Jews picked up stones to stone him.[NIV] For the third time (see 5:17-18; 8:58-59), these Jews wanted to execute this

GOD IS GREATER

The invincibility of God in protecting those who trust in him is attested throughout the Bible. And nowhere else is that power more clear than toward those whom God has promised to save. The following are a sample of biblical affirmations on God's protection (all verses are quoted from NKJV):

God's Greatness	Reference
"LORD, it is nothing for You to help, whether with many or with those who have no power."	2 Chronicles 14:11
"Behold, God is my helper; the LORD is with those who uphold my life."	Psalm 54:4
"Through God we will do valiantly."	Psalm 60:12
"It is better to trust in the LORD than to put confidence in man."	Psalm 118:8
"For sin shall not have dominion over you, for you are not under law but under grace."	Romans 6:14
"For I am persuaded that neither death nor life, nor angels nor principalities nor powers, nor things present nor things to come, nor height nor depth, nor any other created thing, shall be able to separate us from the love of God which is in Christ Jesus our Lord."	Romans 8:38-39
"I am not ashamed, for I know whom I have believed and am persuaded that He is able to keep what I have committed to Him until that Day."	2 Timothy 1:12
"Now to Him who is able to keep you from stumbling, and to present you faultless before the presence of His glory with exceeding joy, to God our Savior, who alone is wise, be glory and majesty, dominion and power, both now and forever. Amen."	Jude 24-25

"blasphemer" (Leviticus 24:11-16). But Jesus withheld their violent act by asking them, **"I have shown you many great miracles from the Father. For which of these do you stone me?"**NIV

The Jews answered that they were not stoning him for any work, **"but for blasphemy, because you, though only a human being, are making yourself God."**NRSV The Jews in Jesus' audience understood accurately enough what Jesus' words meant. Though they didn't believe him, they understood he was claiming equality with God. Ironically, Jesus' greatest critics (especially in modern times) have considered him to be nothing more than a man, while the greatest enemies of his time recognized that he was claiming to be God.

10:34-36 Jesus answered, **"Is it not written in your law, 'I said, you are gods'?"**NRSV The term "law" is often used in the New Testament to encompass the entire Old Testament. By saying "your law," Jesus was claiming common ground with his accusers, for they all agreed that **"scripture cannot be annulled."**NRSV

"If those to whom the word of God came were called 'gods' . . . can you say that the one whom the Father has sanctified and sent into the world is blaspheming because I said, 'I am God's Son'?"NRSV Jesus used Psalm 82:6, where the Israelite judges are called gods (see also Exodus 4:16; 7:1) to counter the Jews' charge of blasphemy. In Psalm 82, the supreme God is said to rise in judgment against those whom he calls "gods," because they had failed to be just to the helpless and oppressed. These "gods" were those who were the official representatives and commissioned agents of God; they were the judges executing judgment for God. If they were called "gods," how was it blasphemous for Jesus to call himself the Son of God when, in fact, he *was* the one the Father sanctified and sent into the world?

10:37-39 **"Even though you do not believe me, believe the miracles."**NIV At least three different kinds of evidence were given to convince people about Jesus: (1) Verbal proof convinced some, such as the people who said "No man has ever taught like this one!" (2) Character proofs convinced others who spent time with Jesus and observed his life. (3) Signs and miracles demonstrated his power. Jesus recognized that some who might not be convinced one way might be open to other evidence. He invited his listeners to consider his miracles if they found his words too difficult to believe.

After all, it was prophesied that the Messiah would do great works (Isaiah 35:4-6).

OLD BUT NEW
How often do you find yourself skipping over the Old Testament because it seems too hard to understand or too outdated? Jesus' words, "scripture cannot be annulled" (also translated, "Scripture cannot be broken") illustrate his high regard for the Old Testament. John records several incidents when Jesus cited the Old Testament. John also wrote in other places of the influence of the Old Testament on Jesus' listeners. For example (all verses are quoted from NRSV):

- Philip said to Nathanael, "We have found him about whom Moses in the law and also the prophets wrote . . ." (1:45).
- Jesus told the Jews he would raise the temple in three days, and after Jesus' resurrection, the "disciples remembered that he had said this; and they believed the scripture and the word that Jesus had spoken" (2:22).
- To explain to Nicodemus the power of faith for salvation, Jesus illustrated from the Pentateuch, "Just as Moses lifted up the serpent in the wilderness, so must the Son of Man be lifted up, that whoever believes in him may have eternal life" (3:14-15).
- Jesus told the Jewish religious leaders: "You search the scriptures because you think that in them you have eternal life; and it is they that testify on my behalf. . . . If you believed Moses, you would believe me, for he wrote about me" (5:39, 46).
- Similarly, after Jesus' triumphal entry into Jerusalem, the disciples, "did not understand these things at first; but when Jesus was glorified, then they remembered that these things had been written of him . . ." (12:16).
- To explain the hardness of people's hearts, John recalled one of Isaiah's prophecies, then explained: "Isaiah said this because he saw [Jesus'] glory and spoke about him" (12:41).
- The incidents of Jesus' final week followed the prophecies in Scripture (see 12:14-15, 38-40; 13:18; 19:24; 28ff).

The Old Testament is filled with prophecies concerning Jesus, incredible stories of the victories and failures of people of faith, and songs and sayings—all are important helps to us today. Don't neglect the Old Testament. Jesus held it in the highest regard—so should we.

"That you may know and understand."NIV This verse contains the Greek words for "know" twice, in two tenses: aorist and present, suggesting beginning knowledge and continuing knowledge. And what does Jesus want his listeners to know and understand? **"That the Father is in Me, and I in Him."**NKJV This statement underscores Jesus' claim to oneness with the Father (see 14:10-11; 17:21).

Jesus' explanations did not change the Jews' minds; they had been intent on stoning him for blasphemy (10:31). But when they attempted to arrest him, **he escaped their grasp.**^{NIV} Once again Jesus demonstrated that his fate would not be determined by the will of crowds or human priorities. Even when "his hour" would come, God would still be ultimately in control. John's readers, who may have faced persecution, would have been encouraged by this report. And we need the same encouragement to know that God cares for us.

10:40-42 Jesus went back across the Jordan to the place where John had been baptizing in the early days.^{NIV} Jesus went to the east

side of the Jordan (see 1:28). It was his final preaching mission out in the countryside. It was the final opportunity for many people to respond to Jesus' preaching and believe. Jesus did not return to Jerusalem again until the day he made his Triumphal Entry.

Many people came to him. They said, "Though John never performed a miraculous sign, all that John said about this man was true."^{NIV} The ministry of John the Baptist had left a permanent impression on those who had heard him speak of the coming Messiah. What they heard here and saw in Jesus confirmed in their minds the genuineness of his forerunner's proclamations. As a result of hearing John's prophetic ministry and then seeing the Messiah himself, **many believed in Jesus.**^{NIV}

Ministry Beyond the Jordan. *Jesus had been in Jerusalem for the Feast of Tabernacles (10:2); then he preached in various towns, probably in Judea, before returning to Jerusalem for the Feast of Dedication (10:22). Jesus again angered the religious leaders who tried to arrest him, but he left the city and went beyond the Jordan to preach.*

MANY CAME . . . MANY BELIEVED
Some people are naturally hesitant about the decision to accept Christ. They hold back because they don't want to be impulsive, they wonder if they have thought it through well enough, or they are concerned about what friends and relatives might say. We must realize that indecision is rejection. Perhaps a clarifying question we can ask ourselves is: Am I looking for a clear reason to believe in Jesus or am I really looking for a clear reason *not* to believe in him? Our honest answer has eternal consequences.

Jesus gave us many reasons to believe in him. The decision process does not have to be difficult. We can read about Jesus, think about him, listen to his words. We can reflect on what others have discovered in trusting him. We do not have to remain tentative or suspicious. We can respond to Jesus, believe in him, and love him. Many are still coming to Christ.

John 11

Up to this point in John's Gospel, Jesus has presented himself as the giver of life to various people:

- to Nicodemus, he offered eternal life (3:16)

- to the Samaritan woman, the water of life (4:14)

- to the official's son and the lame man, the restoring of life (4:50; 5:5-8)

- to the hungry multitude, the bread of life (6:35)

- to the believers in Jerusalem, the rivers of living water (7:38)

- to the blind man, the light of life (8:12; 9:35-38)

- to the sheep who followed him, the abundant life (10:10-11)

In chapter 11, Jesus is "life" in its ultimate expression—he is "the resurrection and the life"—life after death. To the dead man, Lazarus, he offered resurrection life.

The Gospels tell us that Jesus raised others from the dead, including Jairus's daughter (Matthew 9:18-26; Mark 5:41-42; Luke 8:40-56) and a widow's son (Luke 7:11-17). These people represent a cross section of ages and social backgrounds to whom Jesus gave back human life. All of them, including Lazarus, were raised but eventually died again. Lazarus's story stands out because John used it as a *sign* of Jesus' ultimate life-giving power and a picture of his own coming resurrection. And, as with all the miracles recorded in this gospel, it glorifies God. From John's perspective, this miracle was the turning point; it caused the Jewish leaders to take decisive action against Jesus.

However, this chapter contains much more. We observe Jesus relating to different people under real stress. Two sisters were frantic about their sick brother and then devastated by his death. The crowds continued to voice divided opinions about Jesus. The disciples sensed the possible outcome of Jesus' ongoing verbal skirmishes with the religious leaders. Thomas displayed his courage and revealed his resolute attitude when he said: "Let us also go, that we may die with him" (11:16 NIV). The chapter teaches us that in the middle of very difficult circumstances, Jesus the life-giver desires to help and guide us. We must trust him.

11:1-3 Now a man named Lazarus was sick. He was from Bethany, the village of Mary and her sister Martha.NIV Though John only introduces us to the family of Mary, Martha, and Lazarus at the end of Jesus' ministry, Jesus and the disciples often visited their home. Jesus enjoyed their close friendship and hospitality on his visits to Jerusalem, for Bethany was a village just outside of the city. In light of what happened, the meaning of Lazarus's name, "God is my help," became significant. Until he heard Jesus' voice outside the tomb Lazarus probably never realized just how prophetic his name would turn out to be!

At this time, Jesus was on the other side of the Jordan River, also in a town called Bethany. In 10:40 we are told that Jesus crossed the Jordan to the place where John had been baptizing; that place is identified as "Bethany on the other side of the Jordan" (1:28 NIV). The events described in Luke 13:22–17:10 occurred between chapters 10 and 11 of John.

This Mary . . . was the same one who poured perfume on the Lord and wiped his feet with her hair.NIV John identified Mary with an event described in the next chapter (12:1-7) because Mary's display of love for Christ was well known to the first-century Christians (Matthew 26:6-13; Mark 14:3-9).

NOT ISOLATED
Lazarus had been close to Jesus, yet he became deathly ill. The disciples may have asked a question similar to the one asked about the blind man in chapter 9, "Who sinned?" Or perhaps, "What did Lazarus do wrong?" But the Bible helps us see that sickness and death do not indicate that God has rejected someone or that they have done something wrong.

We must remind ourselves that neither we nor our loved ones are exempt. These three disciples of Jesus were his close friends and associates. Jesus loved them. Yet he did not rush to spare them grief. The presence of pain and suffering in the lives of faithful disciples of Jesus can teach us that Christians do not have different experiences in life, rather, they experience life differently. Our hope in Jesus does not insulate us from life's difficulties, but it does provide a way through and beyond them. God can use difficult experiences to make us more compassionate servants for him as we console others.

**The sisters sent a message to Jesus, "Lord, he whom you love
is ill."**[NRSV] Though Lazarus, the brother of Mary and Martha, is
mentioned only in John 11 and 12, this verse and verse 5 show
that Lazarus must have been Jesus' friend for quite some time.

**11:4 When Jesus heard it, he said, "This illness does not lead to
death; rather it is for God's glory."**[NRSV] When Jesus heard of Lazarus's sickness, he knew that it would lead to death, but also that
the glory of God would be revealed. Jesus' words, *"This illness
does not lead to death,"* referred to ultimate, final death. But his
disciples understood him to mean that the illness was not serious.
Again, we see the parallel between Jesus' response here and in 9:3.
In the former passage, Jesus spoke of the man's blindness as an
opportunity for God's works to be seen. Lazarus's death was an
opportunity for **the Son of God [to] be glorified.**[NRSV] As in the case
of the blind beggar who was healed (9:1-5, 24-38), miracles that
alleviate human suffering often give God greater glory than the
more commonplace blessings we experience (Matthew 5:45). In
fact, all of Jesus' healing miracles flow from his compassion. However, God strategically placed some miracles in human history to
demonstrate his wise providence and his sovereignty.

TRIALS OF OPPORTUNITY
Any trial a believer faces can ultimately bring glory to God
because God can bring good out of any bad situation (Genesis
50:20; Romans 8:28). When trouble comes, do you grumble,
complain, and blame God? Or do you see your problems as
opportunities to honor him? Read the following verses and
reflect on their significance for your life:
- Romans 5:3-5
  For early Christians, trials and suffering were the rule rather
  than the exception. We rejoice in suffering, not because we
  like pain, but because we know God is using life's difficulties
  to develop our perseverance. Ask God for strength to deal
  with every difficulty.
- Hebrews 12:4-11
  It is never pleasant to be corrected by hardships, but God
  uses them to discipline us. Trials of this kind are a sign of
  God's love. When hardships redirect our path, we must see
  them as proof of God's fathering care and discover what he
  wants to teach us.
- 1 Peter 1:6-7
  All believers face trials. We must regard them as part of the
  refining process that burns away impurities and thereby prepares us to meet Christ.
- James 1:2-4
  Trials develop strength of character in true disciples. Facing
  trials can help us grow to be mature and complete in our faith.

11:5 Jesus loved Martha and her sister and Lazarus. This parenthetical statement serves two purposes: (1) it affirms Jesus' love for each member of the family, and (2) it serves to explain that it was not lack of love that kept Jesus from going to them. Humanly speaking, Jesus would have wanted to go to them immediately. But he was constrained by the Father's timing.

11:6 Yet when he heard that Lazarus was sick, he stayed where he was two more days.^{NIV} Jesus would not be forced into action by these friends whom he loved dearly, any more than he would be forced by his mother (2:4) or his brothers (7:3-10). Everything he did was according to God's timing alone. Lazarus had been dead for four days by the time Jesus arrived in Bethany (11:39). The messenger(s) must have taken a day to reach Jesus; Jesus waited for two days; then he took a day to reach Bethany. Therefore, Lazarus must have died shortly after the messenger(s) left Bethany. Jesus probably did not even receive the message about the illness until after Lazarus had died. Therefore, it was impossible for Jesus to have arrived in time to prevent Lazarus's death.

WAIT CONTROL
Jesus loved this family and often stayed with them. He knew their pain but did not respond immediately. His delay had a specific purpose. God's timing, especially his delays, may make us think he is not answering or is not answering the way we want. But he will meet all our needs (Philippians 4:19) according to his perfect schedule and purpose. Often when we pray, circumstances seem to actually worsen. We are tempted to doubt and despair. But delay itself builds patience. Our patience improves as we trust in his timing.

11:7 Then he said to his disciples, "Let us go back to Judea."^{NIV} God's time had come, so Jesus headed back into Judea to be with his dear friends in their sorrow. God's timing is always perfect, whether in guiding his Son through his ministry on earth, or in guiding us today and answering our prayers.

Here, even knowing the grief and pain of his dear friends, Jesus waited two days and then returned to Judea. When the time came, Jesus did his Father's will.

> We are not necessarily doubting that God will do the best for us; we are wondering how painful the best will turn out to be. *C. S. Lewis*

TIMING IS EVERYTHING
Sometimes we offer a passionate prayer of need, and God answers quickly. We are thankful and excited, and our faith is often strengthened. At other times it seems that God will never answer our prayers. We can't understand, because we know that we prayed for God's will. What should we do? We should wait in faith, knowing that God has our best interests in mind. We may never see our prayer answered in our lifetime; we may wait many years only to see God answer the prayer in another way altogether; we may find that God's final answer is no. Whatever the case, God's decision is best and his timing is right.

11:8-10 The disciples couldn't understand why Jesus would want to go into Judea again, when the Jews there just recently had been seeking to stone him (see 10:31ff.). Why leave a place where people believe in you and welcome you (10:42) to go back to certain death? But Jesus was not afraid, for he knew that he had to die and that his death would only occur in the Father's timing.

"Are there not twelve hours of daylight?"[NRSV] In response to the disciples' hesitation about returning to Judea, Jesus asked this startling rhetorical question. It had no immediate connection with the disciples' concern. But his answer made his point easier to remember.

The disciples' fears related to the limited sphere of human effort. They worried about what the Jewish leaders might do. Jesus pointed to an unlimited sphere—the sovereignty of God, who transcends the limits of time and over whom people have no control. As Jesus

HOW DO TRIALS GLORIFY GOD?
- They develop our Christian character as we exercise patience (Romans 5:1-5), and they provide an example of strength, courage, and dependence on God to unbelievers.
- They wean us from life's attractions, diversions, and illusions as we focus on God for help.
- They reveal the flimsy grip we have on health and prosperity in this life, as we realize that we must trust in God for our security.
- They intensify our desire to be with God in eternity, where we will receive new bodies and be reunited with loved ones who have gone before us.
- They provide opportunities to portray how God's timing expresses his love to us. Many Christians who have faced calamity testified later how God's timing showed them a new side to his love.

obeyed his Father, he was as confident about the victorious outcome as he was that every day contained twelve hours of daylight.

We should remember that God's sovereignty extends to each moment of our life; otherwise, our trust in him will be limited to only those times when he meets our expectations. We will repeat the disciples' mistake—attempting to limit God to the sphere of human effort.

> Let thy hope of heaven master thy fear of death. Why shouldst thou be afraid to die, who hopest to live by dying! *William Gurnall*

Jesus' answer mentioned an expected number of "hours" during which work may be done. It also clearly implied that time would run out. After twelve hours of daylight the night comes. Our Lord's "day" (his time on earth) was approaching its final hour. But Jesus still had tasks to accomplish, and he would not be sidetracked from his mission.

"Those who walk during the day do not stumble, because they see the light of this world."NRSV The simple lesson of using daylight to get work done illustrates our deeper need to do spiritual work in the "light" of Jesus' presence and God's guidance. Jesus had already used the phrase "the light of the world" to refer to his own presence among people. While he was among them, he was their light (see 1:4; 8:12; 9:5). As long as they did their work in the light of Christ's presence they would not stumble. Sadly, those who live in the dark, without the presence of Jesus' light in them, will stumble.

THE BRIGHTER LIGHT
Jesus received his guidance from the highest source—the Father. The disciples were tempted to receive their guidance from the most immediate source—their circumstances. They worried about what they could "see" nearby; Jesus reminded them to walk by a brighter light.

When making decisions, we should analyze our circumstances but not regard them as infallible guides. If we rely on our circumstances for guidance too much, we will walk in circles. Just as Jesus took charge of his day, we should take charge of our days. We need not rush around, frantically or fearfully trying to stay ahead of uncontrollable circumstances. Rather, we can ask for his help in making wise use of our available time and opportunities. Our first question should be: What would Jesus have me do?

11:11-15 **"Our friend Lazarus has fallen asleep, but I am going there to awaken him."**NRSV The disciples missed the meaning of this euphemism for death (11:12-13; see also Daniel 12:2; 1 Corinthians 11:30; 15:20, 51; 1 Thessalonians 4:14). The disciples expressed their assumption that **"if he sleeps, he will get better,"**[NIV] citing the restoring powers of a good sleep after an illness.

Jesus, realizing their failure to understand what he had said, went on to explain clearly: **"Lazarus is dead, and for your sake I am glad I was not there."**[NIV] Lazarus died so that Jesus could show his power over death to his disciples and others. The raising of Lazarus displayed Christ's power—the resurrection from the dead is a crucial belief of Christian faith. Jesus not only raised himself from the dead (10:18), but he also has the power to raise others.

Even at this point, the disciples still misunderstood Jesus' claim to power over death although he had clearly stated this several times (all are from the NRSV):

- "Indeed, just as the Father raises the dead and gives them life, so also the Son gives life to whomever he wishes" (5:21).

- "This is indeed the will of my Father, that all who see the Son and believe in him may have eternal life; and I will raise them up on the last day" (6:40).

- "Those who eat my flesh and drink my blood have eternal life, and I will raise them up on the last day" (6:54).

- "Very truly, I tell you, whoever keeps my word will never see death" (8:51).

- "I lay down my life in order to take it up again. No one takes it from me, but I lay it down of my own accord. I have power to lay it down, and I have power to take it up again" (10:17-18).

- "My sheep hear my voice. . . . I give them eternal life, and they will never perish" (10:27-28).

WAKE UP!
The disciples heard the word *sleep* and misunderstood Jesus' intention to go there personally to awaken Lazarus from death. Only Jesus can refer to death as sleep because only he has power over death. From a human perspective, death is very real and final. People who call death "sleep" are trying to soften the reality of death and keep the living from taking the issues of death and sin seriously.

For those who believe in the resurrection, death is merely sleep in comparison to eternal life. Those who do not believe need to wake up to Christ's power while they still have the opportunity.

"Let us go to him."^{NIV} Jesus made his intention clear. He would go to Judea, and he expected his disciples to go with him. Jesus had already indicated that he was anticipating their faith growing as a result of what would happen with Lazarus.

DELAYS
Measured by our timetable, many of our prayers' answers may seem delayed. But knowing that we deal with a wise and loving God, we must consider that the problem may be with our time-table rather than God's.

Though we experience delays, we can be sure that Jesus does initiate help for us. He will come to our aid. His help may well come in different ways and forms than we expect, but we can depend on his dependability! God will come to you in your time of need.

11:16 **"Let us also go, that we may die with him."**^{NIV} We often remember Thomas as "the doubter" because he doubted Jesus' resurrection (20:24-25). But he also loved the Lord and was a man of great courage. The disciples knew the dangers of going with Jesus to Jerusalem, so they tried to talk him out of it. Thomas merely expressed what all of them were feeling. When their objections failed, they were willing to go and even die with Jesus. They may not have understood why Jesus would be killed, but they were loyal. We may face unknown dangers in doing God's work. It is wise to consider the high cost of being Jesus' disciple.

> Courage is not simply *one* of the virtues, but the form of every virtue at the testing point, which means at the point of highest reality. A chastity or honesty or mercy which yields to danger will be chaste or honest or merciful only on conditions. *C. S. Lewis*

STEP OUT!
Thomas was ready to move out. Courage often boils down to trusting Jesus and moving out. Emotionally, the experience is much like the first time off a high dive or the first public speech. The stakes may be higher, but so are the benefits. We don't realize God's power until we take the first step. Thomas was the first to step out in faith. Sooner or later you too will have the opportunity to take a step of courage. And your step may moti-vate others to take action too. Ask God for the courage you need.

JESUS COMFORTS MARY AND
MARTHA / 11:17-37 / **166**

Although we get many glimpses of Jesus' compassion throughout
the Gospels, his tender conversations with Mary and Martha are
the most moving. His words reveal patient pastoral concerns.
Elsewhere we see him confront people with the truth; here we
see him console as the gentle Master.

Jesus did not ridicule or belittle grief. He affirmed our need for
comfort by providing it to the sisters without hesitation. It is a
tribute to the family that many from Jerusalem came to Bethany
to pay their respects and offer their support to the sisters.

11:17-19 **Lazarus had already been in the tomb for four days**[NIV] by the
time Jesus arrived (see comments
on 11:6). In the warm climate of
Palestine, a dead body would
decompose quickly, so a person's
body was often buried the same
day of death. *Four days* places
Lazarus well beyond what anyone might call a "near death"
case. When Jesus and the disciples arrived in Bethany, many
Jews from Jerusalem had gathered to console Lazarus's family,
and some of those who had
arrived were religious leaders. In
Jewish society, prolonged mourning for the dead was considered
an essential part of every funeral.
It was convenient for many Jews
to be there because Bethany was
a village on the outskirts of Jerusalem (being **less than two miles
from Jerusalem** [NIV]).

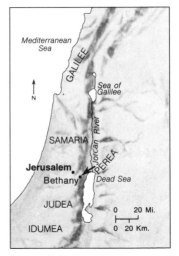

11:20-24 **Martha . . . went and met him,
while Mary stayed at home.**[NRSV]
It was quite natural for Martha, as
the older sister, to be the first to go
out to meet Jesus when he arrived.

*Jesus Raises Lazarus. Jesus
had been preaching in the villages beyond the Jordan, probably in Perea, when he received
the news of Lazarus's sickness.
Jesus did not leave immediately,
but waited two days before
returning to Judea. He knew
Lazarus would be dead when he
arrived in Bethany, but he was
going to do a great miracle.*

In addition, she was the active person, who had busily prepared Jesus a meal (as described in Luke's Gospel; Luke 10:38-42). Mary, more contemplative, remained at home in mourning.

Upon seeing Jesus, Martha said to him, **"Lord, if you had been here, my brother would not have died."**^{NRSV} This was a complaint and a plea. Martha probably realized that Jesus could not have arrived much earlier, but she was confident that Jesus' presence would have prevented Lazarus's death. Mary makes the same comment later (11:32). Despite their pain and sorrow, their faith in Jesus did not waver. The implicaton for us is that we should not quickly assume that God has let us down when we are in the midst of difficulties.

"But even now I know that God will give you whatever you ask of him."^{NRSV} Perhaps Martha thought Jesus would bring her brother back to life. But her reply in verse 24 and subsequent protests at the tomb (11:39) suggest otherwise. She did not realize, understand, or dare to hope that Jesus would ask God to give Lazarus back his physical life and be returned to his family. Instead, she reaffirmed her trust in his power even though she thought Jesus had missed an opportunity to display it by healing her brother.

When Jesus said, **"Your brother will rise again,"** she attributed it to the future resurrection—**"I know that he will rise again in the resurrection at the last day.**^{NKJV} At face value, Jesus' statement did little to console Martha, for she already knew that Lazarus would rise again in the resurrection and live eternally with God, just as she and Mary would when they died. At this point, resurrection was only a future, abstract concept to Martha, not a possible, immediate reality in Christ. But Jesus did not mean an eventual, distant resurrection, he meant that Lazarus would rise again that very day!

NEVER TOO LATE

Lazarus had been dead four days. How could Mary and Martha have imagined that they would soon be feasting with him and with Jesus (12:1-2)? But when Martha said "Even now" she was opening a door of faith wider than she could have anticipated. From the depth of her loss and sorrow she clung in faith to Jesus. The eventual results were astonishing! There is always enough time for Christ to act. We must continue to trust in him.

11:25-27 **"I am the resurrection and the life. Those who believe in me, even though they die, will live, and everyone who lives and believes in me will never die."**^{NRSV} To the woman at the well

(4:25-26), Jesus identified himself as the Messiah; to the ex–
blind man (9:35-37), he disclosed himself as the Son of Man; but
here he enlarged the picture by revealing himself as the source of
resurrection life.

To understand Jesus' statement, we need to see it in two parts.
First, Jesus explained the resurrection: *"I am the resurrection . . .
those who believe in me, even though they die, will live."* Then he
explained the life: *"I am . . . the life . . . everyone who lives and
believes in me will never die."*

The believer will not experience eternal death. Lazarus had
been a believer in Jesus; therefore, even though he died, he
would live. Every believer who has died will yet live, and everyone who is still living and believing will die, but not eternally.
Christ did not promise the prevention of physical death; he guaranteed in himself to give abundant life, including resurrection
and eternity with him. Christ did not prevent Lazarus's physical
death (after being raised, Lazarus would eventually die again),
but Lazarus had the guarantee of eternal life.

Jesus himself *is* the resurrection and he *is* the life. Only
through a relationship with him can we experience this resurrection and this life. Only one kind of life—the life of God (Ephesians 4:18)—is truly life. Only it can overcome death. Jesus is
this life.

**"I believe that you are the Messiah, the Son of God, the one
coming into the world."**[NRSV] Martha is best known for being too
busy to sit down and talk with Jesus (Luke 10:38-42), but here
we see her as a woman of deep faith. Her statement of faith is
exactly the response that Jesus wants from us. This confession
presents a high point in John's Gospel, for here we see a believer
acknowledging that Jesus is the Messiah, the Son of God. In recognizing Jesus as the Messiah, she saw him to be God's envoy
appointed to deliver God's people; in recognizing Jesus as the
Son of God, she saw his divinity.

YOU WILL LIVE!
Jesus has power over life and death as well as power to forgive
sins. This is because he is the Creator of life (see 14:6). He
who *is* life can surely restore life. Whoever believes in Christ
has a spiritual life that death cannot conquer or diminish in any
way. When we realize Christ's power and how wonderful his
offer to us really is, how can we help but commit our lives to
him! Those who believe have wonderful assurance and certainty: "Because I live, you also will live" (14:19 NIV). Is Jesus
the Lord of your life?

11:28-32 She went back and called her sister Mary, and told her privately, "The Teacher is here and is calling for you."^{NRSV} Martha spoke to Mary secretly so that the visiting Jews would not follow her to where Jesus was—somewhere outside the village. However, when Mary arose quickly to go to Jesus, she was followed by the mourners.

"Lord, if you had been here, my brother would not have died.^{NRSV} Mary repeated Martha's statement (11:21). They were both convinced that Jesus would have been able to do something had Lazarus still been living. But they had no idea that death might be reversible.

11:33-36 When Jesus saw her weeping, and the Jews who had come along with her also weeping, he was deeply moved in spirit and troubled.^{NIV} The Greek word for "deeply moved" can mean "intensely agitated." Jesus may have been agitated by the excessive sorrow of the mourners, by Martha and Mary's limited faith, or by the general unbelief. Even more so, Jesus was angry at the power of death, man's ultimate enemy (1 Corinthians 15:26).

Jesus wept.^{NKJV} Among the commotion and the loud wailing of the mourners, Jesus shed tears. What made Jesus cry? Was it his love for Lazarus? Was it the presence of sadness and death? Or was it the faithless grief that surrounded him? For whatever the reason, the situation caused Jesus to shed some tears. The picture of Jesus as being impassive in the face of genuine human suffering is not consistent with the picture in Isaiah, which describes him as a "man of sorrows, and familiar with suffering" (Isaiah 53:3 NIV).

JESUS WEPT
Several views have been put forth to explain Jesus' weeping. The most common are as follows:

- Jesus wept in sympathy for the ones he loved who were grieving.
- Jesus wept for all people who grieve over the death of loved ones.
- Jesus wept over the frailty of life and the ravages of sin and despair.
- Jesus wept in anger over those present who remained in unbelief in the face of death.
- Jesus wept in sorrow for having to call Lazarus back from eternity into a world where he would die again.
  Tears, however, are not self-explanatory; and since Jesus chose not to explain them, we are left with a variety of possibilities for what he might have felt.

**The Jews' interpreted Jesus' tears as a sign of Jesus' great
love for Lazarus: "See how he loved him!"**[NRSV] They assumed
that Jesus wept in frustration and sorrow that he had not arrived
earlier in order to heal Lazarus. But we know that Jesus purposely waited until Lazarus had died before going to Bethany
(11:14-15).

WITH FEELING
John stresses that we have a God who cares. This portrait contrasts with a Greek concept of God that was popular in John's
day—a God with no emotions and no empathy for humans.
Here we see many of Jesus' emotions—compassion, indignation, sorrow, even frustration. He often expressed deep emotion, and we must never be afraid to reveal our true feelings to
him. He understands them, because he experienced them. Be
honest, and don't try to hide anything from your Savior. He
cares.

11:37 Following Martha and Mary, others also asked, **"Could not he
who opened the eyes of the blind man have kept this man
from dying?"**[NRSV] By directly quoting the crowd (who refer to
Jesus' previous miracle—see 9:1ff.), John directed his readers to
consider: "Can the one with power over disease and disablement
have power to prevent death?" But this miracle creates deeper
questions: "Can the one who raised Lazarus from the dead raise
me?" and "What does the one with power over death want to do
in my life right now?"

Jesus' power to overcome death confirmed his power to give
eternal life to those still living. People are dead spiritually without Christ. But to those who trust him, Jesus gives eternal life
now along with the power to live in obedience to him.

JESUS RAISES LAZARUS FROM THE DEAD / 11:38-44 / 167

As this chapter opens, we see Mary, Martha, and the crowd
expressing conditional belief in the power of Jesus. They
believed that Jesus could have worked a miracle if Lazarus had
still been alive. But death intervened, and they thought it was irre-
versible. Little did they know that what they considered impossible would soon be overcome by God's power.

11:38-39 **Jesus, once more deeply moved, came to the tomb.**[NIV] John
once again tells us that Jesus was *deeply moved* (see 11:33).

Jesus' agitation reveals his indignation and outrage that death creates such destructive chaos and suffering in people's lives.

Lazarus was buried in **a cave with a stone laid across the entrance.**^{NIV} Tombs at this time were usually caves carved in the limestone rock of a hillside. A tomb was often large enough for people to walk inside. Several bodies would be placed in one tomb. After burial, a large stone would be rolled across the entrance to the tomb. This burial spot was much like the one in which Jesus would be buried.

Jesus said to the crowd, **"Take away the stone."**^{NIV} When Jesus asked that the stone be removed, Martha protested, saying, **"By this time there is a bad odor, for he has been there four days."**^{NIV} See comments on 11:6.

11:40 **"Did I not tell you that if you believed, you would see the glory of God?"**^{NRSV} The purpose of the whole event was for Jesus to exhibit the glory of God. Jesus had proclaimed this from the moment he heard about Lazarus's sickness (11:4). In order for the miracle to occur and for God to be glorified through it, the sisters would have to believe enough to order the stone to be removed from the tomb's entrance.

GOD LISTENS

Because of Jesus' constant interaction with his Father, we can surmise that he had been praying about Lazarus for some time. Jesus was confident that his Father listened to him. His confidence, "I knew that you always hear me," was expressed for our benefit. He wants us to believe, and he said so (11:42).

Our prayers are arrogant if we assume *how* God will answer. Our prayers are confident if we affirm that God listens. Our confidence comes not from what we pray or how we pray but to whom we pray. God does not require volume or repetition. The whispered simple prayer echoes in the halls of heaven as loudly as the lofty composition voiced in unison by thousands. God listens when you pray!

11:41-44 **"Father, I thank you that you have heard me. I knew that you always hear me, but I said this for the benefit of the people standing here, that they may believe that you sent me."**^{NIV} While the crowd waited beside the tomb—with the stone now rolled away from its entrance—Jesus praised his Father aloud, publicly, so that, upon witnessing the miracle of resurrection, the people might believe in Jesus. His

> Jesus had to call out Lazarus by name for if he hadn't, all the dead would have come out of their graves! *Augustine*

prayer was not a petition, but a prayer of thanks to the Father. Jesus knew that his request would be answered.

He cried with a loud voice, "Lazarus, come forth!"NKJV The voice of Jesus is potent and lifegiving. Lazarus provided proof of Jesus' earlier words: "The dead will hear the voice of the Son of God and those who hear will live" (5:25 NIV).

The dead man came out.NRSV Lazarus was completely wrapped in his graveclothes. There was no question that a dead man had come back to life. The miracle was not only Lazarus's resuscitation. After four days, the body would have seriously decayed. Lazarus's body was raised and restored.

The wailing of grief transformed into gasps of shock and shouts of joy. Even the reticent Mary rushed to her brother. The funeral atmosphere became a joyful party. Perhaps in their excitement over his appearance the people forgot to free him from the burial wraps.

UNWRAP SESSION
Jesus was and is the giver of life. He brings a second birth to those who are dead in sin. But his gift of forgiveness and the indwelling Spirit do not create instant, perfect Christians. We enter Christ's kingdom with many of the old wraps still around us. Old habits and sinful behaviors, painful memories—all these require gentle, loving removal. Like graveclothes, we no longer need them. We need fellow Christians and Christ's power to unwrap us. It is Jesus' command that our healing be complete. Who can you help "unwrap"?

Jesus told them, **"Unbind him, and let him go."**NRSV The power he had just used to return Lazarus to the living could have easily disintegrated or loosed the wraps without help. But Jesus involved those around him in the happy labor of unwrapping Lazarus. His powerful work was completed, but Lazarus needed a personal touch.

RELIGIOUS LEADERS PLOT TO KILL JESUS / 11:45-57 / *168*

The seemingly ever-present religious leaders were not around to see Jesus' friend brought back to life. Perhaps they didn't think Jesus could do such a miracle. Some of the eyewitnesses, however, made it a point to report to the Pharisees in Jerusalem, only a couple of miles away. This fresh evidence of Jesus' power threw the Pharisees into a panic.

What followed is a priceless opportunity for us who know the full story to see how badly mistaken people can be in their assessment of events. We can also observe how desperately people will cling to a lie in the face of truth. The Pharisees and the Sanhedrin thought they were finally at the point of bringing matters to a conclusion with Jesus. But God fit their desperate plans into his own. They thought that killing Jesus would preserve their puny little sphere of power, but God knew that Jesus' death would provide salvation for the world.

11:45-46 Jesus' words and works, even today, divide people into two camps—believers and unbelievers. Many people can see the same miraculous event, yet all walk away being affected differently. The raising of Lazarus was stunning to many, so that **many of the Jews . . . who had come with Mary and had seen what Jesus did, believed in him**NRSV as the Messiah. Yet other Jewish onlookers did not believe; they quickly brought word of what had happened to the Pharisees, who were looking for a reason to destroy Jesus (7:1, 19, 25; 8:37, 40). As is his pattern, John highlighted that Jesus provoked two contradictory responses from those who watched and heard him. Some believed in him, while others could not wait to report his "dangerous" behavior.

11:47 **Then the chief priests and the Pharisees called a meeting of the Sanhedrin.**NIV The Sanhedrin was the highest ruling authority among the Jews in Judea. It was composed of seventy-one members: The high priest presiding over seventy religious leaders, the majority of whom were Sadducees and the minority, Pharisees.

TRUTH OVERLOOKED
In their eagerness to eliminate Jesus, Caiaphas and the Sanhedrin demonstrated their willingness to deliberately misuse truth to serve their own needs.

- They began with the right question ("What are we accomplishing?") but were not open to its most obvious answer ("We are rejecting the Messiah").
- They admitted in private that Jesus did miracles, but they publicly rejected the truth of those miracles.
- They realized that people were actually believing in Jesus, but they regarded their belief as a threat.
- Caiaphas affirmed their ignorance of the real issues.
- Caiaphas proposed the exchange of one person's life to maintain their power. He missed the actual plan of God—exchanging Jesus' life for the salvation of anyone who believes.

"**What are we accomplishing?**"[NIV] The question might have been the beginning of real soul-searching. In fact, we would do well to ask ourselves what we are accomplishing as we evaluate our efforts to obey God. Without Christ, our efforts in life are futile and frustrating. But the immediate meaning of the question was, Are we accomplishing what we have planned to do? The question implied only one answer. The dialogue that follows points clearly to the Jewish leaders' single-minded opposition to Jesus. John captured the irony of their conversation as they used every true statement to lead to wrong conclusions.

11:48 **"If we let him go on like this, everyone will believe in him, and the Romans will come and destroy both our holy place and our nation."**[NRSV] It was Rome's custom to allow conquered people to carry on their religious practices as long as they did not lead to rebellion against Rome. Jesus' miracles, however, often would cause a disturbance. If all the Jewish populace would hail

GREAT EXPECTATIONS
Wherever he went, Jesus exceeded people's expectations.

What was expected	What Jesus did	Reference
A man looked for healing	Jesus also forgave his sins	Mark 2:1-12
The disciples were expecting an ordinary day of fishing	They found the Savior	Luke 5:1-11
A widow was resigned to bury her dead son	Jesus restored her son to life	Luke 7:11-17
The disciples thought the crowd should be sent home because there was no food	Jesus used a small meal to feed thousands, and there were leftovers!	John 6:1-15
The crowds looked for a political leader to set up a new kingdom to overthrow Rome's control	Jesus offered them an eternal, spiritual kingdom to overthrow sin's control	A theme throughout the Gospels
The disciples wanted to eat the Passover meal with Jesus, their master	Jesus washed their feet, showing that he was also their servant	John 13:1-20
The religious leaders wanted Jesus killed and got their wish	But Jesus rose from the dead!	John 11:53; 19:30; 20:1-29

Jesus as their Messiah-King, the leaders feared that the Romans would take away their limited privileges of self-rule, as well as take away what the leaders called "this holy place" (see Acts 6:13; 21:28), the center of their religious life. The Jewish leaders feared that they would lose their limited autonomy and political positions. Furthermore, they feared that Rome's displeasure would bring additional hardship to their nation.

THE THREAT OF CHANGE
A prestigious leadership position can be dangerous, for it can lead to pride. Church leaders may rigidly insist on order or the status quo in order to hold onto their positions indefinitely. The opposition to Jesus was not so much personal as it was that he threatened the status quo and the positions of some of the leaders. Churches, social groups, and other organizations tend to respond to change in the same ways. It is the person doing things differently, making changes, and promoting progress, who is considered dangerous. Some leaders want to keep on doing as they have always done. Jesus' experience with the Jewish religious leaders shows what we can expect if we push for change and what we should watch out for in ourselves.

11:49-50 Caiaphas, who was high priest that year.NRSV Caiaphas led the Sadducees, the elite, educated, and wealthy Jews, who stood on fairly good terms with Rome. Jesus was a special threat to their quiet and secure positions in leadership over Judea's religious life. Caiaphas was proud and ruthless. His usual policy was to remove any threats to his power by whatever means necessary. For him, Jesus' death was not an "if" but a "when, where, and how."

Since Caiaphas served as a high priest for eighteen years (A.D. 18 to 36), the expression *that year* refers to that one year in which Jesus was crucified. The office of high priest was originally instituted by God to be a lifetime position (Numbers 35:25); but the Romans did not want any one person to become too powerful, so they appointed high priests and placed a new one in position whenever they wanted.

"You know nothing at all! You do not understand that it is better for you to have one man die for the people than to have the whole nation destroyed."NRSV Caiaphas was convinced that nothing short of destroying Jesus would save Israel from being destroyed by Rome. The life of one person was considered cheap and expendable as an alternative to endangering the nation. Caiaphas had only a limited perspective. He was stuck in this world and concerned only with the preservation of a system that ensured his power. But God used his words to express an unwitting prophecy of universal proportions: One man did have to die in order that the world, not just a single nation or a fragile political structure, might be saved.

11:51-54 **He did not say this on his own, but . . . he prophesied that Jesus was about to die for the nation, and not for the nation only, but to gather into one the dispersed children of God.**^{NRSV} Or, "for the scattered children of God" (NIV). These words of Caiaphas had great prophetic significance. Though his intent was sinful, God used him to indicate that Jesus would die for the people as a substitutionary sacrifice. And this is the irony of Caiaphas's statement that John didn't want his readers to miss: Jesus' death, intended to spare the nation of Israel from physical destruction, was actually to spare Israel from spiritual destruction. Furthermore, Jesus' death would bring about the gathering together (as

RESPONSES TO JESUS

Throughout chapter 11 we are given a variety of personal responses to Jesus. None of them are neutral. People who met Jesus formed specific opinions about him. Among them are the following.

Response:	*Do you know someone who:*
Some, like Mary and Martha, displayed faith that needed to deepen.	*. . . needs to deepen his/her faith?*
Some saw the miracle of Lazarus's resurrection and concluded that Jesus must be telling the truth about his identity. So they put their faith in him.	*. . . needs to put his/her faith in Christ?*
Some saw the miracle and concluded that it was merely another reason to get rid of Jesus the troublemaker.	*. . . considers Jesus merely a source of trouble?*
Some heard about the miracle and could only see Jesus as a threat to their power and position.	*. . . finds Jesus threatening?*
Some decided that Jesus must be killed and planned accordingly.	*. . . would remove Jesus if that were possible?*
Some arrived in Jerusalem for the Passover still curious about Jesus, moving toward acceptance or rejection.	*. . . is curious and might be open to the Good News?*

Tell them the Good News, that new life is available in Christ!

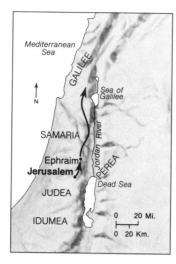

Mediterranean
Sea

N

Sea of
Galilee

SAMARIA

Jordan River

Ephraim
Jerusalem

PEREA

Dead Sea

JUDEA

IDUMEA

0   20 Mi.

0   20 Km.

Time with the Disciples.
Lazarus's return to life became the last straw for the religious leaders who were bent on killing Jesus. So Jesus stopped his public ministry and took his disciples away from Jerusalem to Ephraim. From there they returned to Galilee and stayed there for a while.

opposed to scattering) of all God's children—both Jews and Gentiles, whoever had come to believe in Jesus as the Messiah (see 1:12; 10:11, 16; 17:20-26).

The Jews rejected their only salvation in favor of peace with Rome, but just forty years later, in A.D. 70, they revolted against Rome. As a result, Jerusalem and the temple were destroyed, and the Jews were expelled from their homeland. This had already occurred when John wrote this Gospel.

Of course, the Jewish leaders missed the prophetic implications of Caiaphas's statement, and **from that day on they plotted to take his life.**NIV But evil leaders, no matter how long they have power or how evil their actions, are always under God's control. God permits them to exercise power for a time. Though it may not seem so to those who suffer, all that happens is according to God's timing and under his control. God is always watching over his people.

TOGETHER AS ONE
John's reference to the scattered children of God included not only the Jews spread throughout the world but also all those who would believe. We too are among the scattered for whom Jesus died. This theme is expanded in 2 Corinthians 5:11-21 and Ephesians 2:14-22 and referred to as the doctrine of reconciliation.

Through his death Jesus provides the way all people can be reconciled to God and then to each other. Unity in Christ is not a sentimental feeling but a reality that we can experience even within the limitations of a sinful world. When our sins are pardoned we have the freedom to truly relate to each other in love.

Aware of the plot against his life, Jesus **withdrew to a region near the desert, to a village called Ephraim.**NIV Ephraim may have been the same place as Ophrah, near Bethel (see 2 Chronicles 13:19). Jesus and his disciples stayed there until the time of the Passover.

11:55-57 **When it was almost time for the Jewish Passover, many went up from the country to Jerusalem for their ceremonial cleansing before the Passover.**[NIV] This Passover probably occurred in A.D. 30, the year of Jesus' death. Everyone in Jerusalem during the Passover celebration knew that the chief priests and Pharisees wanted to arrest Jesus. Furthermore, they were under strict orders to report Jesus' whereabouts. Into this tense scene Jesus would make his triumphal entry (12:12ff.).

PRIDE PROBLEMS
Even when confronted point-blank with the power of Jesus' deity, some refused to believe. These eyewitnesses not only rejected Jesus, they plotted his murder. They were so hardened that they preferred to reject God's Son rather than admit they were wrong. Beware of pride. If we allow it to grow, it can lead us into enormous sin.

John 12

The chapter opens with a portrayal of Mary anointing Jesus, accompanied by a wide range of reactions. This anointing concurs with the one described in Matthew 26:6-13 and Mark 14:3-9; but it is different from the one depicted in Luke 7:36-50, which occurred much earlier in Jesus' ministry. The tender attention given to Jesus by his three friends in Bethany contrasts with the treachery Judas planned to commit by the week's end. Lazarus, Mary, Martha, and Judas were all in Jesus' close circle of friends, but their relationship and motives for following him differed greatly. Being close to Jesus is not enough if we don't have heartfelt trust and obedience. Even today, some would reduce the life of faith to a brief weekly appearance at the local church.

12:1-2 Six days before the Passover, Jesus arrived at Bethany.^{NIV} Another Passover was coming, and Jesus arrived in Bethany six days beforehand. John last placed him in Ephraim, where he had gone to be alone with his disciples (11:54). From there, they returned to Galilee for a while (see the map in 11:54). Then, on the way from Galilee to Jerusalem for this Passover, Jesus:

- healed ten lepers in the region between Samaria and Galilee (Luke 17:11-19)

- traveled and taught in the region of Judea beyond the Jordan (Matthew 19:1-12; Mark 10:1-12)

- warned his disciples that on this trip to Jerusalem, he would be crucified but would rise again (Matthew 20:17-19; Mark 10:32-34; Luke 18:31-34)

- healed a blind beggar near Jericho (Matthew 20:29-34; Mark 10:46-52; Luke 18:35-43)

- helped Zacchaeus, a tax collector in Jericho, learn about eternal life (Luke 19:1-10).

From Jericho, Jesus traveled to Bethany, the home of his dear friends. Whenever Jesus visited Jerusalem, he probably went to Bethany (a suburb of Jerusalem, less than two miles away) to stay with Martha, Mary, and Lazarus (see Matthew 21:17; Luke 10:38). This was Jesus' final visit with his friends at Bethany because he was on his way to Jerusalem where, as he had already told his disciples, "The Son of Man will be handed over to the chief priests and scribes, and they will condemn him to death; then they will hand him over to the Gentiles to be mocked and flogged and crucified; and on the third day he will be raised" (Matthew 20:18-19 NRSV).

Where Lazarus lived, whom Jesus had raised from the dead.NIV Only a few weeks had gone by since Jesus had raised Lazarus from the dead. This miracle had caused many Jews to believe in Jesus, but it had angered the Jewish religious leaders so deeply that they were plotting to have Jesus killed. Thus, Jesus had left the region quickly (11:53-54). Jesus was reunited with his dear friends one more time before his death in Jerusalem at the hands of those who were plotting his murder.

Here a dinner was given in Jesus' honor. Martha served, while Lazarus was among those reclining at the table with him.NIV Each person described in this story expressed his or her attitude toward Jesus through specific actions. They were honoring Jesus with this thanksgiving meal. It seems as though Lazarus and his sisters used any occasion as an excuse to celebrate and practice hospitality. Martha, always the self-designated hostess, was doing so here (see Luke 10:38-42), though apparently with a new attitude of meekness. She honored her Lord with hospitality and refreshment. The way in which Lazarus was mentioned implies that the dinner was given in his honor as well as Jesus'. He was reclining at the table with his Lord who had brought him back to life—no doubt

> We should not attach much value to what we have given God, since we shall receive for the little we have bestowed upon Him much more in this life and in the next.
> *Theresa of Avila*

it was a great honor to be with the one he loved and who loved him so much. Mary expressed her great love for and faith in Jesus by offering a very special gift. And Judas betrayed his true character by disapproving of Mary's extravagance.

According to parallel accounts of this story (see Matthew 26:6-13; Mark 14:3-9), this meal was held at the home of Simon the leper, who also lived in Bethany and was very likely healed of his leprosy by Jesus. He too would have had great reason to honor Jesus.

12:3 **Mary took about a pint of pure nard, an expensive perfume; she poured it on Jesus' feet and wiped his feet with her hair. And the house was filled with the fragrance of the perfume.**^{NIV} This ointment or perfume was made from an aromatic herb (also called spikenard) from the mountains of India, and it was imported in alabaster bottles. This expensive imported item carried such value that people used it for investment purposes, as gold is often used today. According to 12:5, this particular nard was worth 300 denarii (the equivalent of a year's wages of a working man). When supper was finished, Mary took this pure, expensive perfume and poured it on (literally, "anointed") Jesus' feet. Nard was used to anoint kings; Mary may have been anointing Jesus as her kingly Messiah.

THE GREAT GIFT
Many centuries later we are still humbled by the extravagance and the appropriateness of Mary's gift. She poured out the very best she could find. Price is not the central issue, but the sincere expression of faith and love. We render similar honor to Jesus when we practice faithful service wherever God has placed us—at home with children, at the office, leading a company, running a financial institution, teaching, preaching, etc. Faithful, honest, diligent service done as unto the Lord can be a gift to God. It is costly. Often others might think the effort wasted, for it seems to make no large or permanent change in the world. But what others may call insignificant or wasteful, God deems to be like the fragrant aroma that filled the house when Mary poured the nard on Jesus' feet.

12:4-6 According to Matthew and Mark, all the disciples were offended that Mary had "wasted" this expensive ointment (Matthew 26:8; Mark 14:4). But in John's Gospel, it is **Judas Iscariot, one of his disciples (the one who was about to betray him),**^{NRSV} who verbalized the offense: **"Why wasn't this perfume sold and the money given to the poor? It was worth a year's wages."**^{NIV}

John then provides a parenthetical explanation as to the motive behind Judas's statement: **He did not say this because he cared about the poor but because he was a thief; as keeper of the money bag, he used to help himself to what was put into it.**^{NIV} The last part of this verse can also be translated "he took [literally, lifted or stole] what was in the money bag." Judas was a thief who had no compassion for the poor, yet Jesus entrusted to him the disciples' money bag (see 13:29). Judas often dipped into the disciples' money bag for his own use. Undoubtedly, Jesus knew what Judas was doing (2:24-25; 6:64), but he never did or said anything about it.

SMOKE SCREEN
In spite of his sharp rebuke, there is no evidence that Judas ever gave to the poor. His objection was actually a smoke screen to cover his own selfishness and greed.

It is common in church life to discover that those most apt to criticize are those who are doing nothing themselves. Those who never go to church criticize the church; those who don't read the Bible are ready to criticize what they have heard are inconsistencies and difficulties; those unwilling to help are ready to criticize when plans fail. Beware of finding fault with others in areas where you are deficient.

When we see what kind of person Judas was, we cannot regard him as a tragic hero for his role in bringing Jesus to the cross. No, he was a man with very base motives.

Judas piously talked about the poor in order to hide his true motives. But Jesus knew what was in his heart; Jesus knew that Judas had a weakness for money and that Judas would betray him for the sum of thirty silver coins. Judas's life had become a lie, and the devil was entering him (13:27). Satan is the father of lies, and a lying person opens the door to his influence. Jesus' knowledge of us should make us want to keep our actions consistent with our words. Because we have nothing to fear with him, we should have nothing to hide.

ON GUARD
Judas was given the position of trustee of the money bag most likely because he had some capability or expressed some interest in doing so. Sometimes the abilities we have enable us to function so effortlessly that we let down our moral or spiritual guard as we carry out those duties. Has God allowed you to assume responsibilities that match your strengths? Whether we are preaching, teaching, or managing money, remember that strengths can become weaknesses if we settle for poor preparation, shortcuts, and acting as if we "own" what truly belongs to another. If Christ is truly Lord of all you do, you will be on guard against greed, self-service, and taking moral shortcuts.

12:7-8 **"Leave her alone. She bought it so that she might keep it for the day of my burial. You always have the poor with you, but you do not always have me."**[NRSV] Jesus pointed out that Mary was not wasting this perfume on him. Certainly, the money could have been given to the poor; there would always be opportunities to care for the poor. But they would not always have Jesus. Mary understood how special Jesus was. Her anointing with a pint (or pound) of nard was like an ointment put on his body in preparation for burial (Matthew 26:12; Mark 14:8). (Later Nicodemus and Joseph of Arimathea would actually wrap Jesus' body with linen and spices—"a mixture of myrrh and aloes, about seventy-five pounds" 19:39 NIV.)

This act and Jesus' response to it do not give us permission to ignore the poor. Rather, Jesus explained that his followers would have many opportunities to help the poor, but only a short time to love and honor the Messiah. Mary's loving act was for a specific occasion—an anointing that anticipated Jesus' burial and a public declaration of her faith in him as the Messiah. Jesus' words should have taught Judas a valuable lesson about the worth of money. Unfortunately, Judas did not learn it. In contrast to Mary's sacrificial gift to Jesus, Judas sold his master's life for thirty pieces of silver (Matthew 26:14-16), the price one paid a slave owner if one's ox killed one of his slaves (see Exodus 21:32).

Jesus was so impressed with this outpouring of affection that he declared that Mary's act would be remembered wherever the gospel was told (Mark 14:9). She had realized how precious it was to have Jesus with them and wanted to demonstrate this before he died. Jesus is precious—to have *him* with us is the best we could ask for in life. Let us seize the opportunities to demonstrate our love to him.

On the human side, too often we delay expressing our love to people until after they have died. The guilt over missed opportunities is an added weight we can avoid by "keeping current" with our relationships. Today is a great day to express our love to our loved ones. Now is the perfect time to express our love for Christ.

UNDETERRED
Mary's gift was criticized by others, but appreciated by the Lord. When you give your best to God, you can be sure he appreciates your gift. Do not allow misunderstanding or criticism to deter you. Mary did not bring the gift because she thought she would receive praise from the others; she brought it because she loved Jesus and wanted to show him.

12:9-11 A large crowd of Jews found out that Jesus was there and came, not only because of him but also to see Lazarus, whom

he had raised from the dead.[NIV] Jews were arriving from all over the world for the Passover celebration. Many had heard of the miracle of Lazarus's resurrection. When they discovered that Jesus had returned to be with Lazarus in Bethany, they came to see both of them.

However, **the chief priests planned to put Lazarus to death as well, since it was on account of him that many of the Jews were deserting and were believing in Jesus.**[NRSV] Note the contrast between the crowd (wanting to see Jesus and Lazarus) and the leaders (wanting to kill both). It is the latter, not the people, who were actually guilty of Jesus' death. The chief priests had already formulated a plan to kill Jesus (11:50-53); then they added Lazarus. His presence, as the one resurrected by the person they wanted to kill, was embarrassing to them. Many Jews were *deserting* or leaving their allegiance to Judaism and to the Jewish religious leaders and *were believing in Jesus.*

The chief priests' blindness and hardness of heart caused them to sink ever deeper into sin. One sin led them to another. From the Jewish leaders' point of view, they could accuse Jesus of blasphemy because he claimed equality with God. But Lazarus had done nothing of the kind. They wanted Lazarus dead simply because he was a living witness to Jesus' power.

SECRET DESIRE
We all like to believe we are above petty jealousy and small retaliations. Unfortunately our behavior often proves the opposite. The chief priests, the guardians of God's royal law, were so driven by jealousy, paranoia, and hate that they enlarged their plan to kill Jesus to include Lazarus.

Most likely you have never been involved in planning someone else's murder; but, have you ever wished someone would disappear, or found yourself hoping they would make some kind of humiliating mistake that would ruin their career or reputation? Have you secretly desired to have their power or position and justified the wish by claiming "I could do a better job"? If our motivation is to do our best at serving God wherever we are, we won't need to compare ourselves to others.

JESUS RIDES INTO JERUSALEM / 12:12-19 / *183*

John's description of the Triumphal Entry, mentioned in all four Gospels, is the most brief of the accounts. John's objective seemed to be to sketch the events, relating them to Old Testament prophecies and explaining that those present did not fully understand all that was going on. He pointed out that these events intensified the animosity of the leaders toward Jesus.

In the other Gospels, we are left with the impression that the crowd's reaction to Jesus was largely spontaneous. John, however, helpfully explained that those who had witnessed the raising of Lazarus had been busily telling others. The news created great anticipation in Jerusalem of Jesus' arrival.

12:12-13 **The next day the great crowd that had come for the Feast heard that Jesus was on his way to Jerusalem.**^{NIV} The day after the feast in Bethany, Jesus made his Triumphal Entry into Jerusalem. Given the importance of the approaching Passover, the road into the Holy City would have been clogged with pilgrims. Among them would have been many people from Galilee, familiar with Jesus from his years of ministry there.

They took branches of palm trees and went out to meet him.^{NRSV} Not only was Jesus part of the large crowd moving toward Jerusalem, others came out to meet him from the city itself. Expectations that something marvelous was soon to happen must have been at fever pitch! The crowd began to shout, **"Hosanna! 'Blessed is He who comes in the name of the LORD!' The King of Israel!"**^{NKJV} As they shouted "Hosanna" (which was the equivalent of saying "Praise God!"), they thought that their conquering king had finally come to liberate them from Roman rule. They believed that the one *who comes in the name of the Lord* was *the king of Israel* (see Psalm 118:25-26; Zephaniah 3:15; John 1:49). Therefore, the Jews thought they were hailing the arrival of their King! But these people who were praising God for giving them a king had the wrong idea about Jesus. They were sure he would be a national leader who would restore their nation to its former glory; thus they were deaf to the words of their prophets and blind to Jesus' real mission. When it became apparent that Jesus was not going to fulfill their hopes, many people turned against him.

Along with the shouted greeting, the people chanted an ancient blessing from the Psalms, *"Blessed is He who comes in the name of the Lord!"* The Passover celebration made special use of the "Hallel" section of the Psalms (113–118), singing them as hymns of worship. The crowds would have been singing these expressions as they approached the City of David. But as they accompanied Jesus, the songs became Messianic greetings.

12:14-15 **Jesus found a young donkey and sat on it.**^{NRSV} Indeed, their King came to them—but not the kind of king they had expected. He did not arrive as a political ruler might, on a mighty horse or

in a chariot. Rather, Jesus came to them in the way prophesied by
Zechariah: **"Fear not, daughter of Zion; behold, your King is
coming, sitting on a donkey's colt."**[NKJV] The Old Testament
prophet Zechariah had prophesied the arrival of a great king, possibly Alexander the Great, in Zechariah 9:1-8. Then contrasting
that, he had prophesied the arrival to Jerusalem's people (called
Daughter of Zion) of *their* King: "Behold, your King is coming
to you; He is just and having salvation, lowly and riding on a donkey, a colt, the foal of a donkey" (Zechariah 9:9, NKJV). In this
coming, Israel's King would be a humble servant, not a con-
queror. He would not be exalted to a throne, but lifted up on a
cross.

12:16 **His disciples did not understand these things at first; but
when Jesus was glorified, then they remembered that these
things had been written of him and had been done to him.**[NRSV]
The same kind of statement was made in 2:22. After Christ's resurrection and subsequent glorification, the disciples remembered
these events and understood what they signified. Prior to Jesus'
resurrection, his followers did not understand the significance of
his Triumphal Entry into Jerusalem. The Holy Spirit would open
their eyes to the meaning of the Old Testament Scriptures and
remind them of this and other messianic predictions (14:26; see
also Luke 24:25-35, 44-48).

RETROSPECTION
After Jesus' resurrection, the disciples understood for the first
time many of the prophecies that they had missed along the
way. Jesus' words and actions took on new meaning and made
more sense. In retrospect, the disciples saw how Jesus had led
them into a deeper and better understanding of his truth. Stop
and think about the events in your life that God has used to
lead you to this point. As you grow older, you will look back and
see God's involvement more clearly than you do now.

12:17-19 As Jesus entered Jerusalem, huge crowds gathered to welcome
him. Many in the crowd had seen him raise Lazarus. **The crowd
that was with him when he called Lazarus from the tomb and
raised him from the dead continued to spread the word.
Many people, because they had heard that he had given this
miraculous sign, went out to meet him.**[NIV] This statement
emphasizes the superficial enthusiasm that possessed most of the
cheering throng. They flocked to Jesus because they had heard
about his great miracle in raising Lazarus from the dead. Their

adoration was short-lived and their commitment shallow, for in a few days they would do nothing to stop his crucifixion. Devotion based only on curiosity or popularity fades quickly.

The Pharisees were exasperated by such exultation. They were hoping to find some sly way to get hold of Jesus and get rid of him while they knew his whereabouts, but it was impossible with the huge adoring crowds surrounding him. Their statement, **"the whole world has gone after him!"**NIV is ironic—for most of those people did not really believe in Jesus.

DESPERATION

The religious leaders were becoming desperate men. Desperation leads to exaggeration. Jesus' popularity seemed to be growing to insurmountable heights. The more they tried to stop Jesus, the more his influence increased.

Those who oppose Christ make a hopeless effort. People who have set out to discredit him have ended up bowing before him in worship. The Pharisees were right when they said "This is getting us nowhere." They were only succeeding as far as their plan coincided with God's plan. People can spend a lifetime resisting and rejecting Christ, only to discover that they have accomplished nothing but their own destruction.

JESUS EXPLAINS WHY HE MUST DIE / 12:20-36 / 185

As if to confirm the fears expressed in verse 19, this section begins with a group of Gentiles trying to approach Jesus. We are not told if their request for an audience with Christ was ever granted, but Jesus replied to their interest with some instruction on the necessity of his own death.

This passage also includes the third instance of God speaking audibly during the ministry of Jesus. The first was at the baptism of Jesus (Matthew 3:13-17; Mark 1:9-11; Luke 3:21-22); the second at the Transfiguration (Matthew 17:1-13; Mark 9:2-13; Luke 9:28-36). God the Father broke the silence of heaven to encourage his Son in the final days of his mission on earth. Jesus himself emphasized again the brief time that remained during which the light would still be present. His invitation was to "put your trust in the light . . . so that you may become sons of light" (12:36 NIV).

12:20-22 There were some Greeks among those who went up to worship at the Feast.NIV Indeed, it seemed as if the "whole world" had gone after Jesus, as illustrated by these Greeks who came to the Feast and sought a meeting with him. These people were

either visitors from Greece or Greek-speaking Jews. They may
have been Jewish proselytes or simply God-fearing Gentiles.
Whoever they were, they had very likely been among the Passover celebrants who greeted Jesus as he rode into Jerusalem on a
donkey (12:12-15).

We can see how God is always in control by noting the timing
of the Passover. This annual celebration would bring many
people and cultures to Jerusalem. Many of these pilgrims were
transplanted Jews who had taken on the characteristics of the cultures in which they lived. Others were Gentile proselytes to the
Jewish faith, thrilled with the opportunity to be in Jerusalem, the
Holy City. This concentration of people presented an ideal setting
for events whose impact would spread across the world. These
pilgrims would take the stories home with them. God was training and preparing missionaries even before Jesus had given the
great commission (Matthew 28:19-20).

**They came to Philip, who was from Bethsaida in Galilee, with
a request. "Sir," they said, "we would like to see Jesus."**NIV
These Greeks probably selected Philip as their emissary to Jesus
because, though Philip was a Jew, he had a Greek name. And
Philip was from Bethsaida, a town in Galilee near the Greek terri-
tory on the eastern side of the Sea of Galilee called Decapolis.
The city of Bethsaida itself had a large Greek population, and
Philip may have been able to speak Greek.

For a moment Philip hesitated to approach Jesus with the
Greeks' request. Probably *everyone* wanted to speak with Jesus,
and the disciples had to screen these requests. So first, **Philip
went and told Andrew**NRSV (with whom Philip is often associated—1:40-44; 6:7-8; Mark 3:18). Then, **Andrew and Philip
went and told Jesus.**NRSV

The very inclusion of Greeks in the events of the final week
has great significance. John continued his pattern of including
Gentiles (the world) all along the way (1:12; 3:16). His readers,
who may have been Gentiles struggling with their acceptability
to God, would have gained encouragement from this incident and
Jesus' response. We Gentiles also ought to be grateful that Christ
includes us in his offer of salvation.

12:23-24 **Jesus replied.**NIV Jesus' words to Philip and Andrew and perhaps
to the other disciples as well were not addressed to the crowd.
The crowd (probably including the Greeks) is not mentioned
again until verse 29.

"The hour has come for the Son of Man to be glorified"NRSV
through death and resurrection. The "whole world" had gone

after Jesus (12:19); even the Greeks wanted to see him (12:20ff). Yet it is exactly at this point, when by human standards Jesus was in a perfect position to consolidate his forces and overwhelm the opposition, that he faced the heart-troubling hour that was upon him. Until this moment, the "hour" had always been a future event. But here Jesus declared that the hour had arrived. It was time, not for kingly honor, but for death. For through Jesus' death, he was to bring us to God.

"Unless a grain of wheat falls into the earth and dies, it remains just a single grain; but if it dies, it bears much fruit."[NRSV] This pictures beautifully the necessary sacrifice of Jesus. Unless a grain of wheat is buried in the ground—where it actually *dies*—it will not become a blade of wheat producing many more grains. The hour had come for Jesus, like *a grain of wheat,* to die. The buried grain would eventually bring forth *much fruit*—more fruit than could have been gained had Jesus become the king of Israel on an earthly throne. Indeed, by being lifted up on the cross, Jesus would draw all people to himself.

Jesus' death becomes our only way to life. Jesus' death would lead to glory and life for him, and also for all those who believe in him. Paul wrote to the Corinthians, "What you sow does not come to life unless it dies. . . . What is sown is perishable, what is raised is imperishable. It is sown in dishonor, it is raised in glory. It is sown in weakness, it is raised in power. It is sown a physical body, it is raised a spiritual body" (1 Corinthians 15:36, 42-44 NRSV). Jesus died to pay the penalty for our sin and also to demonstrate his power over death. His resurrection proves he has eternal life. Because Jesus is God, he can give this same eternal life to all who believe in him.

In his picture of the dying grain, Jesus spoke directly about his own life. He does not necessarily require us to literally give up our lives in sacrificial death as the only way to be fruitful. God does call some believers to die for him. But he calls many more to stay alive for fruitful service (see Romans 12:1-2).

12:25-27 **"Those who love their life lose it, and those who hate their life in this world will keep it for eternal life. Whoever serves me must follow me, and where I am, there will my servant be also. Whoever serves me, the Father will honor."**[NRSV] This message comes from one who lived what he mandated for his followers. True followers of Jesus must have their priorities in order; if they choose to love their own lives more than their Master, they will lose the very life they seek to maintain. True disciples must be willing to suffer and experience rejection, even unto death if need be. How much do we compromise to avoid rejection?

> When we do something we dislike, let us say to God: "My God, I offer you this in honor of the moment when you died for me." *John Vianney*

To serve and follow Jesus means making radical life-style changes. What about your goals, interests, hobbies, career choices, habits? To follow Jesus means going the way he went—not the way of earthly power and honor—but the way of humility and death. Everything Jesus did was for God's glory. When we choose to follow him, we must live for God's glory alone. This does not mean we have no fun, no joy, no security. Rather, it simply means *all that we do is for God's glory alone.* Then God will honor us; then, and only then, will we follow Jesus where he goes—as he explains later, he goes to eternal life with the Father.

The honor from God that Jesus promises may, in fact, be partly experienced in this life, but never entirely. And for many believers, what God has planned by way of honor we can only guess. Meanwhile we can derive real comfort and security from knowing that God observes and remembers each and every act of service we do in his name. None will be forgotten.

COMPLETE COMMITMENT
What does Jesus mean when he tells us to "hate" our life in this world? Jesus wants us to be so committed to living for Christ that we "hate" our life by comparison. Loving our life means that we guard our life so jealously that we squander it on our own pleasures and purposes. In contrast, hating our life means consistently using our resources to follow Christ. It does not mean that we long to die or that we are careless or destructive with the life God has given, but that we are free from self-centeredness and are willing to die if doing so will glorify Christ. We must disown the tyrannical rule of our own self-centeredness. By laying aside our striving for advantage, security, and pleasure, we can serve God lovingly and freely. Releasing control of our life and transferring control to Christ brings eternal life and genuine joy.

Many believed that Jesus came for the Jews only. But when Jesus said, *"Whoever serves me must follow me,"* he was talking about these Greeks (and all Gentiles) as well. No matter who the sincere seekers are, Jesus welcomes them. His message is for everyone. Social or racial differences must never become barriers to the gospel. The Good News is for all people. *"Whoever serves me the Father will honor"* is a great assurance for all who serve Christ.

FOR THIS VERY HOUR

Jesus expressed his desire to be delivered from a horrible death, but he knew that God had sent him into the world to die for our sins in our place. In this Gospel, Jesus speaks of "this very hour" with reference to his crucifixion. This is equivalent to what Jesus said in the other Gospels: "not my will, but yours." Jesus said no to his human desires in order to obey his Father and glorify him. Although we will never have to face such a difficult and awesome task, we are still called to obedience. Whatever the Father asks, we should do his will and bring glory to his name. Let us not fail to say, "your will be done" or "for this very purpose I have come to this hour."

Are you ready for when God may call you "for this very hour" in the lives of others? Are you aware of a friend in trouble, tensions between yourself and other Christians requiring resolution, or the daily challenges of a difficult job and fellow workers? Are you avoiding some specific problems that won't go away? Remember it is human to avoid difficulty and pain, but it is Christlike to obey the Father and endure even those tasks which otherwise we would just as soon decline.

"Now My soul is troubled."NKJV Unlike the synoptic Gospels, John does not record Jesus' agony in the Garden of Gethsemane prior to his crucifixion (Matthew 26:36-46; Mark 14:32-42; Luke 22:39-46). This is the only indication in John that Jesus was troubled by that approaching hour. His agony proves the genuineness of his humanity.

"And what shall I say, 'Father, save Me from this hour'? But for this purpose I came to this hour."NKJV Jesus refused to ask the Father to spare him from the cross (see Romans 8:32) because he knew he had been sent for the very purpose of dying on the cross. Jesus knew his crucifixion lay ahead, and because he was human, he dreaded it. Jesus knew he would have to take the sins of the world on himself (see 2 Corinthians 5:21), and he knew this would separate him from his Father.

12:28-30 **"Father, glorify your name."** Jesus now turns his thoughts back to the Father and back to the purpose for which he had come to earth: to glorify his Father. Thus, the Father responded in a voice from heaven, **"I have glorified it, and I will glorify it again."**NRSV God would glorify his name through the obedience of his Son (13:31-32) and then would glorify his name again when he would be reunited (17:5) with his Son after his resurrection.

The Father's voice was audible but not correctly perceived by the multitude standing around. Some in the crowd **said that it was thunder. Others said, "An angel has spoken to him."**NRSV

Whatever their interpretation of the sound, it could not be denied that the phenomenon was supernatural. Two other times a voice from heaven had been heard—at Jesus' baptism (Matthew 3:17) and at his transfiguration (Matthew 17:5).

IN THE SPOTLIGHT
Glorify is one of those biblical terms we often use without understanding its true meaning. The Greek root word is *doxa,* which refers to brightness, beauty, and even fame. One helpful way to think of the word is to substitute the word *spotlight.* Jesus was consciously giving God, the Father, permission to spotlight himself through what would happen to Christ, God's Son. The Father responded by affirming that he had already spotlighted his name in Jesus and would continue to do so.

When faced with a difficult task or decision, we can turn our thoughts back to why we are on this earth—to glorify God. Our life can spotlight God's beauty and spread his fame. We can pray that God will guide us and work through us to glorify his name.

"This voice was for your benefit, not mine."NIV Jesus made it clear that *he* did not need this "voice" (he knew that the Father would glorify him); the voice had come for the sake of the people. However, only a few (such as John who recorded this event) understood what was said and who said it. To the others it was merely thunderous noise.

WHO IS SATAN?
The prince of this world is Satan, an angel who rebelled against God. Satan is real, not symbolic, and is constantly working against God and those who obey him. Satan tempted Eve in the Garden and persuaded her to sin; he tempted Jesus in the wilderness and did not persuade him to fall (Matthew 4:1-11). Satan has great power, but people can be delivered from his reign of spiritual darkness because of Christ's victory on the cross. Satan is powerful, but Jesus is much more powerful. Jesus' resurrection shattered Satan's deathly power (Colossians 1:13-14). We live in a time when Satan is both "god of this world" (2 Corinthians 4:4 NRSV) and already defeated (John 12:31). When we trust self, he is "god of this world" and we are defeated; when we trust Christ, Satan is defeated and we are victorious. To overcome Satan we need faithful allegiance to God's Word, determination to stay away from sin, and the support of other believers.

12:31-33 Anticipating his glorification through death and resurrection, Jesus proclaimed: **"Now is the time for judgment on this**

world; now the prince of this world will be driven out."[NIV]
From our perspective we see how Christ's death brought judgment on those who had the upper hand in the world's system:
Judas, Caiaphas, Pilate, and the Jewish religious leaders. But
the Son had ultimately come to destroy the works of Satan,
who, as *the prince of this world,* controlled the minds of
people—producing unbelief. Therefore, the world would be
judged in the sense that Satan, the ruler of the world (see
14:30; 16:11; 2 Corinthians 4:4; Ephesians 2:2; 6:12; Revelation 12:9), would be driven out—his final and ultimate weapon,
death, was about to be overcome (see 1 Corinthians 15:26;
Hebrews 2:14).

**"And I, when I am lifted up from the earth, will draw all
people to myself." He said this to indicate the kind of death
he was to die.**[NRSV] As he did earlier, Jesus spoke about his death
in terms of being *lifted up* (see 3:14; 8:28). John's explanation
makes it clear that this expression signified the mode of execu-

LIGHT VS. DARKNESS

In many places in Scripture the realm of God and the realm of evil
are contrasted by the differences between light and darkness:

Darkness	Light	Reference
A condition of despair	The appearance of hope	Isaiah 9:2
Unable to recognize the light	Able to enlighten the world	John 1:4-5, 9
The power of Satan	The power of God	Acts 26:18
Evil deeds	Good deeds	Romans 13:12-14
Natural heart condition	Given by God to shine in our hearts by knowing Jesus Christ	2 Corinthians 4:6
Fruitless works	Source of all that is good, right, true	Ephesians 5:8-11
Spiritual forces of evil	Armor of God	Ephesians 6:12-13
Powerful captivity	Kingdom of the Son, redemption, forgiveness	Colossians 1:12-14
Cannot exist in God's presence	God's presence, fellowship with God, cleansing of sin	1 John 1:5, 7
Passing away	Lasting forever	1 John 2:8-11

tion—the cross onto which Jesus would be nailed and then lifted up and left to die. Jesus knew that he would not die by stoning, something the Jews had already tried to do (8:59), but by crucifixion. That Jesus *will draw all people* to himself does not mean that everyone will ultimately be saved. Jesus has already made it clear that some will not be saved (5:28-29). Rather like his word *whoever* in verse 26, Jesus was saying that his offer of salvation extends to *all* people, not just to the Jews. Jesus' incredible love, expressed in his death for all people, will draw and unify those who believe, so that sin, evil, and death (the weapons of the prince of this world) will be powerless.

12:34 **The crowd spoke up, "We have heard from the Law that the Christ will remain forever, so how can you say, 'The Son of Man must be lifted up'? Who is this 'Son of Man'?"**NIV The people had heard from the Law (i.e., the Old Testament Scriptures—see 10:34) that the Messiah would live and reign forever (see Psalm 72:17; Isaiah 9:6-7; Ezekiel 37:26-28). They had believed that Jesus had been making a claim to be the Messiah, and here they were waving palm branches for a victorious Messiah who they thought would set up a political, earthly kingdom that would never end. So it was difficult for them to believe that Jesus was the Messiah when he spoke of his imminent death— and that on a cross. Therefore, they wanted clarification about what Jesus meant when he used the term *the Son of Man.* Was this Son of Man someone different than the Messiah? And if so, who was the Son of Man?

LIGHTEN UP
Jesus said he would be with them in person for only a short time, and they should take advantage of his presence while they had it. Like a light shining in a dark place, he would point out the way they should walk. If they walked in his light, they would become "children of light," revealing the truth and pointing people to God. As Christians, we are to be Christ's light bearers, letting his light shine through us. How brightly is your light shining? Can others see Christ in your actions?

12:35 **Then Jesus told them, "You are going to have the light just a little while longer. Walk while you have the light, before darkness overtakes you."**NIV Jesus did not attempt to clear up the people's confusion about the Messiah. Rather, he admonished them to live in *the light* while he was still with them (see also 1:5-9; 3:18-21; 8:12; 9:4-5). The ones enlightened by God would recognize their Messiah. The light of Jesus' physical presence on earth was about to be extinguished, and the darkness of Satan's evil influence and sin would overtake those who would refuse to accept Jesus' light.

"If you walk in the darkness, you do not know where you are going."[NRSV] To walk in Satan's darkness is to stumble through life with no guidance, no help, no protection, no understanding, no ultimate goal or meaning.

WHERE ARE YOU GOING?
Our passion for sharing the gospel can almost be measured by how deeply we recognize the lostness of others. Do we really believe that people we see every day are walking in darkness? Have we ever asked them, "Do you know where your life is going?"

We know people who have no purpose, plan, or personal meaning in their lives. They sense no mission in their career, their family lacks unity, and their personal lives are uneasy and empty. They may not accept the directions we offer them in Christ. But what does it say about us if we know they are lost but never offer to help?

12:36 **"While you have the light, believe in the light, so that you may become children of light."**[NRSV] Believe in Jesus, who is the light, and become his children. The opportunity was available to all, but not for much longer, for Jesus was about to depart this world. The following statement affirms this—both actually and symbolically: Jesus spoke these things, and he **left and hid himself from them.**[NIV]

FOLLOW THE LIGHT
Even a small light can guide a person down a dark path or through a darkened room. There only needs to be enough light to see the way. Although we may not see everything clearly in life, we must act on the light we have. We can't wait until everything is clear.

Hear the urgency in Jesus' words, *"Walk while you have the light, before the darkness overtakes you."* Conditions may not be perfect, problems may be unsolved, and questions may be unanswered, but if Christ calls you, follow his light.

MOST OF THE PEOPLE DO NOT BELIEVE IN JESUS / 12:37-43 / **186**

As he does persistently, John never allows his readers to avoid the decision about what to do with Jesus Christ. For those ready to respond, no obstacle will keep them from belief. For those whose hearts are hardened, even the most compelling reasons for faith become obstacles. John soberly reminds us that many of those who believe in Jesus still allow the pressures and fears of people to hinder their faith. Hidden faith may avoid a confrontation with others, but it seldom pleases God.

THE TRUE WAY OF ENLIGHTENMENT
In this section, Jesus mentioned three ways that we can use the light:
- Walk in the light—put into action those lessons and commands that God allows you to see.
- Put your trust in the light—confidently depend on Christ for your present and future.
- Become children of light—allow Christ to shine his light through you so that others might see the light.

12:37-41 **Even after Jesus had done all these miraculous signs in their presence, they still would not believe in him.**[NIV] Jesus had performed enough miraculous signs to cause people to believe in him. The greatest of all signs—raising Lazarus from the dead—should have been enough to elicit faith from all those who saw it and even heard about it. Yet the Jewish people still refused to believe that Jesus was the Messiah.

This unbelief had been predicted by Isaiah. In the opening of his chapter on the suffering Savior, Isaiah asked, **"Lord, who has believed our report? And to whom has the arm of the LORD been revealed?"**[NKJV] (Quoted from Isaiah 53:1.) It took revelation from God to know that Jesus was *the arm of the Lord* (the one through whom God demonstrated his mighty power). But the Jews lacked this understanding. Why? Because it was prophesied, claimed John, who again quoted Isaiah: **"He has blinded their eyes and hardened their hearts, lest they should see with their eyes, lest they should understand with their hearts and turn, so that I should heal them."**[NKJV] This quotation (taken from Isaiah 6:9-10) appears quite often in the New Testament because it provides a prophetic explanation for why the Jews did not perceive Jesus' message nor receive him as their Messiah (see also Matthew 13:14; Mark 4:12; Luke 8:10; Acts 28:26). And because they *would not* believe, they eventually *could not* believe. As a result, the Jews remained unenlightened and hardened. They had not seen what Isaiah had seen, for **Isaiah said this because he saw Jesus' glory and spoke about him.**"NIV Isaiah had seen the Lord of glory, who is none other than Jesus himself—Jesus is God, yet he is also a distinct part of the mysterious Trinity, and he is also Jesus the Son.

HARDENED
People in Jesus' time, like those in the time of Isaiah, would not believe despite the evidence (12:37). As a result, God hardened their hearts. Does that mean God intentionally prevented these people from believing in him? No, he simply confirmed their own choices. After a lifetime of resisting God, they had become so set in their ways that they wouldn't even try to understand Jesus' message. For such people, it is virtually impossible to come to God—their hearts have been permanently hardened. Other instances of hardened hearts because of constant stubbornness are recorded in Exodus 9:12; Romans 1:24-28; and 2 Thessalonians 2:9-12.

As a result of his vision of Jesus' glory (Isaiah 6:1-3), Isaiah predicted the blindness to come. Isaiah spoke much about Jesus, the coming Messiah (see Isaiah 4:2; 7:14; 9:6-7; 11:1-5, 10; 32:1; 42:1-4; 49:1-7; 52:13–53:12; 61:1-3). Isaiah's prophecies gave the people no excuse. He foretold that there would be persistent unbelief in Israel and that God would use their rejection of Christ to open the door to the Gentiles.

DESPITE THE EVIDENCE
Jesus had performed many miracles, but most people still didn't believe in him. Likewise, many today won't believe despite all God does. Don't be discouraged if your witness for Christ doesn't turn as many to him as you'd like. Your job is to continue as a faithful witness. You are responsible to reach out to others, but they are responsible for their own decisions.

12:42-43 **Nevertheless many, even of the authorities, believed in him. But because of the Pharisees they did not confess it, for fear that they would be put out of the synagogue; for they loved human glory more than the glory that comes from God.**NRSV These "authorities" were the leaders of Israel (see 3:1). Several of these leaders had some kind of faith in Jesus, but they were afraid to make an open confession of this faith because the Pharisees would expel them from the synagogue for doing so. John made the point that their faith was weak, and

> Not to feel pleased at being praised is, I am afraid, what has never happened to any man.
> *John Chrysostom*

he described the reason: They were still subject to the lure of human praise (see 5:44). But John primarily warned his readers that secret faith does not ultimately please God. Secrecy may be prudent at times (witness the presence of secret believers and churches in repressive societies like China and the former Romanian state), but that usually comes from a courageous strategy. All too often we remain silent at the very times we ought to be confessing our faith in Christ.

PEER FEAR
Along with those who refused to believe, many believed but refused to admit it. This is just as bad, and Jesus had strong words for such people (see Matthew 10:32-33). Many people will not take a stand for Jesus because they fear rejection or ridicule. Many Jewish leaders wouldn't admit to faith in Jesus because they feared excommunication from the synagogue (which was their livelihood) and loss of their prestigious place in the community. But the praise of people is fickle and short-lived. We should be much more concerned about God's eternal acceptance than about the temporary approval of other people.

JESUS SUMMARIZES HIS MESSAGE / 12:44-50 / **187**

John closes this section in his gospel about Jesus' public ministry with a summary of Jesus' entire testimony. The shared Passover meal will take up the next several chapters. But John leaves his readers with the cry of Jesus' final public speech ringing in their ears. It is an ultimatum set before the crowds: Believe in Jesus, the Light of the World, or live in darkness under God's judgment.

12:44-45 Jesus left the crowds temporarily (12:36-37), but in one final public appearance he appealed to his hearers to believe in him (see also 5:17-44; 6:27-65; 7:16-18; 8:14-58; 10:14-18) and thereby walk in his light. In this appeal, he affirmed his union with the Father: **"Whoever believes in me believes not in me but in him who sent me. And whoever sees me sees him who sent me."**[NRSV] Because the Son sent by the Father is the visible expression of the Father to all people (see 14:9-11), those who believe

in the Son also believe in the Father. Jesus *is* God. We do not
believe in God *or* in Jesus—to believe in God we must believe in
Jesus. If you want to know what God is like, study the person and
words of Jesus Christ.

**12:46 "I have come as light into the world, so that everyone who
believes in me should not remain in the darkness."**^{NRSV} Those
who believe in Jesus have left Satan's dark kingdom and influence, and they have entered the light of God's kingdom. Some
people in the church act as though they still remain in darkness.
Jesus died so that we might be transformed. If our life is not
changing, we may not have begun to really follow the light.

**12:47-48 "I do not judge anyone who hears my words and does not
keep them, for I came not to judge the world, but to save the
world. The one who rejects me and does not receive my word
has a judge; on the last day the word that I have spoken will
serve as judge."**^{NRSV} Jesus repeated the important truth that he
came not to judge the world but to save it (see also 3:17; 8:15-
16); but his rejected words would condemn all unbelievers in the
judgment at the last day (see 3:31-36; 5:22-23, 26-30; 9:39).

The purpose of Jesus' first mission on earth was not to judge
people, but to show them the way to find salvation and eternal
life. When he comes again, one of his main purposes will be to
judge people for how they lived. People will be condemned
because they would *not* accept and obey Jesus. On the day of
judgment, those who have accepted Jesus and lived his way will
be raised to eternal life (1 Corinthians 15:51-57; 1 Thessalonians
4:15-18; Revelation 21:1-8), and those who have rejected Jesus
and lived any way they pleased will face eternal punishment
(Revelation 20:11-15). Decide now your future fate, for the consequences of your decision will last forever.

**12:49 "I have not spoken on my own, but the Father who sent me
has himself given me a commandment about what to say and
what to speak."**^{NRSV} Jesus' mission was to faithfully convey the
words of God to all who would truly listen. He knew that those
who rejected those words would be rejecting life. God himself
instructed Jesus what to say. Jesus did not change that message.
Some, like the Jehovah's Witnesses, have used verses like this to
say that Jesus was not God because he was so subordinate to the
Father. But Jesus' essential, divine being was not subordinate to
the Father—in all things he was equal with God (Philippians 2:5-
6); rather, Jesus coordinated his will to fully comply with the
Father's will. Thus, to respond to Jesus is to respond to God. To
believe in Jesus is to believe in God. To reject Jesus is to reject

God. To hear Jesus' words makes each person responsible before God for what he or she does with them.

12:50 **"I know that his command leads to eternal life. So whatever I say is just what the Father has told me to say."**[NIV] Jesus closed his message with one final appeal to accept the words he had spoken as having come from the Father. To accept those words is to receive eternal life (3:16-17, 35-36; 5:24-29, 39-40).

John 13

The pace of John's writing slowed remarkably beginning with chapter 13. The first twelve chapters cover three years; the next six chapters cover one night.

In chapter 13 John tells his readers that the Passover Feast was about to begin, but he doesn't tell his readers when and if Jesus celebrated the Passover meal with his disciples as their last supper together. This has caused much debate among scholars because John's record doesn't seem to match what is recorded in the synoptic Gospels, which seem to indicate that the Last Supper was the Passover meal. At the very center of the controversy are two questions:

1. Was the Last Supper in fact a Passover meal?

2. On what night of the week did Jesus and the disciples share this meal?

THREE GREAT DISCOURSES OF JESUS
The Gospels record three separate occasions when Jesus taught at great length.

Discourse	Summary
The Sermon on the Mount (Matthew 5–7)	Jesus explained the requirements of repentance and righteousness for those who desire to enter the kingdom of heaven.
The Olivet Discourse (Matthew 24–25; Mark 13; Luke 21)	Jesus described the outcome of history and encouraged us to endure. This discourse was given to Jesus' disciples who would soon need great stability to face the future and resist the temptation to turn away.
The Upper Room Discourse (John 13–16)	Jesus illustrated and defined the love of God. He explained the new relationships necessary to fulfill the new covenant. This discourse was given to the disciples who would need his presence and guidance after he was gone.

Several other questions hinge on how we answer the central ones:

- Why didn't John mention the Eucharist in his description of the meal?

- Does John's Gospel contradict the Synoptics on these matters?

- Are the Gospels reliable, corroborating records of what actually occurred?

Was the Last Supper a Passover meal? Most likely it was. Mark and Luke both identify this meal that Jesus had with his disciples as a Passover meal (Mark 14:12-16; Luke 22:7-16). Certain descriptions in John indicate it was a Jewish seder:

- Everyone ate in a reclining position (13:23). Jews only reclined at Passover. The rest of the time they sat up, thus differentiating themselves from other cultures like the Egyptians and the Romans.

- A traditional Passover contains a hand washing ceremony that could have been the opportunity for the foot washing.

- The use of bread and wine in the seder provided a natural way for Jesus to present the new covenant.

- The dipping of the unleavened bread (13:26) into the preparation of bitter herbs comes from Passover.

- Though eating lamb was not mentioned by any of the Gospel writers, it was not an exact requirement to complete the celebration. A Passover could be celebrated without eating lamb. Those Jews traveling or living away from Jerusalem could not eat the officially slain Passover lambs either. It would be possible to have lamb, but not one of the officially sacrificed ones.

On what night of the week did Jesus and the disciples share this meal? Traditionally, the Passover went from sundown (6:00 P.M.) Thursday to sundown on Friday, the fifteenth day of the month of Nisan. Matthew, Mark, and Luke show that Jesus and the disciples celebrated the Last Supper on Thursday evening. However, seven verses in John suggest that the Last Supper occurred on a Wednesday (see 13:1, 27; 18:28; 19:14, 31, 36, 42).

The following four attempts have been made to solve this apparent problem:

1. The Gospel writers contradict each other. This is highly unlikely since the Passover and the Lord's Supper are so significant to early Christians. The writers would not confuse something so important.

2. There were two calendars being used to determine the day of Passover. The official calendar that the Pharisees and Sadducees followed was lunar. Jesus and the disciples followed a solar calendar, possibly used at Qumran (a monastic Dead Sea community). The two calendars differed by one day, so that Jesus ate the Passover meal one full day before the Jerusalem Passover. There have been no conclusive historic arguments to support this theory.

3. Jesus and his disciples had the Passover meal one day early in anticipation of Passover. This view does explain John 18:28 and allows Jesus to be the Passover Lamb—crucified at the same time as the Passover lambs were slaughtered. If Jesus can heal on the Sabbath because he is the Lord of the Sabbath, he could certainly authorize eating the Passover meal one day early.

   This view harmonizes the chronology of all the Gospel writers and preserves their authority and reliability. Furthermore, it allows for a full three-day period when Jesus was in the grave—not just part of Friday, all of Saturday, and part of Sunday—but from Thursday evening to Sunday morning.

4. Jesus and the disciples did eat the meal on the official day of Passover. In A.D. 30 (the year of Jesus' crucifixion), the Passover was celebrated on Thursday evening (the 14th of Nisan) and was immediately followed by the Feast of Unleavened Bread, which lasted from the fifteenth of Nisan (Friday) to the twenty-first of Nisan. During each day of this celebration, special meals (*chaggigah*) were eaten. According to this view, the other references in John are to the Feast of Unleavened Bread, not the Passover meal (13:29; 18:28; 19:14). In 13:29, after the Passover meal, Judas went out—actually to betray Jesus—but the disciples thought he went out to buy provisions for the upcoming feast. In 18:28 the Pharisees did not want to make themselves unclean (by entering Pilate's palace) so they wouldn't be able to partake of the feast. In 19:14 "the preparation for the Passover" was not for the Passover meal but for the whole week that followed, which in New Testament times was called both the Passover and Feast of Unleavened Bread.

The chronology follows:

Thursday—Lambs slain in the afternoon, Passover begins at 6:00 p.m., Last Supper, Gethsemane, arrest

Friday—Official trial, crucifixion, burial by sundown, Feast of Unleavened Bread, and Sabbath begins at 6:00 p.m.

Saturday—In the tomb

Sunday—Early morning resurrection

13:1-2 Before the Feast of the Passover.NKJV This time period covers the next seven chapters, and locates the events recorded in these chapters as occurring on the fourteenth and fifteenth of Nisan (see the introduction of this section for a detailed explanation about the chronology of these events).

> [The world is] a sea of glass, a pageant of fond delights, a theatre of variety, a labyrinth of error, a gulf of grief, a sty of filthiness, a vale of misery, a state of deceit, a cage full of owls, a den of scorpions, a wilderness of wolves, a cabin of bears, a whirlwind of passions, a feigned comedy, a detestable frenzy. *Arthur Dent*

Jesus knew that His hour had come that He should depart from this world to the Father.NKJV Because Jesus was fully aware that his time had come to leave this world and return to his Father, he devoted his last hours to instructing and encouraging his disciples.

Throughout his writings, John frequently used the term *world* (*kosmos*). The word conveys two distinct meanings in the Bible. On one hand, *world* is used in 3:16 to refer to the object of God's love, "God so loved the world." On the other hand, 1 John 2:15-17 makes the "world" something we should disdain. We are told that "if anyone loves the world, the love of the Father is not in him" (1 John 2:15 NIV).

God does love the world (of which we are a part) as his creation. He even loves the part of his creation that has rebelled against him (including us). His love compelled God to become flesh and visit this planet. Our problem comes when we love the world more than God.

The context determines the meaning of *world*. Sometimes the word refers to humanity and sometimes to the system of values that humans love, but which keeps them apart from God. Our own relationship to the world can take two forms: If we love people as God loves them, we are fulfilling the great commandment; but if we love what people love, and love sinful desires, we are loving the world in a way that God cannot accept. One love redeems the world; the other makes the world our central object of desire.

Having loved His own who were in the world, He loved them to the end.^{NKJV} The last part of this verse could also be rendered, "He loved them to the utmost" or "He now showed them the full extent of his love" (NIV). The statement means that Jesus continued his devotion to his disciples until the very end of his life. Before he left them, he wanted to express his love to them, one by one—and this he would do in a way that would surprise them.

JESUS SHOWS HIS LOVE
Jesus knew that one of his disciples had already decided to betray him. Another would deny him by the next morning. Even this night, they would all desert him. In the next hours they would repeatedly display ignorance, laziness, and lack of trust. It was indeed a sorry lot that gathered in the upper room. Even with good reasons to reject the entire group, Jesus deliberately showed to them the full extent of his love. The actions, words, and feelings that he shared with his disciples conveyed the highest form of love because his disciples did not deserve nor immediately appreciate this love.

Jesus knows us as fully as he knew those disciples. He knows intimately of every time and every way that we have denied or deserted him. Yet knowing us, he willingly died for us. Jesus continually displays his love toward us and reaches out to us. He continues to serve us in the Lord's Supper, and he guides and encourages us by his Spirit. He serves us as we serve one another. Are we prepared to love one another with the same kind of love Jesus demonstrated for us?

The evening meal was being served.^{NIV} This was probably the official time for the Passover meal, indicated by verse 1. And this was a special Passover, for it was the last meal Jesus would eat with his disciples, and during this meal he would institute the "Lord's Supper" (see Matthew 26:17-30; Mark 14:12-26; Luke 22:7-39). The context indicates that the food was being placed before them, but the meal itself had not been eaten (see 13:26, 30).

The devil had already put it into the heart of Judas son of Simon Iscariot to betray him.^{NRSV} Jesus had already called Judas "a devil" in 6:70 because Jesus knew that Judas would cooperate with the devil in perpetrating Jesus' death. Thus, the devil and Judas corroborated in Jesus' betrayal. Indeed, Satan entered Judas to carry out the actual betrayal (see 13:27).

13:3 Jesus, knowing . . . that He had come from God and was going to God.^{NKJV} Jesus, the Son of God, knew his origin and his destiny. He knew that he would soon be returning to his Father. Being assured of his own destiny, he focused his attention on the disciples and showed them what it meant for him to become their Servant and for them to serve one another.

At the time so near to the revelation of Jesus' true identity and glory, he set aside what was rightfully his and expressed his character through an act of humility. Paul described Jesus as one, "Who, being in very nature God . . . made himself nothing, taking the very nature of a servant . . . humbled himself and became obedient to death—even death on a cross!" (Philippians 2:6-8 NIV).

For some people, the desire for approval motivates their service. Their efforts only go as far as the amount of positive feedback they receive. For Jesus, service expressed who he was and did not depend on the response of others. Imagine dying for people who might reject your sacrificial act of service. When we serve freely, without expecting the response or approval of others, we are acting like Jesus.

13:4 Got up from the table, took off his outer robe.^{NRSV} This action portrayed how Jesus was willing to divest himself of being "in the form of God" to take on "the form of a servant" (Philippians 2:5-6). He then **wrapped a towel around his waist**^{NIV} like an apron, and humbled himself by preparing to do a task normally assigned to a servant. The one least compelled to take up the duty was the first to eagerly volunteer. How unlike the natural human response of "Let someone else do it!"

13:5 He poured water into a basin and began to wash his disciples' feet, drying them with the towel that was wrapped around him.^{NIV} Jesus was the model servant, and he showed his servant attitude to his disciples. Foot washing was a common act in Bible times. People traveled mostly on foot in sandals across the dusty roads of Judea. When entering a home, it was customary to wash one's feet. To not offer to wash a guest's feet was considered a breach of hospitality (see Luke 7:44). Washing guests' feet was a job for a household servant to carry out when guests arrived (1 Samuel 25:41). It was a subservient task—wives might wash their husbands' feet; students their teachers' feet, etc., but not the other way around. What was unusual about this act was that Jesus, the Master and Teacher, was doing it *for* his disciples. He wrapped a towel around his waist, as the lowliest slave would do, and washed and dried his disciples' feet.

CURE FOR CONTENTION AND PRIDE
The other Gospel writers record a discussion the disciples had on the way to this meal when they argued about who would have the greatest position in the new kingdom. Jesus' humble service contrasted sharply with their search for high places of prestige in the kingdom (Matthew 20:20-24) and their desire to be considered the "greatest" (Mark 9:33-34; 10:35-44; Luke 22:24-30).

Unselfish service to each other and to those not part of the inner circle was to be one of the distinctive marks of Jesus' true disciples (see 13:34-35). When we feel the temptation to pride or to competitive comparisons with other believers, the antidote will be a healthy dose of service. One great starting place would be to pray for those we serve who most irritate us!

After washing the disciples' feet (a sign of his cleansing ministry), Jesus put his garments on again and returned to his place at the table (13:12). This exhibited his return to glory and to God. Jesus did not wash his disciples' feet just to get them to be nice to each other. His far greater goal was to extend his mission on earth after he was gone. These men moved into the world serving God, serving each other, and serving all people to whom they took the message of salvation. They would be empowered by Jesus' ultimate act of service—dying for their sins. "For even the Son of Man did not come to be served, but to serve, and to give His life a ransom for many" (Mark 10:45 NKJV).

13:6-9 All the disciples accepted the washing until Jesus came to Peter, who questioned Jesus: **"Lord, are you going to wash my feet?"**[NRSV]

Jesus did not provide Peter with an explanation, other than that Peter would understand the significance of the washing some time in the future: **"You do not realize now what I am doing, but later you will understand."**[NIV] Later in the New Testament, Peter explains his understanding of what Jesus had done (1 Peter 5:5-6). Peter came to realize that humble service meant obedience to Christ. When Jesus washed the disciples' feet, he was demonstrating his ultimate sacrificial act—giving his life for them on the cross.

"You will never wash my feet."[NRSV] Imagine being Peter and watching Jesus wash the others' feet, all the while moving closer to him. Seeing the Master behave like a slave must have confused Peter. And Peter did not feel worthy that his Master should be acting like a slave toward him! This was not an expression of arrogance but of confusion. Peter felt he should be washing the

Master's feet—not the other way around. Peter still did not understand Jesus' teaching that to be a leader, a person must be a servant.

IT'S YOUR SERVE
Some people serve naturally. For Jesus' friend Martha, serving others came easily and graciously. For many, hospitality is their gift.

    For others, serving is an ordeal. If they do not feel inept at their efforts, the work exhausts them. Or they become angry when their service goes unappreciated. For these, hospitality becomes an uncomfortable chore.

    Some find it difficult to accept service from others. (Servers may be part of this group.) Being helped makes them feel inadequate or vulnerable. They are unable to be gracious when they are not in control.

    We need to remember that the true point of serving is to obey and imitate Jesus Christ. Likewise, accepting service from others is accepting Christ's service. Christ elevated serving others as the highest pursuit to which we can dedicate our lives.

Jesus responded: **"Unless I wash you, you have no part with me."**[NIV] There are two possible meanings for this sentence: (1) Jesus meant that unless he washed away Peter's sins by his death on the cross, then Peter could have no relationship with him. (2) Jesus meant that unless Peter submitted to him and allowed Jesus to minister in this way, Peter would never learn the lesson of humility.

Either way, Peter seemed to grasp the significance of Jesus' words, for he then wanted to be bathed completely: **"Lord, not my feet only but also my hands and my head!"**[NRSV]

13:10-11 **"One who has bathed does not need to wash, except for the feet, but is entirely clean."**[NRSV] After one has bathed, another bath is not necessary at the end of the day. The person is still clean—except for the feet, which are constantly soiled by the dust of the ground. A clean and bathed person just needs to have his or her feet rinsed. According to the customs of those times, once a person had bathed, he or she needed only to wash his or her feet upon entering a person's home.

To be bathed by Jesus meant to be washed by his living word. Later in the meal Jesus returned to this theme when he told his disciples, "You are already clean because of the word I have spoken to you" (15:3 NIV). It was Jesus' teaching, and the acceptance of his words, that separated the true believers from all the people throughout Jesus' ministry.

To receive Jesus, nothing is required of the believer except humble acceptance of what Jesus has done. Peter had to sit and humbly allow Jesus to wash his dirty feet in order to understand that to accept the salvation Jesus offers means to humbly accept his death on the cross for all sins.

"You are clean, though not all of you." For he knew who was to betray him; for this reason he said, "Not all of you are clean."NRSV Jesus referred to Judas Iscariot (see 13:18), suggesting that Judas was not a true believer in Jesus. Though Jesus had washed Judas's feet, Judas was not clean, for he had not come to believe in Jesus as the Messiah, the Son of God. Jesus already knew that this man would be used by Satan to bring about the events that unfold in the final chapters of this Gospel.

BETRAYAL
John made it clear that Judas was the specific reason Jesus said, "though not all of you." But John must have also had his future readers in mind. If among the original disciples there was one not true, future groups of disciples would also discover among themselves those who were false followers. This happened later in the first century and has continued through the years. Many have betrayed Christ and his people.

Today's readers of John should heed this implicit warning: Are we clean? Will our commitment stand firm and our faith sure? Will we be prepared to endure even when those who have seemed strong in the faith fail?

13:12-13 "Do you understand what I have done for you?"NIV Jesus' act of washing the disciples' feet demonstrated love in action. Jesus was their **Teacher and Lord,** meaning he was on a higher level than they; yet he assumed a position of humility and service because he loved those he served.

13:14-16 "If I then, your Lord and Teacher, have washed your feet, you also ought to wash one another's feet. For I have given you an example, that you should do as I have done to you."NKJV Jesus commanded his disciples to serve one another in love according to the example he set because **"a servant is not greater than his master; nor is he who is sent greater than he who sent him."**NKJV The example is not for us to literally wash one another's feet. Today some churches do practice this, but usually only to teach what Jesus was trying to teach—humble service to others. To refuse to serve others, to refuse to humble yourself, no matter how high your position, is to place yourself above Jesus. Such arrogant pride is not what Jesus taught.

These disciples would soon be *sent* out as the sole planters of the Christian church. They would be leaders in many places—indeed, James, John, and Peter became the leaders of the Christian church in Jerusalem. Jesus taught these soon-to-be leaders that as they labored to spread the gospel, they first and foremost had to be servants to those whom they taught. The disciples must have remembered this lesson often as they labored with the problems, struggles, and joys of the early believers. How many times they must have remembered that they were called to serve. And what a difference it made! Imagine how difficult the growth (even existence) of the early church would have been if these disciples had continued vying for spots of greatness and importance! Fortunately for us, they took Jesus' lesson to heart.

FOOT WASHING TODAY
Some churches and groups still practice foot washing today. In shoe-clad cultures it has little more than symbolic use. But as such, it can still teach a valuable lesson. In Jesus' day, feet were washed for two practical reasons: to remove dirt and to be hospitable. Jesus did not perform a special or unusual act; his taking on a servant's duties stunned the disciples.

Instituting foot washing today would be missing Jesus' primary lesson. He was not inventing a clever way to serve others; he was serving others in a very common way. Today we ought to think of foot washing as an example of servant leadership. Other ways we can show a "foot washing" attitude include:
- Taking on a menial task or accepting a lesser role.
- Not insisting on our "rights" or "privileges."
- Meeting others' needs before meeting our own.
- Looking for a job no one else will do and cheerfully doing it.
- Focusing on the results being achieved, not who is getting credit.

13:17 **"If you know these things, blessed are you if you do them."**NKJV We are blessed (happy, joyful, fulfilled), not because of what we know, but because of what we do with what we know. God's grace to us finds its completion in the service we, as recipients of his grace, perform for others. We will find our greatest joy in obeying Christ by serving others.

13:18-19 **"I am not referring to all of you; I know those I have chosen."**NIV Jesus' previous statements about serving and loving one another did not apply to all of his disciples because, in fact, one of his disciples (Judas) was about to betray him. However, this betrayal was not an unexpected event, for Jesus had known from the beginning that one of the men he chose would betray him (6:70-71).

SPIRITUAL PROCRASTINATION?
When Jesus talked about "knowing" and "doing," he meant a needed service that we have identified but not rendered. Most of us are surrounded with opportunities for service that we have simply left undone. By doing nothing, we forfeit Christ's blessing.

- Do you know someone who needs a visit or a word of encouragement?
- Do you have a possession you no longer use that would help someone else?
- Is there a menial task (like ushering or greeting at church) that regularly goes unfilled?
- Are there trying duties that beg to be done—nursery, teaching classes, being youth sponsors, etc.?
- Do you know a friend or work associate with whom you have never spoken about your faith?

Jesus promised personal spiritual benefits as you act on these opportunities.

"This is to fulfill the scripture: 'He who shares my bread has lifted up his heel against me.'"[NIV] Jesus' betrayal was necessary to fulfill Scripture—specifically, Psalm 41:9. The expression pictures a horse lifting his heel ready for a swift (and sometimes deadly) kick. Jesus drew from Psalm 41 because it describes how one of David's friends turned against him: "Even my close friend, whom I trusted, he who shared my bread, has lifted up his heel against me" (Psalm 41:9 NIV). This may have referred to the story of David's trusted companion, Ahithophel, who betrayed David and then went and hanged himself (see 2 Samuel 16:20–17:3, 23). Judas, who had been with Jesus and was a trusted companion (Judas was keeper of the money), would betray Jesus and then hang himself.

Jesus had known all along that Judas would betray him (see 6:64, 70-71; Matthew 17:22-23; 20:17-19), but he predicted the betrayal in the presence of his disciples so that they would realize, when the betrayal actually occurred, that it had been prophesied in Scripture (see Acts 1:16). This would strengthen their faith.

> Next to the Blessed Sacrament itself, your neighbor is the holiest object presented to your senses. If he is your Christian neighbor, he is holy in almost the same way, for in him also Christ *vere latitat*—the glorifier and the glorified, God Himself, is truly hidden. *C. S. Lewis*

13:20 "Whoever receives one whom I send receives me; and whoever receives me receives him who sent me."[NRSV] This verse follows the thought of verse 16, where Jesus spoke of being a servant to the one who sent him. He would send forth his disciples so that whoever would receive them would receive Jesus and, in turn, receive the one who sent Jesus—God the Father.

THE LAST SUPPER / 13:21-30 / 211

At this point in the dinner, the mood shifted, partly as a reflection of the ominous tone Jesus used in verse 18. Apparently the food was on the table, and they may have already been eating. None of the Gospels record a beginning prayer over the meal itself (though the Synoptics record his praying over the bread and cup before giving them to the disciples). John explains that Jesus was visibly disturbed, indicating that he had been observing the Lord closely.

Moments later, in answer to John's direct question, Jesus indicated his knowledge of Judas's betrayal by handing him the bread that he had dipped in the bowl. The rest of the disciples could not understand the significance behind Judas's abrupt departure. They would have other meals together during the Feast of Unleavened Bread, so they assumed Judas had left on business for the Master.

13:21-26 Jesus was troubled in spirit.[NIV] Jesus was deeply affected by the betrayal, even though he knew that the betrayal had been foreordained—as had been his coming crucifixion. His inner turmoil must have been expressed when he said, **"I tell you the truth, one of you is going to betray me."**[NIV] Jesus' talk about the betrayal became explicit and pointed: one of the twelve disciples would betray him.

Jesus' pronouncement caused great consternation among the disciples. **His disciples stared at one another, at a loss to know which of them he meant.**[NIV] It was not obvious who it was. Judas, as keeper of the money, may have been the one they would *least* suspect.

Peter motioned to John, who was sitting beside Jesus, to ask Jesus who the betrayer was. Perhaps Peter was going to deal with this betrayer then and there! Luke mentions that they had two swords among the group (Luke 22:38) and, later, Peter used a sword to strike at one of those who arrived to arrest Jesus (18:10).

So John leaned back and asked Jesus, **"Lord, who is it?"**[NIV] In those days it was the custom for people to recline only at the Passover meal; usually they ate sitting up. The host would be at the head of the group, and a special guest to the right of the host would have his head near the host's chest. One disciple, here described as **the disciple whom Jesus loved,**[NIV] occupied this special place of honor. While this disciple is usually identified as John, there have been other suggestions. One of the principal candidates is Lazarus, who as recently as 11:3 Mary could call "the one you love." However, since every other indication points to only the Twelve being present for this meal, there seems little reason to look outside that group for this disciple.

Jesus would identify the betrayer as **"the one to whom I will give this piece of bread when I have dipped it in the dish."**[NIV] Jesus dipped the piece of bread into a dish filled with a sauce probably made of dates, raisins, and sour wine. Having said this, Jesus **dipped the piece of bread [and] gave it to Judas son of Simon Iscariot.**[NRSV] Ironically, a host offering a piece of bread to a guest was a sign of friendship. Jesus' act of friendship was his identification of the betrayer. Later, in the Garden, Judas would identify Jesus to the guards with another sign of friendship—a kiss (Luke 22:47-48).

13:27-30 After Judas received the bread, **Satan entered into him.**[NRSV] Thus the betrayal was set in motion. Satan would use Judas as his tool to accomplish his evil plan. But Satan's part in the betrayal of Jesus does not remove any of the responsibility from Judas. Judas may have been disillusioned because Jesus was talking about dying rather than setting up his kingdom, and he may have been trying to force Jesus' hand and make him use his power to prove he was the Messiah. Or perhaps Judas didn't understand Jesus' mission and no longer believed that Jesus was God's chosen one. Whatever Judas thought, Satan assumed that Jesus' death would end his mission and thwart God's plan. Like Judas, Satan did not know that Jesus' death was the most important part of God's plan all along.

WRONG MESSIAH!
Judas had a fatal misconception of who the Messiah would be. Many Jews expected a military or political deliverer who would expel the oppressors and bring peace to Israel. Few were open to having their picture of the Savior clarified.

How well does your view of Jesus match the man who takes shape in the Gospels? From what sources have you developed your view of Christ? Does your picture limit him? To what degree does your view of Jesus put him under your control?

Jesus said to him, "Do quickly what you are going to do." Now no one at the table knew why he said this to him.[NRSV] Because Judas was keeper of the money (see 12:6), the disciples thought Jesus was sending him out **to buy what was needed for the Feast, or to give something to the poor.**[NIV] The *Feast* refers to the seven-day Feast of Unleavened Bread. The disciples had no idea that Judas was going out to betray their Master. Jesus identified Judas so tactfully that all the disciples missed the significance of the act: they did not connect Jesus' earlier statement ("One of you is going to betray me") with his present exchange with Judas. Only John knew the truth. But despite the disciples' misunderstanding, the stage was quickly being set: Judas **went out immediately. And it was night.**[NKJV] The last statement recounts the actual time yet also symbolizes the spiritual condition of Judas. He was in darkness, under the control of the prince of darkness, Satan.

HYPOCRISY
Judas took the bread in what looked like a gesture of fellowship and love between himself and Jesus. Apparently, none of the other disciples knew of his thoughts of betrayal. Judas had completely concealed his hypocrisy from his peers. Yet Christ knew his heart.

If we try to conceal our hypocrisy (professing to live for Christ but not having real commitment), we may succeed in fooling our friends and family. But Christ knows each person's real thoughts and desires. People may be convinced by our exterior sham, but God searches our hearts (see 1 Samuel 16:7). Judas's life teaches us that hypocrisy can lead to satanic control. Judas's betrayal should strengthen our resolve to follow Christ no matter what temptations or opposition we encounter.

JESUS PREDICTS PETER'S DENIAL / 13:31-38 / **212**

After Judas's departure, a heaviness lifted from the room. Jesus spoke of his own glorification and referred to the brief time they would still have together. With a sense of urgency, he commanded them to love each other. He indicated that this single characteristic would set them apart from the world as his disciples.

Peter stopped listening when Jesus mentioned his departure. He wanted to know where Jesus was planning to go that they could not go with him. Jesus simply restated that his destination would not be theirs until later.

Ironically, Peter came close to the truth when he suggested that he would not even allow death to keep him from following Jesus. With profound compassion, which Peter could not possibly fathom until later, Jesus pointed out that Peter was not ready to lay down his life.

That disqualified Peter from going with Jesus at this time. Peter would, in fact, shortly deny that he even knew Jesus.

13:31-32 When he was gone, Jesus said, "Now is the Son of Man glorified and God is glorified in him."[NIV] As Judas was on his way to betray Jesus into the hands of those who would crucify him, Jesus looked past the cross to his glorification at the resurrection. Jesus had allowed Judas to leave and carry out his murderous plans. By this act, Jesus committed himself to following through on what he had come to do. Thus he could say, *Now is the Son of Man glorified.*

Jesus framed his words based on his knowledge that his glorification through death and resurrection already had been accomplished. He anticipated how his resurrection would bring about his spiritual union with the disciples. This is the key to interpreting the following discourse (13:31–17:26).

The word *glorify* is not commonly used in Western language, except in Scripture. In Bible times, the "glory" of something was not only in its appearance but also in what it would accomplish, in its purpose, such as when a field is finally ready for harvest. Thus to "glorify" means to exalt by completing the task, or to express the essential nature of something by bringing it to fruition. The scope and wonder of God's marvelous plan of salvation will only be apparent with Jesus' death and resurrection. Jesus again stated his resolve to see his mission to its completion.

"If God is glorified in him, God will glorify the Son in himself, and will glorify him at once."[NIV] That God will *glorify him at once* refers to the soon-to-come Resurrection and Ascension. Now that Judas had left to complete his treachery, nothing would stop the events leading to the final hour. God's magnificent moral splendor is displayed by Jesus' act of obedience, so God is glorified in Jesus. At the same moment, Jesus is glorified as he resumes the glory he had with the Father before the foundation of the world.

13:33-35 "My children, I will be with you only a little longer. You will look for me, and just as I told the Jews, so I tell you now: Where I am going, you cannot come."[NIV] Jesus told his dear *children* (Greek, *teknia,* which connotes intimacy and fondness) that the time of his departure was nearing. Jesus would be going to the Father (14:6, 28) to rejoin him in the glorious fellowship that the Father and Son enjoyed from all eternity (see 17:5, 24). The disciples would not be able to participate in that fellowship just yet.

"A new commandment I give to you, that you love one another; as I have loved you, that you also love one another."[NKJV] Jesus would be gone, and they would not be able to join him for a while. In the meantime, they were to follow this commandment: *Love one another.* A command to love one another is not a new commandment; it had been mandated in the Old Testament (Exodus 20:12-17; Leviticus 19:18, 33-34; Deuteronomy 5:16-21; 22:1-4; see also Matthew 5:38-48; 7:12; 23:36-40; Luke 10:25-37). The newness

> Love for our neighbor consists of three things: to desire the greater good of everyone; to do what good we can when we can; to bear, excuse and hide other's faults. *John Vianney*

of Jesus' command pertains to the new kind of love that Christians have for one another because they have each experienced the love of Christ.

Jesus commanded his followers to love one another *"as I have loved you."* This was revolutionary, for believers are called to love others based on Jesus' sacrificial love for them. Jesus was a living example of God's love, as we are to be living examples of Jesus' love. This love would be the mark of distinction: **"By this all will know that you are My disciples, if you have love for one another."**[NKJV] One of the major themes in John's first letter is brotherly love (see 1 John 3–4).

Jesus was going to die; he was going to be raised again; he was going to return to the Father. The disciples would be left in the world. Jesus gave them this one all-encompassing command—to love one another. Not only would such love bring unbelievers to Christ; it would also keep believers strong and united in a world hostile to God. And such love, enabled by Jesus' love for them and by the coming Holy Spirit's power in them, would allow them to love all those for whom Christ died, and unite them with Christ spiritually. Then one future day, all believers would be united physically with their Savior.

WHAT DO THEY SEE?
Jesus said that our Christlike love will show that we are his disciples. Do people see petty bickering, jealousy, and division in your church? Or do they know you are Jesus' followers by your love for one another? Love is more than simply warm feelings; it is an attitude that reveals itself in action. How can we love others as Jesus loves us? By helping when it's not convenient, by giving when it hurts, by devoting energy to others' welfare rather than our own, by absorbing hurts from others without complaining or fighting back. This kind of loving is hard to do. That is why people notice when you do it and know you are empowered by a supernatural source. The Bible has another beautiful description of love in 1 Corinthians 13.

13:36 **Simon Peter,** ever the one to voice his thoughts and questions, asked, **"Lord, where are you going?"** Again, Jesus answered, **"Where I am going, you cannot follow now, but you will follow later."**NIV Peter would later follow Jesus in the way of death (see 21:15-19), and Peter would also follow Jesus into glory.

13:37 **Peter asked, "Lord, why can't I follow you now? I will lay down my life for you."**NIV The last statement, made by Peter, repeats what Jesus had said in 10:11, 15, and 17 about laying down his life for his sheep. Peter loved Jesus intensely, and he wanted to be with Jesus always. He did not understand any need for Jesus to die; in fact, he planned to protect Jesus with his life if necessary. As with the foot-washing incident, Peter would much rather lay down his life for Jesus than think that Jesus would lay down his life for him. Peter's brave and proud response resounds across the centuries like many who proudly refuse to accept Jesus' act on their behalf, preferring instead to *do* something in order to obtain salvation. However, obeying Jesus means more than the *intention* to obey or the *promise* to obey. No one can do anything to obtain salvation.

13:38 **"I tell you, before the cock crows, you will have denied me three times."**NRSV When the time of trial came, three times Peter would say that he didn't even know Jesus (see also Matthew 26:69-75; Mark 14:66-72; Luke 22:54-62). The disciples may have started to wonder if Peter (instead of Judas) was the betrayer.

HE NEVER STOPS LOVING
Jesus knew exactly what was going to happen to both Judas and Peter, but he did not change the situation, nor did he stop loving them. In the same way, Jesus knows exactly what you will do to hurt him. Yet he still loves you unconditionally and will forgive you whenever you ask. Judas couldn't understand this, and his life ended tragically. Peter understood, and despite his shortcomings, his life ended triumphantly because he never let go of his faith in the one who loved him.

John 14

After predicting Peter's denial (13:38), Jesus spoke to the deep concerns of the disciples. They were confused; he encouraged them to trust. They needed to anchor that trust in Jesus. He indicated that he and the Father would prepare a place for them while he was gone, but that he would return to gather them.

The disciples could not comprehend Jesus' comments about leaving. Their question about his destination enabled Jesus to identify himself not only as their eternal companion, but also as the very means for them to see the Father. He claimed to be the unique and ultimate resource when he said: "I am the way and the truth and the life. No one comes to the Father except through me" (14:6 NIV).

Characteristically, the disciples responded to Jesus' revelation with a question that reveals how inadequately they grasped Jesus' divine nature. In answering them, Jesus described four aspects of his unique identity: (1) Jesus and the Father share characteristics in such a way that anyone who has seen one has also seen the other. (2) Jesus and the Father are united in such a way that Jesus could speak of either of them being "in" the other. (3) Jesus gives special abilities to those who trust him to accomplish even greater signs than the disciples had already seen. (4) Requests to God made in Jesus' name will be answered.

After this intimate opening dialogue, the Last Supper discourse began. The next several chapters have been among the most treasured of those who follow Jesus. They not only draw us close to him; they also give us compelling reasons to invite others into that fellowship with our Savior. By recording this private discussion between Jesus and his disciples, John hoped to attract all people to Jesus.

14:1 "Let not your heart be troubled."NKJV In the Greek, the pronoun *your* is plural; therefore, Jesus was speaking to Peter (whose denial of Jesus had just been predicted—see 13:38) *and* to all the other disciples. According to Luke, Jesus had told Peter, "Satan has demanded to sift all of you like wheat . . ." (Luke

22:31 NRSV). All of the disciples must have been troubled about Jesus' predictions of betrayal, denial, and departure. After all, if Peter's commitment was shaky, then every disciple should be aware of his own weaknesses.

STRONG WEAK PEOPLE
Jesus did not want his followers to imitate Peter's impulsive self-confidence. Potential weaknesses and possible failures trouble us. So we don't like to think about them. Peter denied his own frailty and claimed more faith than he had. Jesus' solution for troubled hearts requires us to trust in him. Trust does not mean pretending we are strong; it means recognizing our weakness and need for God's help. If we believe for a moment that we can follow Jesus in our own strength, we will fail as miserably as Peter.

"Trust in God; trust also in me."NIV Jesus urged his disciples to maintain their trust in the Father and in the Son, to continue trusting through the next few very difficult days. Jesus later told the disciples why he gave them glimpses of the future that would soon follow: "I have told you now before it happens, so that when it does happen you will believe" (14:29 NIV). They would not need to be afraid because all that he promised would come true.

14:2 "In my Father's house are many rooms."NIV The traditional interpretation of this phrase teaches that Jesus is going to heaven to prepare *rooms* or "mansions" (NKJV) for his followers. Based on that imagery, entire heavenly subdivisions and elaborate "mansion blueprints" have been described. Many commentators think that Jesus was speaking about his Father's house in heaven, where he would go after his resurrection in order to prepare rooms for his followers. Then he would return one day to take his believers to be with him in heaven. The day of that return usually has been regarded as the Second Coming.

The other view is that the passage primarily speaks of the believers' immediate access to God the Father through the Son. The "place" Jesus was preparing has less to do with a location (heaven) as it had to do with an intimate relationship with a person (God the Father). This interpretation does not deny the comfort of heaven's hope in this passage, but it does remove the temptation to view heaven purely in terms of glorious mansions. Heaven is not about splendid accommodations; it is about being with God. The point of the passage is that Jesus is providing the way for the believers to live in God the Father. As such, the way he prepared the place was through his own death and resurrection and thereby opened the way for the believers to live in Christ and approach God.

According to this view, the Father's house is not a heavenly mansion, but Christ himself in whom all the believers reside. By expansion, the Father's house is Christ and the church (see 1 Corinthians 3:16-17; Ephesians 2:20-22; Hebrews 3:2). The believers don't have to wait until the Second Coming to live in this house; once Christ rose from the dead he brought them into a new, living relationship with God (see 20:19-23). He would be the means whereby the believers could come to dwell in the Father and the Father in them. As such, the promise in 14:2-3 relates to the corporate fellowship that would be possible through Christ's departure and return in the Spirit. In this view, the "many rooms" would be the many members of God's household. Christ went to prepare a place for each member in God's household (1 Chronicles 17:9)—the preparation was accomplished by his death and resurrection.

TRUST IN ME?

When we face troubling times we often feel overwhelmed by fear, doubts, grief, and conflict. Our outer resources may evaporate and our inner strength may prove inadequate. Though faced with possible or certain failure, we have assurances in Jesus' words to remain calm and hopeful:

- God is trustworthy, and he has sent Christ, who is also trustworthy, to us. No one else deserves our trust.
- God has a gracious welcome and plenty of space in his "house." We need not fear exclusion or separation from him.
- Jesus spoke the truth. His description of the future was realistic. He has never been proven wrong. We can rely on both Jesus' teaching and his promises.
- Jesus did exactly what he said he would do, return to the disciples after the Resurrection. In so doing, he guaranteed our entrance into God's presence and our place in God's house.
- Jesus is always with us, and someday we will be face to face with him. Whatever the future holds, Jesus promised to be our companion. We know who Jesus is and how much he loves us.

The Greek word for "rooms" (*monai*) could be better translated "abodes" because it shares the same root as the Greek word for "abide" (*meno*). It simply means "a dwelling place." The word *mansions* in the NKJV is misleading because it connotes spacious, luxurious houses. Incidentally, early in church history Origen made popular a similar belief that Jesus was speaking of "stages" or levels of heaven, through which believers advanced as they continued to "develop." But Jesus' words imply no value judgment between "rooms." The "prepared place" is with Christ.

"If it were not so, I would have told you."^{NKJV} Jesus' words give us great encouragement. Throughout his life he had warned the disciples of opposition (see 16:2). He never held back the truth from them. Because he always told the truth, we can trust him with our future as well.

14:3 **"I go and prepare a place for you."**^{NKJV} According to what has been discussed in 14:1-2, there are two ways to understand this statement. Either Jesus was speaking of preparing heavenly dwellings for the future life of the believers, or Jesus was preparing the way for the believers to live in God. Of course, the two views are not mutually exclusive. Now, we live in God because of our living relationship with Christ; in eternity we will live with Christ in the glory he shares with the Father. Eternal life begins in Christ now, not just at some future date when we get to heaven.

In either interpretation, Jesus offers spiritual comfort that begins immediately when we believe. And his Father's many-roomed house represents gracious welcome and provision for us as we live in union with him.

ETERNITY TODAY
There are few verses in Scripture that describe eternal life, but these few verses are rich with promises. Here Jesus says, "I go to prepare a place for you," and "I will come again." We can look forward to eternal life because Jesus has promised it to all who believe in him. But we can actually begin to enjoy eternal life now, for it became ours the moment we believed in Jesus. We can live today with a new destiny in mind. Although we do not know all the details of eternity, we need not fear because Jesus is preparing us to share with him the eternity that he and the Father have prepared for us.

"I will come again and receive you to Myself."^{NKJV} There are three ways to understand this: (1) Jesus' coming again to the disciples would be realized in a short while. This is confirmed by 16:16, "A little while, and you will not see Me; and again a little while, and you will see Me" (NKJV)—note the similar use of *again.* When Jesus said, "I will come again," that coming again occurred on the day of his resurrection. (2) Jesus' "coming again" is the Second Coming. (3) This "coming again" refers to both the Resurrection and the Second Coming—the former foreshadowing the latter. Those who hold this view, therefore, extract a double meaning from Jesus' words in verses 2 and 3; they say the passage speaks both of the believers being brought into the risen Christ as the many "rooms" in the Father's house, and of the believers being brought by the returned Christ into the Father's house in heaven. It does seem that both meanings merge. Christ has us completely in his care.

14:4 **"Where I go you know, and the way you know."**^{NKJV} This statement anticipated Thomas's question (in the next verse) and prepared the groundwork for what Jesus was about to teach regarding himself. Jesus was not naively hoping his disciples understood; he was inviting them to declare their ignorance so they might receive the truth.

THE WAY
Many people are shocked that Christians insist upon Jesus being *the* Way and the only Way. But Christians did not invent the claim. No ancient committee decided that Jesus' uniqueness would be a distinctive teaching of Christianity. Jesus himself made the claim. It really isn't a question of tolerance or being open to diversity; it is a question of whether we want to accept what Jesus said.

Following are three reasons why people reject Jesus' claim to be the *only* way to God:

1. They are satisfied with their own way or with doing nothing; they refuse on principle to examine Christ's claims. Like people in a smoke-filled building who doubt that there is a fire, they will insist that they will find their own way out.
2. They deny their lostness. These people in the smoke-filled building insist on debating whether there is a fire.
3. They are convinced that there must be several valid ways besides Jesus to get to God. These people in the smoke-filled building reluctantly agree that there may be a fire, but that any way of escape is as good as any other, even though they have not actually chosen a way themselves.

Jesus claimed to be the *only* way to God the Father. Some people may argue that this way is too narrow. In reality, it is wide enough for the whole world, if the world chooses to accept it. Instead of worrying about how limited it sounds to have only one way, we should be saying, "Thank you, God, for providing a sure way to get to you!"

14:5-6 Clearly, the disciples didn't think they knew what Jesus said they knew. Thomas expressed the obvious by asking, **"Lord, we don't know where you are going, so how can we know the way?"**^{NIV} Like us, the disciples tended to think first in terms of this world—time and space. So *going* must mean physically moving from one place to another. Thomas was almost giving Jesus a choice: "Tell us where you are going or give us the directions—either one of those, and we can figure out the other."

To which Jesus replied: **"I am the way, the truth, and the life. No one comes to the Father except through Me."**[NKJV] Jesus' response shows that the destination is not a physical place but a person (the Father), and that the way to that destination is another person (the Son). Jesus is the *Way* to the Father; Jesus is the *Truth* (or reality) of all God's promises; and Jesus is the *Life* as he joins his divine life to ours, both now and eternally. Jesus is the way that leads to the truth and life.

THE WAY, THE TRUTH, THE LIFE
Jesus provides for us as much as we need to know and can know about God. "No one has ever seen God. It is God the only Son, who is close to the Father's heart, who has made him known" (1:18 NRSV).

- *He is the WAY:* John 1:18; 8:36; 10:9; Colossians 1:15. Jesus is both God and man, knowing intimately our experience and our needs. He is our path, bridge, transport—not just an example or road sign. He is our guide with dependable directions and powerful protection. Our personal relationship with Christ links us to God. Our response should be to follow his guidance, trusting his ability to do for us what we cannot do for ourselves.
- *He is the TRUTH:* John 1:14, 17; 5:19; 8:29. Jesus is our source of intimate knowledge of the Father. His answers, teaching, and commands were right. No shadow of dishonesty, falsehood, or lying was in his life. He is the reality of all God promised. Our response should be to believe in him and put into practice what he taught.
- *He is the LIFE:* John 1:4; 3:15; 5:26; 10:10; 11:25. Jesus gives us life both now and eternally. His life provides the surest model for our own. He promises to join his life to ours. There is no other source of life beside him. Our response should be to receive that life and allow it to work itself out in our daily experience.

Jesus' exclusive claim is unmistakable. It forces an unconditional response. Jesus invites people to accept or reject him, making it clear that partial acceptance is rejection. His self-description invalidates alternative plans of salvation. Some would say that a single way is entirely too restrictive. But that attitude fails to see the desperate state of the human condition. That there is *a way* at all is evidence of God's grace and love. The state of human rebellion can be seen in this: We are like people drowning at sea who are graciously thrown a life-saving rope but who respond by insisting that we deserve a choice of several ropes along with the option of swimming to safety if we so choose.

14:7 **"If you had known Me, you would have known My Father also."**^{NKJV} In verses 2-6, Jesus told the disciples that he provides the one and only way to the Father. In verses 7 and following, he tries to explain that he is the visible manifestation of the Father. To know Jesus is to know the Father (see 1:18; Colossians 1:15; Hebrews 1:3).

Another manuscript reading treats this phrase like a promise, "Now that you have known me, you will know my father also" (TEV). But it seems more likely that Jesus was not promising the disciples that they would come to know the Father as they had known the Son, but that they should have already known the Father because of their relationship with the Son.

"From now on you know Him and have seen Him."^{NKJV} Jesus shifted the questioning from the future to the present. Instead of being preoccupied with Jesus' going and how they could get there, they were to realize that Jesus opened the way to the Father right now. The disciples needed to discern the meaning of Jesus' time on earth and then respond to him as their Savior. Jesus holds the way open for us today—*from now on,* from this moment forward, we can begin a relationship with the Father by accepting Jesus Christ as our Savior and Lord. The disciples had not yet thoroughly understood this incredible truth, for the death and resurrection of Jesus had not yet occurred (although Jesus had spoken about them), and the Holy Spirit had not yet arrived to help them understand.

14:8-9 **Philip said to him, "Lord, show us the Father, and we will be satisfied." Jesus said to him, "Have I been with you all this time, Philip, and you still do not know me? Whoever has seen me has seen the Father."**^{NRSV} Philip was not satisfied—he wanted to see the Father, as the leaders of Israel had (see Exodus 24:9-10; 33:18) or as the prophet Isaiah had (Isaiah 6:1). But Jesus explained that to see him is to see the Father, for Jesus is God in human form (see 1:14, 18). Philip and the disciples, after their years with Jesus, should have come to know and recognize that the one among them was God in human, physical form. He is the visible, tangible image of the invisible God. He is the complete revelation of what God is like. Jesus' answer contains no rebuke; he explained to Philip, who wanted to see the Father, that to know Jesus is to know God. The search for God, for truth and reality, ends in Christ. (See also Colossians 1:15; Hebrews 1:1-4.)

UNMET DESIRES

Was Philip wrong, shallow, or out of place to question the Lord? Whatever Philip's personal reasons for asking Jesus to "show us the Father," his question shows how much easier it is to ask for more proof than to act on what we already know. We expect God to satisfy our conditions before we will trust him. These conditions take some of the following forms:

- *The desire for assurance:* "Please give us bomb-proof faith in who you are and exactly what you expect from us. Protect us from doubts and ambiguity."
- *The desire for intimacy:* "Please give us such a constant feeling of being close to you that we will never be alone or afraid again. Protect us from the risks of broken relationships and living in a fallen world."
- *The desire for knowledge:* "Please give us a deep understanding of your nature. Protect us from confusion."

These desires may be real, but God is not obligated to satisfy them. Most of us will experience desires that will go unfulfilled in this life. In fact, unmet desires remind us to submit to God. He is in charge; not us. In Christ, God has given us all the resources we need to live, to love, and to serve. Eventually, Christ will help us understand why some of our desires go unmet. In the meantime, we are to trust and go on.

14:10-11 **"Do you not believe that I am in the Father and the Father is in me?"**NRSV This statement conveys the complete unity between Jesus and the Father (see 10:30, 38; 17:21-24). This unity ensures that Jesus truly and completely revealed God to us. This unity goes far deeper than Jesus being of one mind with the Father— merely reflecting the intentions of the Father. Jesus and God were one in essence and purpose. Because of this oneness, Jesus said, **"The words that I say to you I do not speak on my own; but the Father who dwells in me does his works"**NRSV or, if believing in this oneness is too difficult for you just now, Jesus told the disciples, **"At least believe on the evidence of the miracles themselves."**NIV God's power was revealed through Jesus' works. (The word for miracles might better be translated "works," as verse 12 indicates.) For Jesus did many great works and said many great things; not everything Jesus did would be categorized as "miracles."

14:12 **"The one who believes in me will also do the works that I do and, in fact, will do greater works than these, because I am going to the Father."**NRSV Very likely Jesus gave this promise specifically to his disciples concerning evangelism—"bearing much fruit" (see 15:7-8). There are two parts to the *greater works:* There would be a greater number of converts, and there would be a greater scope to the converts. Jesus performed some truly impressive miracles during his earthly ministry; his disciples would perform even greater ones after his resurrection. Furthermore, the disciples, working in the power of the Holy Spirit that would be sent to them after Jesus went to the Father, would carry the gospel of God's kingdom out of Palestine and into the whole world and thus to the Gentiles.

14:13-14 **"Whatever you ask in My name, that I will do, that the Father may be glorified in the Son."**NKJV To pray "in Jesus' name" is to pray in union with Jesus' person and purpose because the "name" of a person symbolized his essence and destiny. We have the promise of answered prayer described in these verses if we properly understand the context of Jesus' last discourse. Jesus promised the disciples that their requests concerning fruit bearing would be answered because it would bring glory to God (see 4:41; 7:18; 8:50, 54). The next chapters clarify this (15:7-8, 16; 16:23-24). In his first epistle, John would later write, "Now this

---

IN JESUS' NAME
Asking in Jesus' name means more than tacking a required phrase at the end of hasty and often self-centered prayers. The privilege to approach God "in Jesus name" ought not to be taken lightly. We demonstrate maturity in our faith as we practice the use of Jesus' name in ways which recognize his enabling power and his unlimited resources. Keep in mind:
- *Christ's kingdom purpose*—Everything Jesus did aimed at glorifying God and bringing those who believe into his kingdom. Do your prayers fit in with Christ's kingdom purpose?
- *Christ's larger perspective*—Christ considers our needs in the context of the needs and desires of his larger family. He knows us individually, but responds to us in community. Do your prayers insist on your will being done or do you seek God's will for all your Christian brothers and sisters?
- *Christ's requirement to follow him*—Because we are his obedient disciples, Christ promises to answer our prayers. Do your prayers flow from an obedient life? Are you willing to fulfill what God has already asked you to do?
- *Christ's promise of peace*—Lack of peace stems from a prayerless life, not from unanswered prayer. Are you overanxious to speed up God's timetable for your benefit? His peace enables us to sort through our desires in order to discover what we really want him to do. We are encouraged to bring all our requests to God—even our desperate and fearful ones.

---

is the confidence that we have in Him, that if we ask anything according to His will, He hears us. And if we know that He hears us, whatever we ask, we know that we have the petitions that we have asked of Him" (1 John 5:14-15 NKJV).

When Jesus says we can ask for anything, we must remember that our asking must be in his name—that is, according to God's character and will. God will not grant requests contrary to his nature or his will, and we cannot use his name as a magic formula to fulfill our selfish desires. If we are sincerely following God and seeking to do his will, then our requests will be in line with what he wants, and he will grant them. (See also 15:16; 16:23.)

JESUS PROMISES THE HOLY SPIRIT / 14:15-31 / **214**

The second half of chapter 14 includes Jesus' teaching on the resources of discipleship. Jesus prepared his followers for his physical absence by telling them that they would experience his presence more fully and intimately because the Counselor, the Holy Spirit, would take up residence in them. Among the resources that the Spirit brings to our lives will be: (1) an awareness of God's love; (2) a sense of guidance and purpose in life; (3) the power to obey Jesus; (4) the realization that we are united in relationship with God; and (5) a recognition and understanding of truth.

> I believe in the Holy Ghost, the Lord and life-giver. In this odd and difficult phrase, the Christian affirms that the life in him proceeds from the eternal creativeness; and that therefore so far as he is moved by that creativeness, and so far only, he is truly alive.
> Dorothy Sayers

Jesus reminded the disciples that his promised resources would be essential for spiritual survival. He would only be with them a while longer, but he did not want them to be unduly troubled. If they endured the difficulties by trusting in his promises, the hard times would prove to be only temporary. Christ's promises are as real and necessary for us today as they were for that first small group of followers.

14:15-17 **"If you love Me, keep My commandments."**NKJV Prior to this, Jesus had urged the disciples to love one another. Then he spoke of their love for him. Truly loving Jesus requires that we do what he commands. Many have a view of the Christian life that under Christ's grace we don't have to do anything. Eternal life is truly a gift that we cannot work for or earn. Once we begin that life in Christ, loving and obeying Christ's commands become the evidence that he is in us. This is John's emphasis in his first epistle (see 1 John 5:2-3).

"And I will ask the Father, and he will give you another Counselor to be with you forever."[NIV] Various translations use different words for the Holy Spirit here: *Advocate* (NRSV), *Helper* (NKJV), *Comforter* (KJV). The Greek word *parakletos* denotes the Helper or Counselor who is always there to give special care in times of need. But the Holy Spirit is more than a Comforter, Helper, and Consoler; he is also an Advocate and an Encourager. In this context, it is also clear that the Holy Spirit is the Son's "Representative," even as the Son was the Father's "Representative."

The expression *another Counselor* (*allon parakleton*) means "another counselor of the same kind as the first." This implies that Jesus was the first Counselor (see 1 John 2:1), and that the Spirit would be the same kind of Counselor. When Jesus would no longer be with the disciples physically, the Holy Spirit would be their constant companion to guide, help, and empower them for the tasks ahead. Jesus identified the Counselor as **the Spirit of truth** because he is the Spirit who reveals the truth about God.

THE HOLY SPIRIT
Jesus would soon leave the disciples, but he would remain with them. How could this be? The Counselor—the Spirit of God himself—would come after Jesus was gone to care for and guide the disciples. The regenerating power of the Spirit came on the disciples just before his ascension (20:22), and the Spirit was poured out on all the believers at Pentecost (Acts 2), shortly after Jesus ascended to heaven. The Holy Spirit is the very presence of God within all believers, helping us live as God wants, and building Christ's church on earth. By faith we can appropriate the Spirit's power each day.

The following chapters teach these truths about the Holy Spirit:

- He will be with us forever (14:16).
- The world at large cannot accept him (14:17).
- He lives with us and in us (14:17).
- He teaches us (14:26).
- He reminds us of Jesus' words (14:26; 15:26).
- He convicts us of sin, shows us God's righteousness, and announces God's judgment on evil (16:8).
- He guides into truth and gives insight into future events (16:13).
- He brings glory to Christ (16:14).

The Holy Spirit has been active among people from the beginning of time, but after Pentecost (Acts 2) he came to live in all believers. Many people are unaware of the Holy Spirit's activities, but to those who hear Christ's words and understand the Spirit's power, the Spirit gives a whole new way to look at life.

"The world cannot accept him, because it neither sees him nor knows him."^{NIV} It may seem at first that the world cannot accept the Spirit because of its sin and disobedience. But if that were the case, *no one* could accept the Spirit, for all of us sin and are disobedient. Instead, the world cannot accept (or receive) this Spirit of truth because the world does not see him or know him— the world does not, indeed refuses to, understand the Spirit; and because of that lack of understanding, they cannot accept him. In the same way that Jesus was not accepted by the world (see 1:11-12), the Spirit would also not be received. But the disciples (and all believers) can receive the Spirit, for Jesus said, **"But you know him, for he lives with you and will be in you."**^{NIV} The disciples, sinful men, not clear in their understanding at this point, even somewhat greedy in their quest for positions in God's kingdom, *would* be able to know the Spirit, for the Spirit would come to live in them, helping them understand and empowering them to do great works for God. The world has refused to know Jesus; but any sincere seeker, no matter how sinful or how ignorant, who humbly comes to Jesus, can receive this gift of the Spirit.

THE CAN'T SEE OR UNDERSTAND
Jesus later pointed out that the Holy Spirit works in the world (16:8) convicting people of sin. People may become aware of their sin but they will not recognize how they came to this awareness. Several factors prevent people's understanding the Holy Spirit until after they have believed in Christ:

- *The Holy Spirit speaks a heavenly message* (the words of Christ). His message of service, sacrifice, and faith is unintelligible to those who have not yet known Christ.
- *The Holy Spirit reverses one's way of thinking.* People naturally place themselves at the center of everything. The Holy Spirit places Christ and his purposes at the center.
- *The Holy Spirit begins with a different starting point.* People tend to refer to their own needs and desires first. The Holy Spirit makes the love for Christ and obedience to God the starting point.

14:18-19 **"I will not leave you as orphans."**^{NIV} This statement showed Jesus' fatherly care for his own, those whom he loved (see 13:1); it also affirmed Jesus' presence with the disciples through the Spirit of truth, for he went on to say, **"I am coming to you."**^{NRSV} After Jesus' resurrection, he appeared to the disciples in his glorious resurrection body and spoke to them prior to returning to the Father (20:19–21:25). At that time he breathed into his disciples the Holy Spirit (20:22). This assured the disciples that *Jesus* would come to them when the Spirit was given to them.

This coming would be but **"in a little while,"**NRSV during which time Jesus would experience crucifixion, burial, and resurrection (see 16:16-23).

"The world will not see me anymore, but you will see me."NIV The disciples and many of Jesus' followers saw him in his resurrection appearances (see 20:20, 26; 21:1, 14). Through the Resurrection, the living Jesus became the disciples' life because they became united to him like branches in a vine. This is the intent behind the words: **"Because I live, you will live also."**NKJV As the Son's life is dependent upon the Father's life (5:26; 6:57), so the believer's life is dependent on the Son's life. The reality of the Resurrection becomes the basis for our hope of eternal life.

YOU WILL LIVE
Jesus spoke with profound confidence even though he faced his own physical death. He affirmed his resurrection as a fact to undergird our way of living and dying. Christ's teaching contradicts the way our culture denies and avoids the reality of death.
    We may freely participate in this life while at the same time we must be ready to let go of it in favor of a life that will not end. We miss the joy of Christ's teaching if we hold desperately to this life. Is there someone who needs to hear us say: "Because Jesus lives, I will live also"? It could be the start of a great conversation, with eternal consequences.

14:20 **"On that day you will know that I am in my Father, and you in me, and I in you."**NRSV *That day* is the day of Jesus' resurrection. After the Resurrection, the disciples would realize by their own experience that Jesus lived in his Father, and they lived in Jesus, and Jesus lived in them. In other words, they would begin to know what it meant to live in God and have God live in them.

14:21 **"They who have my commandments and keep them are those who love me; and those who love me will be loved by my Father, and I will love them and reveal myself to them."**NRSV We who love Jesus demonstrate our love by keeping Jesus' commands. Love means more than words; it requires commitment and action. If we love Christ, then we must prove it by obeying what he says in his Word. In return, the Father and Jesus himself love us. Furthermore, Jesus reveals himself to those who love him. Since the Greek word translated "reveal" means "to appear," it is likely that Jesus was speaking of his appearances to the disciples after his resurrection. But the statement extends beyond that special time to include believers of all time. To all those who love and obey him, he reveals himself as an invisible, spiritual presence (see 20:29; 2 Corinthians 4:6).

IF ONLY
"If only God would show me what to do! I wish God would reveal himself!" In personal experience, most Christians admit to wishing God would reveal himself more openly. We want God to show us exactly what he wants us to do. We may think we are asking God for clear directions so we can carry them out, but our practice shows that we want to know first what God wants us to do so we can decide *if* we want to obey.
  Jesus listed obedience before revelation. He said, in effect, "Obey what you know and you will know more." The Scriptures contain many clear instructions for obedience that are never out of season. If we truly love God, we not only hang on his every word, but we also take our duties seriously. When we feel confused or lack answers, we should ask how we can follow through on directions he has previously given.

14:22 Judas (not Iscariot) said to him, "Lord, how is it that you will reveal yourself to us, and not to the world?"^{NRSV} John clarified for us that this is not Judas Iscariot, but Judas the son of James (see Luke 6:16). This disciple asked Jesus how he would reveal himself to the disciples and not to the world. The disciples may still have been expecting Jesus to establish an earthly kingdom and overthrow Rome; they found it hard to understand why he did not tell the world at large that he was the Messiah. Or at least they felt that if he was going to rise from the dead, everyone should see it and know about it, for surely then they would believe. But Jesus explained that such a revelation to the world was not in the plans—at least not then. Not everyone would understand Jesus' message, and a hardened and unbelieving world would not believe even someone who had come back from the dead (Luke 16:31). Ever since Pentecost, the gospel of the kingdom has been proclaimed in the whole world, and yet not everyone is receptive to it. Jesus reveals himself most deeply to those who love and obey him.

14:23 "Those who love me will keep my word, and my Father will love them, and we will come to them and make our home with them."^{NRSV} In effect, Jesus' response reassured Judas and the disciples that neither he nor the Father would be abandoning them. At first it must have seemed to the disciples that they had no advantage over everyone else—Jesus would die and leave them. In answering Peter's question in the previous chapter, Jesus had explained that, as opposed to the Jewish leaders who had been told they could not go where Jesus was going, the disciples eventually would be able to be with Jesus, but it would be later (see 7:32-34; 13:36). Here Jesus offered the best comfort of all—there wouldn't really be any separation from him for these disciples. Because Jesus would return to the Father, the Holy Spirit would be made available, allowing every believer constant access to the Father and the Son. To those who love Jesus, the Son and the Father will come and make a permanent home with them.

LOVE AND OBEY

Some people have taught that keeping Jesus' words is too stringent or unrealistic. "We are under grace," they say, "not under law, so why should we even worry about keeping commandments?" The key question isn't really about what words to keep or how to keep them, but whether we still love Jesus. Do we relate to him mainly as a traditional religious figure, an object of curious historical study, a source of interesting biblical discussion, or an optional model among many equally qualified persons? Or do we know him as Lord and Savior of our lives? The following questions should clarify our thinking:

- Are we grateful he found us even though we were not truly seeking him?
- Are we glad he rescued us from sin?
- Are we thrilled he chose us to be his followers?
- Are we excited about his presence in us and his words of guidance?
- Are we considering daily how to be more aware of his directions for us?
- Are we making his will the central pursuit in our vocation, education, and family life?

14:24 "Whoever does not love me does not keep my words."NRSV Obedience comes from love and trust. Thus a person who does not love Jesus will not obey him. A sobering way of stating Jesus' point is to say, "The quality of our obedience is a direct reflection of our love for Jesus."

"And the word that you hear is not mine, but is from the Father who sent me."NRSV Jesus repeated that all he said was from God himself (see also 12:49; 14:10).

14:25 "All this I have spoken while still with you."NIV Jesus gave his last words to his disciples. The coming days would bring horrifying and then glorious events, but Jesus would not be able to talk

TWO VERSIONS OF PEACE

The Peace the World Promises and Pursues	*The Peace that Jesus Promises*
Security in this life	*Inner calm*
No needs unmet	*Confidence in God*
No conflicts	*Safety for the soul*
No pain	*Sense of direction and purpose*
No demands	*Hope within conflicts*
	Certain eternal life

to his disciples during those events. Before the disciples could understand any more, Jesus' death and resurrection would have to take place. Then, the disciples' understanding would be heightened by the coming of the Holy Spirit.

14:26 **"The Counselor, the Holy Spirit, whom the Father will send in my name."**NIV The Holy Spirit would be sent by both the Father and the Son (see also 15:26). *In my name* means that the Spirit comes in the Son's name, the name of Jesus Christ, and thereby brings the Son's presence to the disciples. As Jesus represented the Father, the Spirit represents the Son.

"Will teach you all things, and bring to your remembrance all things that I said to you."NKJV The Spirit would continue, for Jesus, the ministry of teaching. The Spirit would also remind the disciples of what Jesus had taught. The apostles remembered and wrote with the help of the Spirit. John's Gospel, even the entire New Testament, would not exist if not for this reminding work of the Holy Spirit.

In the case of the disciples, the reminding role of the Holy Spirit uniquely guided the recording of the New Testament. However, the process is still in place. The disciples first heard Jesus speak; we discover Jesus' words in Scripture. Reading, studying, memorizing, meditating, and obeying place Christ's words firmly inside us, and the Holy Spirit reminds us of their further application as we move through life.

Theologians use the term *illumination* to describe the Holy Spirit's process of helping believers understand Scripture. Without God, sinful people are unable to recognize and obey divine truths. When a person is reborn, the Holy Spirit helps the person to see God's Word with the eyes of faith and love. The Holy Spirit also works in the life of the believer, convincing him of the truth of the Bible, keeping him from misconstruing what it really says, and helping him not be distracted so he can see and remember the true meaning of God's Word.

PLANTED TRUTH
Jesus promised the disciples that the Holy Spirit would help them remember what he had been teaching them. This promise ensures the validity of the New Testament. The disciples were eyewitnesses of Jesus' life and teachings; the Holy Spirit helped them remember without taking away their individual perspectives. We can be confident that the Gospels accurately record what Jesus taught and did (see 1 Corinthians 2:10-14). The Holy Spirit can help us in the same way. As we study the Bible, we can trust the Holy Spirit to plant truth in our minds, convince us of God's will, and remind us when we stray from it.

14:27 **"Peace I leave with you, My peace I give to you; not as the world gives do I give to you."**[NKJV] This verse echoes the first verse of the chapter. Jesus' peace would not guarantee the absence of trouble—for Jesus himself faced excruciating spiritual, physical, and emotional struggles in the coming hours. Instead, Jesus' peace supplies strength and comfort for the burdens we are called to carry. Jesus gave the disciples peace that would help them through their own time of trial ahead. After three days, the risen Jesus would come to them and again bestow his peace upon them (20:19).

Everyone wants peace. The world can give a sort of peace—temporary freedom from distraction that allows us to live with little interference. The world provides the peace of escapism found in our times of daydreams or amusements. The world provides false security. People say, "'Peace, Peace!' when there is no peace" (Jeremiah 6:14 NKJV). In fact, the insatiable quest for peace has often motivated some of the most terrible conflicts in human history. The world hopes that we will work our

True peace comes from yielding all to the will of God. Let him have his way, let him solve the problem, then the heart can be at peace. This is the peace Jesus had as he faced the agony of Calvary. It is peace grounded in the promise of the "joy set before him" (Hebrews 12:2). This is the peace offered to us. Christians do not need pleasures, affluence, influence, gratification of desires. Instead, they obtain peace through fellowship with God. Their peace is within, and the world cannot understand it, nor can it take that peace away. *M. G. Gutzke* way toward peace—that we will arrive there some day, if everyone cooperates.

But the peace Jesus offers his disciples is different. It is *his* peace. It is the peace he modelled every day of his life. Jesus' peace did not flee conflict, pain, or death. In fact, the more intense the difficulties, the more apparent Jesus' peace became. Jesus derived his peace from his relationship with the Father.

As long as Jesus was present, the disciples relied on the peace he gave them. Even a slight alteration demonstrated how little peace the disciples had on their own: when Jesus had been asleep in their boat during a storm on Galilee (Luke 8:22-25), the disciples instantly panicked. But here Jesus promised, along with his presence in them, his peace. It would be a vital resource for them in the days and years to come. He also brings this resource to us. Shortly thereafter, Jesus placed the future in realistic perspective by saying, "I have told you these things, so that in me you may have peace. In this world you will have trouble. But take heart! I have overcome the world" (16:33 NIV).

"Let not your heart be troubled, neither let it be afraid."NKJV The Greek word for *troubled* here is the same one used in 13:21, "Jesus was troubled in spirit" (NIV). Jesus had been able to quiet his own heart and call upon his peace within to sustain him for the events ahead. Here he turns his attention to the disciples, desiring to quiet their hearts in the same way.

Sin, fear, uncertainty, and doubt are at war within us. The peace of God moves into our hearts and lives to restrain these hostile forces and offers comfort in place of conflict. Jesus says he will give us that peace if we are willing to accept it from him. The Holy Spirit's work in our lives brings deep and lasting peace. We have confident assurance in any circumstance; with Christ's peace, we have no need to fear the present or the future. Is your life full of stress? Allow the Holy Spirit to fill you with Christ's peace (see Philippians 4:6-7 for more on experiencing God's peace).

14:28 **"You heard me say, 'I am going away and I am coming back to you.'"**NIV See verse 3 and comments.

"If you loved me, you would be glad that I am going to the Father, for the Father is greater than I."NIV Although Jesus was sad to leave his disciples, he was glad to return to his Father. If the disciples truly loved Jesus, they would understand this and rejoice with him—instead of feeling sorry for themselves. In saying that *the Father is greater than I,* Jesus was asserting his role as the Father's servant, for the Son was the one sent to do the

Father's will. This does not deny his equality with God (see 10:30); rather, it affirms Jesus' humble attitude about his relationship with the Father.

14:29 **"I have told you now before it happens, so that when it does happen you will believe."**NIV Jesus told the disciples about his imminent departure and return so that they would recognize these events, realize that he knew about them, and believe that Jesus upholds his claims. Jesus gave them the tools and resources to understand later events even though at the time he gave them, they did not appreciate their value.

ANTICIPATION
Jesus modeled an important leadership characteristic in preparing his disciples for future events. As leaders we should do all we can to speak truthfully about our own experiences so that others will be warned of the conflicts, struggles, and feelings they will face during various stages of life. Not warning them may lead to disillusionment. Our children ought to benefit from firsthand reflections on what it means to be a spouse, parent, coworker, roommate, employer, retired person, etc. They will not understand all we say, but they may remember some important lessons along the way. Our children, and those we teach, may not learn from our mistakes, but withholding the lesson will make it certain that they won't learn.

Too often, leaders make destructive assumptions, relying on what they think people already know instead of making sure that the people know. When we do not equip people we love, we set them up for failure. For instance, the refusal to talk about sexual abuse has allowed the problem to take on epidemic proportions. Not talking about it did not make it go away.

Talking about problems openly doesn't eliminate them, but it does provide people with preparation for the time of temptation or trial. Move beyond your comfort zone to equip others for survival.

14:30-31 **"I will not speak with you much longer, for the prince of this world is coming. He has no hold on me, but the world must learn that I love the Father and that I do exactly what my Father has commanded me."**NIV The hour was at hand; Jesus was about to leave his disciples and go to the cross. In so doing he would face the *prince of this world* (12:31) who has the power of death (Hebrews 2:14). Although Satan, the prince of this world, was unable to overpower Jesus (Matthew 4), he still had the arrogance to try. Satan's power exists only because God allows him to act. But because Jesus is sinless, Satan has no *hold on* him. Satan would not be able to exert this power over Jesus because Jesus would conquer death. Jesus faced death as one who did so out of love for his Father, for his Father had sent him to die for the sins of the world. Ironically, when Jesus died, Satan thought he had won the battle. He did not realize that Jesus' death had been part of the plan all along. In dying, Jesus' defeated Satan's power over death, for Jesus would rise again (16:11; Colossians 2:15).

CATCHING IT
The lesson may be taught, but the learning hasn't happened until the lesson has been caught. Jesus had taught, in a variety of ways, his identity with the Father as God. He had spoken about and demonstrated his obedience repeatedly. But the world needed an undeniable, irrefutable lesson about obedience to God. Jesus provided this by submitting to the worst kind of death. To the very end, Jesus still trusted the Father and continued to obey. On the cross, when he realized that the Father had forsaken him, he still entrusted himself to his Father.

The feeling that Satan has a hold on us, even when we follow Jesus, may seem overpowering. Hope may vanish. Our family may be disintegrating, children rebelling, income gone, and future grim. We may find ourselves saying, with Jesus, "Why have you forsaken me?" In such a time, we can renew our trust in God or rebel bitterly. Jesus showed that Satan's hold may seem apparent even in death, but God's power can break his hold anytime.

"Rise, let us be on our way."[NRSV] These words suggest that chapters 15–17 may have been spoken en route to the Garden of Gethsemane. Another view holds that Jesus was asking the disciples to get ready to leave the upper room, but they did not actually do so until 18:1. However, it is also likely that these words are spoken, not as a separate sentence, but as an ending to the discourse above. He has just said that the prince of this world is coming, and perhaps by this sentence he is saying, "Let us rise and be ready to meet him." This conveys more of a spiritual movement and preparation than a physical one.

John 15–16:4

Jesus knew that his physical presence with his precious disciples would soon end. He also knew that these men would need a clear understanding of their position with God, as well as what was expected of them. So he consciously filled their minds with pictures and ideas to help them survive the days to come. But these same lessons also provide vital resources for preparing future generations of disciples to grow in their faith.

Jesus regularly used objects and customs from daily life to illustrate profound spiritual lessons. Many of these are no longer available or common in our times. The introduction of machinery has made farming, for instance, remarkably different from what it was in Jesus' time. But the growing and care of grapevines has changed little over the centuries. The following facts about grapes help us understand Jesus' use of that particular plant to illustrate the relationship he expected between himself and his disciples:

- Grapes are the most widely grown fruit in the world.
- Archaeological evidence from Egyptian tombs shows that grapes were being cultivated 2,500 years before Christ.
- Even today, grapes are central to Israel's agriculture and economy.
- The grapevine is part of Israel's national emblem.
- Grapes are consumed in three popular forms: fresh, raisins, wine.
- Grapes grow in a multitude of colors, sizes, and flavors.
- The quality of a vine is only as good as the rooted stock. Individual branches are grafted into a healthy, productive stock.
- Vines are adaptable, but require attentive care: water, fertilizer, pruning.
- New plants are pruned for three to five years to "train" them before they are allowed to produce a crop.
- Good roots produce for as many as a hundred years.
- For their size, vines are very productive, yielding as much as eighty pounds of grapes in a single season.

- Disease and lack of productivity can spread from dead branches that have not been removed.
- Well-tended grapevines are beautiful and aesthetic plants.

15:1-2 **"I am the true vine."**NKJV The grapevine is a prolific plant; a single vine bears many grapes. In the Old Testament, grapes symbolized Israel's fruitfulness in doing God's work on earth. The prophets had written of Israel as God's vine, carefully planted and cared for. But the vine was a disappointment because it yielded only rotten fruit; that is, they refused to give him love and obedience. This is very graphic and poignant in Isaiah 5:1-7, a passage Jesus seems to have drawn upon here (see also Jeremiah 2:2, 21; 6:9; Ezekiel 15; 17:5-10; 19:10-14; Hosea 10:1; 14:7). Jesus, with all believers "abiding" in him, is the *true* vine—the true fulfillment of God's plan for his people (see Psalm 80:8-17). The new society of God's people—Christians—originates from Christ and is united to him as branches to a vine.

BARRIERS TO FRUITFULNESS

Barrier	Explanation	Implication
Lack of proper nourishment	Poor supply of water or nutrients will destroy the vine.	If Christ's life and love do not flow in us, we will be spiritually unproductive.
Disease	Insects and disease move from dead wood into healthy plants.	Ongoing sin and unresolved past issues will lead to spiritual ineffectiveness.
Immature branches	New branches require several years of pruning before they can produce.	We need time to grow. Growth may involve suffering.
Improper pruning	A wise gardener knows what to remove in order to bring about fruitfulness.	Our priorities and the focus of our energies must be guided by Christ and his Word, not our own wisdom and desires.
No gardener	Vines need constant attention.	Resistance to God's guidance and pruning leads to unfruitfulness.
Separated from the Vine	Branches must be attached to a healthy root stock.	We must not think for a moment that we are capable of surviving apart from Jesus Christ. He is the giver and sustainer of life!

"My Father is the vinedresser."^{NKJV} God is the Gardener, the cultivator of the Vine and the branches. In order to achieve their best productivity, grapevines need the attention of a loving gardener. Wild vines are unproductive. God's role in producing growth is recognized throughout the Bible. Paul described his work as merely part of God's plan when he wrote, "I planted the seed, Apollos watered it, but God made it grow" (1 Corinthians 3:6 NIV, see also Colossians 2:19).

"Every branch in Me."^{NKJV} Believers, both sincere and false, are pictured here as the branches. The union between the Vine and the branches is characterized by the expression *in Me*. Christ is the Vine, and God is the Vinedresser who cares for the branches to make them fruitful. The branches are all those who claim to be followers of Christ. The fruitful branches are true believers who by their living union with Christ produce much fruit. But this union can be broken. The Father **"cuts off every branch . . . that bears no fruit."**^{NIV} Those who become unproductive—those who turn back from following Christ after making a superficial commitment—will be separated from the Vine (see 15:6 for more discussion on the specific identity of the unproductive branches). Unproductive followers are as good as dead and will be cut off and tossed aside. *Fruit* is not limited to soul winning. In this chapter, answered prayer, joy, and love are mentioned as fruit (15:7, 11-12). Galatians 5:22-24 and 2 Peter 1:5-8 describe additional fruit, explained as qualities of Christian character.

In contrast, **"every branch that bears fruit He prunes, that it may bear more fruit."**^{NKJV} The combination of the Greek words, *airei* (translated "takes") and *kathairei* (translated "prunes") provides an interesting word play that English cannot match. Jesus made a distinction between two kinds of pruning: (1) removing what does not bear fruit, and (2) cultivating what does. Successful gardeners know that pruning, cutting back the branches, increases fruit bearing. Each spring vinedressers cut back each vine to its root stock to enhance its fruitfulness. Sincere believers, the fruitful branches, will be "pruned," meaning that God must sometimes discipline us to strengthen our character and faith. But branches that don't bear fruit are "cut off" at the trunk and completely discarded because they are worthless and often infect the rest of the plant. People who won't bear fruit for God or who try to block the efforts of God's followers will be cut off from his life-giving power.

PAINFUL GROWTH
The act of pruning appears harsh. The vinedresser cuts back the lush, growing branches just as they are about to flower. The wise gardener knows that good must sometimes be sacrificed for better. Grape branches or tendrils can grow very fast and very long (twelve to twenty feet). But as they develop length and size, they use resources that could be channeled into making fruit. Pruning focuses the growth and energy of the plant. A lush vine with little fruit has failed its purpose.

God's pruning of our lives can be painful. He may limit or remove achievements, objects, and abilities. These may not be wrong in themselves, but God knows they will detract from our fruitfulness. We must not resent God's pruning. Instead, God's discipline should cause us to turn to him with renewed desire to be productive.

15:3-4 **"You have already been cleansed by the word that I have spoken to you."**[NRSV] The Greek word for "cleansed" (*katharoi*) means "purged" or "pruned." (It is the participle form of the verb *kathairei* appearing in verse 2.) Jesus' illustration here shifts to a different level. This cleansing is spiritual, taking away the contamination of sin. This verse indicates that the disciples were already clean because they had accepted the Lord's word; they were ready for fruit bearing. But not so with Judas, the betrayer; he was not clean—therefore, he was one of those branches that had been cut off.

"Abide in Me, and I in you."[NKJV] This verse presents an important theme in this passage: Believers are to *abide* or remain in Jesus, the Vine. The Greek word for "abide" is spoken as a command. It also has an ongoing emphasis; that is, the command to "abide" is not fulfilled in a single act. Abiding, for the disciples and for all believers today, means to make a constant, moment-by-moment decision to follow Christ. And we must not be passive—believers don't just sit and "abide" until they die. Instead, we must be active—we have a lot to do.

ABIDE IN ME
Abiding in Christ means:
- believing that he is God's Son (1 John 4:15)
- receiving him as Savior and Lord (John 1:12)
- doing what God says (1 John 3:24)
- continuing to believe the gospel (1 John 2:24)
- relating in love to the community of believers, Christ's body (John 15:12)

Each of these activities begins at some point, but the long-term (branch-to-vine) practice is "abiding."

"As the branch cannot bear fruit of itself, unless it abides in the vine, neither can you, unless you abide in Me."[NKJV] Curiously, a grapevine branch can survive and produce foliage for a while after it has been severed, but it cannot produce fruit unless it is connected to a root stock. As Jesus had a living dependence on the Father (see 6:57), so believers in Jesus need to have a living dependence on him.

15:5-6 **"Those who abide in me and I in them bear much fruit, because apart from me you can do nothing."**[NRSV] Each branch that continues to remain in the Vine will continually produce fruit. This "fruit" could be new converts (15:5), or "the fruit of the Spirit" (see Galatians 5:22), or both. The fruit of the Spirit displayed in our lives should attract people to Jesus and thereby make them new members of

> The essential idea of fruit is that it is the silent natural restful produce of our inner life. *Andrew Murray*

God's vine. Jesus' emphasis here was not to dwell on our glaring inadequacies, but to remind us of the incomparable adequacy that comes from our relationship with him.

ARE YOU ATTACHED?
Many people try to be good, honest people who do what is right. But Jesus says that the only way to live a truly good life is to stay close to him, like a branch attached to a vine. Apart from Christ our efforts are unfruitful. Are you receiving the nourishment and life offered by Christ, the Vine? If not, you are missing the key to living the Christian life.

"Whoever does not abide in me is thrown away like a branch and withers; such branches are gathered, thrown into the fire, and burned."[NRSV] Each branch that does not continue to abide in the vine is removed from the vine. The branch seems physically attached, but is not organically part of the plant because it does not participate in the life-giving flow of the vine. Sooner or later, that branch will drop off and have to be discarded. Three traditional interpretations have tried to identify who these discarded branches might represent:

1. For some, these branches are true believers who have lost their salvation because they were cut off from Christ and burned. Some think this is also what is described in Romans 11:20-22 and Hebrews 6:8. This view challenges those whose security had become a point of pride. However, it leaves a much larger group (who believe that "something more is required" of

them) in a constant state of turmoil and doubt and also contradicts other passages like John 3:16, 36; 5:24; 10:28-29; Romans 8:1.

2. For others, these burned branches are Christians who will lose rewards but not salvation on the day of judgment (1 Corinthians 3:15). But this is probably not true because Jesus was speaking of *dead* branches. This view would actually fit better under the idea of extreme pruning (discipline), rather than the picture of separation and loss that Jesus gives.

3. For still others, these burned branches refer to those professing to be Christians who, like Judas Iscariot, are not genuinely saved and therefore are judged. Judas, a disciple of Jesus, seemed like a branch, but he did not truly believe. Therefore, he was cut off; his fate was like that of a dead branch. Given John's concern to make committed disciples of his readers and Jesus' goal to bring people into an "abiding" relationship with himself, this view provides a healthy balance. It keeps the decision of destiny as God's responsibility while preserving an emphasis on our responsibility to "remain" in the relationship. In any case, the verse is not so much aimed at creating discomfort and doubt as it is in teaching the importance of daily connectedness with Christ.

15:7-8 **"If you abide in me, and my words abide in you."**^NRSV The Greek expression for "words" (*rhemata*) indicates the individual utterances of Jesus; another Greek expression (*logos*) indicates Jesus' entire message. True disciples do more than just believe what Jesus says; they let Jesus' words *abide* in them. Jesus' words had cleansed them (15:3), so Jesus equated abiding in him with abiding in his words.

MORE THAN WORDS
How do we let Jesus' words abide in us? The word *abide* implies intimate knowledge of what a person has said. But it also implies that the words become a vital part of the way a believer lives. So Jesus' words abide in us when we know what he said and did, and when we allow those words and actions to affect the way we live. By reading and memorizing, we take in God's Word; by obeying, we indicate that the words abide in us:
- We learn from Jesus' actions and teaching what to do.
- We learn from his responses how we should respond.
- We learn from his compassion how we should love others.
- We learn from his obedience how we should submit to the Father.
- We learn from his self-control how to stay pure and strong.

"Ask for whatever you wish, and it will be done for you. My Father is glorified by this, that you bear much fruit and become my disciples."[NRSV] In this passage and in 14:13-14, "asking God" is connected with fruit bearing and doing greater things for God. When a believer abides in Christ and Christ's words abide in him, that person's prayers will be answered. This does not mean that all requests are granted—for the context suggests that the prayers should pertain to fruit bearing (either helping others believe, or showing more of the fruits of the Spirit in one's life) and glorifying the Father. An essential part of being a disciple requires bearing fruit for the Lord. And in order to pray for results, a person must abide in Christ. For when we abide in him, our thoughts and desires conform to his, and we can pray "in his name" (14:13), knowing that our requests please God. We can be assured then that whatever we ask will be done.

A vine that bears *much fruit* glorifies God, for daily he sends the sunshine and rain to make the crops grow, and he constantly nurtures each plant and prepares it to blossom. What a moment of glory for the Lord of the harvest when the harvest is brought into the barns, mature and ready for use! He made it all happen! This farming analogy shows how God is glorified when we come into a right relationship with him and begin to "bear much fruit" in our lives.

15:9 "As the Father loved Me, I also have loved you; abide in My love."[NKJV] Believers must abide in Jesus (15:4), abide in his words (15:7), and abide in his love. For the Son to love us in the same way that his Father loves him means we receive the greatest love possible. We should respond with total dedication, commitment, and obedience.

 FRUIT BEARING
While it would be natural to take "much fruit" as the standard for comparing ourselves with others, it would also be wrong. Use these criteria to gauge your spiritual productivity:
1. Is my life bringing God glory?
2. Is my life an example of discipleship?
Depending on skills, gifts, and opportunities, a believer may produce "much fruit" in a limited area of service or a forgotten corner of the world. God does not want quantity to determine how pleasing we are to him.

15:10 "If you keep My commandments, you will abide in My love."[NKJV] We can abide in Jesus' love by keeping his commands—just as he kept his Father's commands. If we do so, we will experience the daily joy of obedience to our Lord.

"Just as I have kept My Father's commandments and abide in His love."^{NKJV} Jesus himself modeled two important behaviors for true disciples: (1) since he obeyed his Father's commands, they can obey his; (2) and he loved them, so they should love one another. Jesus not only tells us what to do; he shows it through his life.

FULL JOY
When things go well, we feel elated. When hardships come, we sink into depression. But true joy rises above the rolling waves of circumstance. Joy comes from a consistent relationship with Jesus Christ. When our lives intertwine with his, he helps us walk through adversity without sinking into debilitating lows, and we can manage prosperity without moving into deceptive highs. The joy of living with Jesus Christ daily keeps us level-headed no matter how high or low our circumstances.

15:11 **"These things I have spoken to you, that My joy may remain in you, and that your joy may be full."**^{NKJV} Jesus does not call Christians to a dull existence of being hated by the world, obeying commands, and waiting to get to heaven. Instead, he offers us fullness of joy! Nothing else in all the world can bring the joy that we find in serving, abiding in, and obeying Christ. Jesus had promised, "I have come that they may have life, and have it to the full" (10:10 NIV).

15:12-13 Jesus summed up all his commands in one: **"Love one another as I have loved you."**^{NKJV} And how did Jesus ultimately express his love?

LOVING HIS WAY
We are powerless to obey Jesus' command to love unless he lives within us. He must enable us to love in his way. Consider all the provisions he gives us to enable us to love others:
- He frees us from the tyranny of self-love.
- He frees us from crippling guilt.
- He focuses our thoughts on others, not on our own problems or shortcomings.
- He restrains our selfish desires.
- He comforts us by the Holy Spirit.
- He challenges us with his own example of patience and concern for others.
- He encourages us with the support of Christian brothers and sisters.
  With his powerful life within us, we can be channels for his love to others.

"**Greater love has no one that this, than to lay down one's life for his friends.**"NKJV The highest expression of love we could have for another would be laying down our life for someone else—just as Jesus did for those he loved. We must love each other sacrificially, as Jesus loved us, and he loved us enough to give his life for us (see Romans 5:7-8). We may not have to die for someone, but we can practice sacrificial love in many other ways: listening, helping, encouraging, giving. We do not need to *feel* love for everyone. Some people will be difficult to love, but still we are commanded to act lovingly toward our fellow believers.

15:14-15 "**You are my friends if you do what I command you. I do not call you servants any longer, because the servant does not know what the master is doing; but I have called you friends, because I have made known to you everything that I have heard from my Father.**"NRSV In those days, the disciples of a rabbi were considered his servants. Jesus would now change that relationship; the disciples were to be not his servants but his friends. Jesus considered them his friends because he had told them everything he had heard from the Father. This showed that Jesus trusted them to receive these communications and then pass them on to others as the gospel. In fact, he had chosen and appointed them for this task.

> Superficiality is the curse of our age. The doctrine of instant satisfaction is a primary spiritual problem. The desperate need today is not for a greater number of intelligent people, or gifted people, but for deep people.
> *Richard Foster*

CLOSE FRIENDSHIP
What kind of relationship do you have with Jesus? Do you picture yourself as a reluctant servant or an intimate friend? The following questions will help you determine the quality of your relationship with Jesus:
- Do you do what he commands? (He wants you to love him enough to love others.)
- Do you know what he wants to do in the world? (He wants others to experience his love and know who he is.)
- Do you know how Jesus thinks? (He wants you to be familiar with what he heard from the Father.)

15:16 "**You did not choose me but I chose you. And I appointed you to go and bear fruit, fruit that will last.**"NRSV Jesus chose these disciples and appointed them to spread the gospel and bear fruit for God's kingdom. The Lord chooses each believer to be a branch in the Vine—a branch that bears *fruit that will last*. The remaining, or lasting, fruit means either new believers whose faith perseveres, or the enduring quality of the fruit of the Spirit—especially brotherly love.

THE CHOICE
Jesus made the first choice—to love and to die for us, to invite us to live with him forever. We make the next choice—to accept or reject his offer. Unless he chose us, we would have no choice to make.

Then, Jesus speaks of making requests to the Father: **"That whatever you ask the Father in My name He may give you."**^{NKJV} As in verses 7-8, Jesus linked the request making with the fruit bearing. The Father would answer their requests in order to help them accomplish the mission he gave them—to produce "fruit that will last."

Then, Jesus speaks of making requests to the Father: **"That whatever you ask the Father in My name He may give you."**^{NKJV} As in verses 7-8, Jesus linked the request making with the fruit bearing. The Father would answer their requests in order to help them accomplish the mission he gave them—to produce "fruit that will last."

15:17 **"This is my command: Love each other."**^{NIV} This verse capsulizes the theme that Jesus introduced in verse 12 and yet also serves as a contrast for what follows. The disciples must love one another because they would take Jesus' message to a world that despised them. Christians get plenty of hatred from the world; from each other we need love and support.

Jesus legislated love. He required his disciples to make peace with one another, to place the interests of others above their own, to solve differences quickly. He knew they were diverse in background, but he ordered them to love each other. Jesus knew that setting this high standard was essential to preserving the unity of the church. If he required it, the believers would accept

The role for all of us is perfectly simple. Do not waste time bothering whether you "love" your neighbor; act as if you did. As soon as we do this we find one of the great secrets. When you are behaving as if you loved someone, you will presently come to love him. If you injure someone you dislike, you will find yourself disliking him more. If you do him a good turn, you will find yourself disliking him less. *C. S. Lewis* and live out this standard. Backbiting, disrespect, and bitterness toward fellow believers strips the church of its power.

GET-FRUIT-QUICK SCHEME
Jesus wants our fruitfulness to have enduring quality. Whether the fruit appears in our lives or in others, the fruit should be lasting. Results should not be so rushed that they lack dependable roots; superficial results may appear flowery but actually lack substance. A phony spiritual image is deeply dishonest and cannot generate new growth. Ministers or ministries that distort the truth or utilize statistics to make their growth seem more impressive actually undermine the good they may actually accomplish. Jesus has not given us a get-fruit-quick scheme for spiritual living. Genuine growth takes time and lasts much longer than instant successes. Jesus intends our fruit to last for eternity!

Do you allow small problems to get in the way of loving other believers? Jesus commands that you love them, and he will give you the strength to do it.

COMMANDED TO LOVE
Our world wants love to be spontaneous and driven by feeling. But Jesus knows our deeper need. We know we ought to love even when we don't feel like it because we want others to love us when we are unlovable. In Jesus we find both the supreme model for loving and the supreme resource. He commands us to to love, and he helps us accomplish his command.

Jesus knew that if we would practice love, then the feelings of love would follow naturally. If we waited to be motivated by affection for others, we would never love others. Treating others with honor and respect (even when we don't feel they deserve it) may generate good will and affection. If we understand how deeply we are loved by God in spite of our sin, we will be pushed in the direction of loving others ourselves. Those who do not realize God's love for them find it difficult to love others.

JESUS WARNS ABOUT THE WORLD'S HATRED / 15:18–16:4 / *216*

Jesus called the disciples to abide in him and to love one another. But their relationship with the world would be entirely different. Because they loved Christ and were so like him, the world would transfer its hatred of Christ to the disciples. Yet they must take the Good News to the world. This section explains how the disciples, with the help of the Comforter, would continue Jesus' work of glorifying the Father in a hostile world.

Disciples today have the same calling. Because we can do nothing apart from Christ, we must abide in him. The world hates us. Why? Because we have left the kingdom of darkness and entered the kingdom of light (Colossians 1:12-13). As light, we expose the evil deeds of unbelievers. People don't like to have their sinfulness exposed. On top of that, Christians should have a contented life-style, inner joy and peace, certainty of the future, lack of fear of death, and love for their enemies. People without God feel, sometimes unconsciously, threatened. Atheistic governmental systems know that allegiance to Jesus keeps people spiritually free who may be under their control in every other way. Refusal to worship Caesars, even though done with respect, had an impact similar to armed rebellion. So the government hated Christians, and the world will hate us. We need to love and support other believers, who share our same goals.

By warning the disciples, Jesus disarmed their disappointments. When oppression would come, they would remember that he had told them what to expect. Jesus did not want them to lose hope when the days became difficult.

 LIVING THREATS
Though people cannot always verbalize why they reject Christianity, they have specific reasons. Christianity, by its very existence, threatens the systems of this world. Fundamentally, we believe in a God the world cannot accept. Here are several reasons the world rejects Christianity:

- Christians' values contradict the values of those who do not follow Jesus. The world rejected the way Jesus lived, and will reject the way we live, if we live like Jesus.
- Christians submit to God in a world that deifies either independence or rigid conformity to a human system. Christians are free from all authority except God (and those authorities that God has ordained). The world resented Jesus' freedom; it will resent ours.
- Christians believe in absolutes in a world that proclaims absolute pluralism and the absence of divine standards.
- Christians return love for hatred and are therefore hated even more. Jesus forgave those who crucified him. Christians who show Jesus' kind of love are misunderstood and hated even more.

15:18-19 **"If the world hates you, be aware that it hated me before it hated you."**[NRSV] Jesus was hated from the very beginning (when

Jesus was a young child, King Herod sought him out to kill him—
Matthew 2:13-16). He was hated at the end when the people
rejected him as the Savior and called for his crucifixion. The
same world would surely hate those who proclaim allegiance to
the crucified Lord.

**"If you belonged to the world, it would love you as its own. As
it is, you do not belong to the world, but I have chosen you
out of the world. That is why the world hates you."**NIV Jesus
wants believers to be distinctive; he sets us apart from the world.
His choosing and setting us apart makes us holy and helps us
grow. Our very separation from the world arouses the world's animosity. The world would prefer that we were like them; since we
are not, they hate us (see 1 Peter 4:3-4).

WELCOMED REJECTION
Jesus taught us to expect rejection. Rejection may be difficult
to take, but if we never experience it, we may be hiding our
Christianity from others. If we profess Christ and are warmly
embraced by the world, we should reexamine our commitment
and life-style. If we remain silent about our faith in order to gain
acceptance by the world, we have made a poor trade. In fact,
we are being dishonest in two ways: We deny the faith we
claim as central in our lives, and we deceive those whose
acceptance we want by not revealing our Christian faith. The
Scriptures warn us, "Friendship with the world is hatred toward
God" (James 4:4 NIV; see also 2 Timothy 3:10-12; 1 John 2:15-
17; 3:1; 4:5-6).

15:20-21 "Remember the word that I said to you, 'A servant is not greater
than his master.'"NKJV Jesus had told the disciples this earlier that
evening (13:16; also Matthew 10:24). He had been speaking of
their need to imitate his acts of humble service. They also needed
to understand that if their Lord was not respected or honored by
the world, they should expect even harsher treatment.
**"If they persecuted me, they will persecute you also. If they
obeyed my teaching, they will obey yours also."**NIV To persecute believers is to persecute Christ because believers are an
extension of Christ, as branches are an extension of the vine. Yet
despite certain persecution, believers are called to share the gospel—this includes not just telling the story, but giving the invitation to accept Jesus as Savior and Lord. Before Jesus ascended to
heaven, he commanded his disciples, "Go therefore and make disciples of all nations, baptizing them in the name of the Father and
of the Son and of the Holy Spirit, teaching them to observe all

things that I have commanded you" (Matthew 28:19-20 NKJV). Believers can claim that they have been sent in the same way that Jesus claimed to have been sent by the Father. The gospel begins by rescuing others, but it also recruits them for service in carrying on the gospel.

CLOSE ENCOUNTERS
Every believer is a witness for Jesus—either good or bad. Unbelievers will develop their opinion about Jesus by watching Jesus' followers. If you are following Jesus and trying to be a good witness for him, you will encounter some who will scoff, some who will ignore your witness, and some who will downright hate (even persecute) you. But there will also be those who will believe, turn to Christ, and find salvation. Each day, ask God to help you see those people he wants you to reach!

15:22-25 **"If I had not come and spoken to them, they would not be guilty of sin. Now, however, they have no excuse for their sin."**NIV Jesus did not mean that the Jews would have been without sin had he not come to live among them. He meant that they would not have been guilty of rejecting God if they had not rejected Jesus Christ—who was God in the flesh. But since they did reject Jesus, who came to reveal God the Father to all humanity, they had no excuse for their sin. Their rejection of Jesus caused their sin to be fully exposed because, as Jesus said, **"Whoever hates me hates my Father also. If I had not done among them the works that no one else did, they would not have sin."**NRSV They actually hated the Son and the Father—even after seeing the marvelous works Jesus performed.

"But now they have seen these miracles, and yet they have hated both me and my Father."NIV Like Nicodemus, the entire nation should have responded, "No one could perform the miraculous signs you are doing if God were not with him" (3:2 NIV). Ironically, their own Scriptures predicted this rejection and hatred. Jesus knew this was **"to fulfill what is written in their Law."**NIV Jesus quoted Psalm 69:4: **"They hated me without a cause."**NRSV (See also Psalm 35:19.) The Jews had no reason to hate Jesus—he came as their Savior, fulfilling their Scriptures, healing many, and promising eternal life to those who believed in him. Yet the people thought they were serving God by rejecting Jesus, when in reality, they were serving Satan (8:44).

15:26-27 **"When the Counselor comes, whom I will send to you from the Father, the Spirit of truth who goes out from the Father,**

he will testify about me."NIV In 14:26 Jesus had said that the Father would send the Counselor, the Spirit of truth, in the name of his Son. This verse states that the Son would send the Counselor, the Spirit of truth, from the Father. There is actually no contradiction, for Jesus said that he would send the Spirit *from the Father.* (In fact, Jesus emphasized that the Spirit *goes out from the Father.*) Therefore, both 14:26 and 15:26 identify the Father as the one who would send the Spirit. The verse adds an extra detail: the Son would also send the Spirit. Thus, the Father and Son together would send the Spirit.

Jesus used two names for the Holy Spirit—*Counselor* and *Spirit of truth.* The word *Counselor* conveys the helping, encouraging, and strengthening work of the Spirit as he represents Christ. "The Spirit of truth" points to the teaching, illuminating, and reminding work of the Spirit. The Holy Spirit ministers to both the head and the heart, and both dimensions are important.

> As Christians, we are tempted to make unnecessary concessions to those outside the Faith. We give in too much. Now, I don't mean that we should run the risk of making a nuisance of ourselves by witnessing at improper times, but there comes a time when we must show that we disagree. We must show our Christian colours, if we are to be true to Jesus Christ. We cannot remain silent or concede everything away. *C. S. Lewis*

"You also must testify, for you have been with me from the beginning."NIV The disciples would *testify* (or witness) that Jesus is the Messiah. The Holy Spirit would testify by preparing people's hearts and minds, persuading them of the truth of the gospel, and enabling them to receive the message. *You* refers to Jesus' original disciples, since only they had been with him from the beginning of his ministry (see Luke 1:2; Acts 1:21-22). These disciples were the vital link between Jesus Christ and all subsequent believers. They would need the Holy Spirit to remind them so that as they preached, taught, and wrote, they would spread the *truth* of the gospel. The Holy Spirit would see to it that their witness would not be impaired by persecution. Jesus has already forewarned these men about the persecution to come so that they would not be surprised.

By application, this verse extends to all Christians. All Christians are called to testify of Jesus, allowing the Holy Spirit to help them through times of persecution and to remind them of the truth of God's Word and work in the hearts and minds of their listeners.

16:1-2 **"All this I have told you so that you will not go astray."**^{NIV} In
the last two chapters (13:31–15:27) (and especially 15:18-27,
which deals with persecution the disciples will face) Jesus
warned and safeguarded the disciples against the trials that
awaited them. He did not want them to be caught off guard, to
stumble, or to fall when trials came. Jesus wanted his disciples
to remember that he had predicted his own persecution and
theirs in order to fortify them for the difficult times to come.
He also wanted them to remember the rest of his teaching (*all
this*). His accurate predictions would increase their trust in his
instructions.

"They will put you out of the synagogues."^{NRSV} In 9:22 and
12:42 we are told that the religious leaders had decided that anyone who confessed Jesus as the Messiah would be expelled from
the synagogue. Jesus predicted that this would happen to the disciples. By the time John's Gospel was recorded, Christians were
already frequently barred from the synagogues.

**"In fact, a time is coming when anyone who kills you will
think he is offering a service to God."**^{NIV} This prophecy would
come true very soon. An early deacon in the church, Stephen,
would become the first martyr for the faith (Acts 7:54-60).
James, one of the disciples present with Jesus during this teaching, would be put to death by King Herod (Acts 12:1-2). Saul of
Tarsus—before his conversion—went through the land hunting
down and persecuting Christians, convinced that he was serving
God by killing those who proclaimed Jesus as their Messiah
(Acts 9:1-2; 26:9-11; Galatians 1:13-14; Philippians 3:6).

DOING GOD A FAVOR
Some of the most shameful acts throughout history have been
perpetrated by those who thought they were offering a service
to God. Attempts have been made to convert pagans by force.
People have been tortured and killed in the name of religion.
For the sake of orthodoxy, Christians have persecuted one
another with remarkable lack of mercy or love. Some of the
issues may have been valid, but the methods have offended
Christ.
　　Jesus knew that devout Jews like Saul of Tarsus would persecute Christians. These Jews would be fully convinced they
were protecting the true faith. We must not harm others in our
zeal for his concerns. That would be a horrible error. It is better
to err on the side of mercy. Our methods in obeying Christ's
commands must be consistent with his greatest command: to
love!

16:3-4 "They will do such things because they have not known the
Father or me."ᴺᴵⱽ Those who would persecute believers would
do so out of ignorance. Many of them would know about God,
but not knowing God's true nature or will for people they would
not recognize the Son of God. They did not understand that God
was at work through Jesus; so, when they rejected Jesus, they
also rejected God. Paul, who had traveled across the land searching out Christians to persecute, later wrote, "Even though I was
once a blasphemer and a persecutor and a violent man, I was
shown mercy because I acted in ignorance and unbelief" (1 Timothy 1:13 NIV).

"I have told you this, so that when the time comes you will
remember that I warned you."ᴺᴵⱽ Thus, the disciples were forewarned. When the persecutions would actually occur, they would
be prepared because they would remember what Jesus had said.
Jesus' predictions hold today. The world is still hostile toward
Jesus and his disciples. When a tree in the forest stands taller
than the rest it must endure the full force of the wind. When
Christians take a stand for Christ in their cultures, they will experience the full force of the opposition.

 IT WILL COST
Like Jesus, we must warn new and younger disciples that
hatred from the world and hard times are ahead. We must dis-
pel illusions and deal honestly with unrealistic expectations. In
our eagerness to promote the benefits of following Christ we
must not shrink back from also presenting the cost of discipleship. Preparing new believers for times of discouragement will
teach them to rely on the Holy Spirit's comfort and guidance
along the way. When Christians assume that following Christ
will be easy, they neglect the daily spiritual resources provided
for them. These include Bible study, prayer, and the promises
and directions that Jesus gives us.

"I did not tell you this at first because I was with you."ᴺᴵⱽ
Jesus waited until the very last evening to warn his disciples
because he himself had been their protection from the beginning.
Jesus had deflected any criticism and opposition away from the
disciples. But after Jesus was crucified, the persecution would
shift to his followers and would focus on these men, his inner
circle.

John 16:5-33

Not all the news for the disciples was grim. There would be persecution, but Jesus comforted his followers with the promise that they would not be alone; he would send them the Counselor, the Spirit of truth. John highlighted five important tasks of the Holy Spirit: (1) to convict the world of its sin and call it to repentance, (2) to reveal the standard of God's righteousness to anyone who believes because Christ would no longer be physically present on earth, (3) to demonstrate Christ's judgment over Satan, (4) to direct believers into all truth, and (5) to reveal even more about Jesus Christ.

16:5 "But now I am going to him who sent me; yet none of you asks me, 'Where are you going?'"NRSV The verb tense for *asks* is present; otherwise, this statement would contradict 13:36 and 14:5. The disciples *had asked* (past tense) where Jesus was going. In this verse, Jesus was looking for an immediate reaction to his words about his departure. But instead of asking, "Where are you going?" at that time when Jesus was ready to answer, they reacted in sorrow.

16:6 "Because I have said these things to you, sorrow has filled your hearts."NRSV Although the disciples had previously talked with Jesus about his death (see 7:33-34), they had never truly understood its meaning because they had been mostly concerned about themselves. If Jesus went away, what would become of them? If they had asked where Jesus was going, and then had understood that he was going to the Father, they would not have been filled with such sorrow—they would have realized that Jesus' departure was for their good.

16:7 "It is for your good that I am going away. Unless I go away, the Counselor will not come to you."NIV Without Jesus' death and resurrection we could not be saved. His death made it possible for him to remove our sins. Before Jesus could defeat death by his resurrection, he had to submit to death. And if he would not go back to the Father, the Holy Spirit would not come in the way God had planned. "Up to that time the Spirit had not been given, since Jesus had not yet been glorified" (7:39 NIV). After his glorification—through the process of crucifixion, resurrection, and ascension—Jesus could send the Spirit to the believers. Christ's presence on earth was limited to one place at a time. His leaving meant he could live, through the Holy Spirit, in every believer in the whole world. Thus, it was for their good that he had to go away. The Spirit would carry Jesus' work to a more intense level during the history of the church. By the Spirit the gospel would go out to all the world.

> The work of the Holy Spirit in the church is done in the context of persecution. The Spirit is not a guide and a helper for those on a straight way perfectly able to manage on their own. He comes to assist men caught up in the thick of battle, and tried beyond their strength. *Leon Morris*

16:8 "And when He has come, He will convict the world of sin, and of righteousness, and of judgment."[NKJV] To *convict* (*elencho*) means "to expose the facts, to convince someone of the truth, to accuse, refute, or to cross-examine a witness." As a prosecuting attorney, the Holy Spirit carries out his convicting work in at least three ways:

1. The Holy Spirit proves the world wrong by exposing the world's error and convincing people they are sinners. Even general admissions of guilt are evidence of the Spirit's work.

2. The Holy Spirit legally convicts people of their sin, representing the righteous judgment of God. In legal terms, the Holy Spirit's role is to read aloud the verdict of the court. There is no appeal to the Holy Spirit's judgment.

3. The Holy Spirit shows people their sin in order to bring them to repentance. He personalizes God's accusation from "all are guilty" to "you are guilty." He breaks through our defenses and rationalizations and confronts us with at least a glimpse of our true selves in relation to God's standards.

For purposes of evangelism, the third way that the Spirit works is the one that matters. By themselves, the first two communicate little more than a strong sense of God's justice. But the third explanation not only includes the first two, it also brings to bear God's mercy. God graciously makes us aware of our sin that he might make us receptive to his grace. The Holy Spirit prepares the human heart and then applies the healing work of Jesus Christ to that person.

FOR YOUR OWN GOOD
Who among us does not react with skepticism to the statement,
"I'm doing this for your own good"? Yet who beside Christ has
better credentials to carry out his beneficial purposes for us? If
Jesus had not gone away, the disciples would never have
learned to walk by faith, and neither would we. When Jesus
seems distant or our problems threaten to overwhelm us, let us
keep walking by faith. Trusting during a trial means waiting to
see what good Jesus can bring out of what may seem like complete chaos. Christ uses trials to strengthen us for even greater
service.

16:9 **"Of sin, because they do not believe in Me."**^{NKJV} The greatest
sin is the refusal to believe in Jesus (3:18). Those who reject
Jesus are in danger of eternal separation from God.

THE JUDGMENT OF SATAN
Satan has been judged so that his darkness cannot overcome
believers' light.

Reference	Quotation	Explanation
Luke 10:18	"I watched Satan fall from heaven like a flash of lightning" (NRSV)	Pride was Satan's downfall. Jesus spoke of his fall from glory and pointed to his total destruction.
John 12:31	"The prince of this world will be driven out" (NIV)	Jesus' crucifixion gave him the victory over Satan.
John 16:11	"The prince of this world now stands condemned" (NIV)	Jesus announced that Satan's judgment was complete.
Hebrews 2:14	"He Himself likewise shared in the same, that through death He might destroy him who had the power of death, that is, the devil" (NKJV)	Jesus' crucifixion shattered Satan's deadly power.
1 John 3:8	"The Son of God was revealed for this purpose to destroy the works of the devil" (NRSV)	Jesus' purpose was fulfilled in overcoming Satan.
Revelation 20:10	"The devil, who deceived them, was cast into the lake of fire and brimstone ... forever and ever" (NRSV)	Jesus will have the complete and final victory over Satan.

16:10 **"Of righteousness."**^{NKJV} There are two ways to understand "convict the world . . . of righteousness": (1) The Spirit's function will be to show all people that Christ alone provides the standard of God's righteousness. The Holy Spirit must make unbelievers recognize God's perfect standard before they will admit their own deficiency. As long as people can maintain the idea that God is somehow less than perfect, they can hide from their own condition. The Holy Spirit lifts that veil and displays to the human heart God's holiness. (2) It can also mean that the Spirit will show the world the futility of religious self-righteousness. The Holy Spirit will show the inadequacy of ceremony and ritual in making one right with God (see Matthew 5:20; Romans 10:3; Philippians 3:6-9).

"Because I go to My Father and you see Me no more."^{NKJV}Jesus was the one who convicted the world of its unrighteousness by exposing the hearts of men. Once Jesus left this earth, the Holy Spirit would continue Jesus' work.

16:11 **"[Of] judgment, because the prince of this world now stands condemned."**^{NIV} The Spirit will show that, through Jesus' death and resurrection, Satan has already been judged and condemned. Though Satan still actively attempts to harden, intimidate, and delude those in this world (1 Peter 5:8), we are to treat him like a condemned criminal, for God has determined the time of his execution (see Revelation 20:2, 7-10).

Convicting us of our sin, convicting us of God's righteousness, and convicting us of Satan's (and our) impending judgment describes three approaches that the Holy Spirit uses. We do not all require all three in order to be convinced that we need God's grace. The Holy Spirit does not crush those who only require prodding. Some are simply more stubborn and resistant than others. God demonstrates his grace by approaching each of us with that level of conviction necessary for our response.

One question that we will all have to answer at some point is not how many times we heard the gospel, but how we responded to the convicting work of the Holy Spirit?

This convicting may be done with the help of believers, through whom the Holy Spirit works. Jesus had already told his disciples, "When the Counselor comes . . . he will testify about me. And you also must testify . . ." (15:26-27 NIV).

16:12 Having indicated what the Spirit would be doing in the world (16:7-11), Jesus then related to the disciples what the Spirit would be doing in believers. But most of what Jesus told the disciples would be unclear to them until after the events of the Crucifixion and Resurrection. Thus Jesus said: **"I still have many things to say to you, but you cannot bear them now."**[NRSV]

16:13 **"When he, the Spirit of truth, comes, he will guide you into all truth."**[NIV] The prominent role of the Spirit of truth is to guide the believers *into* (Greek *eis*) *all truth.* By *truth* Jesus meant the truth about his identity, the truth of his words and actions, and the truth about all that was to happen to him. In time they would fully understand that he was the Son, come from the Father, sent to save people from their sin. But only after these events occurred, and only through the Holy Spirit's guidance would the disciples be able to understand. The Holy Spirit is the true guide for all believers; his primary task is to instruct us about the truth (1 John 2:20).

THE PATHFINDER
The Holy Spirit is our guide, navigator, and pathfinder. Jesus gave us a reliable map when he gave us his life and his words. These essential resources assist us to find our way as his disciples. Jesus has also given us time. The original disciples could not absorb all Jesus had to teach them at once. Some steps of discipleship cannot even be comprehended until we have taken previous steps of obedience. We must never resent the limitations we have. Our knowledge of the way and the future will always be limited. Instead, we must trust and follow the pathfinder Christ has given us.

"He will not speak on his own; he will speak only what he hears."[NIV] In addition to revealing Christ and guiding the believers into the truth of Christ, the Spirit would convey Jesus' words both by way of teaching and by way of reminding the disciples of what Jesus had said during his ministry. The Spirit would also affirm Jesus' ministry by bearing witness to him (15:26). The Lord had many things he wanted to tell the disciples before he departed from them, but they would not be able to **bear them** at that time. When the Spirit came, he would speak to the disciples whatever he heard from Jesus.

"He will tell you what is yet to come."[NIV] The disciples were not given power to predict the future, but the Spirit would give them insight into *what is yet to come*—that is, the events of the Crucifixion, Resurrection, Ascension, and perhaps the Second Coming. The disciples would not fully understand until the Holy Spirit had come after Jesus' death and resurrection. Then the

Holy Spirit would reveal truths to the disciples that they would write down in the books that now form the New Testament.

GOD'S TIMING

Have you ever wondered what it must have been like to have been one of the original disciples? Perhaps you have thought, *Back then, my life would have been so different. Knowing Jesus and then being filled with his Spirit would have made me* one of those dynamic Christians. But if looking backward makes us dissatisfied with the present, we will not fully appreciate God's present plan.

Jesus wants each believer to be empowered by his same Holy Spirit who filled the disciples. His Spirit lives in us today, and God's best time for us to be alive is now. We don't need to dwell on the past or be preoccupied with the future. God has plenty of work for us and power to help us this day.

16:14 **"He will bring glory to me by taking from what is mine and making it known to you."**[NIV] The Spirit does not glorify his own personality; rather, he glorifies the Son's. The Spirit takes what the Son is and reveals it to believers. In so doing, he individualizes the teaching of Christ and calls people to obey. The Holy Spirit makes us want to apply, teaches us to apply, and then helps us apply Christ's words!

16:15 **"All that belongs to the Father is mine. That is why I said the Spirit will take from what is mine and make it known to you."**[NIV] Jesus explained that the Holy Spirit works in complete submission to and in harmony with the Son and the Father. The Spirit reveals the Son (in all his true splendor) to the believers. Yet as he reveals the Son, the Spirit is also revealing the Father because all the attributes of the Son are the attributes of the Father. Thus the Spirit reveals the Son, who, in turn, expresses the Father. This verbal picture of what cannot be fully seen by finite humans helps us understand the profound unity of God.

What we call the doctrine of the Trinity is a summary of what Jesus taught about his relationship to the Father and the Spirit. Without in any way diminishing the awesome revelation of God as one, Jesus demonstrated that God's oneness is at the same time a threeness: Father, Son, and Holy Spirit. God exists in perfect, unbroken harmony while at the same time functioning in the person of the Father, the Son, and the Holy Spirit. They are one; yet they relate to one another. They are beyond our complete grasp; yet they have graciously revealed themselves to us so that we may trust and be saved!

SUSPICIOUS
Jesus' teaching about the Holy Spirit explains why Christians should be suspicious of those who claim to have new and special revelations from God. We should be very cautious when these "new revelations" call into question the words and character of Jesus. Jesus promised that the Holy Spirit would continue to make him known, to bring honor to him, and to complete his work. All that the Holy Spirit does clarifies and glorifies Jesus. Believers have the authority to question and repudiate any religious system claiming to have new knowledge or understanding that contradicts God's Word or any leader claiming to have special power and status equal with Christ.

JESUS TEACHES ABOUT USING HIS NAME IN PRAYER / 16:16-33 / **218**

Jesus explained to the disciples that his departure would only last "a little while" (actually only three days), for he would see them again on the day of his resurrection. Then a new relationship between the disciples and Jesus' Father would begin. They would then be able to approach God the Father as his children and bring to him their requests through prayer.

Jesus concluded this section with yet another prediction and teaching to prepare them. He informed the disciples that, while they thought they believed, within hours they all would abandon him. Jesus did not berate them for their weakness but prepared them to endure in spite of it. Jesus wanted the disciples to know that he knew their deepest tendencies, so that when failure came, they would remember he still loved them. The disciples were to have peace, even in a world of trouble. The peace offered by Jesus is maintained in those who remind themselves that Jesus has overcome the world!

16:16-19 **"A little while, and you will no longer see me, and again a little while, and you will see me."**NRSV Jesus was referring to his death, only a few hours away, and his resurrection three days later. But the disciples didn't understand this, so they were grieved and perplexed. They kept asking each other what he could possibly mean: **"We don't understand what he is saying."**NIV Jesus had already told the disciples that he would go to the Father and return to them after his resurrection (chapter 14), but they didn't understand.

16:20-21 Following his explanation of the time between his departure and return, Jesus used a figure of speech to depict how quickly the disciples' grief would turn to joy: **"You will weep and mourn while the world rejoices. You will grieve, but your grief will turn to joy. A woman giving birth to a child has pain because her time has come; but when her baby is born she forgets the anguish because of her joy that a child is born into the world."**[NIV] The disciples would grieve for their crucified Master, and the world (the mass of people opposed to Jesus) would rejoice that this "madman" had finally been silenced. But the disciples' *grief will turn to joy,* for they would see their resurrected Lord. In addition, the Holy Spirit would help them understand the true purpose of Jesus' crucifixion and resurrection—that it meant salvation from sin and eternal life for everyone who believes! This would indeed bring them great joy—just as a woman has great joy after the pains of giving birth to a child. They, with Jesus, were now suffering the birth pangs; soon the pain would be over (both for Jesus and for them), when they would see their risen Lord!

ENDLESS JOY
Because Jesus lives forever, the disciple's joy would be endless. No one, not the persecutors, not the doubters, not the unbelievers, not the murderers, could take away their joy. This is a tremendous promise for all believers. *No one* can take away our joy!

When we understand Christ's resurrection, it will have a powerful impact on our iives. The Resurrection guarantees our forgiveness and assures us that Jesus will return. Jesus' resurrection realizes our hope to be reunited with believing friends and loved ones beyond death. No opposition or criticism should ever destroy or diminish our joy!

16:22 "So with you: Now is your time of grief, but I will see you again and you will rejoice, and no one will take away your joy."[NIV] The disciples would grieve right then and over the next couple of days as the predicted events unfolded. But their time of rejoicing would come, for Jesus would rise again to live forever:

- "We know that Christ, being raised from the dead, will never die again; death no longer has dominion over him. The death he died, he died to sin, once for all; but the life he lives, he lives to God" (Romans 6:9-10 NRSV).

- "For our light affliction, which is but for a moment, is working for us a far more exceeding and eternal weight of glory" (2 Corinthians 4:17 NKJV).

■ "Jesus lives forever, he has a permanent priesthood. Therefore he is able to save completely those who come to God through him, because he always lives to intercede for them." (Hebrews 7:24-25 NIV)

■ The promise "I will see you again" refers both to the resurrection appearances of Jesus to his disciples (20:19-29) and to the Second Coming, when he will receive all the believers, who will live with him forever (1 Thessalonians 4:17).

16:23-24 **"On that day you will ask nothing of me."**^{NRSV} This "day" refers to the time subsequent to the day of Jesus' resurrection. On that day, their questions about his departure and return would be answered. The phrase is awkward out of context. Just as Jesus previously promised that his absence would mean the presence of the Holy Spirit, so now, "on that day," the disciples could take their requests directly to the Father. While the preceding context of "ask nothing of me" brings to mind questions, in the verses that follow Jesus clearly broadens the point of asking to include "anything."

"If you ask anything of the Father in my name, he will give it to you."^{NRSV} From that day forward, the disciples should begin to make their requests to the Father directly, who would answer their requests in Jesus' name (see 14:13-14; 15:7). This was another reminder that Jesus would not remain on earth indefinitely after he rose from the dead. Requests asked in Jesus' name are requests that the believer knows Jesus would be pleased to answer, requests that are in accordance with the Father's will. Any such request will be given.

"Ask, and you will receive, that your joy may be full."^{NKJV} Answered prayer brings joy—just ask any believer! Jesus encouraged the disciples to ask, so that they might receive and have full and complete joy (see also 1 John 5:13-15).

GO STRAIGHT TO THE TOP
Jesus clarified a new relationship between the believer and God. Previously, people approached God through priests. After Jesus' resurrection, any believer could approach God directly in Jesus' name. A new day has dawned; now all believers are priests, talking with God personally and directly (see Hebrews 10:19-23). We approach God, not because of our own merit, but because Jesus, our great High Priest, has made us acceptable to God. When was the last time you asked God for what you really need?

16:25-27 **"I have said these things to you in figures of speech."**^{NRSV} Specific predictions about future events would have been too much
for the disciples at this point (16:12-13), so Jesus spoke to them
in figures of speech.

**"A time is coming when I will no longer use this kind of lan-
guage but will tell you plainly about my Father."**^{NIV} After Jesus
arose, the disciples were given a new, living relationship with the
Father (see 20:19). And through the Holy Spirit, Jesus would give
them fresh and clear understanding of the Father (16:13-15).

**"On that day you will ask in my name. I do not say to you
that I will ask the Father on your behalf."**^{NRSV} The disciples
would have direct, personal access to the Father. Jesus would not
have to make their requests for them; instead, they would go
straight to God, asking in Jesus' name. Jesus was not withdraw-
ing from representing us before the Father. He still makes inter-
cession for us (Romans 8:34; Hebrews 7:25). Jesus was preparing
the disciples for the reality that his death would allow them direct
access to the Father in prayer and that they ought to make use of
it (Hebrews 10:19-25)! The Father would respond to the disciples
because, as Jesus said, **"The Father himself loves you because
you have loved me and have believed that I came from
God."**^{NIV} All who love Jesus and believe in him as God's Son are
loved by the Father. Why? Because they have loved him whom
the Father dearly loves. God remembers our faithfulness to his
Son, Jesus Christ. Jesus not only encouraged the disciples to love
him and remain faithful, but he also reminds us how essential our
faithfulness really is.

16:28-30 Then Jesus plainly said, **"I came from the Father and entered
the world; now I am leaving the world and going back to the
Father."**^{NIV} In this sentence, Jesus plainly described his entire
mission—he was incarnated (*came from the Father*), he was
made a human being in order to secure the salvation of human
beings (*entered the world*), and he would be resurrected from
death and ascend back to the glory from which he came (*going
back to the Father*).

The disciples responded, **"Now you are speaking plainly, not
in any figure of speech!"**^{NRSV} The disciples finally realized that
Jesus had been speaking of his departure to the Father. Then they
said, **"Now we can see that you know all things and that you
do not even need to have anyone ask you questions. This
makes us believe that you came from God."**^{NIV} Jesus' repeated
predictions of his imminent death, resurrection, and ascension
(7:33; 10:11-18; 12:23-24, 30-36; 13:18-38; 14:1-5, 15-31;

16:5-7) finally left their mark on the disciples. Now they were convinced that Jesus' knowledge about future events marked him unquestionably as the Son of God come from God. The disciples believed Jesus' words because they were convinced that he knew everything. He even knew the questions on their minds before they asked them (16:19). They were making a claim, not about their own knowledge, but about his. Jesus' omniscience was another proof of his divinity. But their belief was only a first step toward the enduring faith they would receive when the Holy Spirit came to live in them.

JESUS KNOWS
John portrayed Jesus' sensitivity toward his disciples. He knew them. He based his words and actions toward them on his intimate awareness of them. He knows us just as well. None of our problems, griefs, questions, and concerns are hidden from him. He knows about them, and he knows them. Hebrews describes Jesus as the High Priest who can sympathize with our weaknesses, having experienced them first hand, and who is therefore approachable (Hebrews 2:18; 4:15-16).

No matter how great our unfaithfulness or weakness, Jesus knows and understands our situation and our needs. Although he knows us, he still loves us and calls us to return and remain faithful.

16:31-32 **"Do you now believe?"**NRSV The implied exasperation in the statement is conveyed better by "You believe at last!"NIV. The disciples had taken a small but real step forward in understanding. Jesus continued to tell them what was going to happen so that their faith would be strengthened in the end: **"A time is coming, and has come, when you will be scattered, each to his own home. You will leave me all alone."**NIV *Scattered* alludes to Zechariah 13:7: "Strike the shepherd, and the sheep will be scattered" (NIV). (Jesus also quoted from Zechariah in Matthew 26:31 and Mark 14:27.) As predicted, the disciples abandoned Jesus when he was arrested in the Garden of Gethsemane (Matthew 26:56; Mark 14:50). Even though Jesus was abandoned by his disciples, he was not completely alone. As Jesus said previously (8:29), here he says, **"Yet I am not alone because the Father is with me."**NRSV

16:33 **"These things I have spoken to you, that in Me you may have peace. In the world you will have tribulation; but be of good cheer, I have overcome the world."**NKJV In a final note of encouragement, Jesus promised the disciples peace through their union with him—for he would overcome the world by rising from the grave. The world, Satan's system that is opposed to God, will give the believers terrible trouble and opposition. But Jesus has beaten Satan's system, won the victory, and overcome the world. Before his own trial, Jesus could already speak of an accomplished task. This adds impact to his victory over

> When it is all over, you will not regret having suffered; rather you will regret having suffered so little and suffered that little so badly. *Sebastian Valfre*

Satan since he not only accomplished it, he predicted it! The disciples could constantly rejoice in the victory because they were on the winning team.

Jesus summed up all he had told them this night, tying together themes from 14:27-29; 16:1-4; and 16:9-11. With these words he told his disciples to take courage. Despite the inevitable struggles they would face, they would not be alone. Just as Jesus' Father did not leave him alone, Jesus does not abandon us to our struggles either. If we remember that the ultimate victory has already been won, we can claim the peace of Christ in the most troublesome times. Jesus wants us to have peace.

TROUBLESOME PEACE
In contrast to our assumption that peace means the absence of conflict, Jesus promises that his peace becomes apparent in the very middle of trouble and conflict. Troubles remind us to ask for Jesus' peace. God's answer will not usually mean that the problem will be over, but that Christ's peace will see us through it. How much have you relied on the peace of Jesus when you face trouble?

John 17

John 17 contains Jesus' great intercessory prayer. It is not the prayer of agony in the Garden of Gethsemane but an open conversation with the Father about his followers. This prayer brings to a close Jesus' discourse in 13:31–16:33. It expresses the deepest desires of Jesus' heart for his return to the Father and for the destiny of his chosen ones. Jesus asked the Father to grant the believers the same kind of unity that he and the Father enjoyed from eternity—a unity of love.

From Jesus' prayer in this chapter, we see the world as a tremendous battleground where the forces under Satan's power war against those under God's authority. Satan and his forces are motivated by bitter hatred for Christ and his forces. Jesus prayed for his disciples, including those who follow him today, that God would keep his chosen believers safe from Satan's power, setting them apart and making them pure and holy, uniting them through his truth.

As Jesus began to pray, he spoke first of himself. The focus of Jesus' request, however, was that his Father would be glorified. These few sentences are packed with profound truths: Jesus has authority over all people to give eternal life; the essence of eternal life is knowing the Father; Jesus had been sent to earth to complete his Father's work; Jesus existed in glory with the Father before creation. As Jesus was about to finish his work on earth, he asked to be glorified and thereby bring glory and honor to the Father.

17:1 Jesus began his petition by praying for himself: **"Father, the time has come. Glorify your Son, that your Son may glorify you."**NIV Jesus knew that his "hour" of suffering had come—several times previously in the Gospel, John had pointed out that Jesus time had *not* come (2:4; 7:6, 8, 30; 8:20). But the time for Jesus' glorification had arrived. As stated earlier (see 13:31), Jesus' glorification is one of the central themes of the extended discourse (13:31–16:33). Jesus' motives are quite clear. If the Father would glorify the Son in the Crucifixion and Resurrection, the Son could, in turn, give eternal life to the believers and so glorify the Father. Jesus asked the Father to restore to him the full rights and power as Son of God (as described in Philippians 2:5-11).

17:2 **"You have given him authority over all people, to give eternal life to all whom you have given him."**^{NRSV} Jesus made his requests to the Father, knowing that from eternity past the Father had given him authority over all people so that he could give eternal life to as many as (literally, "all which") the Father had given him.

17:3 **"And this is eternal life, that they may know You, the only true God, and Jesus Christ whom You have sent."**^{NKJV} Jesus here defines eternal life. *Eternal life* means to know experientially God and his Son, Jesus Christ—having personal knowledge of the eternal God. And the God we know is *the only true God,* not some man-made religion or some feel-good ideas. We find eternal life only by knowing the one true God. This knowledge is ongoing and personal (see also Matthew 11:27).

KNOWING GOD
How do we know God? Jesus explained knowing God as the essence of having eternal life. Eternal life is a gift we receive when we enter into a personal relationship with God in Jesus Christ. We cannot know God unless we have eternal life; and at the core of eternal life is intimate knowledge of God.

Eternal life means having the capacity for intimacy with others who have eternal life. Jesus is the source of eternal life. Our first step toward eternal life includes realizing we don't have it. That sense of separation, rebellion, lostness, or inadequacy before God is defined as "sin" in the Bible. When we admit our sin, turn away from it and then to Christ, Christ's love lives in us through the Holy Spirit. Eternal life is not just being around forever; for believers it means eternity with God, their loving Father.

17:4 **"I have glorified You on the earth."**^{NKJV} In this statement, Jesus affirmed that he had glorified the Father on earth by finishing **"the work which You have given Me to do."**^{NKJV} The last phase of Jesus' revealing work was about to be accomplished through his death on the cross. Jesus spoke of his work as though it had already happened—his obedience to death on the cross was a certainty. Jesus requested again to be returned to glory based on the certainty of his completing the work of the cross.

JESUS' PREVIOUS GLORY
Before the Son of God became a man, he lived eternally with the Father. In this preincarnate form, he shared the glory of the Father. John 1:18 shows that his preexistence enabled him to fully reveal the Father to people. In John 8:58 KJV, Jesus said, "Before Abraham was, I am," thereby revealing his eternal existence. All throughout this Gospel, Jesus declares that he has come from heaven (see 3:13). The one who existed from all eternity with the Father laid aside his glory and rights to become a man (Philippians 2:5-11).

17:5 **"So now, Father, glorify me in your own presence with the glory that I had in your presence before the world existed."**NRSV Looking beyond the Cross to his resurrection and ascension, Jesus asked the Father to restore the glory he had enjoyed with the Father *before the world existed.* In saying this, Jesus gives us a glimpse of his relationship with the Father before the beginning of time. Jesus wanted to return to the glory he had with the Father before the world was created (see 1:1, 18). Jesus would enter into that glory as the crucified and risen Lord Jesus Christ. Thus, Jesus' return to God was not simply a return to his preincarnate state, since Jesus would have his resurrected body. Jesus' resurrection and ascension—and Stephen's dying exclamation (Acts 7:56)—attest that Jesus' prayer was answered. He returned to his exalted position at the right hand of God.

GET TO WORK
Jesus gave us a remarkable example in his prayer. He asked the Father to glorify him because he was completing the work God had given him to do (see John 4:34). He prayed confidently as the obedient Son. Do our prayers lack confidence because we are not committed to do what God wants? Jesus' work was to reveal God to his disciples and to enable them to continue that work through others to the present day.
How do we bring glory to God? By completing the work he has given us to do. What is God's work for us?
■ Show mercy, justice, and humility before God (Micah 6:8).
■ Pass on the gospel and make disciples to the ends of the earth (Matthew 28:19-20).
■ Care for those who are needy around us (James 1:27).
■ Do good and share with others (Hebrews 13:16).
As we practice obedience in these areas, God will strengthen us.

JESUS PRAYS FOR HIS DISCIPLES / 17:6-19 / **220**

Jesus could have closed his opening personal remarks to his Father about their relationship by repeating what he said outside Lazarus's grave: "Father, I thank you that you have heard me. I knew that you always hear me, but I said this for the benefit of the people standing here, that they may believe that you sent me" (John 11:41-42 NIV). Jesus turned his attention to his followers. He wanted them to hear what he had to say to his Father about them and his desires for their future. The prayer almost takes the form of a progress report on the success of Jesus' ministry. He reviewed their identity as owned by God. He repeated his own objective to give them the words that came from the Father. He formally turned them over to the Father for safekeeping. He was pointed in stating that his prayer was not for their safe removal from the world, but for their safe conduct within the world. They would need that protection because he was sending them into the world in the same way the Father had sent him into the world.

This prayer is one of several mentioned in the Bible that focused on the disciples. Before choosing the Twelve, Jesus spent the night in prayer (Luke 6:12). During their ministry together (John 6:15; Luke 10:18-22), we assume Jesus' prayers included his disciples. We know that before the final days, Jesus had been praying specifically for Peter (Luke 22:32). The Scriptures also tell us that part of Jesus' present activity is to pray for us (Romans 8:34; Hebrews 7:25). Jesus made it clear that although we have direct access to the Father (16:26-27), we are still the objects of his loving concern.

17:6-7 "I have revealed you to those whom you gave me out of the world. They were yours; you gave them to me and they have obeyed your word. Now they know that everything you have given me comes from you."NIV After praying for his own glorification, Jesus turned the direction of his petition to his disciples. These were the men God had selected to give to his Son as his disciples (see 15:19). To these men, Jesus had *revealed* the Father; in other words, he had expressed the reality of the Father's person to them (see 1:18). And they had *obeyed*. Sure, their faith wasn't perfect, and they would fail their Savior in the coming hours; but their commitment was in the right place, and they would return to this faith and to obedience to God.

17:8 "For I gave them the words you gave me and they accepted them. They knew with certainty that I came from you, and

they believed that you sent me."ᴺᴵⱽ The disciples had received
Jesus' words as coming from God; as a result, they had come to
believe that Jesus had been sent from the Father (see 16:28-30).
Before Jesus instituted God's plan of salvation by dying on the
cross, he introduced it to his disciples. They had to believe the
words of Christ to benefit from the work of Christ. Jesus effectively demonstrated that what he said came from God. The disciples were not in a position to accept the saving purpose of Jesus'
death until they had accepted the fact that God had sent him.
Once they knew God had sent Jesus, they were ready to learn
that God had sent him to die! Jesus was declaring that the disciples were ready for the next lesson, as difficult as it might be.

**17:9 "I pray for them. I am not praying for the world, but for
those you have given me, for they are yours."**ᴺᴵⱽ We know that
God loves the world (3:16), but at this time Jesus was focusing
on the disciples, not the world. These disciples were the object of
Jesus' affection and Jesus' prayer. He was not praying for *the
world,* for the world was hostile and unbelieving. Instead, he was
praying for the ones the Father had given him. He prayed that
they would be protected (17:11) and sanctified (17:17).

17:10 "All I have is yours, and all you have is mine."ᴺᴵⱽ Jesus' words
reveal his oneness, closeness, and equality with God the Father.
These disciples belonged to both him and the Father, and they
were the ones in whom Jesus would be glorified on earth after he
had returned to the Father. The disciples' lives would reveal
Jesus' essential character to those who had not yet believed, so
Jesus was present in the world through them.

HOW CAN WE GLORIFY CHRIST?
While you cannot predict exactly how Jesus will receive glory
through your life, you can remove any hindrances to his glory.
- *Get rid of any immorality.* The moral quality of your life must
  not even tarnish Jesus' good name. Is Jesus honored by your
  life?
- *Get rid of pride.* Focus on Christ so that he receives honor
  and acclaim rather than you. Does he get the credit?
- *Get rid of ambiguity.* Your words and actions must clearly
  show that you are his disciple. Does anyone know you are a
  Christian?

**17:11 "And now I am no longer in the world, but they are in the
world, and I am coming to you. Holy Father, protect them
in your name that you have given me—so that they may be**

one, as we are one."^{NRSV} Jesus would leave the world to rejoin the Father; the disciples would stay in the world to carry out God's plan by spreading the good news of salvation. Such a mission would arouse great hostility from the evil one, so the disciples needed special protection from the evil one. Therefore, Jesus asked that the Holy Father would keep his disciples *in his name*—the name that the Father had given him, for "the name of the LORD is a strong tower; the righteous run to it and are safe" (Proverbs 18:10 NIV). Nowhere else in John does Jesus use this term *Holy Father* in prayer. By adding *Holy* to his usual, familiar way of addressing the Father, Jesus emphasized the significance of being kept "in your name." Being able to approach God as "Father" is an acknowledgment of his love, but *Holy* reminds us that the one to whom we pray is God.

The prayer itself indicates confidence in God's ability to "keep" his children, while at the same time allowing the disciples to hear Jesus' desire for how they are to be kept. Jesus' use of "in your name" could be a reference to the authority and power represented by the divine title (as is conveyed in the NIV, "by the power of your name"), but the context indicates that Jesus was speaking of a relationship between the believers and himself. In other words, Jesus wasn't saying "Holy Father, use the power connected with your name to keep my disciples"; rather, he was praying, "Holy Father, keep these disciples intimately connected with yourself."

STILL IN THE WORLD

We, like Jesus' original disciples, still live in the world. What is "the world"? It is a system of values typified by Satan himself, centered on power, deceit, and self-will. While we're in the world, Satan wants to neutralize or destroy us. In 1 John 2:16, John explains that "the world" is the cravings of sinful human beings, the lusting of the eyes, and the boasting of what one has and does. As Christ's disciples today, we are on a collision course with the world's values. We need God's protection more than ever because it is so easy for us to emulate the world's character.

The fact that we are *in* the world does not grant us license to become *of* the world. We must not betray Jesus by loving the world. We must recognize and resist the pervasive attractions presented to us through advertising, self-help psychology, public opinion polls, and charismatic public figures. We must be sure that we allow Christ—not the media and the world around us—to define who we are.

Jesus prayed for this connection because it would help the believers be unified with a unity patterned after that of the Father and the Son. They would have a unified desire and purpose to serve and glorify God. Jesus prayed that they would be *one,* even as the Son and Father are one. Just as the Father, Son, and Holy Spirit are united in harmony, so should all believers be united. Then they would have the strongest of all possible unions.

17:12 **"While I was with them, I protected them in your name that you have given me. I guarded them."**[NRSV] Jesus' physical presence had provided the obvious point of unity for the disciples. The more they were "in Christ," the more they were united and protected. Jesus had carefully protected these disciples as a precious gift given to him from the Father; here he gave an account of the job he had done. All of the disciples had been guarded—**"and not one of them was lost except the one destined to be lost, so that the scripture might be fulfilled."**[NRSV] The one who had been lost was Judas Iscariot, who by his own volition betrayed Jesus. Thus, Jesus sadly identified Judas as one who had rejected the protection offered. This fulfilled Scripture is Psalm 41:9, "Even my bosom friend in whom I trusted, who ate of my bread, has lifted the heel against me" (NRSV). Judas, though never a true follower, indeed had been a bosom friend (he was one of the twelve disciples), who had eaten with Jesus yet had lifted his heel against him by selling him out to the religious leaders. (For more about Judas, see 13:2, 11, 18, 27).

The place of Judas among the disciples and his choice to betray Jesus highlight the balance that we find throughout the Bible between the awesome sovereignty of God and the freedom he allows people to exercise. We would tip the balance toward error if we would say that Jesus intentionally withheld his protection of Judas to expose him to the temptation of Satan so that the betrayal could happen. We would also be in error if we would say that the temptation of Satan was stronger than Jesus' ability to protect Judas. Judas was not a puppet on a string. Judas shared the protection offered by the presence of Jesus all during their time together. Judas made his decision to betray Jesus, and by so doing he removed himself from Christ's protection. He passed the point of no return and thereby fulfilled the scriptural prediction.

The extent of God's protection over us every single day is beyond our comprehension. His sovereignty is complete, including his choice to allow us to actually be able to effectively reject him. God could have created persons whose choices didn't really matter. Instead, because of his love for us, he created us with enough freedom to live in relationship with him.

17:13 **"But now I am coming to you, and I speak these things in the world so that they may have my joy made complete in themselves."**^{NRSV} Jesus had told his disciples all about his coming death—hardly a joyful topic. But after these events would take place—especially after the Resurrection—the disciples *would* be filled with joy, for they would then understand that Jesus had conquered death and Satan and had brought eternal life to all who believe in him.

Joy is a common theme in Christ's teachings—he wants us to be joyful (see 15:11; 16:24, 33). The key to immeasurable joy is living in intimate contact with Christ, the source of all joy. When we do, we will experience God's special care and protection and see the victory God brings, even when defeat seems certain.

17:14 **"I have given them your word and the world has hated them, for they are not of the world any more than I am of the world."**^{NIV} The world hates Christians because Christians' values differ from the world's, and because Christians expose the world's values for what they are—absolutely worthless. Because Christ's followers don't cooperate with the world by joining in their sin, they are living accusations against the world's immorality. The world follows Satan's agenda, and Satan is the avowed enemy of Jesus and his people (see 15:18; 16:2).

17:15 **"I am not asking you to take them out of the world, but I ask you to protect them from the evil one."**^{NRSV} Jesus did not pray that the disciples would be removed from the hatred and persecution to come, rather that they would be protected *through* the difficult circumstances from falling prey to the devil. The only way believers can be witnesses *to* the world is to be witnessing for Christ *in* the world. We must carry our message, trusting God for his protection.

17:16 **"They do not belong to the world, just as I do not belong to the world."**^{NRSV} Jesus was not a part of the world's system, headed by Satan (indeed, he had been tempted to that end and had refused—see Matthew 4:1-11). Neither are believers a part of the world; instead they belong to "the kingdom of the Son" (Colossians 1:13 NIV) because they have been born again (3:3).

A BRAND-NEW GAME

Imagine a young boy's experience as a baseball fanatic. He plays the game, collects the cards, memorizes statistics, and idolizes the players. In fact, all the boys in his neighborhood follow his leadership. But then a new boy moves next door and introduces a new game none of them have ever played. His personality draws the other boys to him. Soon, along with the new game, there is also a new leader, with new rules and new loyalties. The former leader feels alienated, angry, and confused. He regards the new game as an intrusion and the new leader as an enemy. He is torn between his desire for friendship and his fear of betraying "his" game. He wants to be loyal to the old game.

The world sees our allegiance to Jesus Christ in the same way. Christ threatens to shatter the neighborhood structure. His rules are different. His words are attractive. But loyalty to Christ means disloyalty to the world. We can understand the world's confusion, but we should never forget that we were also part of that life. But precisely because we *have* been there, we need to build bridges and find common ground with unbelievers so they can see the difference Christ makes in our lives. But we must never return to the old game.

17:17 **"Sanctify them by Your truth. Your word is truth."**NKJV Three distinct views have emerged to explain what Jesus meant by "Sanctify them by Your truth": (1) The truth found in God's Word accomplishes our sanctification. (2) The central truth of God's saving love sets into motion God's sanctifying work in us. (3) The process of passing on (preaching, teaching) God's truth would have a sanctifying effect in the disciples' lives. These views are actually complementary, describing different aspects of sanctification: the second view highlights the initial pouring of God's grace into our lives through the truth of the gospel; the first view summarizes the ongoing effects of the applied truths from God's Word; and the third view emphasizes that progress in sanctification will be seen in our desire and practice of communicating the gospel. God's Word, then, works as a divine cleansing agent that God uses to bring about our sanctification.

17:18 **"As you have sent me into the world, so I have sent them into the world."**NRSV Jesus came *into* the world on a mission for the Father; so he sent these disciples *into* the world on a mission by the Son. That mission was to make God known. This is an important and exciting theme in John's Gospel. The Father sent the Son into the world, the Father and the Son send the Spirit to the disciples, and the disciples are sent by the Father and Son into the world.

SET APART
A follower of Christ becomes sanctified (set apart for sacred use, cleansed and made holy) through believing and obeying the Word of God (Hebrews 4:12). He or she has already accepted forgiveness through Christ's sacrificial death (Hebrews 7:26-27). But daily application of God's Word has a purifying effect on our minds and hearts. Scripture points out sin, motivates us to confess, renews our relationship with Christ, and guides us back to the right path.

It is up to us to carry on Jesus' mission—to make God known to others. Because Jesus sends us into the world, we should not try to escape from the world, nor should we avoid all relationships with non-Christians. We are called to be salt and light (Matthew 5:13-16), and we are to do the work that God has sent us to do.

17:19 **"For them I sanctify myself."**^{NIV} Jesus set himself apart to do the Father's will like a priest consecrating himself to make the sacrifice. His final act of dedication was his offering himself on the cross (see Hebrews 10:10). The purpose of that death was so that the disciples (and all believers) would **"be truly sanctified."**^{NIV} Jesus died to set us apart for him.

JESUS PRAYS FOR FUTURE BELIEVERS / 17:20-26 / *221*

Jesus concluded his prayer by including us. His words, "I pray also for those who will believe in me through their message" (17:20), can bring real comfort during times of discouragement. We can easily replace "those" with our own names and realize that Jesus had us in mind as he prepared for the cross.

The pattern of Jesus' prayer provides a helpful outline for us. He prayed for himself, for those close to him, and for those beyond his immediate sphere who would be affected by the ministry of his friends.

The purpose of Jesus' prayer should be our purpose in praying. He asked for unity. He desired to see a deep connection between those who were connected to him. The unity of which he spoke was clearly a reference to his earlier command to "love one another" (13:34) In Jesus' words, both unity and love have the same purpose: "to let the world know" (17:23) or so that "all men will know" (13:35). In a world where unity means to broaden the labels or enlarge the structure, Jesus commands us to be united in him. Passionate commitment to Jesus Christ leads a believer to discover fellow believers in the most unusual places. The unity

that the world seeks to impose, whether it is sociological, governmental, legal, or religious, will actually bring discord. The unity
that Christ offers brings peace within and between persons. "I
have said this to you, so that in me you may have peace. In the
world you face persecution. But take courage; I have conquered
the world!" (16:33 NRSV).

17:20 **"My prayer is not for them alone. I pray also for those who will
believe in me through their message."**[NIV] After praying for his disciples, Jesus prayed for all those who would believe in him *through
their message.* In a sense, everyone who has become a Christian
has done so through the apostles' message because they wrote the
New Testament and were the founders of the Christian church. So
Jesus was praying for all the believers who would ever exist. He
was praying for you and others you know. And he was praying for
those he wants us to reach! Knowing that Jesus prayed for us
should give us confidence as we work for his kingdom.

17:21 There are three requests in verse 21, each beginning with the
word *that:* (1) **"that they all may be one, as You, Father, are in
Me, and I in You"**; (2) **"that they also may be one in Us"**; (3)
"that the world may believe that You sent Me."[NKJV] All the
requests hinge on one another. In the first request, the Lord asked
for unity—that *all* the believers would be one. This all-encompassing petition includes all the believers throughout time. This
oneness does not readily fit the idea of one unified church structure. Rather, this unity becomes most visible through love, obedience, and commitment to the Father's will.

BECOMING ONE
Jesus' great desire for his disciples was that they would
become one. He wanted them unified as a powerful witness to
the reality of God's love. Unity between believers is not often
mentioned as the catalyst for someone becoming a Christian.
However, Christian unity does provide an environment for the
gospel message to make its clearest impact, and lack of unity
among Christians frequently drives people away. Are you helping to unify the body of Christ, the church? You can pray for
other Christians, avoid gossip, build others up, work together in
humility, give your time and money, exalt Christ, and refuse to
get sidetracked by arguing over divisive matters.

In the second request, Jesus prayed for a unity among the
believers that is based on the believers' unity with him and the
Father. Christians can be unified if they live in union with God.
For example, each branch living in union with the Vine is united

CHRIST IS IN US; WE ARE IN CHRIST

Christ is in us	We are in Christ
He takes up residence in our lives by his Spirit.	Our salvation is guaranteed by him.
He goes everywhere with us.	We live in his protection.
We represent Jesus everywhere we go.	Our purpose for living is focused in Christ.
Jesus helps us obey him.	We seek to obey Jesus.
His presence guarantees our hope.	He accomplished what we now look forward to with hope.

with all other branches (see 15:1-17); or each part of the body is united with the other parts so that when one hurts, they all hurt, and when one rejoices, they all rejoice (1 Corinthians 12:12-27).

This union with the Father and Son would result in people all over the world believing that Jesus had been sent by God as the world's Savior—and not only believing, but receiving this Savior as their own. This is the third request.

17:22-23 Jesus further explained this oneness in terms of mutual indwelling: **"The glory that you have given me I have given them."**NRSV Jesus was still referring to all his followers, not just the immediate disciples. The phrase is a promise. Jesus gave all true believers his glory by completing his mission of revealing God (17:4-6). Jesus' work was not only to speak and model the character of God. His ultimate purpose was to present both the splendor and character of God (God's glory) in such a way that God would become personally real to the disciples. They, in turn, were to pass on what they had received to others who would also believe. Those who, in fact, received the glory would become unified by their shared relationship with Christ.

17:23 "That they may be one as we are one: I in them and you in me. May they be brought to complete unity to let the world know that you sent me and have loved them even as you have loved me."NIV Complete and perfect unity between God and believers results in worldwide belief. When we demonstrate this oneness, we will convince the world that the Father sent the Son, and that the Father loves believers deeply and eternally, just as he loves the Son.

VISIBLE UNITY
Christian unity begins in the heart of individual believers. Are we willing to be unified with others who may be completely different from us other than the fact that we both follow Jesus Christ?

Unity in Christ grows as local church groups practice Christ's teachings. This unity can expand as groups of local churches discover they can practice larger efforts in obedience to Christ. Because Satan's power is directly challenged by these examples of unity, we can expect resistance. We can also expect simple resistance from people who confuse human loyalties and traditions with the command to obey Jesus. To achieve Christian unity, we need Christ's help and the Holy Spirit's restraining power.

To promote unity in Christ, take these steps:
- Focus on the nature, attributes, splendor, and holiness of God. Filling our minds with God will keep us from being occupied with ourselves.
- Keep mind, heart, and ears open while keeping the mouth closed longer. Realize that not all believers use the same terms, nor speak the same "language." Impulsive conclusions can prevent us from getting along with those who share allegiance to Jesus Christ.
- Steer clear of persons who closely measure everyone else by their standards. We may be the next to be "dissected" and judged.
- Remember that Jesus died for persons, not principles or a system.
- Stay out of endless arguments over various denominational methods and church traditions. Satan uses these to distract the church from obeying its commission. Better to fail as we obey than to neither fail nor obey!

17:24 **"Father, I want those you have given me to be with me where I am, and to see my glory, the glory you have given me because you loved me before the creation of the world."**[NIV] Jesus wants all believers (the eleven disciples and all others) to be with him where he is so they can see his glory. What wonderful assurance Jesus' prayer gives us to know that the Lord of heaven wants us to be with him. This request impacts our present experience and future hope. In the present, we unite with Christ in God the Father (see 14:6; Colossians 3:3). In the future, we will be with Christ in eternal glory and enjoy with him the love he experienced with the Father forever.

OUR RESOURCES IN CHRIST
John 17 contains a storehouse of resources God makes available to us as disciples of Jesus. What more could we ask for? What else could we need?

- Jesus give us eternal life (17:2).
- Jesus prays for us (17:9, 20).
- The Holy Father protects us (17:11).
- Jesus gives us the words of God (17:8, 14).
- Jesus sets us apart for special service (17:17-18).
- We are unified with God and Christ (17:21, 23).
- We have God's love (17:23-24, 26).
- Christ is in us (17:23).
- Jesus reveals God to us (17:26).

Because we have these wonderful resources, we can persevere in our faith.

17:25-26 Jesus addressed his Father as **"Righteous Father"** because God's righteous judgment reveals that the world's knowledge of God is incorrect and that the disciples' knowledge is correct. Just as Jesus had chosen the name "Holy Father" (17:11) to present his request for protection of the disciples, so here Jesus added *righteous* as a highlight to the gulf that exists between the world and God. Jesus knew he was the living connection between the lost world and his loving, righteous Father.

> The end of all knowledge is to know God, and out of that knowledge to love and imitate Him. *John Milton*

"Though the world does not know you, I know you, and they know that you have sent me."[NIV] The world failed to recognize that Jesus was God's communication to them. The disciples did recognize this, for they had come to believe that Jesus was the one sent from God. Jesus, who knew the Father personally and intimately, had revealed the Father to his disciples and would continue to do so. Thus, Jesus could say, **"I have made you known to them, and will continue to make you known."**[NIV] Finally, Jesus asked the Father to love the disciples with the same love he (the Father) had for his Son.

FAULTY KNOWLEDGE
The world does not know Jesus truly, for its information comes from biased sources. Consider where most people get what they know about Jesus:
1. Television/cinema—These media constantly portray God, Christians, evangelists, and the Bible in connection with perversion, mental illness, child abuse, and dishonesty.

Religious characters are stereotyped as deranged or weak and often are objects of destructive humor.

2. History—Accounts are written blaming Christians for most of the evils in the world. They highlight serious failures of Christians (the Crusades, the Inquisition, genocidal acts) so as to imply that God and the Bible prompted these injustices. Many of these acts were done in ignorance or blatant disobedience to God's revealed commands. Often injustices were done as by-products of political moves by people who used the Bible to justify their sinful desires.

3. Religious training—Some people were forced to adopt a church's or religious school's "view" of God without opportunity for questions or real understanding. Required religious instruction can cause students to rebel. They not only resist the system but dismiss what may well be the truth. Wrong views taught by well-meaning teachers, or even right truths conveyed to children in an unloving manner can devastate a person's adult understanding of God. Those who "haven't paid much attention to God since Sunday school (or confirmation)" should be challenged to think again.

4. Philosophy—In philosophy, God is reduced to a concept for purposes of discussion and understanding. Unfortunately, many attempt to keep him in that state. As long as God is nothing more than a concept, people will invent any number of creative ways of "seeing" him. When we allow God's revelation, the Bible, to guide our thinking about God, many of the philosophies of the world will be shown to be in serious error about God.

Believers need to be aware of the mistakes and biases against Christianity that they will face in the world. One of our bridge-building efforts with nonbelievers will be to guide them in questioning their sources of knowledge about God.

"In order that the love you have for me may be in them and that I myself may be in them."[NIV] Jesus asked that the Father's love would be in believers and that he himself (Jesus) would be in them. This expresses the heart of the Father's desire, which is to have his Son in his people: "I . . . in them." And because it is the Father's desire, he will make sure it is accomplished. How do you understand your relationship with God the Father. Is his love in you?

John 18–19:16

After the prayer recorded in John 17, Jesus again predicted Peter's denial (Matthew 26:31-35; Mark 14:27-31). The synoptic Gospels then record Jesus' agony in the Garden of Gethsemane (see Matthew 26:36-46; Mark 14:32-42; Luke 22:39-46). Here is a summary of that section: After arriving in Gethsemane, Jesus sat his disciples down and told them to wait for him while he went and prayed. Then he took Peter, James, and John aside, expressed his great distress to them, and asked them to stay awake with him. How touching that Jesus, in this great hour of distress, sought human companionship from his closest friends—just someone to stay awake and be with him.

Jesus agonized in prayer to the Father, "O My Father, if it is possible, let this cup pass from Me; nevertheless, not as I will, but as You will" (Matthew 26:39 NKJV). Three times Jesus prayed this prayer; three times he returned only to find his disciples asleep. Finally he said, "Get up, let us be going. See, my betrayer is at hand" (Matthew 26:46 NRSV).

According to John's account, we do not see Jesus agonizing in the Garden prior to his arrest. However, Jesus did not pass through this time of trial without any human feelings. He, indeed, was troubled (see 13:21), but he accepted his destiny with divine serenity and supernatural confidence in the outcome: resurrection and ascension to the Father. The arrest scene especially demonstrates Jesus' divinity. He is Lord of all, subject to no other human being. He was in complete control of the situation. He could have escaped being arrested, as he did before (10:39; 11:54), but he boldly faced his betrayer and those coming to arrest him, and he allowed himself to be arrested in order to carry out the divine plan of salvation.

18:1 After Jesus had spoken these words, he went out with his disciples across the Kidron valley to a place where there was a garden, which he and his disciples entered.NRSV To get to the Garden of Gethsemane, Jesus and the disciples had to cross the Kidron Valley, a ravine that starts north of Jerusalem and goes between the hill where the temple is built and the Mount of Olives, then moving on to the Dead Sea. During the rainy season, the valley filled with water torrents, but at this time it was dry.

18:2 Now Judas, who betrayed him, knew the place, because Jesus had often met there with his disciples.^{NIV} Though Judas had left the group while they were still in the upper room (13:26-31), he calculated that Jesus would go to Gethsemane with his disciples because that seemed to be a favorite place for Jesus and the disciples to get away from the crowds when they were in Jerusalem (see Luke 21:37).

18:3-4 So Judas brought a detachment of soldiers together with police from the chief priests and the Pharisees.^{NRSV} Judas acted as a guide to two groups: (1) *a detachment of soldiers,* who would be Romans (probably a "cohort" which is a tenth of a legion, or about 600 men), and (2) *police from the chief priests and the Pharisees,* who would be Jewish temple police. The Jews were given authority by the religious leaders to make arrests for minor infractions. The soldiers probably did not participate in the arrest but accompanied the temple guard to make sure matters didn't get out of control. The Jewish leaders may have asked the Romans for help in arresting Jesus because their ultimate intention was to obtain assistance in executing Jesus. Apparently the Jews had accused Jesus of being a rabble-rouser (see Luke 23:2), so the Romans would be interested in getting such a person who might incite riots into custody. The police and the

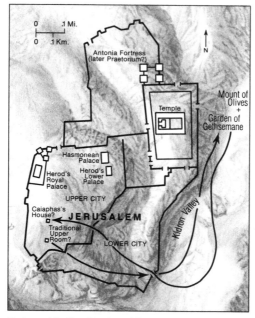

Betrayal in the Garden. *After eating the Passover meal in the upper room, Jesus and his disciples went to Gethsemane, where Judas led the temple guard to arrest Jesus. Jesus was then taken to Caiaphas' house for his first of many trials.*

guards were prepared to meet violent resistance, for they carried **lanterns and torches and weapons.**[NRSV] The mention of lanterns and torches also reminds us that it was still night—Judas's departure into the night to go and betray Jesus had occurred only hours earlier (13:30).

John did not record Judas's kiss of greeting (Matthew 26:49; Mark 14:45; Luke 22:47-48), but the kiss marked a turning point for the disciples. With Jesus' arrest, each one's life would be radically different. For the first time, Judas openly betrayed Jesus before the other disciples. For the first time, Jesus' loyal disciples ran away from him (Matthew 26:56). The band of disciples would undergo severe testing before they were transformed from hesitant followers to dynamic leaders.

Jesus, knowing all that was going to happen to him, went out and asked them, "Who is it you want?"[NIV] Jesus' betrayal, arrest, and crucifixion transpired according to the prearranged, divine plan. The betrayer, Judas Iscariot, had been selected by Jesus. He knew from the beginning that Judas was a devil and would be his betrayer (see 6:64, 70). The time of his arrest was predetermined; it would happen during Passover, not before or after. The method of execution (crucifixion) was predetermined, so Jesus knew that he would be lifted up on the cross (see 12:32-33).

18:5-6 **They answered Him, "Jesus of Nazareth." Jesus said to them, "I am He."**[NKJV] Jesus' response is literally "I am." With these words, he declared his deity (as in 8:58). The reaction this utterance produced in those who were there to arrest him (including **Judas the traitor**[NIV]) indicates that Jesus' words startled this mass of armed men, for they **stepped back and fell to the ground.**[NRSV] The men were startled by the boldness of Jesus' question, and they fell prostrate when they heard him say "I am" (literally), for this was a declaration of his divinity (see Exodus 3:14 where God used this name to identify himself as the God of the Hebrews). Because some temple guards were among the Roman soldiers, quite possibly they understood the significance of Jesus' claim. Or perhaps they were overcome by his obvious power and authority. Among them may have been some

> This relates the great power which Jesus breathed with a single word, that we might learn that the ungodly had no power over him except so far as He permitted. He replies mildly that it is He whom they seek; and yet, as if they had been struck by a violent hurricane, or rather by lightning, He prostrates them on the ground. *John Calvin*

of those who earlier (7:46) had concluded that, "We've never heard anything like [his words]!" (TLB). The response of the guards shows that Jesus could have exercised his power to thwart his arrest, but chose not to.

18:7-9 **Again he asked them, "Whom are you looking for?" And they said, "Jesus of Nazareth." Jesus answered, "I told you that I am he."**NRSV Jesus was willing to turn himself over to the soldiers, but he asked them, **"If you are looking for me, then let these men go,"**NIV referring to the eleven disciples who were with him.

This was to fulfill the word that he had spoken, "I did not lose a single one of those whom you gave me."NRSV Jesus was referring to words recorded in 6:39 and 17:12. Jesus was the Good Shepherd who would lay down his life for the sheep (10:11).

18:10-11 **Then Simon Peter, who had a sword, drew it and struck the high priest's servant, cutting off his right ear. (The servant's name was Malchus.)**NIV Peter had promised to die for Jesus (Matthew 26:33-35), and he wasn't going to let Jesus be taken without a fight. Peter's sword (Greek *machairan*) was probably a dagger. Luke mentions that the disciples had two swords among them (Luke 22:38); he also wrote of this event, but did not name the servant, and he did add that Jesus then healed the servant's ear (Luke 22:50-51).

> There was much in it from which his spirit recoiled, but he chose to do the will of God, however the flesh might start and shrink. Let us even take the cups of life's pain and sorrow direct from the hand of God, not seeing Judas, but the Father. *F. B. Meyer*

Jesus said to Peter, "Put your sword back into its sheath. Am I not to drink the cup that the Father has given me?"NRSV Jesus was determined to do his Father's will. (This is the only mention of the cup of suffering in John's Gospel. See Mark 14:36.) In the Old Testament, the "cup" often referred to the outpouring of God's wrath (see Psalm 75:8; Isaiah 51:17; Jeremiah 25:15; Ezekiel 23:31-34). For Jesus, the cup meant the suffering, isolation, and death that he would have to endure in order to atone for the sins of the world. Peter may have shown great loyalty, but he missed the point. All that was happening was part of God's plan.

Immediately after the same reference to the cup of suffering, both Matthew and Mark mention that all the disciples deserted Jesus and fled (Matthew 26:56; Mark 14:50).

IT MAY BE BETTER NOT TO GET OUR WAY
Trying to protect Jesus, Peter pulled a sword and wounded the
high priest's servant. But Jesus told Peter to put away his
sword and allow God's plan to unfold. At times it is tempting to
take matters into our own hands, to force the issue, or at least
try to dictate the direction. Most often such moves lead to sin.
Instead we must trust God to work out his plan. Think of it—if
Peter had had his way, Jesus would not have gone to the
cross, and we still would be dead in our sins.

ANNAS QUESTIONS JESUS / 18:12-24 / 225

Once the religious leaders had Jesus in their power, the events
began to move with planned precision. Since the point of the
effort was to kill Jesus, determining his guilt or innocence was a
mere formality. To the chief priests, the issue of timing the death
was more important than asking whether Jesus deserved to die.

Only Peter and John followed the crowd at a distance, and they
soon found themselves at Annas's house, where the preliminary
phase of the trial would begin. Anything Jesus said could and
would be used against him, including some things he didn't actually say (see Mark 14:53-61). For Peter, the admission into the
high priest's courtyard cost him his first denial of knowing Jesus.

In the verbal skirmishes between them, Jesus challenged
Annas and the others into declaring openly any truthful accusation they had against him. His calm responses infuriated one person enough to strike Jesus in anger.

18:12-13 **Then the detachment of soldiers with its commander and the
Jewish officials arrested Jesus. They bound him.**[NIV] The Jews
and the Romans, led by a commander (Greek *chiliarch*), arrested
Jesus.

**First they took him to Annas, who was the father-in-law of
Caiaphas, the high priest that year.**[NRSV] Both Annas and Caiaphas had been high priests. Annas was Israel's high priest from
A.D. 6 to 15, when he was deposed by Roman rulers. Caiaphas,
Annas's son-in-law, was appointed high priest from A.D. 18 to
36/37. According to Jewish law, the office of high priest was held
for life. But the Romans didn't like such concentration of power
under one person, so they frequently changed the high priest.
However, many Jews still considered Annas to be the high priest
and still called him by that title. But although Annas retained
much authority among the Jews, Caiaphas made the final deci-

sions. Very likely, Annas had asked to interrogate Jesus and was given the first rights to do so (see 18:19-23).

Jesus was immediately taken to the high priest's residence even though it was the middle of the night. The religious leaders were in a hurry—they wanted to complete the execution before the Sabbath and get on with the Passover celebration.

18:14 Caiaphas was the one who had advised the Jews that it was better to have one person die for the people.NRSV In 11:49-52, Caiaphas had advised the Jewish leaders that it was expedient for one man to die on behalf of the people. Caiaphas said this because he feared the Romans. The Jews had limited religious freedom so long as they kept the peace. The Jewish leaders feard that Jesus' miracles and large following would cause Rome to react and clamp down on them.

AMBITION
Both Caiaphas and Annas cared more about their political ambitions than about their responsibility to lead the people to God. Though religious leaders, they had become evil. As the nation's spiritual leaders, they should have been sensitive to God's revelation. They should have known that Jesus was the Messiah about whom the Scriptures spoke, and they should have pointed the people to him. But when deceitful men and women pursue evil, they want to eliminate all opposition. Instead of honestly evaluating Jesus' claims based on their knowledge of Scripture, these religious leaders sought to further their own selfish ambitions and were even willing to kill God's Son, if that's what it took, to do it.

18:15-18 Simon Peter and another disciple followed Jesus. Since that disciple was known to the high priest, he went with Jesus into the courtyard of the high priest, but Peter was standing outside at the gate. So the other disciple . . . went out, spoke to the woman who guarded the gate, and brought Peter in.NRSV Although all the disciples had fled when the soldiers arrived with their weapons and torches, two of them returned and decided to follow Jesus. So these two disciples followed Jesus to Annas's house where Annas questioned him. This house was more like a compound surrounded by walls with a guarded gate. Only one disciple was identified: Peter; the other was apparently a disciple who was an acquaintance of the high priest. This other disciple only entered with Jesus into the court of the high priest.

Some scholars think the other disciple was John because of

similar references to himself as "the other disciple" in 20:2 and 21:20, 24. But many scholars argue that John, the son of Zebedee from Galilee, would not have been known by Annas. Whoever this disciple was, he secured permission for Peter to enter the courtyard.

Immediately Peter was put on the defensive. Just as he entered, the woman who was guarding the gate (actually a servant) asked Peter a question (the Greek construction of the question expects a negative answer): **The woman said to Peter, "You are not also one of this man's disciples, are you?"**NRSV In striking contrast to Peter's earlier declaration that he would lay down his life for his Lord (13:37), Peter gave the expected answer and denied being a disciple of Jesus: **"I am not."** He thought that lying was his only option. Most people do not believe in situation ethics, but we tend to live as if we do. The incidental dishonesties that crowd our lives cannot be dismissed with the "everyone does it" excuse. If truth is compromised in small matters, it isn't even considered when the stakes are high!

> In spite of his brave talk, he was swept off his feet—as we shall be, unless we have learned to avail ourselves of that power which is made perfect only in weakness. Peter's fall was due to his self-confidence and lack of prayer. Those who are weak should beware of exposing themselves in places and company where they are liable to fail. Do not warm yourself at the world's fires. *F. B. Meyer*

It was cold, and the servants and officials stood around a fire they had made to keep warm. Peter also was standing with them, warming himself.NIV It was a spring evening, and the city of Jerusalem sits 2,500 feet above sea level. People occupied in ghastly business under the cover of darkness were chilled. The fire kept the cold and their guilt at bay for a while.

18:19 **Meanwhile.**NIV John employed a literary technique of alternating scenes—from Jesus' ongoing trial to Peter's ongoing denial.

The high priest questioned Jesus about his disciples and his teaching.NIV If a rebellion was feared by the authorities, Annas may have wanted to know how many disciples Jesus had gathered so as to estimate the force of their retaliation. Or Annas may have wanted to question the disciples about what Jesus had taught them. Jesus said nothing about his disciples, so as to protect them (as in 18:8), but was willing to talk about his teaching.

THE FAILURE
This would not be Peter's only denial, for there in the courtyard he would deny even knowing Jesus two more times (18:25-27), just as Jesus had predicted (13:37-38; see also Matthew 26:33-35; Mark 14:29-31). Peter's three denials were not merely instant responses to an immediate threat, but were intentional lies spoken at different times. We can learn from Peter's experience:

1. Moments of peace allow us to recover from past troubles and prepare for the next. Peter and the other disciples had slept in the Garden of Gethsemane when they should have been praying (as Jesus had asked them to do). Instead of being prepared with the armor of God (see Ephesians 6:10-18), they were left with nothing but a short, human sword.

2. Moments of confusion and pressure require that we imitate Jesus. The disciples were out of sync with Christ—attacking when they should have been still; then running when they should have stood their ground. Claiming God's protection means little until the time of trial comes. Depending on our own resources means that we have turned away from God's help.

3. Moments of doubt and challenge should be met with honest estimates of our own strength. Instead of seeking Jesus' help when told he would deny his master, Peter impulsively claimed more courage than he possessed. When we don't admit our weaknesses and fears, we keep ourselves from recognizing God's strength.

18:20-23 **"I have spoken openly to the world; I have always taught in synagogues and in the temple, where all the Jews come together. I have said nothing in secret."**[NRSV] Jesus was not the leader of a cult or secret organization. He was not planning a religious coup. Instead, Jesus noted that everything he taught had been taught in public. Even the quiet and private talks with his disciples included no secret or subversive teachings. Everything he said to the disciples was told to the crowds, but they refused to understand. If Annas wanted to know the substance of Jesus' teachings, he could ask anyone who had heard Jesus speak on several occasions. Interrogating the disciples would not be necessary. So Jesus turned the questioning back to Annas: **"Why do you ask me? Ask those who heard what I said to them; they know what I said."**[NRSV]

This incited anger. One of Annas's officers, seeing Jesus' answer as a sign of contempt for the high priest, struck Jesus in the face (probably a good hard slap) saying, **"Do You answer the high priest like that?"**[NKJV] Jesus defended himself, for he had been slapped unjustly: **"If I have spoken wrongly, testify to the**

wrong. But if I have spoken rightly, why do you strike me?^{NRSV} This incident is similar to that recorded in Acts 23:2-5, where Paul was struck for not answering the high priest "correctly." Jesus denies that he spoke any evil.

18:24 Then Annas sent him, still bound, to Caiaphas the high priest.^{NIV} After being interrogated by Annas, Jesus was sent on to Caiaphas, the ruling high priest. However, John does not give us any record of the interview Caiaphas had with Jesus. Mark records that this questioning before Caiaphas included the entire Sanhedrin (Mark 14:53-65). The religious leaders knew they had no grounds for charging Jesus, so they tried to build evidence against him by using false witnesses.

HAVE YOU DENIED HIM?
We can easily get angry at the Jewish council for their injustice in condemning Jesus, but we must remember that Peter and the rest of the disciples also contributed to Jesus' pain by deserting and disowning him (Matthew 26:56, 75). While most people are not like the religious leaders, we are all like the disciples, for all of us have been guilty of denying that Christ is Lord in vital areas of our lives or of keeping secret our identity as believers in times of pressure. Don't excuse yourself by pointing at others whose sins seem worse than yours. Instead, come to Jesus for forgiveness and healing.

PETER DENIES KNOWING JESUS / 18:25-27 / 227

While Jesus was countering the questions of Annas (see 18:19-24), who was trying to gather information against the disciples, Peter denied knowing Jesus three times. Jesus displayed his great moral character by not disowning his disciples, even though they had denied him. John captured the pathos of the moment by merely reporting that Peter's final denial was made with the rooster crowing in the background.

18:25 As Simon Peter stood warming himself.^{NIV} These verses are a continuation of verses 15-18. Peter was still in the courtyard of Annas's house and was standing beside a fire with several other people—all warming themselves on that cold spring evening (see 18:18). Again Peter was asked a leading question that, in Greek, expected a negative answer: **"You are not also one of his disciples, are you?"**^{NRSV} Peter denied it saying, **"I am not!"**^{NKJV} The vehemence of Peter's denial may have caught the attention of sev-

eral others who were gathered around the fire. To at least one of
them, Peter looked very familiar.

ON TRIAL
What situations might cause you to deny knowing Jesus?
Strength and help are only sought when we recognize our
weaknesses. What would be your response to:
- Intimidation from being alone and surrounded by hostile
  unbelievers?
- Possible rebukes, punishment, or death for standing up for
  Christ?
- Embarrassing circumstances when exposed as one who
  loves and follows Jesus?
- Entanglements from habits or relationships that tie you too
  closely to the enemies of Christ?
  Most of us will probably never face as intense a trial as Peter
did. But moments of truth occur almost every day. We know the
feeling of being paralyzed by surprise, fear, or possible shame.
We must pray for God's instant help so that when the
ambushes come, we rely on his strength and Word for our
response.

**18:26-27 One of the servants of the high priest, a relative of the one
whose ear Peter cut off, said, "Did I not see you in the garden with Him?" Peter then denied
again; and immediately a rooster
crowed.**NKJV This, the third denial,
happened exactly as Jesus had predicted (see 13:38; Mark 14:30). The
other three Gospels say that Peter's
three denials happened near a fire in
the courtyard outside Caiaphas's palace. John places the three denials outside Annas's home. This was very

> No one ought to be
> confident in his own
> strength when he
> undergoes temptation.
> For whenever we endure
> evils courageously, our
> long-suffering comes
> from Christ. *Augustine*

likely the same courtyard. The high priest's residence was
large, and Annas and Caiaphas undoubtedly lived near each
other.

Luke records that after Peter had denied Jesus the third time,
"The Lord turned and looked straight at Peter. Then Peter remembered the word the Lord had spoken to him. . . . And he went outside and wept bitterly" (Luke 22:61-62 NIV). How like Peter we
are! He had been warned, and he was given three opportunities to
stand up for Christ. He failed them all. It took a crowing rooster
and the piercing look of Jesus to make him realize how quickly
and how fast he had abandoned his Lord.

GREAT SIN

Imagine standing outside while Jesus, your Lord and Master, is questioned. Imagine watching this man, whom you have come to believe is the long-awaited Messiah, being abused and beaten. Naturally Peter was confused and afraid. It is a serious sin to disown Christ, but Jesus forgave Peter (21:15-19). No sin is too great for Jesus to forgive if you are truly repentant. He will forgive even your worst sin if you turn from it and ask his pardon.

JESUS STANDS TRIAL BEFORE PILATE / 18:28-37 / **230**

The same rooster that announced the third denial of Peter also welcomed the day that Jesus was to be crucified. John gives us none of the details of Jesus' further questioning before Caiaphas, since the

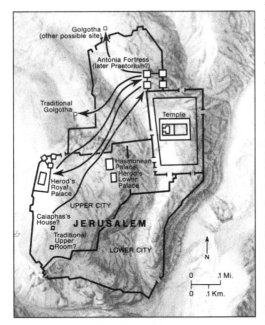

two parts of the preliminary "trial" were perfunctory and repetitious. The faces changed, but the false accusations remained the same. Early morning found Jesus and his accusers at Pilate's gate demanding an audience. Roman permission to crucify Jesus was an inconvenient requirement, but it did allow the leaders to shift any blame for murder on to the foreign occupiers. In short, the Jewish leaders were eliminating one enemy and framing another for the death.

Jesus' Trial and Crucifixion. Jesus was taken from trial before the Jewish Sanhedrin to trial before the Roman governor, Pilate, in Pilate's palace. Then Pilate sent him to Herod (Luke 23:5-12), but after questioning Jesus, Herod returned Jesus to Pilate. Responding to threats from the mob, Pilate finally turned Jesus over to be crucified.

Pilate did not welcome the manipulation. He quickly concluded that the charges against Jesus were groundless. But he was also clearly puzzled that Jesus refused to defend himself. The imperial representative of Rome found himself uncomfortably pressed between a rock and a hard place.

THE EARLIEST MANUSCRIPT
Here is an interesting historical fact about this section in John's Gospel: the earliest extant manuscript of the New Testament is dated A.D. 110–125. This papyrus manuscript, containing John 18:31-33 on one side and 18:37-38 on the other, must have been one of the very earliest copies of John's Gospel. This manuscript testifies to the fact that the autograph of John's Gospel must have been written before the close of the first century.

18:28 Then the Jews led Jesus from Caiaphas to the palace of the Roman governor.^{NIV} This palace was also called the Praetorium, the headquarters of the governor of the province—in this case, Pilate.

By now it was early morning, and to avoid ceremonial uncleanness the Jews did not enter the palace; they wanted to be able to eat the Passover.^{NIV} If we understand the Last Supper to have been at the same time as the Passover meal (see introduction to chapter 13), then this refers to the week of Passover and/or the Feast of Unleavened Bread, which was also commonly called the Passover. By Jewish law, entering the house of a Gentile would cause a Jewish person to be ceremonially defiled. As a result, the Jew could not take part in worship at the temple or celebrate the feasts until he or she was restored to a state of "cleanness." Afraid of being defiled, these men stayed outside the house where they had taken Jesus for trial—it was not against the law to be in the courtyard or on a porch. They kept the ceremonial requirements of their religion while harboring murder and treachery in their hearts. Because the Jews were outside, Pilate had to come out to them.

18:29-31 So Pilate came out to them and asked, "What charges are you bringing against this man?"^{NIV} This Roman governor, Pilate, was in charge of Judea (the region where Jerusalem was located) from A.D. 26–36. Pilate was unpopular with the Jews because he had taken money from the temple treasuries to build an aqueduct. Pilate resided in Caesarea, but he came to Jerusalem during the major feasts in order to handle any riots or insurrections that

THE SIX STAGES OF JESUS' TRIAL

Although Jesus' trial lasted less than 18 hours, he was taken to six different hearings.

BEFORE JEWISH AUTHORITIES	Preliminary hearing before Annas (John 18:12-24)	Because the office of high priest was for life, Annas was still the "official" high priest in the eyes of the Jews, even though the Romans had appointed another. Thus Annas still carried much weight among the Sanhedrin.
	Hearing before Caiaphas (Matthew 26:57-68)	Like the hearing before Annas, this hearing was conducted at night in secrecy. It was full of illegalities that made a mockery of justice.
	Trial before the Sanhedrin (Matthew 27:1-2)	Just after daybreak, members of the Jewish council met to approve of the previous hearings to make them appear legal. The purpose of this trial was not to determine justice but to justify their own preconceptions of Jesus' guilt.
BEFORE ROMAN AUTHORITIES	First hearing before Pilate (Luke 23:1-5)	The religious leaders had condemned Jesus to death on religious grounds, but only the Roman government could grant the death penalty. Thus, they took Jesus to Pilate, the Roman governor, and accused him of treason and rebellion, crimes for which the Roman government gave the death penalty. Pilate saw at once that Jesus was innocent, but he was afraid that the religious leaders would report him to Caesar for not dealing with a rebel.
	Hearing before Herod (Luke 23:6-12)	Because Jesus' home was in the region of Galilee, Pilate sent Jesus to Herod Agrippa, the ruler of Galilee, who was in Jerusalem for the Passover celebration. Herod was eager to see Jesus do a miracle, but when Jesus remained silent, Herod wanted nothing to do with him and sent him back to Pilate.
	Last hearing before Pilate (Luke 23:13-25)	Pilate didn't like the religious leaders. He wasn't interested in condemning Jesus because he knew Jesus was innocent. However, he knew that another uprising in his district might cost him his job. First he tried to compromise with the religious leaders by having Jesus beaten, an illegal action in itself. But finally he gave in and handed Jesus over to be executed. Pilate's self-interest was stronger than his sense of justice.

might take place. Passover was a very important feast to the Jews as they remembered their freedom from bondage in Egypt. Such thoughts could bring their desire for freedom from Roman occupation to a fever pitch. Indeed, rebellions were occurring all over the country—Barabbas, the man who would be released in place of Jesus, had been imprisoned because of his part in a rebellion.

So to go to Pilate, these Jewish leaders must have been really desperate to get rid of Jesus. Normally, the Jews would never turn one of their own people over to the hated Romans. Pilate must have known about their charges against Jesus, for he had to give permission to the Roman soldiers to participate in Jesus' arrest (18:3). If Jesus was going to start a riot or a coup, then it was best that he be brought into custody.

But Pilate realized that something wasn't normal about this case. He must have sensed the jealousy of the Jewish leaders who brought this popular teacher to him. Pilate certainly had seen or at least had heard about Jesus' glorious entry into Jerusalem only a few days earlier, so he understood the motives of these religious leaders. Therefore, Pilate demanded that they provide a bona fide legal charge against Jesus. The Jewish leaders answered as vaguely as possible: **"If this man were not a criminal, we would not have handed him over to you."**NRSV It was as if they were saying, "You already know the charges—your soldiers helped us arrest him. Now let's get on with this!"

But Pilate, uninterested in the constant squabbling among the Jews, was satisfied that this potential troublemaker was in custody. He had no reason to push the trial any farther, so he tried to dismiss them: **"Take him yourselves and judge him by your own law."**NIV

But the Jewish leaders persisted and gained Pilate's attention by insinuating that they had already found reasons in their own law for Jesus' execution. According to Luke's Gospel, the Jewish leaders accused Jesus of three things, "And they began to accuse him, saying, 'We have found this man subverting our nation. He opposes payment of taxes to Caesar and claims to be Christ, a king'" (Luke 23:2, NIV). But the Jews needed Pilate to give Jesus a trial because the Jews were **not permitted to put anyone to death.**NRSV Being under Roman rule, the Jews were not permitted to carry out the kind of execution they were planning without the sanction of the Roman government. It seems that "spontaneous" executions like the stoning of Stephen or the woman taken in adultery were overlooked by the Romans. But in the eyes of the Jewish leaders, Jesus needed to be executed publicly. Thus, the Jews needed the Romans to execute Jesus for them.

18:32 **This was to fulfill what Jesus had said when he indicated the kind of death he was to die.**^{NRSV} Jesus knew all along that his would be a Roman execution, for he had predicted that he would die on a cross. Capital punishment for the Jews was by stoning and for the Romans by crucifixion. Jesus had always foretold his death in terms of crucifixion, not stoning (Matthew 20:19).

IT HAD TO BE A CROSS
Jesus sacrificial death was an inevitable necessity for our salvation. But the very means of that death was designated by God in order to accomplish several detailed purposes of God. Among the reasons for the Crucifixion are the following:
- The Crucifixion preserved the accuracy of long-standing messianic prophecies, or typology—that none of Jesus' bones would be broken, whereas stoning broke bones (Exodus 12:46) and that piercing would occur (Zechariah 12:10).
- The Crucifixion combined the Jews and Gentiles in a conspiracy of death. The responsibility and guilt for the death of Jesus was thereby placed upon the world (Acts 2:23; 4:27).
- The Crucifixion actualized another Old Testament type, the serpent lifted on a pole as a sign of salvation (John 3:14).
- The cross also represented God's commanded form of death for anyone who was under divine curse. He was to be hanged from a tree in judgment for his sin (Deuteronomy 21:23; Galatians 3:13).

God used the cross of Jesus to work out every detail of his eternal plan to accomplish our salvation!

18:33-34 **Pilate then went back inside the palace, summoned Jesus and asked him, "Are you the king of the Jews?"**^{NIV} Since Jesus' enemies had accused him of sedition against Rome (Luke 23:1-2), Pilate asked Jesus if he really claimed to be a king.

Jesus then asked Pilate, **"Is that your own idea . . . or did others talk to you about me?"**^{NIV} If Pilate was asking this question in his role as the Roman governor, he would have been inquiring whether Jesus was setting up a rebel government. But the Jews were using the word *king* to mean their religious ruler, the Messiah. Israel was a captive nation, under the authority of the Roman Empire. A rival king might have threatened Rome; a Messiah could have been a purely religious leader.

18:35-36 **"I am not a Jew, am I? Your own nation and the chief priests have handed you over to me. What have you done?"**^{NRSV} Pilate's response indicates that his interrogation was motivated by the Jews. The impression is that he was merely performing his task.

Jesus explained: **"My kingdom is not from this world. If my**

kingdom were from this world, my followers would be fighting to keep me from being handed over to the Jews. But as it is, my kingdom is not from here."NRSV Pilate asked Jesus a straightforward question, and Jesus answered clearly. Jesus is a king, but one whose kingdom is not of this world. Therefore, Jesus' followers would not be trying to take control by force. By his *kingdom (basileia)*, Jesus was referring to all he had done and would do as God's Son and all that is under his authority. When believers are born again, they become subjects of this kingdom—a spiritual kingdom. To the degree, then, that believers live out their obedience to Christ in whatever system, to that degree the kingdom of God becomes apparent in this world. Although the final victory has not been won, Jesus planted the flag of his kingdom in this world, and God began rescuing citizens from the kingdom of darkness and bringing them into the kingdom of Christ (see Colossians 1:12-13). The kingdom of God is wherever Christ's rule is acknowledged by men and women.

> When Christ commanded His followers to "seek first the kingdom of God," He was exhorting them to seek to be ruled by God and gratefully acknowledge His power and authority over them. That means that the Christian's goal is not to strive to rule, but *to be ruled. Chuck Colson*

NOT FROM THIS WORLD
Jesus' claim to the throne and his reign are beyond the limitations of this world. The goals, principles, and methods of Christ's kingdom come from heaven. They are not the invention of evolving people or even of prophets and wise men. The way the kingdom affects our lives demonstrates that it is not rooted in this world. For instance, citizens of the kingdom hold all of life in such high regard that they are ready to lay down their own lives in obedience to Christ for the sake of other lives. Jesus' kingship requires, not a choice of options for action, but real obedience to a wise Savior-King.

18:37 Pilate tried to get his original question answered (see 18:33): **"So you are a king?"**NRSV. Some versions make this statement an exclamation (see NIV). In any case, the fact that John describes Jesus' response as an "answer" indicates that Pilate was asking for further clarification.

"You are right in saying I am a king. In fact, for this reason I was born, and for this I came into the world, to testify to the

truth. Everyone on the side of truth listens to me."[NIV] Jesus was the king of a different realm, who had come to earth to *testify to the truth*. Jesus did not enter the world for any political purpose; instead he came to testify to the truth. There seems to have been no question in Pilate's mind that Jesus spoke the truth and was innocent of any crime. It also seems apparent that while recognizing the truth, Pilate chose to reject it. It is a tragedy when we fail to recognize the truth. It is a greater tragedy when we recognize the truth but fail to heed it.

YOU MUST DECIDE
Pilate made four attempts to deal with Jesus: (1) he tried to put the responsibility on someone else (18:31); (2) he tried to find a way of escape so he could release Jesus (18:39); (3) he tried to compromise with having Jesus flogged rather than handing him over to die (19:1-3); and (4) he tried a direct appeal to the sympathy of the accusers (19:15). Everyone has to decide what to do with Jesus. Whatever desire Pilate had to free Jesus was negated by his refusal to do so. Pilate let everyone else decide for him—and in the end, he lost.

PILATE HANDS JESUS OVER TO BE CRUCIFIED / 18:38–19:16 / **232**

Pilate mused on the possibility of truly comprehending "truth" and then declared Jesus "not guilty." He had no basis for a charge against Jesus and certainly no evidence that required a death penalty. But it wouldn't be that easy.

18:38 Pilate asked him, "What is truth?"[NRSV] Pilate was cynical; he thought that all truth was relative—it could be whatever Rome wanted it to be. To many government officials, truth was whatever the majority of people agreed with or whatever helped advance their own personal power and political goals. When there is no basis for truth, there is no basis for moral right and wrong. Justice becomes whatever works or whatever helps those in power. In Jesus and his Word we have a standard for truth and for our moral behavior.

How ironic it is that Pilate should ask his question to the one who claimed to be the embodiment of truth. Jesus could have corrected him by saying, "You

> If knowledge can cause most people to become vain, perhaps ignorance and lack of learning can make them humble. Yet now and then you do find men who pride themselves on their ignorance.
> *John Climacus*

mean, *'Who* is truth?'" Pilate was never closer to the truth than he was that very moment!

With this he went out again to the Jews and said, "I find no basis for a charge against him."^{NIV} At that point, Pilate had the power and authority to simply set Jesus free. But he lacked the courage to stand by this conviction in the face of opposition from these Jews and a possible ensuing riot. Problems like that could mean that Pilate would be removed from his position because of being unable to keep the peace. So Pilate tried first to pass Jesus off on Herod, who was ruler of Galilee, the region of Jesus' hometown (Luke 23:6-7). But Herod only mocked Jesus and then sent him back to Pilate.

18:39-40 **"But it is your custom for me to release to you one prisoner at the time of the Passover. Do you want me to release 'the king of the Jews'?"**^{NIV} Pilate hoped to escape passing judgment on Jesus by allowing the Jews to determine Jesus' fate. If they asked for Jesus' release, then Pilate would be free from convicting an innocent man. If they refused Jesus, then the onus of Jesus' execution would be on them, not Pilate.

They shouted back, "No, not him! Give us Barabbas!" Now Barabbas had taken part in a rebellion.^{NIV} The screaming Jewish officials demanded that a convicted rebel, Barabbas, be pardoned instead of Jesus. (The Greek word *lestes* was used to describe rebels against Roman authority.) Barabbas was a rebel against Rome (Mark 15:7), and although he had committed murder, he was probably a hero among the Jews. The Jews hated being governed by Rome and paying taxes to the despised government. Barabbas, who had led a rebellion and failed, was released instead of Jesus, the only one who could truly help Israel.

WHO WAS BARABBAS?
Jewish men had names that identified them with their fathers. Simon Peter, for example, is called Simon son of Jonah (Matthew 16:17). Barabbas is never identified by his given name, and this name is not much help either—*bar-abbas* means "son of *Abba"* (or "son of daddy"). Barabbas, son of an unnamed father, committed a crime. Jesus died in his place, so this man was set free. We too are sinners and criminals who have broken God's holy law. Like Barabbas, we deserve to die. But Jesus died in our place, for our sins, and we have been set free. We don't have to be "very important people" to accept our freedom in Christ. In fact, thanks to Jesus, God adopts us all as his own sons and daughters and gives us the right to call him *Abba*—"daddy" (see Galatians 4:4-6).

19:1 Then Pilate took Jesus and had him flogged.^{NRSV} Pilate handed Jesus over to the soldiers to be flogged. According to Luke 23:16 and 22, Pilate intended to teach Jesus a lesson by flogging and then releasing him. It was also another attempt by Pilate to set Jesus free. Pilate knew that Jesus was innocent of any crime, and he desperately wanted Jesus freed to quiet his own conscience. So Pilate thought

> No Christian should ever forget that the source of his joy was the pain and suffering of his Lord.
> *M. G. Gutzke*

the flogging would appease the Jews. This was ruthless but not intended to kill him. Nevertheless, it was not uncommon for prisoners to die of floggings. Some of the whips used for flogging were designed to inflict terrible damage to the human body. The leather thongs that formed the striking surfaces were embedded with shards of metal so that victims were both bruised and cut severely. Punishment was applied to the bared upper body of a bound prisoner. Apparently, Pilate thought this flogging was a humane alternative to crucifixion. He was avoiding condemning Jesus to death.

19:2-3 The soldiers twisted together a crown of thorns head. They clothed him in a purple robe and went up to him again and again, saying, "Hail, king of the Jews!" And they struck him in the face.^{NIV} The Roman soldiers jammed a crown of thorns onto Jesus' head and obtained a purple robe (purple was the color of royalty) in order to mock Jesus' supposed kingship. According to Matthew 27:28, they first stripped Jesus of his outer garment. Matthew and Mark add that the soldiers spit on Jesus as well (Matthew 27:30; Mark 15:19). Then the Roman soldiers mocked Jesus further by bowing before him and striking him. They took devilish delight in repeatedly mocking and pummeling their prisoner.

Again, all this had been prophesied. Listen to Isaiah: "I offered my back to those who beat me, my cheeks to those who pulled out my beard; I did not hide my face from mocking and spitting" (Isaiah 50:6 NIV; see also 52:14–53:6).

19:4 Pilate went out again and said to them, "Look, I am bringing him out to you to let you know that I find no case against him."^{NRSV} After Jesus' beating and the display of mockery, Pilate, for the second time (see 18:38), declared Jesus "not guilty"—that is, not guilty of a crime warranting death.

19:5-7 Then Jesus came out, wearing the crown of thorns and the purple robe,^{NKJV} **and Pilate uttered the now-famous words, "Behold the Man!"**^{NKJV} (Latin, *Ecce homo*). He hoped the sight of this beaten, bloody person would elicit pity and make the crowd realize that there could be no possible threat from this poor fellow. The tone of these words implies ridicule, as if he said, "How can you possibly believe this pitiful man's claim to be a king?"

But the bloodthirsty chief priests and officials responded: **"Crucify him! Crucify him!"**[NRSV] That they demanded crucifixion reveals their intense hatred of Jesus. Crucifixion was a shameful death reserved for criminals, slaves, and rebels. Jesus was none of these, and Pilate knew it. But the Jewish enemies of Christ wanted not only to kill him but also to discredit and humiliate him thoroughly.

"You take him and crucify him. As for me, I find no basis for a charge against him."[NIV] Pilate dared the Jewish leaders to usurp the exclusive Roman authority of capital punishment by crucifying their "King" themselves. But the Jewish leaders were too shrewd to fall into this trap, and they weren't about to lose the battle now. So they revealed the *real* reason for their hatred of Jesus: **"We have a law, and according to that law he ought to die because he has claimed to be the Son of God."**[NRSV] The law they were referring to is Leviticus 24:16: "Anyone who blasphemes the name of the LORD must be put to death" (NIV) For anyone to claim to be God (as Jesus did) was a clear case of blasphemy and thus required that the person be put to death. The irony here is that Jesus was not violating the law, for what he had said was true! The Jews just didn't believe it.

GOLDEN MOMENT

Pilate let his golden moment slip away. Three times he pronounced Jesus "not guilty" (18:38; 19:4; 19:6). He even tried to set Jesus free (19:12). But Pilate would not stand for truth or justice in the face of opposition. Instead, he tried to preserve his position at the expense of doing what was right.

Under pressure, we too may feel our power or security threatened. But unlike Pilate, we must stand for what is right even if the consequences mean personal loss. If we don't, we will lose something even more valuable—our integrity. When we face tough choices, we can take the easy way out or with God's help speak out for what is right. When we know what is right yet do not act on it, we sin (James 4:17).

19:8 When Pilate heard this, he was even more afraid.[NIV] Pilate's fear may have had its origin in a combination of three factors:

1. Romans were inclined to believe in human deities; so Pilate may have sensed that the man in his presence was a god.

2. According to Matthew 27:19, Pilate's wife may have influenced his thoughts about Jesus, for she had had a troublesome dream, and had sent word to Pilate: "Have nothing to do with that just Man, for I have suffered many things today in a dream because of Him" (NKJV).

3. Pilate may well have been concerned that a riot was about to break out among the Jews. Hatred for Romans and the extremely crowded conditions in Jerusalem created a powder keg of unrest that needed only a good spark to become explosive.

19:9-11 Pilate therefore asked Jesus about his origin: **"Where are you from?"**NRSV But Jesus gave him no answer. Some commentators see Jesus' silence as fulfilling Isaiah 53:7 ("He was oppressed and afflicted, yet he did not open his mouth" NIV). Pilate, astounded by Jesus' silence, reminded Jesus: **"Don't you realize I have power either to free you or to crucify you?"**NIV

Pilate's power did not intimidate Jesus because God's authority overrules all human authority. Therefore Jesus answered, **"You would have no power over me unless it had been given you from above."**NRSV Pilate had no power over Jesus, for Jesus lived and died completely under control of divine authority. Jesus' statement about the source of all power further clarified the meaning of his earlier words, "My kingdom is not of this world" (18:36, NIV).

Jesus continued, **"The one who handed me over to you is guilty of a greater sin."**NRSV Jesus referred to Caiaphas, the high priest, who handed Jesus over to the Romans, not to Judas, who had betrayed him to the Jews. For a Jewish high priest to deliver the Jews' King and Messiah over to the Romans for execution was an even more heinous sin than for the Roman governor to sentence him to death. Pilate was merely a pawn in a very elaborate game, but the high priest would be more severely judged because he should have known better. Caiaphas turned from the "light" in order to side with the darkness and made excuses for disobeying God's law. However, Jesus was at the same time clearly charging Pilate with sin. Pilate was responsible for his choices.

19:12 Pilate tried to set Jesus free.NIV By this time Pilate was apparently convinced that Jesus was some kind of extra-special, supernatural person, so he tried still another time to let him go.

But the Jews were not about to let Jesus escape at this point in the trial; so in a final desperate ploy, they played their trump card: **"If you let this man go, you are no friend of Caesar. Anyone who claims to be a king opposes Caesar."**NIV Since the Jews despised Roman rule, this was blatant hypocrisy. But these Jews hated Jesus so much that to get rid of him they were claiming their allegiance to Rome and to Caesar! If it were not so tragic, these Jewish leaders would almost appear comical. At any rate, their strategy worked—very likely Pilate was afraid that he would be reported to Caesar as having released a man who had been charged with claiming to be a king. Historical records indicate that the Jews had already threatened to lodge a formal complaint against Pilate for his stubborn flouting of their traditions. Most likely such a complaint would have led to being recalled by Rome, losing his job, or even losing his life. The Roman government could not afford to put large numbers of troops in all the regions under its control, so one of Pilate's main duties was to do whatever was necessary to maintain peace.

The Jews' use of the term *friend of Caesar* (*philos tou Kaisaros*) probably alluded to the technical Roman term (*amicus Caesaris*). The emperor awarded privileged status of "friend of Caesar" to loyal subjects. There is evidence that Pilate may have enjoyed this status by virtue of his association with the strongly anti-Semitic Aelius Sejanus. (Tacitus wrote in *Annals* 6.8 that "whoever was close to Sejanus had a claim on the friendship of Caesar.") But Sejanus lost his own status in the year A.D. 31 (or 32), and for this reason Pilate may have been especially vulnerable—especially to threats from the Jews.

THE TRAP CLOSES
Pilate tried to avoid or disarm the conflict over Jesus, but he waited too long to take decisive action. A mob mentality was beginning to form, and Pilate knew that events were almost beyond his control. Because Pilate had not really tried to beat the Jewish leaders, he found himself forced to join them. When we continually compromise with sin, we risk falling so deeply under its control that we cannot extricate ourselves. Pilate's actions also demonstrate that we must never conclude that we have fallen so far that going along with sin is better than repentance.

19:13-14 Pilate **brought Jesus out and sat down on the judge's seat at a place known as the Stone Pavement.**NIV Although the text does not explicitly state that Pilate passed judgment on Jesus, the fact that Pilate seated himself on the judgment seat indicates that the judgment originated from him; thus, he was responsible. The Stone Pavement was the courtyard of the Fortress of Antonia that was built next to the northwest corner of the temple area. This judgment came on **the day of Preparation of Passover Week, about the sixth hour.**NIV In this context, the day would be Friday, the day of preparation for the weekly Sabbath. Passover refers to the week-long Feast of Unleavened Bread. By this time in history, the term *Passover* was used for the entire week-long celebration.

But the judgment was very indirect. Perhaps Pilate was too guilt-ridden to summarily condemn Jesus, and he was angry at having his hand forced against his better judgment. So his words ring with anger and mockery at these Jews by saying to them: **"Behold your King!"**NKJV It is as if he were saying, "You are a pitiful bunch, and this really *is* your pitiful king."

19:15-16 But the Jews continued with their shouting: **"Away with him! Away with him! Crucify him!"**NRSV Again Pilate retorted, **"Shall I crucify your King?"**NKJV His repetition of Jesus as "your King" angered the leaders all the more, to the point where they made a ludicrously hypocritical statement . . .

"We have no king but Caesar!"NKJV Nothing could be farther from the truth than this pronouncement of loyalty to Caesar from the Jewish religious leaders. These religious men, in the heat of the moment and in their blindness, had forgotten their faith—the Jews were God's people. God was their King (Judges 8:23; 1 Samuel 8:7). But perhaps the words rang with truth, for in their murderous plans against Jesus, God's Son, they showed that God was no longer their king. And if that was they case, they, the Jewish leaders, were committing blasphemy.

NO KING BUT CAESAR
In rejecting Christ's rightful control over their lives, the religious leaders claimed Caesar as king. They acknowledged a human power that they thought would guarantee their own status. Instead, that power destroyed Jerusalem and the temple and killed 500,000 Jews. The next generation paid dearly for the sins of their leaders.

Today people still refuse to let God have any control or influence over their decisions. They make choices based on short-term goals. They grasp present "benefits" without regard for the long-term costs. We must not give allegiance or cooperation to leaders and systems that have no regard for God's authority. Who or what holds the position of king in your life?

Finally Pilate handed him over to them to be crucified.^{NIV}
According to the Greek text, the pronoun *them* would refer to the
"chief priests" in verse 15. But the Roman soldiers actually carried out the crucifixion (as is conveyed by the next statement:
The soldiers took charge of Jesus^{NIV}). Therefore, the text must
mean that Pilate gave in to the Jews' desire to have Jesus executed. This idea is captured in the NEB: "Then at last, to satisfy
them [the chief priests], he handed Jesus over to be crucified."
(See also Luke 23:25, where it says Pilate "surrendered Jesus to
their will" NIV).

John 19:17-42

We must never forget the reason Christ died. Unless we recognize the eternal tragedy that would have occurred to the human race without the Cross, we will not be able to see the Cross as our victory. At great personal cost, Jesus won eternal life for us. He paid the price for our sin with his own life. That he offers us life as a free gift ought to give us deep joy. We must be touched by Christ's death, for he died in our place!

19:17 **Carrying his own cross, he went out to the place of the Skull (which in Aramaic is called Golgotha).**[NIV] Jesus carried the cross (usually the horizontal cross beam) at first, but he became weak because of the flogging that Simon was commanded to take over (see Matthew 27:32; Mark 15:21; Luke 23:26). Jesus went to *Golgotha,* meaning *place of the Skull.* This hill may have been called this because of its stony top or because it was shaped like a skull. *Golgotha* is the Hebrew word for "skull." The familiar name *Calvary* is derived from the Latin *calvaria* (also meaning "skull").

As the drama of the cross unfolds, John's writing captures the simple ironies of the tragedy. The soldiers who escorted Jesus to Calvary didn't know who he was, they were just doing their duty. Pilate knew that Jesus wasn't guilty of death, but he still didn't understand *who* Jesus was. The people, roused to a fever pitch by the religious leaders, didn't take the time to care about who Jesus was (even though they had hailed him as their king a few days earlier. Obviously, they were disappointed by the mocking display of him as a pitiful king). The chief priests per-

> So in all this welter of confusion, with people doing certain things for a good or a bad reason, for a short or a long reason, for their own benefit or just in the doing of their duty: in all of this, God's will was carried out! There is no indication that God's will varies because of circumstances or the selfish ideas of men. God always carries out His purpose, and the believer may share in that with Him, if he will but trust Him. *M. G. Gutzke*

haps were the most blind of all, for they had totally lost sight of
everything they stood for, seeking Jesus' death only to hold onto
their precious positions and to stop the teachings that were threat-
ening their status quo.

JESUS IS PLACED ON THE CROSS / 19:18-27 / 235

Jesus knew his destiny (see 18:37), and he approached death
boldly and courageously—carrying his own cross to Calvary
(19:17). Jesus endured the shame of crucifixion, the ridicule of
the crowd, and the insults of those who cast lots for his clothing
as he died. Though he was in agony, his thought included the care
of his aged mother, whose care he entrusted to the disciple he
loved.

The Jews and the Romans were not taking Jesus' life from
him; he was laying it down of his own accord. When Jesus had
accomplished salvation—when it was all "finished," of his own
volition he gave up his spirit (19:30). As Jesus had foretold, no
one had taken his life from him; he had the authority to give it up
and then to retake it in resurrection (10:18). Thus, the royal Messiah went to the cross as if going to his throne, which had a universal proclamation of his royal status written in three languages:
"This is the King of the Jews."

**19:18-22 There they crucified him, and with him two others, one on
either side, with Jesus between them.**NRSV The *others* were criminals (see Matthew 27:38; Mark 15:27; Luke 23:32). This again
fulfilled prophecy: "He poured out his life unto death, and was
numbered with the transgressors" (Isaiah 53:12 NIV). Luke
records that one of the criminals insulted Jesus, while the other
turned to Jesus and said, "Jesus, remember me when you come
into your kingdom" (Luke 23:42 NIV). To which Jesus replied,
"Today you will be with me in paradise" (Luke 23:43 NIV).

**Pilate had a notice prepared and fastened to the cross. It
read: JESUS OF NAZARETH, THE KING OF THE JEWS.**NIV Pilate
wrote this notice in three languages so that anyone passing into
or out of the city would be able to read it. Pilate provided a tribute to Jesus' kingship with this trilingual placard that all the
world could read in Hebrew (or, Aramaic—the language of the
Jews), Latin (the Roman language, the official language), and
Greek (the *lingua franca,* the common tongue).

Probably bitter over his political defeat at the hands of the Jewish leaders, Pilate posted a sign over Jesus that was meant to be
ironic. The sight of a humiliated king, stripped of authority, fas-

tened naked to a cross in public execution could only lead to the conclusion of complete defeat. But the irony that Pilate hoped would not be lost on the Jews pales before the irony that God wanted to communicate to the world. The dying King was actually taking control of his kingdom. His death and resurrection would strike the death blow to Satan's rule and would establish Jesus' eternal authority over the earth. Few people reading the sign that bleak afternoon understood its real meaning, but the sign was absolutely true. Jesus was King of the Jews as well as the Gentiles, the universe, and you. This sign became a universal proclamation, an unconscious prophecy, that Jesus is the royal Messiah.

CRUCIFIXION
Both the Greeks and the Romans used crucifixion to execute victims and criminals. Alexander the Great crucified 2,000 prisoners of war at one time. For the Romans, it was a slave's punishment; it was not used against freeborn citizens. It was a death for the worst criminals and terrorists. Before the crucifixion, the prisoner was flogged; the blood loss hastened the death. The prisoner was then nailed to the crosspiece by the wrists and to the stake by the ankles. He died completely naked to complete the humiliation. The death was slow and painful; the person died of shock or suffocation when the lungs collapsed.

For Jesus to die this way was hideous; Deuteronomy 21:23 says that anyone who is hung on a tree is cursed. But Jesus' crucifixion was the path to his exaltation; he was "lifted up on the cross" and then exalted into glory for his ultimate act of sacrifice on our behalf.

The chief priests wanted Jesus' crime posted as a false claim to kingship, but no persuasion from the chief priests could induce Pilate to change his mind. He dismissed them by saying, **"What I have written, I have written."** Again, if this whole scenario weren't so tragic, it would be quite humorous to see Pilate's "last laugh" against the chief priests. Pilate had given in long enough; he was determined to have the final word.

19:23-24 When the soldiers had crucified Jesus, they took his clothes and divided them into four parts, one for each soldier.[NRSV] Contrary to the paintings depicting the Crucifixion, Jesus died naked, another horrible part of his humiliation. The Roman soldiers who performed the Crucifixion divided the victim's clothes among themselves. Clothing was not a cheap commodity in those days as it is today. Thus this was part of the "pay" the executioners received for performing their gruesome duties. But one part of Jesus' clothing was not divided. **The tunic was seamless, woven in one piece from the top.**NRSV The soldiers decided to cast lots (somewhat like rolling dice) for it. In so doing they fulfilled the Scripture: **"They divided My garments among them, and for My clothing they cast lots"**NKJV (quoted from Psalm 22:18).

TRAGIC FATE OR GOD'S PLAN
A miscarriage of justice, a jaded political figure, and now soldiers gambling over his torn clothing. On the surface it appeared that Jesus' life was as wasted as a treasure lost in a game of chance. Little did the Jews or Romans know that God's divine plan was being worked out. In this dark and terrible humiliating moment, God was completely in control. Out of the greatest evil people could commit, God brought immeasurable good. No matter how bleak our outlook may be or how terrible our circumstances, we must remember the results of our Lord's suffering. He suffered beyond anything we could ever endure, yet triumphed through it. His courage should motivate us and his power enable us to persevere.

19:25 **Near the cross of Jesus stood his mother, his mother's sister, Mary the wife of Clopas, and Mary Magdalene.**NIV The four women, in contrast to the four soldiers, are the faithful; they stayed with Jesus until the end. Even more so, in contrast to the disciples who had fled after Jesus was arrested, these women followed Jesus to the cross and became eyewitnesses of his crucifixion. The first woman mentioned is Jesus' mother (see 2:1ff.). Imagine her incredible grief, helplessly watching her son suffer and die unjustly. Indeed the prophet Simeon, who had spoken to her in the temple just after Jesus' birth, had been correct when he had told her, "A sword will pierce your own soul too" (Luke 2:35, NIV). Surely Mary was feeling that "sword" at that very moment.

The other women mentioned here have not appeared earlier in John's Gospel. Mary's sister could have been Salome (see Matthew 27:55ff.; Mark 15:40ff.), the mother of John (the Gospel writer) and James. If this is true, Jesus, John, and James were cousins. Mary the wife of Clopas was the mother of James the younger and of Joses. Mary Magdalene is mentioned here for the first time in this Gospel. She will be a prominent figure in the next chapter—for Jesus appears first to her after his resurrection.

19:26-27 **When Jesus saw his mother there, and the disciple whom he**

loved standing nearby, he said to his mother, "Dear woman, here is your son," and to the disciple, "Here is your mother." From that time on, this disciple took her into his home.**NIV** Seeing his mother and *the disciple whom he loved* (John, the Gospel writer), Jesus directed his disciple John to take care of Mary, his mother, in his absence. Mary had apparently been widowed and was being cared for by Jesus himself. Even while suffering in agony, Jesus demonstrated his care for his mother. Jesus' compassion for Mary teaches us to care for our aging parents. Jesus' brothers were not there; they had been sceptical of Jesus and had probably remained in Capernaum. So Jesus commissioned John to care for Mary. In Christ's greater family, the church, fellow believers may be more of a family to us than our blood relatives.

This was the third of the seven statements made by Jesus from the cross—the seven statements gleaned from all the Gospel accounts (where quoted, from the NIV):

1. He spoke to God of his executioners, asking that they be forgiven. (Luke 23:34, in some manuscripts)

2. He assured the penitent criminal crucified beside him that they would be together in paradise. (Luke 23:43)

3. He asked John to care for his mother, Mary. (recorded here, in John 19:26-27)

4 "My God, my God, why have you forsaken me?" (Matthew 27:46; Mark 15:34)

5. "I am thirsty." (John 19:28)

6. "It is finished." (John 19:30)

7. "Father, into your hands I commit my spirit." (Luke 23:46)

JESUS DIES ON THE CROSS / 19:28-37 / 236

19:28 After this, Jesus, knowing that all things were now accomplished, that the Scripture might be fulfilled, said, "I thirst!"NKJV As he had stated in 17:4, Jesus knew he had carried out the mission his Father had given him. His success was complete at the moment of his death. He was about to surrender his life to his Father who would carry out the crowning touch of the plan by raising the Son from the grave.

Some scholars believe this Scripture is Psalm 69:21, "They . . . gave me vinegar for my thirst" (NIV); thus, Jesus said, "I thirst." This emphasizes Jesus' humiliation. Others point to Psalm 42:2, "My soul thirsts for God, for the living God. When can I go and meet with God?" (NIV). This affirms Jesus' submission to the Father. In either case, scripture was fulfilled.

19:29 A jar full of sour wine was standing there. So they put a sponge full of the wine on a branch of hyssop and held it to his mouth.^{NRSV} This sour wine was not the same as the drugged wine offered to Jesus earlier ("wine mixed with myrrh," Mark 15:23 NIV). Jesus did not take the wine earlier because he wanted to be fully conscious through the entire process.

19:30 "It is finished"^{NRSV} According to the Greek, the one word, *tetelestai,* means "it is accomplished," "it is fulfilled," or even, "it is paid in full." Jesus' death accomplished redemption—"paid in full"; and his death fulfilled all the Old Testament prophecies. It was time for Jesus to die (see 4:34; 17:4). Up to this point, sin could be atoned through a complicated system of sacrifices. Sin separates people from God, and only through the sacrifice of an animal, a substitute, and faith in God's promise could people be forgiven and become clean before God. But people sin continually, so frequent sacrifices were required. Jesus, however, was the final and ultimate sacrifice for sin. With his death, the complex sacrificial system ended because Jesus took all sin upon himself. Now we can freely approach God because of what Jesus did for us. Those who believe in Jesus' sacrificial death and resurrection can live eternally with God and escape the penalty that comes from sin.

He bowed his head and gave up his spirit.^{NRSV} The language describes Jesus' voluntarily yielding his spirit to God. Luke records Jesus' last words from the cross: "Father, into your hands I commit my spirit" (Luke 23:46 NIV, echoing Psalm 31:5). Jesus' life was not taken from him; he gave his life of his own free will (see 10:11, 15, 17-18; 15:13). This shows Jesus' sovereignty over all—he was even in control of his death!

19:31-34 It was the day of Preparation, and the next day was to be a special Sabbath. . . . The Jews did not want the bodies left on the crosses during the Sabbath.^{NIV} The Jewish leaders were concerned that the dead bodies would remain on the crosses during the Sabbath. The Sabbath began on Friday evening—and this was a very *special Sabbath* because it coincided with the Passover festival. The Jews did not want to desecrate their Sabbath (Deuteronomy 21:22-23) by allowing the bodies of three crucified Jews to remain hanging on crosses overnight. Thus, **they asked Pilate to have the legs broken and the bodies taken down.**^{NIV} A person being crucified could use his legs to lift up his body in an attempt

to take more oxygen into his collapsing lungs. To break the legs
of one being crucified would, therefore, speed up the death.
Pilate agreed with the request.

However, when the soldiers **came to Jesus and saw that he
was already dead, they did not break his legs. Instead, one of
the soldiers pierced his side with a spear, and at once blood
and water came out.**NRSV This piercing would make sure that
Jesus was really dead. Medical experts have tried to determine
what was punctured to create a flow of blood and water. Some
think the pericardial sac was ruptured. John's testimony of this
occurrence was important to affirm a major argument in this Gospel against the Docetists who were denying Jesus' humanity.
Jesus was indeed a man composed of *blood and water.* He actually experienced death as a human being (see 1 John 5:6-7). The
mention of the blood and water also answers the argument by
some that Jesus did not really die but fell into some type of coma
from which he later awakened in the tomb. But the eyewitness
account of the blood and water refutes that. The piercing itself
would have killed Jesus, but he was already dead as the separation of blood and water reveal. Jesus did indeed die a human
death. In addition, the Roman soldiers, who had participated in
numerous crucifixions, reported to Pilate that Jesus was dead
(Mark 15:44-45). Questioning Jesus' death was one way that
people used to reject the news of his resurrection.

**19:35 The man who saw it has given testimony, and his testimony is
true. He knows that he tells the truth, and he testifies so that
you also may believe.**NIV The man who saw the Crucifixion and
witnessed the issue of blood and water is John the apostle (see
20:30-31 and 21:24-25). Luke's prologue (Luke 1:1-4) and
John's words demonstrate that the Gospel writers were writing
reliable history, not just a subjective description of what they felt
(see also 2 Peter 1:16-18).

Some question the identity of the witness as John, claiming
that he probably took Mary home before this time. They interpret
verse 27 ("From that time on") to mean immediate action. But
"taking someone into your home" is as much an expression of
acceptance as it is a description of someone moving their belong-
ings into a new house. The witness may have been a Roman soldier or someone else, but it is more likely that John himself heard
and saw these events.

**19:36-37 These things were done that the Scripture should be fulfilled,
"Not one of His bones shall be broken." . . . "They shall look
on Him whom they pierced."**NKJV Without knowing it, the sol-

diers fulfilled two biblical prophecies when they lanced Jesus instead of breaking his bones: (1) *Not one of his bones shall be broken.* Exodus 12:46 and Numbers 9:12 speak of the bones of the Passover lamb that are not to be broken. Because Jesus was the final sacrifice, these verses apply to him; and (2) *They shall look on Him whom they pierced.* This is from Zechariah 12:10; see also Revelation 1:7. The risen Christ bore this mark in his side (20:19ff.).

JESUS AND THE EXODUS EXPERIENCE
John shows the parallels between events in Exodus and the life of Jesus. God filled the wilderness experience of his people with illustrations of his eternal plan to save the world. The rescue of a people from captivity itself became a prophetic clue that God would offer a way of escape to the world through Jesus Christ. John indicated:

- As God temporarily took up residence in a tent among the people, Jesus is the living tabernacle of God. (John 1)
- As Moses lifted the serpent in the wilderness, Jesus is the perfect bronze serpent. (John 3)
- As God provided bread from heaven to feed the people, Jesus is the real manna. (John 6)
- As God provided water from the rock, Jesus is both source and substance of living water from the rock. (John 7)
- As God's presence was seen in the column of fire in the wilderness, Jesus is the Light of the World. (John 8)
- As God instituted the memorial of the sacrificed lamb and the blood of Passover, Jesus is the perfect Passover Lamb. (John 1:29; 18:28; 19:14, 36)

JESUS IS LAID IN THE TOMB / 19:38-42 / 237

Two secret disciples of Jesus came forward to take care of Jesus' burial. They both had feared persecution from the Jewish religious leaders, so they had not openly declared their faith in Jesus as the Messiah (see 12:42).

Secrecy and true belief are only temporary allies. Those who try to be permanent, secret disciples have no way of knowing if their faith is real. God will create moments along the way when even those who are secret disciples will have to declare themselves or be forced to admit that they are not disciples after all. In the case of Joseph and Nicodemus, late was certainly better than never!

19:38-42 The first man: **Joseph of Arimathea asked Pilate for the body of Jesus. Now Joseph was a disciple of Jesus, but secretly because**

he feared the Jews. With Pilate's permission, he came and took the body away.NIV Joseph was from Arimathea, a town not exactly pinpointed today but generally considered to have been about twenty miles northwest of Jerusalem. Matthew's Gospel says Joseph was "a rich man" (Matthew 27:57 NIV); Mark describes him as "a prominent member

> We fear men so much, because we fear God so little. One fear cures another. When man's terror scares you, turn your thoughts to the wrath of God.
> *William Gurnall*

of the council, who was himself waiting for the kingdom of God" (Mark 15:43 NIV); and Luke adds further that he was "a good and upright man, who had not consented to [the council's] decision and action" (Luke 23:50-51 NIV).

Joseph would not have been able to stop the council's planned murder of Jesus, but he did what he could afterwards by boldly going to Pilate to ask for Jesus' body so he could give it a proper burial. He had to ask for permission because the Romans usually left the bodies exposed without burial, both as a lesson to anyone passing by, and as a final humiliation for those executed. So Joseph went to ask Pilate, and Pilate agreed to let him take and bury the body.

The second man: **Nicodemus, who had at first come to Jesus by night, also came.**NRSV Jesus had talked at length with Nicodemus about being born again (3:1ff.), and Nicodemus had stood up for Jesus among the chief priests and Pharisees (7:50-52). Nicodemus joined Joseph in embalming and wrapping Jesus' body in regal style. **Nicodemus brought a mixture of myrrh and aloes, about seventy-five pounds.**NIV This was an extraordinarily large amount of embalming spices and must have been extremely expensive.

STANDING UP
Joseph and Nicodemus were secret believers, but after seeing the horrible treatment of Jesus, they decided that it had gone far enough and they were going to stand up, show their loyalty, and take care of Jesus' body for burial. Today, many treat the Bible and Jesus with similar horrible treatment. Now is the time for believers to step forward. Now is the time to come forward and testify to what God has done for you. Now is the time to join "that courageous and faithful band who are not afraid to stand up and be counted!"

Perhaps the action of Joseph and Nicodemus points to a lesson in teamwork. Both men were naturally cautious. Perhaps they had been chastised repeatedly for not openly rejecting Jesus. But when the moment for boldness came, they worked together. When we join with other believers we can often accomplish what we would not dare to try alone. Though Joseph and Nicodemus were probably each very much afraid, they nevertheless acted courageously. Obedience will often require us to act in spite of our fears.

Taking Jesus' body, the two of them wrapped it, with the spices, in strips of linen. This was in accordance with Jewish burial customs.NIV The *Jewish burial customs* did not include mummifying or embalming; instead, they washed the body, then wrapped it in a cloth soaked with aromatic oils and spices (thus the *myrrh and aloes* brought by Nicodemus).

At the place where Jesus was crucified, there was a garden, and in the garden a new tomb, in which no one had ever been laid.NIV According to Matthew 27:60, this was Joseph's own tomb that he gave up for Jesus (see also Luke 23:53). Such rock-hewn tombs were expensive. Even in burial, Jesus fulfilled prophecy: "He was assigned a grave with the wicked, and with the rich in his death . . ." (Isaiah 53:9, NIV). It was fortuitous that Joseph had a tomb nearby and that he wanted to put Jesus' body there; the burial had to happen quickly **because it was the Jewish day of Preparation,**NIV prior to the coming of the Sabbath.

CHANGES
The death of Jesus made a dramatic change in the lives of four people. The criminal, dying on the cross beside Jesus, asked Jesus to include him in his kingdom (Luke 23:39-43). The Roman centurion proclaimed that Jesus was the Son of God Mark 15:39). Joseph and Nicodemus, members of the Jewish council and secret followers of Jesus (John 7:50-51), came out of hiding. Each of these men were changed more by Jesus' death than by his life. As a result of realizing who Jesus was, they believed and put their faith into words and actions. When confronted with Jesus and his death we should also be changed—to believe, proclaim, and act.

John 20

The truth of Christianity rests heavily on the Resurrection. If Jesus rose from the grave, who saw him? How trustworthy were the witnesses? Those who claimed to have seen the risen Jesus went on to turn the world upside down. Most of them also died for being followers of Christ. People rarely die for halfhearted belief. Chapter 20 of John's Gospel contains the record of Jesus' resurrection and first appearances to his followers and John's personal discovery of the empty tomb. The four Gospels provide different accounts of Jesus' resurrection appearances. These appearances occurred over a forty-day period (Acts 1:3). See the chart below.

Matthew's Gospel records that after Jesus was buried by Joseph of Arimathea and Nicodemus, the chief priests and Pharisees again went to Pilate. This time they requested that the tomb be made secure. The religious leaders remembered Jesus' claims to rise again on the third day, so they wanted to make sure that no one could get into the tomb (or maybe that no one could get *out*). Because the tomb was hewn out of rock in the side of a hill, there was only one entrance. The tomb was sealed by stringing a cord across the stone that was rolled over the entrance. The cord had a clay seal at each end.

The religious leaders took a further precaution, asking that guards be placed at the tomb's entrance. Their explanation to Pilate: "His disciples may go and steal him away, and tell the people, 'He has been raised from the dead,' and the last deception would be worse than the first" (Matthew 27:64 NRSV). The religious leaders didn't know that at that moment the disciples were cowering in fear for their lives, not even thinking about the Resurrection. And such a sham would be unbelievable, for any thinking person would ask: "If Jesus rose again, where is he?" But the Pharisees were terrified of Jesus; and Pilate was still quaking in his Roman sandals from all that had occurred, so he agreed: "You have a guard of soldiers; go, make it as secure as you can" (Matthew 27:65 NRSV). But they did not understand that no rock, seal, or guard could prevent the Son of God from rising again.

20:1-2 **Early on the first day of the week, while it was still dark, Mary Magdalene went to the tomb.**[NIV] Mary Magdalene was one of several women who had followed Jesus to the cross, watched his crucifixion (19:25), and then remained to see where he was buried (Matthew 27:61). She, along with other women, was an early follower of Jesus who traveled with him and helped provide for the financial needs of the group: "The twelve were with [Jesus], as well as some women who had been cured of evil spirits and infirmities: Mary, called Magdalene, from whom seven demons had gone out . . . and many others, who provided for them out of their resources" (Luke 8:1-3, NRSV). Mary was obviously grateful to Jesus for freeing her from the torment of demon possession. She was from Magdala, a town near Capernaum in Galilee, and had followed Jesus to Jerusalem and, ultimately, to the foot of his cross and to his tomb.

> Christ the Lord is ris'n
> today, Alleluia!
> Sons of men and angels
> say: Alleluia!
> Raise your joys and
> triumphs high, Alleluia!
> Sing, ye heav'ns and
> earth reply, Alleluia!"
> *Charles Wesley*

Because of the short interim between Jesus' death and the coming of the Sabbath on Friday evening, the women who had stood by the cross had not had time to anoint Jesus. When the Sabbath arrived with the sunset on Friday, they had to go to their homes and rest. But after sundown on Saturday, the end of the Sabbath, they probably purchased and/or prepared the spices, then *early on the first day of the week,* (the day after the Sabbath, that is, Sunday), *Mary Magdalene* (also called Mary of Magdala in some versions) came to anoint the body of Jesus with certain spices. According to the other Gospel accounts, she was joined by Mary the mother of James, Salome (Matthew 28:1; Mark 16:1), and perhaps other women as well.

WHAT CAN YOU DO?
These women had followed Joseph to the tomb, and so they knew exactly where to find Jesus' body when they returned after the Sabbath with their spices and ointments. These women could not do great things for Jesus—they were not permitted to stand up before the Jewish council or the Roman governor and testify on his behalf—but they did what they could. They stayed at the cross when most of the disciples had fled, and they got ready to anoint their Lord's body. Because of their devotion, they were the first to know about the Resurrection. As believers, we may feel we can't do much for Jesus. But we are called to take advantage of the opportunities given us, doing what we *can* do and not worrying about what we cannot do.

Mark records that as the women were on their way to the tomb, they were saying to one another, "Who will roll away the stone for us from the entrance to the tomb?" (Mark 16:3 NRSV). But this would not be a problem, because as they approached they **saw that the stone had been removed from the entrance.**NIV John writes specifically from Mary Magdalene's perspective, as if she were the only one at the tomb. The other women were there, but in the following verses they are gone, for Mary Magdalene is the first person to see the resurrected Christ. At this point, however, the women arrived at the tomb and saw that the stone had been removed. They assumed that Jesus' body had been stolen. But the stone had been rolled away, not by grave robbers, and not so that Jesus could get out, but so they, and others, could get *in* and see that Jesus was gone.

ANGELS
The conception, birth, and resurrection of Jesus Christ are supernatural events beyond human logic or reasoning. Because of this, God sent angels to help certain people understand the significance of what was happening (see Matthew 2:13, 19; Luke 1:11, 26; 2:9; 24:4-7).

Angels are spiritual beings created by God who help carry out his work on earth. They bring God's messages to people (Luke 1:26ff.; 24:4-7), protect God's people (Daniel 6:22), offer encouragement (Genesis 16:7ff.), give guidance (Exodus 14:19), carry out punishment (2 Samuel 24:16), patrol the earth (Zechariah 1:9-14), and fight the forces of evil (2 Kings 6:16-18; Revelation 20:1-2). There are both good and bad angels (Revelation 12:7), but because bad angels are allied with the devil, or Satan, they have considerably less power and authority than good angels. Eventually the main role of angels will be to offer continuous praise to God (Revelation 7:11-12).

The other Gospel accounts record that angels spoke to the women. According to Mark's Gospel, as they went to the tomb, they wondered among themselves how they were going to get in. "When they looked up, they saw that the stone, which was very large, had already been rolled back. As they entered the tomb, they saw a young man, dressed in a white robe" (Mark 16:4-5 NRSV). Luke records two angels who, in no uncertain terms, questioned the women with a slight reprimand: "Why do you look for the living among the dead? He is not here, but has risen. Remember how he told you, while he was still in Galilee, that the Son of Man must be handed over to sinners, and be crucified, and on the third day rise again" (Luke 24:5-7 NRSV). Then the angels told the women to "go quickly and tell His disciples that He is risen from the dead" (Matthew 28:7 NKJV).

She ran and went to Simon Peter and the other disciple, the one whom Jesus loved, [that is, John the Gospel writer] **and said to them, "They have taken the Lord out of the tomb, and we do not know where they have laid him."**NRSV According to Luke's account, several women ran to tell the disciples: "Now it was Mary Magdalene, Joanna, Mary the mother of James, and the other women with them who told this to the apostles. But these words seemed to them an idle tale, and they did not believe them. But Peter got up and ran to the tomb; stooping and looking in, he saw the linen cloths by themselves; then he went home, amazed at what had happened" (Luke 24:10-12 NRSV). Peter was not alone when he dashed in amazement to the tomb; John adds his personal account (as "the other disciple") to his narrative.

20:3-5 Peter and the other disciple set out and went toward the tomb. . . . The other disciple outran Peter and reached the tomb first. He bent down to look in and saw the linen wrappings lying there, but he did not go in.NRSV Though John's youthful legs carried him more swiftly to the grave, once he was there he looked in, but he waited for Peter's arrival before entering the cave. Resurrection would not have been their first thought. None of the possible natural explanations for the missing body were of any comfort. If Jesus' body had been stolen or moved by the religious leaders, the disciples would have reason to worry about their own fate.

20:6-7 Then Simon Peter, who was behind him, arrived and went into the tomb. He saw the strips of linen lying there. . . . The cloth was folded up by itself, separate from the linen.NIV Close examination revealed that the graveclothes had been left as if Jesus had passed right through them. The headpiece was rolled up separately from the other wrappings that had enveloped Jesus' body. A grave robber couldn't possibly have made off with Jesus' body and left the linens as if they were still shaped around it. The neatness and order indicated that there was not a hasty removal of Jesus' body. Rather, Jesus arose and left the wrappings lying there, empty.

20:8-9 Finally the other disciple, who had reached the tomb first, also went inside. He saw and believed.NIV When John saw the empy tomb and the empty graveclothes, he instantly believed that Jesus must have risen from the dead. The text stresses the importance here of John "seeing and believing" to affirm the eyewitness account of an apostle. Most believers would not have this opportunity; they would have to base their faith on what the witnesses reported.

Though John believed that the graveclothes and open tomb indicated Jesus' resurrection, he **still did not understand from Scripture that Jesus had to rise from the dead**^{NIV} (see 2:22). John believed, but without complete understanding; that would come later and affirm his belief. The *Scripture* they would come to understand probably included Psalm 16:10 ("You will not abandon me to the grave, nor will you let your Holy One see decay," NIV) and Isaiah 53:11 ("After the suffering of his soul, he will see the light of life and be satisfied" NIV).

The disciples did not fabricate this story about the Resurrection; in fact, they were surprised that Jesus was not in the tomb. When John saw the graveclothes looking like an empty cocoon from which Jesus had emerged, he believed that Jesus had risen. It wasn't until after they had seen the empty tomb that they remembered what the Scriptures and Jesus had said—he would die, but he would also rise again!

John's account also demonstrates that the disciples couldn't have "invented" the Resurrection in order to fulfill the Old Testament prophecies because they did not immediately see any Old Testament connection. The *fact* of the Resurrection opened the disciples minds to see that God had foretold his plan through the prophets.

THE KEY
Why is Jesus' resurrection the key to the Christian faith?
- Jesus rose from the dead, just as he said. We can be confident, therefore, that Jesus will accomplish all he has promised.
- Jesus' bodily resurrection shows us that the living Christ, not a false prophet or impostor, is ruler of God's eternal kingdom.
- Because Jesus was resurrected, we can be certain of our own resurrection. Death is not the end—there is future life.
- The divine power that brought Jesus back to life is now available to us to bring our spiritually dead selves back to life.
  The Resurrection is the basis for the church's witness to the world.

20:10 Then the disciples went back to their homes.^{NIV} Perplexed, John and Peter left and went back home. They "believed" in something miraculous; that is, they did not fear that Jesus' body had been stolen, as Mary had, but they did not know for sure what they believed or what they should do next. So they just went home. Later they joined with the other disciples behind locked doors (see 20:19).

JESUS APPEARS TO MARY MAGDALENE / 20:11-18 / **240**

We see Jesus' humility in his resurrection as well as in his crucifixion. Jesus did not rise and then march into the temple to confront the religious leaders or Caiaphas; he did not dash to the Praetorium to say to Pilate, "I told you so"; he did not go stand in the center of Jerusalem to impress the crowd. Instead, Jesus revealed himself only to believers. The first person to see him was a woman who had been healed and forgiven and who tearfully stayed at the cross and followed his body to the tomb.

As Jesus demonstrated throughout his life, he responded to those who waited attentively and faithfully. Jesus dissolved the perplexities of the disciples. He dried their tears. He dispelled their doubts. Jesus knows how similar we are to his original disciples, and he does not overpower us either. Even though our faithfulness wavers, Jesus faithfully stays with us.

JESUS' APPEARANCES AFTER HIS RESURRECTION

1. Mary Magdalene	*Mark 16:9-11; John 20:10-18*
2. The other women at the tomb	*Matthew 28:8-10*
3. Peter in Jerusalem	*Luke 24:34; 1 Corinthians 15:5*
4. The two travelers on the road	*Mark 16:12-13; Luke 24:13-35*
5. Ten disciples behind closed doors	*Mark 16:14; Luke 24:36-43; John 20:19-25*
6. All eleven disciples (including Thomas)	*John 20:26-31; 1 Corinthians 15:5*
7. Seven disciples while fishing on the Sea of Galilee	*John 21:1-14*
8. Eleven disciples on a mountain in Galilee	*Matthew 28:16-20; Mark 16:15-18*
9. A crowd of 500	*1 Corinthians 15:6*
10. Jesus' brother James	*1 Corinthians 15:7*
11. Those who watched Jesus ascend into heaven	*Mark 16:19-20; Luke 24:44-49; Acts 1:3-8*

20:11-12 Mary stood outside the tomb crying.^{NIV} Mary apparently followed Peter and John back to the tomb. When the two disciples left, she was there alone, still crying, still hoping that somehow she could discover where Jesus' body had been taken, but fearing the worst.

As she wept, she bent over to look into the tomb and saw two angels in white.^{NIV} The angels actually looked like humans—not beings with halos and wings. The angels had appeared to the women and then sent them to spread the good news that Jesus was alive (Matthew 28:1-7; Mark 16:1-7; Luke 24:1-12), but apparently they were not in the tomb when Peter and John arrived. Yet they are here again to speak to Mary.

20:13 They asked her, "Woman, why are you crying?"^{NIV} Under normal circumstances this would seem to be an odd question. People might be expected to be crying beside the tomb of a loved one, and even more so if one thought the tomb had been desecrated and the body stolen. However, the angels knew the incredible *joy* of the empty tomb. They also knew that if these people had listened to Jesus' words about his resurrection while he was alive, they would not be sad and confused; instead, they would be leaping for joy. So the angels' question was not odd, but obvious. It was not meant as a rebuke, but as a reminder of heaven's perspective.

Every tragedy provides us with an opportunity to see Jesus in a new way. As we experience sorrow, we can recall Christ's suffering for us. Our pain is a result of living in a fallen world; his pain was the result of his love for us who inhabit this sinful world. Our pain is deserved, or at least unavoidable; his pain was freely chosen. Our pain reminds us that beyond it lies all the blessing that Christ provided for us by his pain. Because Jesus died, we can be forgiven. Because he lives, we too shall live! Christ's resurrection gives us hope for a future restoration with loved ones and the gift of new bodies in the heavenly kingdom.

Mary simply answered the angels' question, **"Because they have taken away my Lord, and I do not know where they have laid Him."**^{NKJV}

20:14-15 At this, she turned around and saw Jesus standing there, but she did not realize that it was Jesus.^{NIV} Something caused Mary to turn around, probably a feeling that a person had come up behind her. And indeed, next to the tomb stood Jesus, but Mary didn't recognize him. Perhaps this was the same kind of blindness that afflicted the two who walked with the risen Jesus on the road to Emmaus (see Luke 24:15-16). Or perhaps Mary's eyes

were so full of tears and her grief so intense that she literally
could not see who was standing there.

"Woman," he said, "why are you crying? Who is it you are looking for?"NIV Jesus repeated the angels' question and added an
additional question, asking Mary to specify her request.
Thinking he was the gardener, she said, "Sir, if you have carried
him away, tell me where you have put him, and I will get him."NIV
Mary imagined that this man was the gardener. She was trying to
grasp what might have happened to Jesus' body. The shock of
having the grave disturbed must have been devastating.

20:16-17 **Jesus said to her, "Mary!" She turned and said to him in
Hebrew, "Rabbouni!" (which means Teacher).**NRSV Mary had
been looking for the body of her dead Lord; suddenly, to her
amazement, she stood face to face with her living Lord. Mary
didn't recognize Jesus at first. Her grief had blinded her, and she
couldn't see him because she didn't expect to see him. Then
Jesus spoke her name, and immediately she recognized him. A
gardener would not have known her name. Imagine the love that
flooded Mary's heart when she heard her Savior saying her name!

JESUS KNOWS YOUR NAME
Your heart may be filled with grief and despair, but Jesus knows
your name. Suffering does not mean that you have been forgotten! Jesus knows every tear and every trial you face. In sorrow,
he seeks you out by his comforting Holy Spirit, to minister to you.

Mary's immediate response was to touch Jesus and cling to
him. But Jesus stopped her: **"Do not hold on to me,"**NRSV which
could also be translated, "Stop clinging to me." Perhaps Mary
wanted to hold Jesus and not lose him again. She had not yet
understood the Resurrection. Perhaps she thought this *was* his
promised Second Coming (14:3). Though Mary's title of
"teacher" was endearing, Jesus did not want to be detained at the
tomb. He was not to remain on this earth in physical form. If he
did not ascend to heaven, the Holy Spirit could not come. Both
he and Mary had important work to do.

**"But go to my brothers and say to them, 'I am ascending to
my Father and your Father, to my God and your God.'"**NRSV
Prior to his death, Jesus had called the disciples his "friends"
(15:15). But here, because of the Resurrection, Jesus' disciples
had become his *brothers* (see also Matthew 28:10). Christ's resurrection creates this new level of relationship because it provides

for the regeneration of every believer (see 1 Peter 1:3). After his resurrection, Jesus called his disciples "my brothers" (see Hebrews 2:11-14). After Jesus ascended to his Father, he would come to his disciples and give them this new life and relationship by breathing into them the Holy Spirit. Thus, for the first time in the Gospel, it is made clear that Jesus' Father is *our* Father, that Jesus' God is *our* God. The death and resurrection of Jesus ushered in a new relationship between believers and God.

20:18 Mary Magdalene went to the disciples with the news: "I have seen the Lord!"[NIV] Thus, Mary was the first person to see the risen Christ.

THE TOMB IS EMPTY
Mary did not meet the risen Christ until she had discovered the empty tomb. She responded with joy and obedience by going to tell the disciples. We cannot meet Christ until we discover that he is indeed alive, that his tomb is empty. Are you filled with joy by this good news? How can you share it with others?

And she told them that he had said these things to her.[NIV] Jesus' words should have been a great comfort to the disciples. Despite their deserting him in the Garden, he was calling them his "brothers" and explaining that his Father was theirs, his God was theirs. But this report was no more believed by the disciples than the women's report of the angels' words (see Luke 24:10-11). "She went and told those who had been with him and who were mourning and weeping. When they heard that Jesus was alive and that she had seen him, they did not believe it" (Mark 16:10-11 NIV). The disciples were still hiding behind locked doors, for fear of the Jews.

HE AROSE!
People who hear about the Resurrection for the first time may need time before they can comprehend this amazing story. Like Mary and the disciples, they may pass through four stages of belief. (1) At first, they may think the story is a fabrication, impossible to believe (20:2). (2) Next, like Peter, they may check out the facts and still be puzzled about what happened (20:6). (3) Only when they encounter Jesus personally will they be able to accept the fact of the Resurrection (20:16). (4) Then, as they commit themselves to the risen Lord and devote their lives to serving him, they begin to understand fully the reality of his presence with them (20:28).

At this point, Matthew records the humorous anecdote about the religious leaders and the guards, who had obviously been unable to stop this "deception" that they had so much feared (Matthew 27:62-66). Matthew alone records that the guards were present at the tomb but "became like dead men" at the appearance of the angels (Matthew 28:4 NRSV). So picture them hightailing it to the chief priests—breathlessly telling the story of an angel descending, an earthquake, and the tomb opening—and then not being able to remember anything else! Notice that they did not go to Pilate, for to do so might have meant their lives. Roman soldiers who let a prisoner escape (even a dead one) would often pay for their negligence with their lives.

The religious leaders dealt with the soldiers as they had with Judas—with money. They gave the frightened men a large sum of money and told them to forget whatever they saw: "You must say, 'His disciples came by night and stole him away while we were asleep.' If this comes to the governor's ears, we will satisfy him and keep you out of trouble" (Matthew 28:13-14 NRSV). These soldiers "took the money and did as they were directed. And this story is still told among the Jews to this day" (Matthew 28:15 NRSV).

Meanwhile, a very alive Jesus was making himself known to his beloved followers: the women (Matthew 28:8-10), Peter (Luke 24:34), and two travelers on the road to Emmaus (Mark 16:12-13; Luke 24:13-35). Then he went to see his disciples.

JESUS APPEARS TO THE DISCIPLES BEHIND LOCKED DOORS / 20:19-23 / *244*

Mary's announcement (20:18) must have stunned the disciples. Later the news that the Lord was alive came from two travelers who had unknowingly spent the day walking to Emmaus with Jesus (Luke 24:15-16). Confused, elated, doubtful, and fearful, the disciples stayed close together, hoping to endure the waiting in one place. They were huddled behind locked doors when Jesus appeared to all of them.

There is no real safe place in the world without Jesus, but his presence makes the most dangerous places bearable. When Jesus appeared to his disciples on this occasion he left them five gifts: (1) his own presence; (2) his peace (20:19, 21); (3) a mission: "I am sending you"; (4) a companion—the Holy Spirit; and (5) a message of forgiveness.

20:19 On the evening of that first day of the week, when the disciples were together, with the doors locked for fear of the Jews,

Jesus came and stood among them.[NIV] The disciples were still perplexed and apparently had gotten together that night behind bolted doors. They probably were discussing the women's reported sighting of angels, what Peter and John saw at the tomb, and Mary's astounding claim that she had seen Jesus. At some point during the day, Jesus had appeared to Peter (Luke 24:34), and the women had reported the angel's words that the disciples were to go to Galilee and meet Jesus there (Matthew 28:7). But for some reason, they did not go; instead they stayed in Jerusalem, hiding from the Jewish leaders. Before long, however, their confusion would be dispelled.

The first news arrived in the night with the sounds of excited knocking on the door. Two disciples were allowed in, breathlessly telling the rest of the group that they had met Jesus on the road to Emmaus and had talked with him most of the day (Luke 24:13-35). The variety of reports must have had an effect. Shock and disbelief began to be replaced with wild hope. Luke recounts that this was when Jesus made his first appearance to his gathered disciples (although we find out later that Thomas was missing from the group). This appearance is astounding because Jesus *came and stood among them,* somehow appearing to them in a locked room. Jesus could do this because his resurrection and subsequent glorification had altered his bodily form. In this new spiritual form, he was able to transcend all physical barriers.

 DON'T HIDE . . . SEEK!
Though the Resurrection had occurred, the disciples were hiding out! The happy news had not driven their doubts away. But we are like them when we lock ourselves behind closed doors:
- Doors of isolation—If we never make friends with non-Christians or interact with the world, we deny God's power to change lives. Hiding in church, or refusing to make contact with anyone suspected to be a nonbeliever, limits Christ's work. The truth does not have to hide or isolate itself.
- Doors of anonymity—If we relate to those around us but never tell them that we are Christians, we deprive them of discovering what God has done in our lives.
- Doors of superficiality—If we only talk of sports and weather and keep to safe subjects with people around us, we cooperate with the world's intention to ignore God and any subject that might lead someone to seriously consider God's perspective.

Christ can make his presence known behind closed doors, but he will not unlock them for us. Unless we step out of our hiding places, we will never see all that Christ can do through us.

"Peace be with you."^{NKJV} This was a standard Hebrew greeting, but here it was filled with deeper meaning (see 14:27; 16:33). Jesus would repeat these words in verse 21.

20:20 He showed them his hands and side. The disciples were overjoyed when they saw the Lord.^{NIV} Due to Jesus' sudden, miraculous appearance among them, the disciples "were startled and frightened, thinking they saw a ghost" (Luke 24:37 NIV). Jesus needed to convince them that he, including his touchable physical body, was present with them. When they realized who he was, they rejoiced. Jesus had said, "In a little while you will see me no more, and then after a little while you will see me. . . . You will grieve, but your grief will turn to joy" (16:16, 20, NIV). The "little while" was over, joy had replaced grief, and "no one will take away your joy" (16:22, NIV).

20:21-23 Jesus said to them again, "Peace be with you. As the Father has sent me, so I send you."^{NRSV} Jesus gave his peace to them and then commissioned them to be his representatives, even as he had been the Father's (see 17:18). Jesus again identified himself with his Father. He told the disciples by whose authority he did his work. Then he gave the task to his disciples of spreading the gospel message around the world. They were sent with authority from God to preach, teach, and do miracles (see Matthew 28:16-20; Luke 24:47-49)—in essence, to continue across the world what Jesus had begun in Palestine. Whatever God has asked you to do, remember: (1) Your authority comes from God, and (2) Jesus has demonstrated by words and actions how to accomplish the job he has given you. As the Father sent his Son, Jesus sends his followers . . . and you. Your response is to determine from day to day those to whom the Father has sent you.

When He had said this, He breathed on them, and said to them, "Receive the Holy Spirit."^{NKJV} Before the disciples could carry out this commission, however, they needed the power of the Holy Spirit. And Jesus gave them this power by breathing into them the Holy Spirit. It could be said that this verse consummates the Gospel of John because the Spirit who had been promised (7:37-39; 14:16-20, 26; 15:26; and 16:7-15) at last was given to the disciples.

This act reminds us of what God did to make the first man come alive—he breathed into him and he became a living soul (Genesis 2:7). There is life in the breath of God. Man was created but did not come alive until God had breathed into him the breath of life (Genesis 2:7). God's first breath made man different from all other forms of creation. Here, through the breath of Jesus,

God imparted eternal, spiritual life. With this breathing came the power to do God's will on earth.

If you forgive the sins of any, they are forgiven them; if you retain the sins of any, they are retained[NRSV] Jesus gave the disciples their Spirit-powered and Spirit-guided mission—to preach the Good News about him so that people's sins might be forgiven. The disciples did not have the power to forgive sins (only God can forgive sins), but Jesus gave them the privilege of telling new believers that their sins have been forgiven because they have accepted Jesus' message. All believers have this same privilege. We can announce the forgiveness of sin with certainty when we ourselves repent and believe. Those who don't believe will not experience the forgiveness of sins; their sins will be retained (i.e., not forgiven).

JESUS APPEARS TO THE DISCIPLES INCLUDING THOMAS / 20:24-31 / **245**

Thomas was not with the other disciples for Jesus' first visit in 20:21-23. Consistent with his character elsewhere in the Gospel (see 14:5), Thomas was skeptical toward his friends' report about seeing Jesus. He epitomized hardheaded realism by insisting that seeing and touching Jesus for himself would be the only proof that would satisfy him. When Jesus did appear to him, Thomas realized the inappropriateness of his demand.

A week after the first appearance of Jesus, Thomas was with the other disciples, but they had no particular reason to believe that Jesus was coming to them again. But Jesus did visit and, it seems, specifically for Thomas's sake. His words to Thomas about believing without tangible proof also speak directly to us.

> It is the office of faith to believe what we do not see, and it shall be the reward of faith to see what we do believe.
> *Thomas Adams*

Jesus made it clear that our faith must be based on the testimony of those who were with him. Insisting on seeing and touching Christ ourselves would indicate a reluctance to believe. We have no right to require God to prove himself; but he has every right as our Creator to expect our belief and obedience. The fact that God blesses those who believe is simply an added gift of his grace.

John concludes this section with a summary of his reason for writing. After quoting Jesus' words to Thomas about the importance of acting on the witness that has been given to us, John reminds his audience that the very words that they are reading are proof enough to believe in Jesus. Have you submitted in faith to the truth about Jesus that you have been told?

20:24 But Thomas . . . was not with them when Jesus came.^{NRSV} When the disciples told Thomas that Jesus had appeared to them, he did not believe. Sometimes people overemphasize the doubtful part of Thomas's character. John 11:16 reveals Thomas as tough-minded and committed, even if he tended to be pessimistic. And Matthew points out (Matthew 28:17) that all the disciples shared Thomas's skepticism. It was part of his character to put the group's feeling into words. None of the other disciples believed until they saw Christ face-to-face.

20:25 "Unless I see the nail marks in his hands and put my finger where the nails were, and put my hand into his side, I will not believe it."^{NIV} Thomas insisted that he see the Jesus who had been crucified. He wanted bodily proof—to see and touch the nail scars in his hands and the scar of the lance thrust into his side.

20:26-28 After eight days^{NKJV} Thomas got his chance. This time he was present when Jesus appeared. The disciples were still behind locked doors when Jesus appeared among them as he had before and gave the same greeting, **"Peace be with you!"**^{NIV} But this time he spoke directly to Thomas, supernaturally knowing of Thomas's doubt and what he needed in order to be convinced.

Then he said to Thomas, "Put your finger here; see my hands. Reach out your hand and put it into my side. Stop doubting and believe."^{NIV} Jesus' resurrected body was unique. It was not the same kind of flesh and blood Lazarus had when he came back to life. Jesus' body was no longer subject to the same laws of nature as before his death. He could appear in a locked room; yet he was not a ghost or apparition because he could be touched and could eat. Jesus' resurrection was *literal* and *physical*—he was not a disembodied spirit.

> I long to understand in some degree thy truth, which my heart believes and loves. For I do not seek to understand that I may believe, but I believe in order to understand. For this also I believe, that unless I believed, I should not understand.
> *Anselm*

When he saw Jesus, doubting Thomas became believing Thomas. His response rings through the ages as the response of many doubters who finally see the truth, **"My Lord and my God!"** This clear affirmation of Jesus' deity provides a good conclusion to John's Gospel, which continually affirms Jesus' deity (see 1:1, 18; 8:58; 10:30).

YOU CAN TOUCH JESUS
Have you ever wished you could actually see Jesus, touch him, and hear his words? Are there times you want to sit down with him and get his advice? Thomas wanted Jesus' physical presence. But God's plan is wiser. He has not limited himself to one physical body; he wants to be present with you at all times. Even now he is with you in the form of the Holy Spirit. You can talk to him, and you can find his words to you in the pages of the Bible. He can be as real to you as he was to Thomas.

20:29-31 "Because you have seen me, you have believed; blessed are those who have not seen and yet have believed."[NIV] Though Thomas proclaimed Jesus to be his Lord and God, Jesus reproved Thomas because he had to see before he could believe. The blessed ones are they who have not seen and yet have believed. Some people think they would believe in Jesus if they could see a definite sign or miracle. But Jesus says we are blessed if we can believe without seeing. We have all the proof we need in the words of the Bible and the testimony of believers.

DOUBTING DOS AND DON'TS
Jesus wasn't hard on Thomas for his doubts. Despite his skepticism, Thomas was still loyal to the believers and to Jesus himself. Some people need to doubt before they believe. If doubt leads to questions, questions lead to answers, and the answers are accepted, then doubt has done good work. It is when doubt becomes stubbornness and stubbornness becomes a life-style that doubt harms faith. When you doubt, don't stop there. Let your doubt deepen your faith as you continue to search for the answer.

In the last two verses of the chapter, John explains why he wrote this Gospel: **Jesus did many other signs in the presence of His disciples, which are not written in this book; but these are written that you may believe that Jesus is the Christ, the Son of God, and that believing you may have life in His name.**[NKJV] John wrote this Gospel to encourage belief in Jesus as the Christ and as the Son of God. All the *signs* in this Gospel point to Jesus as being the Christ and God's Son, who came to give life to all those who believe. Most likely, John wrote this Gospel to encourage those who already believed to continue in their faith. We who believe are encouraged to read and reread John in order to continue in our belief. And this Gospel has also been used far beyond that as a powerful tool for evangelism, bringing people to faith in Christ.

To understand the life and mission of Jesus more fully, all we need to do is study the Gospels. John tells us that his Gospel records only a few of the many events in Jesus' life on earth. But the Gospels include everything we need to know to believe that Jesus is the Christ, the Son of God, through whom we receive eternal life.

John 21

Chapter 21 is an epilogue to John's narrative. Very likely, John
decided to add this chapter some time after he completed his Gospel in order to clarify the misconception about the relationship between his (John's) death and the Lord's return. The rumor that
John would not die before the Lord's return (21:23) had to be corrected, otherwise the church might experience great trouble at his
death before the Lord's return. John, therefore, decided to add a
chapter that would make it clear that Jesus did *not* say that he
would return before John died.

John also used this chapter to show Peter's restoration after
having denied the Lord three times. In none of the post-Resurrec-
tion appearances recorded in chapter 20 had John mentioned any
kind of special attention given to Peter by Jesus. Both Luke and
Paul mention that the Lord made a special appearance to Peter
(Luke 24:34; 1 Corinthians 15:5), but there is no record of what
transpired. This chapter clearly depicts Jesus restoring Peter to be
an effective leader in the church. Furthermore, John used this epilogue to show that Peter's death (by crucifixion) had been foretold by Jesus. At the time John wrote his Gospel and the epilogue
(A.D. 85–90), Peter had been dead twenty years (A.D. 67).

**21:1 Afterward Jesus appeared again to his disciples, by the Sea of
Tiberias.**^{NIV} This chapter records Jesus' appearance to the disciples beside the Sea of Tiberias (another name for the Sea of Galilee). Jesus had made at least six appearances in (or around)
Jerusalem (see the chart in chapter 20). After the Jerusalem
appearances, the disciples evidently had returned to Galilee.
Jesus made several appearances in this region: to five hundred
believers (1 Corinthians 15:6); to James, his brother (1 Corinthians 15:7); to the seven disciples who went fishing on the Sea of
Tiberias, including a personal conversation with Peter (recorded
here in John). So Jesus first appeared to them in Jerusalem and
then in Galilee. According to John's account, Jesus' appearance
to the seven disciples by the Sea of Galilee was his third appear-

ance to the disciples (see 21:14). He had appeared to them twice in Jerusalem (20:19, 26).

Prior to his resurrection, the Lord had told his disciples that he would meet them at an appointed place in Galilee after he arose (Matthew 28:10; Mark 14:28). But due to the disciples' unbelief and fear, they had remained in Jerusalem. Consider what the disciples had experienced over the last few weeks: the Triumphal Entry into Jerusalem of their beloved Jesus and their high hopes for high places in Christ's kingdom; a supper with Jesus that proved to be his last—a supper filled with mysterious actions and words, and the sudden departure of a trusted friend, one of their own; surprise in Gethsemane by several hundred men with torches and weapons who had come to arrest everyone, and the disciples had turned tail and run; Jesus going with the authorities without a fight; Peter, their leader, denying three times that he was a disciple of Jesus; Jesus, their supposed leader and King, crucified on a cross like a common criminal, then buried in a borrowed tomb; then an incredible resurrection with Jesus appearing to them and saying more mysterious words. What were they supposed to do now? They did as they were told and returned to Galilee. But as they waited there, they remained unsure, confused. So they did what they knew how to do best—they went fishing.

21:2 Seven disciples were together at this time:

1. **Simon Peter** (mentioned first because he was the leader)

2. **Thomas** (mentioned specifically at the end of chapter 20)

3. **Nathanael** (first introduced in chapter 1 and not mentioned again until now)

4. and 5. **The sons of Zebedee** (John, the author, and James)

6. and 7. **Two other disciples** (unnamed).

21:3 Simon Peter said to them, "I am going fishing." They said to him, "We will go with you."NRSV Having returned to Galilee, the disciples did not know what to do next, so it was natural for some of them to return to their occupation. Simon, Andrew, and James and John (the sons of Zebedee) had been fishermen (see Mark 1:16-20). Peter took the lead, and the other six disciples went with him.

They went out and got into the boat, but that night they caught nothing.NRSV These disciples had gone back to their occupation, only to completely fail at that too, so it seems. Although fishing was often good during the night while the fish were active and feeding closer to the surface, the disciples' nets were empty. When daybreak arrived, they were tired, hungry, and probably more than a little frustrated. It did not help that a voice called to them from the beach.

EMPTY NETS
Jesus never criticized the disciples for going fishing. Whatever their motives, fishing was a familiar activity that gave them a sense of normalcy and comfort. It gave them something to do and time to sort out their thoughts. But their efforts yielded nothing. Many times our efforts at work, parenting, or ministry leave us with only "empty nets." The Lord allows us to experience lack of productivity, frustrations, and failure to bring us closer to him and to help us rely on him, not on our own resourcefulness. When you feel tired and empty, listen for Jesus' words to you.

21:4 Just after daybreak, Jesus stood on the beach; but the disciples did not know that it was Jesus.^{NRSV} Jesus had come to make another appearance to the disciples, especially to Peter. Perhaps because of the distance, haze over the water, or lack of light this early in the morning, the men in the boat did not recognize the man on the shore.

SURPRISED BY JESUS
Once again the disciples failed to recognize Jesus. This time the poor light gave them a good reason not to realize who he was. Perhaps they were preoccupied with fishing; surely they weren't expecting him; maybe they were avoiding the issue of what to do next. Are you involved in some area or activity where you think a visit from Christ would be unlikely? Guard against being so preoccupied with your own work that you miss seeing Christ. Expect that he can do the miraculous in ordinary events. Look for him throughout each day.

21:5-6 Jesus called out to the disciples, asking about their catch (they were only about a hundred yards out, see 21:8), only to receive the answer that they had caught nothing. **He said to them, "Cast the net to the right side of the boat, and you will find some." So they cast it, and now they were not able to haul it in because there were so many fish.**^{NRSV} The disciples, tired as they were, responded to the obvious authority in the voice, and cast their nets to starboard—and a miracle occurred! This recalls Luke 5:1-11, another occasion where Peter and the other disciples were fishing on the sea, catching nothing. Jesus gave a command to go out into the deep water. Peter, though doubtful, followed Jesus' orders. When they obeyed, a miracle occurred! When Peter saw the first miracle, "he fell down at Jesus' knees, saying, 'Go away from me, Lord, for I am a sinful man!'" (Luke 5:8 NRSV). He recognized beyond Jesus' power a holiness that was not part of his own life.

On this occasion, Peter is again a central character. Jesus identified himself by his unexpected and seemingly useless request. The fishermen's actions involved them in another miracle. If the request did not give them a clue, the results unmistakably pointed to the power of their Lord. Both John and Peter recognized that Jesus was behind the overwhelming catch of fish.

Though he must have been ashamed of his sinfulness (the recent denial of Jesus was still fresh in his mind), Peter rushed to be with Jesus. A little later Jesus had some special words for him.

21:7 Therefore that disciple whom Jesus loved said to Peter, "It is the Lord!"NKJV John may have immediately recognized the repeated miracle, for he was part of the incident recorded in Luke 5 (see Luke 5:10). As John peered through the morning mist, his sensitive and thoughtful nature revealed to him that the man on the shore was Jesus.

Now when Simon Peter heard that it was the Lord, he put on his outer garment (for he had removed it), and plunged into the sea.NKJV Peter's impulsive nature came through in this sentence. Peter had always been the one to act, speak, react—whether in climbing out of the boat to walk on the water to Jesus (Matthew 14:28-31), offering to build shelters on the Mount of Transfiguration (Mark 9:5-6), refusing to let Jesus wash his feet (13:8-9), striking out with a sword at those who had come to arrest Jesus (18:10), or denying his Lord (18:26-27). Here he jumped into the lake to swim to Jesus. Though his love for Jesus was very great, Peter may have thought a barrier still existed between the Lord and him because of his denial.

Peter was beginning to think twice before speaking. John had to say what they must have all immediately suspected. Once he knew that he wasn't imagining Jesus presence, Peter leaped out of the boat and swam for shore. Impulsiveness is deeply ingrained.

21:8-9 The other disciples followed in the boat, towing the net full of fish, for they were not far from shore. . . . When they landed, they saw a fire of burning coals there with fish on it, and some bread.NIV We can only guess what Peter did when he came out of the water, dripping wet, facing the one he had denied. He may have been at a loss for words. No doubt Peter appreciated the fire that Jesus had burning; there he dried off while he felt the inward chill of remembering what he had done the last time he had stood by a fire warming himself. If any words were said, they were kept between Jesus and Peter, since the others were still too far away to hear.

What a welcome pleasure for the senses to find a warm fire, a hot meal, and the greatest friend of all waiting for them after a frustrating night and an exhausting conclusion to their fishing expedition.

DISCOURAGED WORKERS
Tired, hungry, and frustrated, these discouraged disciples needed a lift. They lacked direction and they were uncertain of the Lord's presence and help. Jesus came to them, made his presence known, and gave them direction. Are you discouraged in your work for the Lord? Jesus is prepared for you; he has a gracious welcome waiting. He offered the disciples a warm fire and breakfast. He also wants to give you sustenance, comfort, and fellowship.

21:10-11 Jesus said to them, "Bring some of the fish that you have just caught. So Simon Peter went aboard and hauled the net ashore, full of large fish, a hundred fifty-three of them; and though there were so many, the net was not torn.NRSV The miraculous catch of fish must have affected Peter profoundly. Peter did not say a word as he dragged the heavy net full of 153 large fish to shore and then, with the other disciples ate the breakfast of bread and fish the Lord had prepared even before they caught the fish.

The amount of fish probably has no other significance than that it was a very large amount of large fish after having caught nothing all night. And the exact number is recorded simply as a matter of historical fact. It was the usual procedure for a group of fishermen to count the day's catch and then divide it among themselves. Once again, John observed that when Christ takes action, the results bring overabundance.

21:12 None of the disciples dared ask him, "Who are you?" They knew it was the Lord.NIV Any question or any comment seemed trite at that moment. They stood around in awed silence before this one who, as always, was doing the serving.

JESUS KNOWS
The fact that the net was not torn attested not only to the miracle, but to the attention of the miracle worker. Jesus would supply their catch of fish and would take care that their nets were not torn. Such attention to detail is characteristic of the Holy Spirit's work in circumstances in every believer's life—from these disciples who would soon begin to carry out the great commission, to us, today, as we struggle through the confusion in our daily lives.

21:13 Jesus then came and took the bread and gave it to them, and likewise the fish.^{NKJV} This special meal with the risen Jesus had a profound effect on these seven disciples. Peter would later make claim to his reliability as a witness of Jesus by saying, "He was not seen by all the people, but by witnesses whom God had already chosen—by us who ate and drank with him after he rose from the dead" (Acts 10:41 NIV). John does not record that Jesus ate anything, but Luke 24:41-43 describes an appearance of Jesus where he did eat some fish.

21:14 This was now the third time Jesus appeared to his disciples after he was raised from the dead.^{NIV} Jesus had come to them to encourage these disciples, especially Peter, concerning their future work. The text seems to imply that Jesus had come to remind them that they were not to return to their old life of fishing. He had called them to be fishers of people (Luke 5:10) and to start the church (Matthew 16:19). Peter, the leader among them, needed to be ready for the responsibilities he soon would assume. He would lead and feed the flock—not with physical food (which Jesus would provide) but with spiritual food.

JESUS TALKS WITH PETER / 21:15-25 / *247*

After the meal, Jesus and Peter had a talk. During their conversation, Jesus led Peter through an experience that would remove the cloud of guilt that came from Peter's denial. The Master-Teacher conveyed both forgiveness and usefulness to this disciple who must have concluded he was beyond being useful to Jesus.

Peter had disowned Jesus three times. Three times Jesus asked Peter if he loved him. When Peter answered yes, Jesus told him to feed his sheep. It is one thing to say you love Jesus, but the real test requires actually doing it. Peter had repented, and here Jesus was asking him to commit his life. Peter's life changed when he finally realized who Jesus was. His occupation changed from fisherman to evangelist; his identity changed from impetuous to rock solid; and his relationship to Jesus changed—from one who had denied him to one who was forgiven. And Peter finally understood the significance of Jesus' words about his death and resurrection.

John closed his Gospel with a second summary statement. The earlier one (20:30-31) focused on the reason for the book; this one highlights John's awareness that all he had written about Jesus was only a glimpse of what Jesus had said and done.

21:15-17 When they had finished breakfast, Jesus said to Simon Peter, "Simon son of John, do you love me more than these?"[NRSV] *Simon son of John* was the name Jesus had said when he first met this man who would become his disciple: "'You are Simon son of John. You are to be called Cephas' (which is translated Peter)" (1:42, NRSV). But Peter had not yet proven himself to live up to that name—Peter, "the rock." According to Luke 24:34, Jesus had probably met with Peter previously.

Jesus' first question to Peter could be translated in three ways: (1) "Do you love me more than these men love me?" (2) "Do you love me more than you love these men?" (3) "Do you love me more than these things?" (that is, the fishing boat, nets, and gear). Of the three options, the first seems the most appropriate because Peter had boasted that he would never forsake Jesus, even if all the other disciples did (see Matthew 26:33; Mark 14:29; John 13:37). This was the same as saying that he had more love for Jesus than the others did.

BROKENNESS
Jesus helped Peter grasp his most valuable life lesson—he must learn humility before he could obtain leadership. Peter needed to confront realistically his shortcomings before he could guide the flock. This strong, powerful person had to be broken before he could deal compassionately with others. Do you aspire to lead others? It takes more than talent to gather followers. To have Jesus' style of leadership takes a spirit broken from pride, linked to God, and tender toward others.

Peter did just the opposite of what he boasted: He denied Jesus three times. As a consequence, Jesus asked Peter three times, *"Do you love me?"* to affirm Peter's love and commitment. Each time Peter told Jesus, "I love you," Jesus exhorted Peter to care for his flock: **"Feed my lambs"** (21:15, NIV); **"Take care of my sheep"** (21:16, NIV); **"Feed my sheep"** (21:17, NIV). *Lambs* and *sheep* can be taken as words of endearment. Jesus' love and concern is for all believers—the entire "flock" that would grow as a result of the apostles' ministry.

Peter was charged to care for this flock by feeding and shepherding them. Jesus used action words to describe Peter's role as a disciple. Jesus did not ask Peter to be the leader, but to take specific action: "Feed and take care of my sheep." If people in leadership assume that holding a position or being in charge is all they must do, they miss the point. Leadership in ministry requires a servant's heart: contributing to others, not just directing; developing people, not just demanding that tasks be done. Peter always remembered this commission; he became a dedicated shepherd of the flock (see 1 Peter 5:1-4). And as a good shepherd, caring for the sheep, Peter would, like Jesus, be called upon to lay down his life.

21:18-19 **When you were younger you dressed yourself and went where you wanted; but when you are old you will stretch out your hands, and someone else will dress you and lead you where you do not want to go. Jesus said this to indicate the kind of death by which Peter would glorify God.**^{NIV} Jesus used a proverbial statement about old age to depict Peter's death, which was by crucifixion. Tertullian (c. A.D. 212), referring to these verses, said that Peter was "girt by another" when his arms were stretched out and fastened to the cross. From this day onward, Peter knew what death lay before him. Peter never forgot this prophecy from Jesus; Peter referred to it in his Second Epistle when he spoke about his imminent death (see 2 Peter 1:14). Peter was crucified in Rome under Nero around A.D. 65–67.

And when He had spoken this, He said to him, "Follow Me."^{NKJV} By his words, Jesus was reinstating and restoring Peter as his disciple. What assurance these words must have been for Peter. Despite what glory or trial or death lay ahead, he would always be under the Savior's care, for he would be following Jesus.

Three years earlier, along the same lake, Jesus had said the same words to Peter—"Follow me." All the learning and the miles, all the miracles and the stories, all the impulsiveness and failures did not change the basic challenge Jesus gave to Peter and to us—Follow me. Following Jesus is not a step. Rather it is a lifelong walk of faith. Jesus' constant invitation reminds us not to think as often about where we are or where we are going but rather to think constantly about how well we are following him.

"Follow Me" is a present tense imperative meaning "Keep on following." Stripped of pride, impulsiveness, and false expectations of leadership, Peter was ready to follow Christ in a new way because of new experiences and a clearer picture of himself. "Follow Me" means consistent discipleship and steadfast pursuit of Christ, even if that requires martyrdom. It means continuing Christ's work in the way he wants it done, not in a way we want it done.

21:20-23 **Peter turned and saw the disciple whom Jesus loved . . . [and] said to Jesus, "Lord, what about him?"**NRSV Having been told his destiny, Peter wanted to know what would happen to John (called *the disciple whom Jesus loved* and identified as the one who had asked Jesus at the Last Supper who would betray him, see 13:23-25).

"If it is my will that he remain until I come, what is that to you? Follow me!"NRSV In this profound but loving rebuke, Jesus explained to the impulsive Peter that he was not to be concerned about God's plans for anyone else but himself. Indeed, Peter's contri-

> Let everyone be sure that he is doing his very best, for then he will have the personal satisfaction of work well done and won't need to compare himself with someone else.
> *Apostle Paul (Galatians 6:4* TLB)

bution to the beginnings of the Christian church would be astounding (from his sermon on Pentecost in just a few weeks, to his leadership of the Jerusalem church, to his being the first to understand that Gentiles too could become Christians), and both his miraculous escape from death (Acts 12:1-19) and his death by martyrdom would be heroic. John, although he would remain alive, would be called to a different kind of service, even through exile on a remote island—for John would write this incredible Gospel, three letters, and the astounding account of the triumphant return of the Son of God in the book of Revelation. Peter, the impulsive one, would write two epistles to encourage patience while we wait for Christ's return. Peter and John were called to different kinds of service for their Lord; neither was to question why.

When Jesus had called these men to be his disciples, he had said, "Come, follow me" (Mark 1:17 NIV). He repeated the command here: *"Follow me!"* Although Jesus was soon to leave the earth and would no longer be present with the disciples, he could still be *followed* because his Holy Spirit would be their guide. What an incredible comfort this was to these confused disciples and is for us today. Jesus was not going to leave them in their confusion; he was going to commission them and then give them guidance every step of the way. Thus, the Lord's command to Peter, "Follow me!" applies to each and every believer. He is not behind us; he is beside us, with us, and ahead of us, calling us to follow.

DON'T COMPARE
If we want to follow Jesus, we must be totally committed to obeying him, but God's call and the result of that obedience are different for every person. God can use all kinds of people. He has specific plans and service for the impulsive Peters, the thoughtful and sensitive Johns, and the forceful Pauls. God takes into consideration each person's nature and abilities. Each Christian is called and guided by God and is accountable to no one but God. Christians should not make comparisons among themselves or judge others regarding how each is fulfilling God's plan (Galatians 6:4). We must be content with where God has placed us and not be jealous about what he has given others to do.

Jesus' statement to Peter had been interpreted to mean that John would remain alive on earth until the Second Coming of the Lord. The first century was not immune to the rumor mill—for a rumor had started that said John would not die. (For if John remained alive until the Lord's coming, he would never have to experience death.)

John had to correct this rumor. Although the Second Coming is not a major theme in John's Gospel, it was the hope of the church and of all believers. If John died and the Lord still had not come, this tiny rumor could throw many believers, and the church itself, into confusion.

> It is of great importance to be obedient, to respect authority, and to let someone else captain our ship. It is far safer to follow than to lead.
> *Thomas à Kempis*

But Jesus did not say that he would not die.^{NIV} John insisted that Jesus' words had been misunderstood. Jesus had not said that John would not die; rather, he simply said to Peter, **"If it is my will that he remain until I come, what is that to you?"**^{NRSV} The point is that the decision was up to Jesus—not John or Peter. What Jesus was communicating to Peter was that it was not for Peter to be concerned about what would become of John's life. He, Peter, was responsible to follow the Lord according to what the Lord had revealed to him. And so was John.

YOU FOLLOW ME
Peter asked Jesus how John would die. Jesus replied that Peter should not concern himself with that. We tend to compare our lives to others, whether to rationalize our own level of devotion to Christ or to question God's justice. Jesus responds to us as he did to Peter: "What is that to you? You must follow me."

JESUS' MIRACLES

John and the other Gospel writers were able to record only a fraction of the people who were touched and healed by Jesus. But enough of Jesus' words and works have been saved so that we also might be able to know him and be his disciples in this day. There follows a listing of the miracles that are included in the Gospels. They were supernatural events that pointed people to God, and they were acts of love by one who is love.

	Matthew	Mark	Luke	John
Five thousand people are fed	14:15-21	6:35-44	9:12-17	6:5-14
Calming the storm	8:23-27	4:35-41	8:22-25	
Demons sent into the pigs	8:28-34	5:1-20	8:26-39	
Jairus's daughter raised	9:18-26	5:22-24, 35-43	8:41-42, 49-56	
A sick woman is healed	9:20-22	5:25-34	8:43-48	
Jesus heals a paralytic	9:1-8	2:1-12	5:17-26	
A leper is healed at Gennesaret	8:1-4	1:40-45	5:12-15	
Peter's mother-in-law healed	8:14-17	1:29-31	4:38-39	
A shriveled hand is restored	12:9-13	3:1-5	6:6-11	
A boy with an evil spirit is healed	17:14-21	9:14-29	9:37-42	
Jesus walks on the water	14:22-33	6:45-52		6:17-21
Blind Bartimaeus receives sight	20:29-34	10:46-52	18:35-43	
A girl is freed from a demon	15:21-28	7:24-30		
Four thousand are fed	15:32-38	8:1-9		
Cursing the fig tree	21:18-22	11:12-14, 20-24		
A centurion's servant is healed	8:5-13		7:1-10	
An evil spirit is sent out of a man		1:23-27	4:33-36	
A mute demoniac is healed	12:22		11:14	
Two blind men find sight	9:27-31			
Jesus heals the mute man	9:32-33			
A coin in a fish's mouth	17:24-27			
A deaf and mute man is healed		7:31-37		
A blind man sees at Bethsaida		8:22-26		
The first miraculous catch of fish			5:1-11	
A widow's son is raised			7:11-16	
A crippled woman is healed			13:10-17	
Jesus heals a sick man			14:1-6	
Ten lepers are healed			17:11-19	
Jesus restores a man's ear			22:49-51	
Jesus turns water into wine				2:1-11
An official's son is healed at Cana				4:46-54
A lame man is healed				5:1-16
Jesus heals a man born blind				9:1-7
Lazarus is raised from the dead				11:1-45
The second miraculous catch of fish				21:1-14

21:24 This is the disciple who testifies to these things and who wrote them down.^{NIV} The last two verses of John's Gospel contain the finishing touch to the book that attests to the truth of John's written testimony. The testimony is trustworthy because John was an eyewitness of Jesus Christ. After many years of experience and reflection, John wrote an account that reflects his spiritual insight into the life of Jesus Christ (see 1:14; 1 John 1:1-3).

We know that his testimony is true. This statement is probably from some of John's contemporaries who knew that what John wrote was true. Some scholars think these contemporaries were the Ephesian elders, who had been told and/or read the preceding narrative. Early church history reports that after John spent several years as an exile on the island of Patmos (see Revelation 1:9), he returned to Ephesus where he died as an old man, near the end of the first century.

21:25 And there are also many other things that Jesus did, which if they were written one by one, I suppose that even the world itself could not contain the books that would be written. Amen.^{NKJV} This final statement is not mere hyperbole. It is an affirmation of the fact that John's one book is far from being exhaustive because John recorded only some of the things that Jesus had done. If John had covered every event, how many more books would be required to contain all the material? Some of this material can be found in the other three Gospels. But there is so much more that could have been said about Jesus. Nonetheless, what was written has provided believers with a true biography of the greatest person who ever lived: Jesus Christ, the Son of God.

READ AND DECIDE
John's stated purpose for writing his Gospel was to show that Jesus was the Son of God. He clearly and systematically presented the evidence for Jesus' claims. When evidence is presented in the courtroom, those who hear it must make a choice. Those who read the Gospel of John must also make a choice—is Jesus the Son of God, or isn't he? You are the jury. The evidence has been clearly presented. You must decide. Read John's Gospel and believe in Jesus!

---

250 EVENTS IN THE LIFE OF CHRIST/
A HARMONY OF THE GOSPELS

All four books in the Bible that tell the story of Jesus Christ—Matthew, Mark, Luke, and John—stand alone, emphasizing a unique aspect of Jesus' life. But when these are blended into one complete account, or harmonized, we gain new insights about the life of Christ.

This harmony combines the four Gospels into a single chronological account of Christ's life on earth. It includes every chapter and verse of each Gospel, leaving nothing out.

The harmony is divided into 250 events. The title of each event is identical to the title found in the corresponding Gospel. Parallel passages found in more than one Gospel have identical titles, helping you to identify them quickly.

Each of the 250 events in the harmony is numbered. The number of the event corresponds to the number next to the title in the Bible text. When reading one of the Gospel accounts, you will notice, at times, that some numbers are missing or out of sequence. The easiest way to locate these events is to refer to the harmony.

In addition, if you are looking for a particular event in the life of Christ, the harmony can help you locate it more rapidly than paging through all four Gospels. Each of the 250 events has a distinctive title keyed to the main emphasis of the passage to help you locate and remember the events.

This harmony will help you to better visualize the travels of Jesus, study the four Gospels comparatively, and appreciate the unity of their message.

I. BIRTH AND PREPARATION OF JESUS CHRIST

	Matthew	Mark	Luke	John
1 Luke's purpose in writing			1:1–4	
2 God became a human being				1:1–18
3 The ancestors of Jesus	1:1–17		3:23–38	
4 An angel promises the birth of John to Zechariah			1:5–25	
5 An angel promises the birth of Jesus to Mary			1:26–38	
6 Mary visits Elizabeth			1:39–56	
7 John the Baptist is born			1:57–80	
8 An angel appears to Joseph	1:18–25			
9 Jesus is born in Bethlehem			2:1–7	
10 Shepherds visit Jesus			2:8–20	
11 Mary and Joseph bring Jesus to the temple			2:21–40	
12 Visitors arrive from eastern lands	2:1–12			
13 The escape to Egypt	2:13 18			
14 The return to Nazareth	2:19–23			
15 Jesus speaks with the religious teachers			2:41–52	
16 John the Baptist prepares the way for Jesus	3:1–12	1:1–8	3:1–18	
17 John baptizes Jesus	3:13–17	1:9–11	3:21, 22	
18 Satan tempts Jesus in the desert	4:1–11	1:12, 13	4:1–13	
19 John the Baptist declares his mission				1:19–28

	Matthew	Mark	Luke	John
20 John the Baptist proclaims Jesus as the Messiah				1:29–34
21 The first disciples follow Jesus				1:35–51
22 Jesus turns water into wine				2:1–12

II. MESSAGE AND MINISTRY OF JESUS CHRIST

	Matthew	Mark	Luke	John
23 Jesus clears the temple				2:12–25
24 Nicodemus visits Jesus at night				3:1–21
25 John the Baptist tells more about Jesus				3:22–36
26 Herod puts John in prison			3:19, 20	
27 Jesus talks to a woman at the well				4:1–26
28 Jesus tells about the spiritual harvest				4:27–38
29 Many Samaritans believe in Jesus				4:39–42
30 Jesus preaches in Galilee	4:12–17	1:14, 15	4:14, 15	4:43–45
31 Jesus heals a government official's son				4:46–54
32 Jesus is rejected at Nazareth			4:16–30	
33 Four fishermen follow Jesus	4:18–22	1:16–20		
34 Jesus teaches with great authority		1:21–28	4:31–37	
35 Jesus heals Peter's mother-in-law and many others	8:14–17	1:29–34	4:38–41	
36 Jesus preaches throughout Galilee	4:23–25	1:35–39	4:42–44	
37 Jesus provides a miraculous catch of fish			5:1–11	
38 Jesus heals a man with leprosy	8:1–4	1:40–45	5:12–16	
39 Jesus heals a paralyzed man	9:1–8	2:1–12	5:17–26	
40 Jesus eats with sinners at Matthew's house	9:9–13	2:13–17	5:27–32	
41 Religious leaders ask Jesus about fasting	9:14–17	2:18–22	5:33–39	
42 Jesus heals a lame man by the pool				5:1–18
43 Jesus claims to be God's Son				5:19–30
44 Jesus supports his claim				5:31–47
45 The disciples pick wheat on the Sabbath	12:1–8	2:23–28	6:1–5	
46 Jesus heals a man's hand on the Sabbath	12:9–14	3:1–6	6:6–11	
47 Large crowds follow Jesus	12:15–21	3:7–12		
48 Jesus selects the twelve disciples		3:13–19	6:12–16	
49 Jesus gives the Beatitudes	5:1–12		6:17–26	
50 Jesus teaches about salt and light	5:13–16			
51 Jesus teaches about the law	5:17–20			
52 Jesus teaches about anger	5:21–26			
53 Jesus teaches about lust	5:27–30			
54 Jesus teaches about divorce	5:31, 32			
55 Jesus teaches about vows	5:33–37			
56 Jesus teaches about retaliation	5:38–42			
57 Jesus teaches about loving enemies	5:43–48		6:27–36	
58 Jesus teaches about giving to the needy	6:1–4			
59 Jesus teaches about prayer	6:5–15			
60 Jesus teaches about fasting	6:16–18			
61 Jesus teaches about money	6:19–24			
62 Jesus teaches about worry	6:25–34			
63 Jesus teaches about criticizing others	7:1–6		6:37–42	
64 Jesus teaches about asking, seeking, knocking	7:7–12			
65 Jesus teaches about the way to heaven	7:13, 14			
66 Jesus teaches about fruit in people's lives	7:15–20		6:43–45	
67 Jesus teaches about those who build houses on rock and sand	7:21–29		6:46–49	
68 A Roman centurion demonstrates faith	8:5–13		7:1–10	
69 Jesus raises a widow's son from the dead			7:11–17	
70 Jesus eases John's doubt	11:1–19		7:18–35	
71 Jesus promises rest for the soul	11:20–30			
72 A sinful woman anoints Jesus' feet			7:36–50	
73 Women accompany Jesus and the disciples			8:1–3	
74 Religious leaders accuse Jesus of being under Satan's power	12:22–37	3:20–30		

	Matthew	Mark	Luke	John
75 Religious leaders ask Jesus for a miracle	12:38–45			
76 Jesus describes his true family	12:46–50	3:31–35	8:19–21	
77 Jesus tells the parable of the four soils	13:1–9	4:1–9	8:4–8	
78 Jesus explains the parable of the four soils	13:10–23	4:10–25	8:9–18	
79 Jesus tells the parable of the growing seed		4:26–29		
80 Jesus tells the parable of the weeds	13:24–30			
81 Jesus tells the parable of the mustard seed	13:31, 32	4:30–34		
82 Jesus tells the parable of the yeast	13:33–35			
83 Jesus explains the parable of the weeds	13:36–43			
84 Jesus tells the parable of hidden treasure	13:44			
85 Jesus tells the parable of the pearl merchant	13:45, 46			
86 Jesus tells the parable of the fishing net	13:47–52			
87 Jesus calms the storm	8:23–27	4:35–41	8:22–25	
88 Jesus sends the demons into a herd of pigs	8:28–34	5:1–20	8:26–39	
89 Jesus heals a bleeding woman and restores a girl to life	9:18–26	5:21–43	8:40–56	
90 Jesus heals the blind and mute	9:27–34			
91 The people of Nazareth refuse to believe	13:53–58	6:1–6		
92 Jesus urges the disciples to pray for workers	9:35–38			
93 Jesus sends out the twelve disciples	10:1–16	6:7–13	9:1–6	
94 Jesus prepares the disciples for persecution	10:17–42			
95 Herod kills John the Baptist	14:1–12	6:14–29	9:7–9	
96 Jesus feeds five thousand	14:13–21	6:30–44	9:10–17	6:1–15
97 Jesus walks on water	14:22–33	6:45–52		6:16–21
98 Jesus heals all who touch him	14:34–36	6:53–56		
99 Jesus is the true bread from heaven				6:22–40
100 The Jews disagree that Jesus is from heaven				6:41–59
101 Many disciples desert Jesus				6:60–71
102 Jesus teaches about inner purity	15:1–20	7:1–23		
103 Jesus sends a demon out of a girl	15:21–28	7:24–30		
104 The crowd marvels at Jesus' healings	15:29–31	7:31–37		
105 Jesus feeds four thousand	15:32–39	8:1–10		
106 Religious leaders ask for a sign in the sky	16:1–4	8:11–13		
107 Jesus warns against wrong teaching	16:5–12	8:14–21		
108 Jesus restores sight to a blind man		8:22–26		
109 Peter says Jesus is the Messiah	16:13–20	8:27–30	9:18–20	
110 Jesus predicts his death the first time	16:21–28	8:31–9:1	9:21–27	
111 Jesus is transfigured on the mountain	17:1–13	9:2–13	9:28–36	
112 Jesus heals a demon-possessed boy	17:14–21	9:14–29	9:37–43	
113 Jesus predicts his death the second time	17:22, 23	9:30–32	9:44, 45	
114 Peter finds the coin in the fish's mouth	17:24–27			
115 The disciples argue about who would be the greatest	18:1–6	9:33–37	9:46–48	
116 The disciples forbid another to use Jesus' name		9:38–41	9:49, 50	
117 Jesus warns against temptation	18:7–9	9:42–50		
118 Jesus warns against looking down on others	18:10–14			
119 Jesus teaches how to treat a believer who sins	18:15–20			
120 Jesus tells the parable of the unforgiving debtor	18:21–35			
121 Jesus' brothers ridicule him				7:1–9
122 Jesus teaches about the cost of following him	8:18–22		9:51–62	
123 Jesus teaches openly at the temple				7:10–31
124 Religious leaders attempt to arrest Jesus				7:32–52
125 Jesus forgives an adulterous woman				7:53–8:11
126 Jesus is the light of the world				8:12–20
127 Jesus warns of coming judgment				8:21–30
128 Jesus speaks about God's true children				8:31–47
129 Jesus states he is eternal				8:48–59
130 Jesus sends out seventy-two messengers			10:1–16	
131 The seventy-two messengers return			10:17–24	
132 Jesus tells the parable of the Good Samaritan			10:25–37	
133 Jesus visits Mary and Martha			10:38–42	
134 Jesus teaches his disciples about prayer			11:1–13	
135 Jesus answers hostile accusations			11:14–28	
136 Jesus warns against unbelief			11:29–32	

	Matthew	Mark	Luke	John
137 Jesus teaches about the light within			11:33–36	
138 Jesus criticizes the religious leaders			11:37–54	
139 Jesus speaks against hypocrisy			12:1–12	
140 Jesus tells the parable of the rich fool			12:13–21	
141 Jesus warns about worry			12:22–34	
142 Jesus warns about preparing for his coming			12:35–48	
143 Jesus warns about coming division			12:49–53	
144 Jesus warns about the future crisis			12:54–59	
145 Jesus calls the people to repent			13:1–9	
146 Jesus heals the crippled woman			13:10–17	
147 Jesus teaches about the kingdom of God			13:18–21	
148 Jesus heals the man who was born blind				9:1–12
149 Religious leaders question the blind man				9:13–34
150 Jesus teaches about spiritual blindness				9:35–41
151 Jesus is the Good Shepherd				10:1–21
152 Religious leaders surround Jesus at the temple				10:22–42
153 Jesus teaches about entering the kingdom			13:22–30	
154 Jesus grieves over Jerusalem			13:31–35	
155 Jesus heals a man with dropsy			14:1–6	
156 Jesus teaches about seeking honor			14:7–14	
157 Jesus tells the parable of the great feast			14:15–24	
158 Jesus teaches about the cost of being a disciple			14:25–35	
159 Jesus tells the parable of the lost sheep			15:1–7	
160 Jesus tells the parable of the lost coin			15:8–10	
161 Jesus tells the parable of the lost son			15:11–32	
162 Jesus tells the parable of the shrewd manager			16:1–18	
163 Jesus tells about the rich man and the beggar			16:19–31	
164 Jesus tells about forgiveness and faith			17:1–10	
165 Lazarus becomes ill and dies				11:1–16
166 Jesus comforts Mary and Martha				11:17–37
167 Jesus raises Lazarus from the dead				11:38–44
168 Religious leaders plot to kill Jesus				11:45–57
169 Jesus heals ten men with leprosy			17:11–19	
170 Jesus teaches about the coming of the kingdom of God			17:20–37	
171 Jesus tells the parable of the persistent widow			18:1–8	
172 Jesus tells the parable of two men who prayed			18:9–14	
173 Jesus teaches about marriage and divorce	19:1–12	10:1–12		
174 Jesus blesses little children	19:13–15	10:13–16	18:15–17	
175 Jesus speaks to the rich young man	19:16–30	10:17–31	18:18–30	
176 Jesus tells the parable of the workers paid equally	20:1–16			
177 Jesus predicts his death the third time	20:17–19	10:32–34	18:31–34	
178 Jesus teaches about serving others	20:20–28	10:35–45		
179 Jesus heals a blind beggar	20:29–34	10:46–52	18:35–43	
180 Jesus brings salvation to Zacchaeus's home			19:1–10	
181 Jesus tells the parable of the king's ten servants			19:11–27	
182 A woman anoints Jesus with perfume	26:6–13	14:3–9		12:1–11
183 Jesus rides into Jerusalem on a donkey	21:1–11	11:1–11	19:28–44	12:12–19
184 Jesus clears the temple again	21:12–17	11:12–19	19:45–48	
185 Jesus explains why he must die				12:20–36
186 Most of the people do not believe in Jesus				12:37–43
187 Jesus summarizes his message				12:44–50
188 Jesus says the disciples can pray for anything	21:18–22	11:20–26		
189 Religious leaders challenge Jesus' authority	21:23–27	11:27–33	20:1–8	
190 Jesus tells the parable of the two sons	21:28–32			
191 Jesus tells the parable of the wicked tenants	21:33–46	12:1–12	20:9–19	
192 Jesus tells the parable of the wedding feast	22:1–14			
193 Religious leaders question Jesus about paying taxes	22:15–22	12:13–17	20:20–26	
194 Religious leaders question Jesus about the resurrection	22:23–33	12:18–27	20:27–40	
195 Religious leaders question Jesus about the greatest commandment	22:34–40	12:28–34		
196 Religious leaders cannot answer Jesus' question	22:41–46	12:35–37	20:41–44	

	Matthew	Mark	Luke	John
197 Jesus warns against the religious leaders	23:1–12	12:38–40	20:45–47	
198 Jesus condemns the religious leaders	23:13–36			
199 Jesus grieves over Jerusalem again	23:37–39			
200 A poor widow gives all she has		12:41–44	21:1–4	
201 Jesus tells about the future	24:1–25	13:1–23	21:5–24	
202 Jesus tells about his return	24:26–35	13:24–31	21:25–33	
203 Jesus tells about remaining watchful	24:36–51	13:32–37	21:34–38	
204 Jesus tells the parable of the ten bridesmaids	25:1–13			
205 Jesus tells the parable of the loaned money	25:14–30			
206 Jesus tells about the final judgment	25:31–46			

III. DEATH AND RESURRECTION OF JESUS CHRIST

	Matthew	Mark	Luke	John
207 Religious leaders plot to kill Jesus	26:1–5	14:1, 2	22:1, 2	
208 Judas agrees to betray Jesus	26:14–16	14:10, 11	22:3–6	
209 Disciples prepare for the Passover	26:17–19	14:12–16	22:7–13	
210 Jesus washes the disciples' feet				13:1–20
211 Jesus and the disciples have the Last Supper	26:20–30	14:17–26	22:14–30	13:21–30
212 Jesus predicts Peter's denial			22:31–38	13:31–38
213 Jesus is the way to the Father				14:1–14
214 Jesus promises the Holy Spirit				14:15–31
215 Jesus teaches about the vine and the branches				15:1–17
216 Jesus warns about the world's hatred				15:18—16:4
217 Jesus teaches about the Holy Spirit				16:5–15 ·
218 Jesus teaches about using his name in prayer				16:16–33
219 Jesus prays for himself				17:1–5
220 Jesus prays for his disciples				17:6–19
221 Jesus prays for future believers				17:20–26
222 Jesus again predicts Peter's denial	26:31–35	14:27–31		
223 Jesus agonizes in the garden	26:36–46	14:32–42	22:39–46	
224 Jesus is betrayed and arrested	26:47–56	14:43–52	22:47–53	18:1–11
225 Annas questions Jesus				18:12–24
226 Caiaphas questions Jesus	26:57–68	14:53–65		
227 Peter denies knowing Jesus	26:69–75	14:66–72	22:54–65	18:25–27
228 The council of religious leaders condemns Jesus	27:1, 2	15:1	22:66–71	
229 Judas kills himself	27:3–10			
230 Jesus stands trial before Pilate	27:11–14	15:2–5	23:1–5	18:28–37
231 Jesus stands trial before Herod			23:6–12	
232 Pilate hands Jesus over to be crucified	27:15–26	15:6–15	23:13–25	18:38—19:16
233 Roman soldiers mock Jesus	27:27–31	15:16–20		
234 Jesus is led away to be crucified	27:32–34	15:21–24	23:26–31	19:17
235 Jesus is placed on the cross	27:35–44	15:25–32	23:32–43	19:18–27
236 Jesus dies on the cross	27:45–56	15:33–41	23:44–49	19:28–37
237 Jesus is laid in the tomb	27:57–61	15:42–47	23:50–56	19:38–42
238 Guards are posted at the tomb	27:62–66			
239 Jesus rises from the dead	28:1–7	16:1–8	24:1–12	20:1–9
240 Jesus appears to Mary Magdalene		16:9–11		20:10–18
241 Jesus appears to the women	28:8–10			
242 Religious leaders bribe the guards	28:11–15			
243 Jesus appears to two believers traveling on the road		16:12, 13	24:13–35	
244 Jesus appears to the disciples behind locked doors			24:36–43	20:19–23
245 Jesus appears to the disciples including Thomas		16:14		20:24–31
246 Jesus appears to the disciples while fishing				21:1–14
247 Jesus talks with Peter				21:15–25
248 Jesus gives the Great Commission	28:16–20	16:15–18		
249 Jesus appears to the disciples in Jerusalem			24:44–49	
250 Jesus ascends into heaven		16:19, 20	24:50–53	

BIBLIOGRAPHY

Adels, Jill Haak. *The Wisdom of the Saints.* New York: Oxford University Press, 1987.

Barclay, William, trans. *The Gospel of John.* Vols. 1 and 2. Philadelphia: The Westminster Press, 1975.

Barrett, C. K. *The Gospel According to St. John.* Philadelphia: The Westminster Press, 1978.

Beasley-Murray, George R. "John." In *Word Biblical Commentary.* Waco, Tex.: Word, 1987.

Brown, Raymond E. *The Gospel According to John.* Vols. 29 and 29A. New York: Doubleday, 1966.

Bruce, F. F. *The Gospel of John.* Grand Rapids: William B. Eerdmans Publishing Company, 1983.

Carson, D. A. *The Gospel According to John.* Grand Rapids: William B. Eerdman's Publishing Company, 1991.

Ferguson, S. B., D. F. Wright, and J. I. Packer, eds. *New Dictionary of Theology.* Downers Grove, Ill.: InterVarsity Press, 1988.

Filson, Floyd V. *The Gospel According to John.* Vol. 19 of *The Layman's Bible Commentary.* Edited by Balmer H. Kelly. Atlanta: John Knox Press, 1963.

Gutzke, Manford George. *Plain Talk on John.* Grand Rapids: Zondervan Publishing House, 1968.

Kent, Homer A., Jr. *Light in the Darkness.* Grand Rapids: Baker Book House, 1974.

Metzger, Bruce. *A Textual Commentary on the Greek New Testament.* New York: United Bible Societies, 1971.

Michaels, J. Ramsey. *John. The New International Biblical Commentary Series.* New Testament edited by W. Ward Gasque. Peabody, Mass.: Hendrickson Publishers, 1989.

Morris, Leon. "The Gospel According to John." In the *New International Commentary on the New Testament.* Grand Rapids: William B. Eerdmans Publishing Company, 1971.

Newman, Barclay, and Eugene Nida. *A Translator's Handbook on the Gospel of John.* New York: United Bible Societies, 1980.

Nicoll, W. Robertson, ed. *The Expositor's Greek Testament.* Vol. 1. Grand Rapids: William B. Eerdmans Publishing Company, 1961.

Schnackenburg, Rudolph. *The Gospel According to St. John.* Translated by Kevin Smyth. New York: Crossroad Publishing Company, 1982.

Tasker, R. V. G. *The Gospel According to St. John: An Introduction and Commentary. Tyndale New Testament Commentaries.* Grand Rapids: William B. Eerdmans Publishing Company, 1988.

Tenney, Merrill C. "The Gospel of John." In *The Expositor's Bible*

Commentary. Vol. 9. Edited by Frank E. Gaebelein. Grand Rapids: Zondervan Publishing House, 1981.

Walvoord, John F., and Roy B. Zuck. *Bible Knowledge Commentary: New Testament Edition.* Wheaton, Ill.: Victor Books, 1983.

Westcott, B. F. *Gospel According to St. John.* 1881. Reprint. Grand Rapids: Zondervan Publishing House, 1973.

Westcott, B. F. and F. J. A. Hort. *Introduction to the New Testament in the Original Greek,* with "Notes on Select Readings." New York: Harper and Brothers, 1882.

Yarbrough, Robert W. *John.* Chicago: Moody Press, 1991.

GENERAL INDEX

Pharisees, Sadducees,
Teachers of the Law)
Jewish Ruling Council
description of—51, 238
Nicodemus was member of—51
plot to have Jesus
killed—237–43, 359
Jews/Jewish Nation
persecute Jesus because he
healed on the Sabbath—106
reject Jesus—8, 135–37, 189
John, Apostle
disciple of Jesus—*x, xi,* 24,
278–79, 356–57, 378–79,
381, 402–04, 412
disciple of John the Baptist—*xi,*
23–24
fisherman—*x, xi, xvii,* 402–04
eyewitness of the
Resurrection—*xvii–xviii, xxiii,*
388–90
how Jesus changed his
personality—*x, xii*
leader of church in
Jerusalem—*xi–xii*
ministry of—*xi–xii,* 399
nicknamed "Son of
Thunder"—*ix–x, xi*
others letters of—*xii,* 409
rumor that he would not
die—401, 409–10
John, Gospel of
audience of—*xiii–xiv*
message of—*xvi–xxiv*
prologue of—1–17
purpose of—*ix, xiv–xvi,*
399–400, 412
Chart: Parallels between John's
Prologue and His Gospel—11
Chart: Miracles Recorded in
John's Gospel and Their
Significance—36–37
John the Baptist
baptized Jesus—*xxi,* 22–23
baptized his followers—67
cousin of Jesus—21
his disciples follow Jesus—*xi,*
23–24
his miraculous birth—17
humility of—19–21, 68–71
prepared the way for
Jesus—6–7, 14, 17–24,
68–71, 220

questioned by the
Pharisees—18–19, 75, 113
Jordan River—20, 68
Joseph—26, 32, 135–36
Joseph of Arimathea—382–84
Joy
in the Resurrection—391, 396
Jesus gives—312, 329–31, 342
application for today—312, 330
Judas *(Son of James)*
disciple of Jesus—298
Judas Iscariot
betrays Jesus—142–43, 145,
271, 275, 278–80, 341,
352–53
disciple of Jesus—247–48
Judging/Judgment
future judgment—176–78
Jesus' judgment—109–12,
173–75, 265–66
application for today—173, 176,
410
Chart: The Judgment of
Satan—325
Kingdom of God
founded by Jesus Christ—28,
365–67
must be born again to
enter—53–59
application for today—53–55,
366
Chart: The Kingdom of God—54
Last Supper—267–83
Lazarus—223–37, 245–51, 252,
279
Law
ceremonial laws followed by the
Jews—33–34, 67–68, 79,
103–04, 362, 380
given by Moses—15–16, 26,
118–19, 156, 200
Jesus and the—218–19
spoke of the Messiah—26,
118–19
application for today—104, 219
Leadership
application for today—303, 407
Levites
and priests question John the
Baptist—17–20
Lie/Lying
Satan is father of—185
application for today—185
Life *(see Eternal Life)*